Alfred O. Hero, Jr., holds a Master's in Psychology from Vanderbilt University and a Ph.D. in Political Science from George Washington University. He is Director of the World Peace Foundation and author of numerous books and articles on the roles of public opinion in foreign policy.

AMERICAN RELIGIOUS GROUPS VIEW FOREIGN POLICY

AMERICAN RELIGIOUS GROUPS VIEW FOREIGN POLICY: TRENDS IN RANK-AND-FILE OPINION, 1937-1969

Alfred O. Hero, Jr.

World Peace Foundation

Duke University Press   Durham, North Carolina   1973

© 1973, Duke University Press
L. C. C. card no. 72–81335
I. S. B. N. Q–8223–0253–5
Printed in the United States of
America by the Seeman Printery, Inc.

PREFACE

The potential impacts of religious institutions on the thought and action of Americans with respect to world affairs, and, ultimately, on American foreign policy, remain substantial. The United States is one of the few industrialized societies in which a majority of the population is still affiliated with one or another religious organization and participates more or less frequently in masses, services, or other church or synagogue activities. Though American adults who attend church during a typical week declined from 49 percent in 1955 to 40 percent in 1971, in the early 1970's over half of men as well as women, whites as well as Negroes, Protestants as well as Catholics, independents as well as Democrats and Republicans, the highly urbanized Northeast as well as the more rural South and Midwest, and better educated as well as less well educated citizens were members of a religious body and went to church at least as often as once a month. Church-connected schools maintain contact with millions of youngsters during their formative development. Books, magazines, newspapers, and other literature sponsored by or connected with religious institutions reach into a large fraction of American homes.

Most American presidents, their senior foreign-policy aides, and members of the Senate and House of Representatives, including those on key committees involved in international affairs, have been among this numerous element of the population involved in religious institutions to one degree or another. Anticlericalism and active criticism of religious bodies and their leaders have seldom been evident among the federal Executive or Congress. Both legally and in practical political terms the churches have more latitude than most other tax-exempt voluntary institutions to take part in the controversial political processes involved in foreign-policy making. If the churches do not assist policymakers, foreign-policy elites, and the body politic generally in examining particularly ethical aspects of that important field of public policy, it is very unlikely that any other influential institution with wide contacts in American society will do so.

Increasingly since the interwar period, theologians, ethicists, and other intellectuals and leaders connected with the mainline Protestant churches have studied, discussed, and written about implications of religious faith and ethics for international issues. Virtually all major Protestant denominations, except for more fundamentalist ones, have issued a number of public statements on ethically relevant world problems, the overall tones of which have been rather consistent over the years since the Second World War. The Vatican and the Catholic hierarchy in the United States, though less articulate on most world issues than their Protestant counterparts during the earlier part of this period, have since the late 1950's issued encyclicals and other public pronouncements the general content and tone of which have differed on most questions in but relatively minor respects from those of the World Council of Churches, the National Council of Churches, and their member denominations.

This book and the study from which it is derived attempt primarily to examine as systematically as available data permit the impacts of the churches, and especially of the public stances of their international and national leaderships, on intermediate and lower levels of their respective organizations, including local clergy and laymen in the pews or, conversely, the degree to which these public utterances have reflected the views of their respective grass roots. Secondarily, the volume considers the implications of these findings, along with more direct evidence, for impacts on foreign-policy making itself. Finally, a number of hypothetical interpretations of the causes and significance of the phenomena observed and speculative suggestions of more effective ways of achieving the objectives of the religious group leaderships in this field will be offered.

The origins of this study go back to the mid-1950's when the author began examining opinion polls, surveys, and social science data relevant to mass public opinion and communications in the United States bearing on international affairs for his contributions to a series of monographs, *Studies in Citizen Participation in International Relations*, published by the World Peace Foundation in 1959–61.[1] It became evident as this research proceeded that even when other demographic factors such as level of education and urbanization were held constant, American Jews were significantly better informed, more interested, more apt to follow the media, and more likely to harbor relatively liberal views with respect to world problems than were other religious and ethnic groups. Lesser differences seemed to obtain between Catholics and members of certain Protestant denominations, but it was less clear than in the case of Jews whether these were traceable to religious or to other factors.

1. *Americans in World Affairs, Mass Media and World Affairs, Voluntary Organizations in World Affairs Communication*, and *Opinion Leaders in American Communities*.

A subsequent study in the early 1960's in collaboration with the late
Charles O. Lerche, Jr., of the international behavior of the American
South (the former Confederacy) discovered significant differences among
the major religious groups of that region and devoted some attention
to the sources of those differences and their implications for the political
process.[2] Later research in which the author was involved on trade
union members; Negroes as contrasted with whites; and reactions of
major social and demographic groups in America to such diverse issues
as the United Nations system, aid, trade, and development with respect
to the third world, and interrelationships of liberalism versus conservatism
in regard to international and domestic issues revealed further differences
related to religious beliefs, preferences, or affiliations.[3]

Meanwhile, service on the International Relations Committee of the
Massachusetts Council of Churches, on the Committee of the International Affairs Department of the National Council of Churches, and
on the Joint Project Committee on International Affairs Education of
the Departments of International Affairs and of Educational Development
of the National Council of Churches, and involvement as a consultant
and participant in a number of church-sponsored programs in world
affairs beginning in the early 1960's exposed the author to both the
complexity and the difficulty of the practical problems of religious institutions in this field and demonstrated the urgency of improving their
effectiveness.

The study reported below began in 1967 with a systematic search
of national survey data and empirical social science research wherein
questions about international issues of continuing importance and about
religious affiliation, church involvement, and other aspects of religious
behavior were posed to the same individuals. While the findings of these
studies were being examined and new computer tabulations being re-

2. Reported in Alfred O. Hero, Jr., *The Southerner and World Affairs* (Baton Rouge,
La.: Louisiana State University Press, 1965), pp. 435–503; "Southern Jews, Race
Relations, and Foreign Policy," *Jewish Social Studies* 27, no. 4 (Oct. 1965), pp. 213–35;
and "Southern Protestants, Southern Catholics, and International Affairs: A Comparative
Analysis," unpublished paper delivered to the April 1966 meeting of the American
Society of Church History at Union Theological Seminary in Richmond, Virginia.

3. Reported respectively in (with Emil Starr) *The Reuther-Meany Foreign Policy
Dispute* (Dobbs Ferry, N.Y.: Oceana Publications, 1970); "American Negroes and U.S.
Foreign Policy: 1937–1967," *Journal of Conflict Resolution* 13, no. 2 (June 1969),
pp. 220–51; "The American Public and the UN, 1954–1966," *Journal of Conflict
Resolution* 10, no. 4 (Dec. 1966), pp. 436–75; "Foreign Aid and the American Public,"
Public Policy 14 (1965), pp. 71–116; and "Liberalism-Conservatism Revisited: Foreign
vs. Domestic Federal Policies, 1937–1967," *Public Opinion Quarterly* 33 (Fall 1969),
pp. 400–408.

quested and run, Miss Theresa Wyszkowski and Mr. Russell Alcorn, students respectively at the Harvard Divinity School and the Boston University School of Theology, conducted an extensive critical inventory of relevant literature, including doctoral theses and other unpublished material, relevant to the public stances of American religious groups in world affairs and their impacts on the public and the policy-making process itself. The author later conducted open-ended interviews with some seventy participant observers in the churches, other nongovernmental organizations, and the federal government.

The systematic examination of data and interviews on which this volume is largely based ended in mid-1970. Some of the more detailed findings reported herein, such as some of those pertaining to Vietnam and China, may have been overtaken by more recent events. Nevertheless, surveys through the summer of 1972 generally support or reinforce the validity of observations and interpretations to follow.

Alfred O. Hero, Jr.

Boston, September 1, 1972

ACKNOWLEDGMENTS

The contributors to the research on which this book is based, to the interpretations of the empirical findings of that study, to speculations about their implications for the present and the future, and to the various papers, memoranda, "think pieces," and drafts of chapters which were later revised into this published version have been too numerous for individual mention here.

The citations from others' research and thought in the pages that follow were derived primarily from a systematic inventory and abstracting of existing research, publications, theses, and other unpublished materials pertinent to the international stances of American churches and the flow of information and ideas relevant to world affairs within them performed in the winter, spring, and summer of 1969 by Theresa Wyszkowski, at that time a graduate student at the Harvard Divinity School, with the assistance of Russell Alcorn, a Canadian clergyman at that time a graduate student at the Boston University School of Theology. The resulting bibliography and abstracts, introduced by a critical essay on the inclusiveness and quality of research and thought in this field, what we know and do not know from previous studies, and phenomena particularly worthy of future study, are available in Alfred O. Hero, Jr., "Communication of World Affairs Within and By American Churches: Bibliography and Abstracts," mimeographed (Boston: World Peace Foundation, 1969), 234 pp.

The observations that follow concerning comparative reactions of American religious groups to foreign aid, trade, and other aspects of U.S. relations with the less-developed world were derived mainly from secondary analyses of survey data financed by a grant from the New World Foundation. A number of other tabulations were by-products of earlier studies of international attitudes in the American South financed by the World Peace Foundation[1] and of comparative international behavior of American trade unionists financed by the United Automobile, Aerospace, and Agricultural Implement Workers of America and the American Philosophical Society.[2] These and other tabulations appearing herein were performed for the most part by the Roper Public Opinion

---

1. Reported in Alfred O. Hero, Jr., *The Southerner and World Affairs* (Baton Rouge: Louisiana State Univ. Press, 1965).

2. Reported in Alfred O. Hero, Jr., and Emil Starr, *The Reuther-Meany Foreign Policy Dispute: Union Leaders and Members View World Affairs* (Dobbs Ferry, N.Y.: Oceana Publications, 1970).

Research Center at Williams College, the Interuniversity Consortium for Political Research at the University of Michigan, and Louis Vexler, at that time with the Gallup Organization.

The interpretations of these data and suggestions for church action in the future benefited greatly from the author's participation as a member in the Committee of the Department of International Affairs of the National Council of Churches (N.C.C.) and as a consultant in the Joint Project Committee on International Affairs Education of the Departments of International Affairs and of Educational Development of the N.C.C., as well as from his involvement in various ad hoc seminars, meetings, and discussions sponsored by agencies of the N.C.C., the Division of World Justice and Peace of the U.S. Catholic Conference, the Massachusetts Council of Churches, the Council of Religious and International Affairs, and other religious and quasi-religious agencies. Particularly the last two chapters in this volume profited from thoughtful written comments and suggestions on successive drafts by individual fellow participants in the Joint Project Committee on International Affairs Education and the Committee of the Department of International Affairs of the N.C.C., as well as those received from several dozen busy senior members of the staffs of the N.C.C., the U.S. Catholic Conference, and the Massachusetts Council of Churches. Helpful suggestions were likewise provided by a number of other perceptive observers of church life in America and the role of American churches in international affairs.

The errors of fact, interpretation, and judgment herein are, however, attributable to the author alone.

CONTENTS

CONTENTS

AMERICAN RELIGIOUS GROUPS
VIEW FOREIGN POLICY

INTRODUCTION

This volume considers how American Protestants, Catholics, and Jews compare with one another in their reactions to issues of foreign policy since the late 1930's. The book is based on national surveys which have posed questions about both religion and world affairs; on this basis it examines empirically a number of differences between the religious groups in their thinking on international questions.

What are these differences? Many and conflicting impressions are in circulation, and thus many questions need to be answered in this field. For instance, the anticommunist stance of the Vatican was long taken for granted, expressed by articulate American Catholic spokesmen like Cardinals MacIntyre and Spellman and in the Catholic press of the 1930's, 1940's, and 1950's. But to what extent was this stance reflected in the views of the Catholic population in the United States? Do Catholics in fact favor firmer and less compromising policies toward the communist powers than do Protestant Americans? Do Catholics a great deal more than Protestants approve of ultraconservative "anticommunist" regimes of supposedly pro-Catholic sympathies in Spain, Portugal, and Latin America? Are Catholics likewise more inclined than Protestants to favor conservative, pro-Western governments over progressive governments in the less-developed world generally? In the 1950's, when Senator Joseph McCarthy was at the height of his influence, and later, were Catholics more apt to consider communism at home a major threat to U.S. security? Many Catholics are of relatively recent immigrant origins, largely peasant. Are such origins in fact associated with super-patriotism, provincialism, neo-isolationism, and generally conservative sentiments in international issues, as some observers claim?

Others argue quite to the contrary: Roman Catholics can be expected to support the Democratic Party and to have more liberal views on such domestic issues as Negro-white relations, trade unions, social welfare, and transfer of wealth from rich to poor; surely, they say, these attitudes in domestic politics are associated with more liberal preferences in foreign policy as well. But is this true? Are Catholic Americans really more sympathetic than their Protestant compatriots to liberal domestic programs, and if so, what connections have views on domestic issues with thinking on international questions?

Some observers also suggest that the composition of the Catholic Church, generally more cosmopolitan than that of particular Protestant denominations, and the more diverse cultural and political experience of its hierarchy around the world result in greater emotional and rational sensitivity to international developments among its adherents. Is this the case? The world ponders the *aggiornamento* of the Catholic Church under Popes John XXIII and Paul VI, their internationally oriented encyclicals, the flexible recent posture of the Vatican toward communist and neutralist states, and its more vigorous support of the United Nations, of economic assistance to the less-developed world, and the like. Are these shifts in Vatican policy paralleled by similar shifts in attitude of rank-and-file Catholics?

If a person's religious beliefs and affiliation with religious bodies are associated with his thinking about the world beyond the nation's frontiers, then his theological preferences and degree of identification with his church should have some relationship with his opinions on international matters. But in fact, are the more fundamentalist, i.e., theologically conservative, Protestants and Catholics also more conservative on foreign relations than their coreligionists who happen to be more liberal theologically? Do regular churchgoing Protestants differ from their religiously indifferent colleagues with respect to major issues of foreign policy— particularly issues with ethical overtones? And do parishioners who attend the Catholic mass once a week or oftener diverge significantly in their views on international questions from Catholics who are less devoted?

Protestant denominations come in all shapes and sizes, and one denomination is apt to differ sharply from another in socioeconomic and ethnic composition, in doctrinal emphases—and in conceptions of the churchman's role with respect to international questions. On the other hand, there is much resemblance between the pronouncements of bodies that represent many Protestant denominations—e.g., the Federal Council of Churches (F.C.C.) and its successor the National Council of Churches (N.C.C.)—and pronouncements of the heads of affiliated denominations. These pronouncements have been typically liberal, internationalist, and multilateralist in tenor. But have they reflected the foreign-policy views of the rank-and-file memberships of these denominations? Or has the rank and file often shown more resemblance in its opinions to members of other denominations whose leaders have taken more conservative positions or remained silent on international issues? How aware are church members of the public stances of the national and international religious bodies that speak in their name on world issues, and how is any such awareness related to the layman's attitudes on the same questions?

Are American Jews really much more cosmopolitan or liberal in their world attitudes than most Christians, as many observers suggest? How do their sentiments about Israel and the Middle East compare with Catholic feelings about relations of the federal government with the Vatican, Franco Spain, and Catholic regimes elsewhere, and with Protestant Negroes' reactions to Africa south of the Sahara? When we find differences in opinion on international questions between people of different faith, how far can we account for the differences by other factors than the religious—by racial, ethnic, or national origins, by differential educational or socioeconomic background, by disproportionate concentration of one or another religious group in some particular geographic region or cultural milieu of the United States?

How do the views of local clergymen on international questions differ from the views of their parishioners? How far do local clergymen agree with the public stances of their national and international leaderships in such questions? What is the clergyman's role in transmitting to his own congregation the ideas relevant to ethical reflection on world affairs that come to him from denominational and ecumenical bodies and from intellectual and other elites?

PROBLEMS OF CONCEPT AND METHOD

The Continual Shifting of Issues, Attitudes, and Definitions

International issues changed markedly between 1937 and 1969, even where popular labels remained the same. For example, foreign aid shows much change, in its purposes, its contents, its recipients. These were not the same in the '60's as in the late '40's and early '50's, and not the same in the '40's and '50's as before Pearl Harbor. National defense, conscription, collective security, and the like responded to very different military and economic challenges and enemies between 1937 and 1945 than in the decades that followed. Since V-J Day, the less-developed world has been transformed from a minor to a major consideration of U.S. policy. Tariffs dropped sharply during the decades after the Reciprocal Trade Agreements Act of 1934. International trade, regarded as mostly a matter of domestic economics in the interwar years, came into closer and closer connection with other aspects of U.S. foreign policy, with implications for the reconstruction and economic health of western Europe and Japan during the first ten years after the war, for the development of Asia, Africa, and Latin America more recently, and for commerce with the communist countries, and so on.

Thus trends in attitudes of particular religious groups may be due as much to changes in the issues themselves as to real shifts in opinions. Time has also altered the connotations of labels for some patterns of opinions in international affairs and brought new, more apposite labels. The old terms have not departed; they still turn up in the literature on U.S. public opinion, and that is why we need to define them and follow the shifts they have undergone.

The old term "isolationist" was applied to any person who opposed efforts of the Roosevelt administration to help opponents of the Axis, reduce barriers to trade, or otherwise take an active role in international affairs. The number of such isolationist Americans fell promptly with American entry into the war. Isolationists, once a majority on many of these issues, shrank to small minorities who went on to oppose the Marshall Plan, U.S. involvement in the United Nations and NATO, and other postwar commitments. In these pages, an "isolationist," except when the term is applied to attitudes toward a particular issue, is a person who favors a general withdrawal from foreign affairs in the postwar era as well.

"Neo-isolationism" suggests a loose syndrome of policy preferences in recent decades, shown by somewhat larger minorities than expressed immoderate isolationist opinions in the Roosevelt years. Some neo-isolationists venture Fortress America (or Fortress North America) views. Others feel that the U.S. should concentrate on the defense of the Western Hemisphere, and that any moves it makes beyond the two oceans should hold fast to military action, either unilateral or in collaboration with a few "trustworthy" allies. There is often associated with such views a preference for U.S. support of rightest governments in Latin America and elsewhere against regimes viewed as less pro-American or less anticommunist.

The term "internationalist" is less familiar now than before the '60's. Until Pearl Harbor it often connoted approval of U.S. collaboration with the League of Nations. "Internationalists" favored liberalization of the Johnson Act and the Neutrality Act to permit more help for opponents of the Axis. They wanted lower tariffs and liberalized quotas and more U.S. involvement abroad. In some eyes, the "internationalist" was the same thing as an "interventionist." After the war, "internationalist" connoted approval of most of the international programs of the Truman administration—emergency relief for Europe and the Far East, economic aid, military supplies for NATO allies, cooperation with the UN, liberalization of trade, and so forth. Since the 1950's, "internationalist" has come to suggest support not only for freer trade, economic aid, and the UN but also for cooperation with nonaligned or leftist regimes, especially in the less-developed world, and for broader contacts and compromises with communist regimes, even Peking, to reduce armaments and other sources of tension. In these pages, the "internationalist" of the late 1950's and 1960's is one who approves such multilateral cooperation.

A more accurate term for this cluster of opinions in recent years is "multilateralist," at the opposite pole of "unilateralist" and "unilateral interventionist."[1] The "unilateralist," as the public views him, favors the Fortress America postures of neo-isolationism. The unilateralist syndrome emphasizes U.S. intervention for the nation's own interests, going it alone if other powers do not join, and high priority for military means in dealing with forces in the world which oppose U.S. interests. The unilateralist orientation tends to belittle nonmilitary means for achieving long-range ends. It turns away from mutual reductions of trade barriers, expansion of economic and other nonmilitary aid, intercultural exchange, diplomatic negotiation and its mutual compromises, and the channeling of more U.S. efforts through international organizations.

The terms "liberal" and "conservative" mark distinctive attitudes, but the distinction is a stronger one in domestic issues than in international issues (see below, pp. 140–43). In fact, those who call themselves liberals may entertain views on most international questions that are only a little different from the views of those who call themselves conservatives (see below, pp. 141–42). Even in the utterances of sophisticated observers these terms often bear ambiguous meanings when applied to world affairs.

Before the war, "liberal" was often interchangeable with "internationalist"—an advocate of the League of Nations, wider trade, aid to the Loyalists in Spain and to Britain, France, and China in their resistance to the Axis powers, support of Lend-Lease, and so on. "Conservative" suggested the reverse, even out-and-out isolationism. Meanwhile a number of New Deal liberals were conservatives when foreign involvement was in ques-

1. For further discussion of the concept of unilateralist versus multilateralist orientations, see Charles O. Lerche, Jr., *The Uncertain South: Its Changing Patterns in Politics in Foreign Policy* (Chicago: Quadrangle Books, 1964).

tion—just where quite a few opponents of the New Deal were liberals, internationalists, or interventionists.

For ten years or so after World War II, liberalism in world affairs implied approval, conservatism disapproval, of the foreign programs of the federal government. But by the 1960's "liberal," like "international-ist," tended to become a synonym of "multilateralist," particularly as favoring less-military and more-accommodating stances in U.S. policy. "Conservative" developed connotations of "unilateralist," cooperation with conservative and anticommunist governments, stress on security and defense policy, U.S. sovereignty, and a hard line toward communist regimes—in fact, even neo-isolationist views.

Such strong and clear attitudes exist in consistent form among only the small minorities of the American public composed of the rare and atypical Americans who are interested in international affairs. Most Americans express one or another blend of attitudes, likely to include views which the well-informed and sophisticated regard as logically and ideologically inconsistent. "Liberal" and "conservative" are nonetheless terms that will occur in the pages that follow, where their meaning is not likely to be obscure for the issue in question or in connection with the data cited. When the terms are employed to compare more general attitude patterns, they will bear the senses summarized above.

Limitations Inherent in Available Data

Terms that keep shifting in meaning can be a source of interference in the perpetual effort to ascertain facts, but they are perhaps not the most troublesome source. More crucial are certain limitations that affect the research projects themselves. True, many projects have been devoted since the mid-1930's to the attitudes of religious groups toward political issues. But most research available as of 1970 comes to a focus in either ethical reflections on international affairs or in the public stances of de-nominations, ecumenical bodies, and other ecclesiastical institutions at the national or international level. Only very limited attention has been devoted to how such issues are viewed in local pews, and virtually none to the transmission of ideas in American churches.[2]

The primary source for any study of local views is still the extensive body of national survey data gathered by the American Institute of Public

2. For a critical inventory of existing research, see Alfred O. Hero, Jr., "Communica-tion of World Affairs Within and By American Churches," mimeographed (Boston: World Peace Foundation, 1969).

Opinion (AIPO, the Gallup Polls), Elmo Roper and Associates (formerly Fortune Poll), the National Opinion Research Center (NORC) of the University of Chicago (formerly of the University of Denver), and the Survey Research Center (SRC) of the University of Michigan. As for the years before the mid-thirties and the international opinions of religious groups of that period, these cannot be examined empirically; few reliable surveys were made earlier. Even after 1937 for a decade or so, no questions or only questions of little value for our purposes were posed on a number of issues which later turned out to be important ones. The questions asked often dealt with only part of the major issues of the period, and not the most salient part. When anyone undertakes a secondary analysis of data gathered years earlier for a variety of purposes all different from his own, he is typically busied with issues and aspects that are by no means of central concern to him. Thus the issues that we consider in these pages and the aspects we examine are not always picked out because they are of great importance for religion or international policy, but because the data on them are available.

We also run into problems in the wording of the original questions. What is a person's religion? Surveys made during World War II and before asked for church membership; more recent surveys have asked only for religious preference. This shift affects statistics. Many Americans are not members of any church or synagogue; yet only a few of these consider themselves, or are willing to declare themselves, atheists, agnostics, or wanting in religious preference. The effect of the change in questions is to add to the ranks of Protestants and Jews, and to a lesser extent Catholics, many persons who give themselves a nominal religious identification that would not have appeared in earlier surveys.

Jews present special problems of identification. The term "Jew" has an ethnic as well as a religious connotation. Jews are also less apt than Protestants and much less apt than Catholics to attend religious functions on a regular basis. Thus fewer people were counted as Jews in earlier statistics based on church membership than in later ones based on religious preference. More than half of the American ethnic Jews probably appear before 1945 among non-church-members, whereas for more recent years they make up a disproportionate fraction of the categories of no religious preference and of liberal (non-trinitarian) denominational preferences other than Jewish.

How can attachment to a religious group be measured? The usual measure has been frequency of church attendance, but the question has been probed in only a few surveys, and those touched little on international issues. Only a handful of surveys attempted to determine church attendance over an extended period. Most asked only whether the respondent had attended within the last week or on the preceding Sabbath. We look in vain for opinion on world affairs that includes multiple indicators of church involvement—financial contributions, participation in communion, confession, or church organizations, and relationships with parish clergy.

Data that are even more narrowly limited underlie our comments on how theological views jibe with attitudes on international questions. The doctrinal differences that may turn up among clergymen and others who have an interest in theology and doctrine are only feebly manifested among parishioners. Few surveys examining Americans' theological preferences have included many questions on international affairs. Conversely, only a handful of studies devoted to international questions have asked about theological beliefs. Most of that handful probed only the literal versus the liberal interpretations of the Bible, or whether clergy and church should stress individual conversion and salvation or should rather apply their faith to controversial social issues. Such questions have appeared so seldom that we will need to consult other correlates of religious literalism and conservatism—e.g., frequent Bible reading, affiliation with fundamentalist Protestant sects, and advocacy of liquor prohibition.

A further limitation affects our study because the samples of some religious groups are quite small. Accordingly, our criterion for statistical significance of differences between any two groups is a liberal one—the 10 percent level of confidence. That is, we accept as significant differences in any one survey only those which could have occurred no more than once in ten times through sampling errors alone (see the Appendix for tables of statistical significance of differences). After all, many surveys included no more than 1,200 interviewees, and few contained more than 3,000. Jews, a slowly decreasing fraction of the American population since the late 1930's, have constituted only 2 to 5 percent of most samples since roughly 1945. Before then they were typically a much smaller identifiable fraction of national samples, since it included only synagogue members. Self-identified Jews in some surveys numbered even fewer than 40, and seldom did they exceed 100. Therefore, differences between Jews and other religious or ethnic groups have to be quite large to be statistically significant.

To deal with this problem, we regard as significant the differences which turn up consistently between Jews and Christian groups in several surveys conducted independently, even when no difference in any one survey was significant. Since Jews in fact differ notably from others on most international questions, consistency of differences is a frequent phenomenon. However, in some cases where fewer than, say, 60 Jews appeared in a survey, the differences that the survey registered between them and other Americans were erratic.

The problem of small samples is more serious when groups are compared that differ less from other groups than Jews do. Consider the differences between similar Protestant denominations—say, Episcopalians and Presbyterians—or between white ethnic groups other than Americans of third or later generation, or between Catholics in the South and Catholics in the West, or between college-educated Catholics and Protestants of similar education. These differences are hard to interpret in a definitive way, unless they appear consistently over time in several surveys.

Changes in sampling methods probably introduced more important sources of error. Until the late forties or early fifties (depending on the survey organization) the kind of sampling most frequently employed was quota sampling. In this, the selection of interviewees is left to the interviewer in each locale; all he is expected to do is make sure of including specified numbers in each of certain demographic categories. Interviewees so selected were liable to be less representative of the real population than interviewees selected in later years by probability methods; in quota sampling the very wealthy and the wretchedly poor were often underrepresented.

Again, surveys prior to the early 1950's were more often than not studies of people who had voted in some immediately preceding election. But voters are on the average better educated, more sophisticated, more affluent, better informed, more interested in world affairs, and less provincial in their international thinking than nonvoters who are not included. Women, rural people, Southerners, and especially Negroes (see below, p. 84) were likewise disproportionately few in most of the early samples. Thus Protestants, especially those of fundamentalist persuasion, were often underrepresented.

In the last fifteen years or so, sampling has become more nearly representative of the national population among all major survey agencies; but as late as the end of the 1960's, actual samples still typically included disproportionate numbers of the groups easier to interview—Jews more than Negro Protestants, the better educated more than the poorly educated, i.e., precisely the demographic groups most informed and cosmopolitan about foreign affairs. However, in recent years the art of ascertaining just how opinions on international questions are distributed in the population has been based on weighting systems which try to compensate for these distortions in actual samples interviewed. Because of such shifts in method, replies over the years to similar or even identical questions are not entirely comparable. Yet comparisons of one religious group with others in one and the same survey should be less affected by such systematic errors in sampling.

Some methodological reservations are especially advisable for data on this or that racial, ethnic, regional, theological, denominational, or other subgroup within the two major Christian persuasions. These reservations will be mentioned as such groups are discussed.

The combination of all the limitations we have mentioned has probably produced errors which may affect some of our more detailed findings. Yet it is our strong impression that the more general comparative trends noted in the pages that follow very probably correspond with real trends among the total American population of the religious orientations indicated. Since there is no way to gather more nearly representative evidence on international attitudes among religious groups in decades past, it may well be that the data leading to our generalizations are the best we can hope for.

THE PAGES THAT FOLLOW

Part I examines differences between religious groups in respect of issues that were pressing on the eve of formal U.S. entry into the Second World War. We shall observe that Catholics were the least well informed of the three major religious groups, even when Negroes are included within Protestant statistics. Jews were by far the most aware of international developments, the most generally liberal or internationalist, and the most supportive of more active U.S. involvements abroad—differences which persist to the present day. Catholics were in general more isolationist than Protestants on most of the international questions of the time— reciprocal trade, cooperation with the League of Nations, liberalization of the Johnson Act and the Neutrality Act, material assistance to the opponents of the Axis, aid to Finland during its winter war with the

U.S.S.R., Lend-Lease, and especially, sale of U.S. arms to the Spanish Loyalists.

Such differences are apparent even when education, socioeconomic status, and like variables are held constant. However, ethnic differences and regional factors were at least as important as religion—particularly the lesser willingness of Catholics of Irish, German, and especially Italian origins to support Britain against Germany and Italy, and the widespread interventionist sentiments in the predominantly Protestant Southeast.

Part II considers postwar trends in attitudes toward world affairs of the three major American religious groups, a period of gradual disappearance and, later, reversal of a number of pre–Pearl Harbor differences between Catholics and Protestants. Differences in average level of awareness and general knowledge between the two major Christian groups became inconsequential in most aspects of international relations. By the late forties most attitudinal differences between the two groups had likewise narrowed to insignificance. It was only in relation to a few postwar issues that Catholics remained less favorably disposed toward international collaboration. Even these small differences had disappeared for the most part by the beginning of the 1960's.

Finally, by the mid-sixties many prewar differences between the two Christian groups had become inverted. Both Catholics and Jews in 1963–69 were significantly more favorable than Protestants to a number of types of international cooperation and negotiation—the UN, relaxation of tensions with the communist world, admission of Mainland China to the UN, liberalizing immigration, expanding cultural exchanges and other contacts with foreigners, and particularly, foreign aid, of economic and nonmilitary kinds. Catholics had also become somewhat more optimistic than Protestants about most public issues, including the possibilities of avoiding another major war, America's future role in the world, and the general course of international relations. On most other issues the two Christian groups differed in no consistent respects—international trade, military aid to "friendly" governments, national defense, collective security, and most aspects of the war in Vietnam. Even earlier Catholic-Protestant differences with respect to the Franco regime and world population control had declined considerably.

Part III begins by considering the relevance of such demographic factors as differential racial, ethnic, educational, socioeconomic, and regional composition of Catholic versus Protestant religious groups to the differences in attitude on international questions which are noted in Part

II. Nonwhite (mostly Negro) Protestants have been much less aware of international developments, less interested in them, and less inclined to hold opinions on them than whites of any religion. Negro Protestants were likewise less supportive than their white coreligionists of most U.S. international commitments prior to the early 1950's. Thus the Negro component lowered the Protestant averages of support for U.S. assistance to the opponents of the Axis, for Lend-Lease, for aid to Greece and Turkey under the Truman Doctrine, for the Marshall Plan, for military supplies for NATO members, and for most other U.S. commitments of the period.

However, the differences between the attitudes of Negro and of white Protestants on most international questions had disappeared by the mid or late fifties, and by the mid-sixties a number of them had got reversed. Negro Protestants, insofar as they expressed any views, grew more favorably inclined than white Protestants to economic aid, the Peace Corps, cooperation with neutralist governments, expanding negotiation and mutual compromise to reduce disagreements with Moscow and Peking, collaboration with the UN, expanding international trade, intercultural exchange, and immigration, and even establishing diplomatic relations with the Vatican. Thus when Negroes are eliminated from Protestant and Catholic statistics, there are usually larger differences between Protestants and Catholics on questions of support for multilateral cooperation, because Negroes, mostly Protestants, oftener share the views of white Catholics.

On the other hand, Negro Protestant reactions to large U.S. defense expenditures and to military service do not differ significantly from those of white Protestants or Catholics. Although Negro Protestants accord higher priority to U.S. relations with black Africa than do whites of either religious persuasion, they are on the average no better informed about developments there, and their identification with that area is much less pronounced than the identification of American Jews with Israel.

By the late 1960's most differences in international views among non-Jewish white ethnic groups apparent before World War II had virtually disappeared. Certainly such small differences as persisted did not explain the more widespread support for most types of multilateral cooperation among Catholic than Protestant whites. Southern white Protestants had become distinctly less supportive than Protestant whites elsewhere of economic aid for nonaligned regimes, of compromises with the Soviet Union and Communist China to reduce disagreements, and of some other forms of multilateral cooperation. However, even when Southerners are eliminated from the figures, the non-Southern Protestants were somewhat less approving of such policies than Catholic whites outside the South. Interregional differences with respect to views on foreign affairs outside the South within each of the two major Christian groups during the sixties were small or nonexistent. Except in the Northeast, where Catholic whites did not differ significantly in most of their foreign-policy preferences from Protestant whites, Catholics were consistently more favorable to multilateral collaboration than Protestant whites in the same region.

The gradual narrowing of the prewar gaps in education, income, and occupation between the two Christian groups can account only in part for the differences between them, evident by the 1960's, in their attitudes on international questions. Even when such factors are held constant, Catholics of each general educational and socioeconomic level were somewhat more favorable to nonmilitary aid, admission of Mainland China to the UN, and negotiation with communist leaders to relieve international tensions than were Protestants of similar backgrounds. Nor were such differences confined to younger groups; they were apparent at all age levels. Rural and small-town white Protestants have been less supportive than their urban coreligionists of economic aid for nonaligned regimes, Peking's membership in the UN, and expanded negotiations with communist governments. But even when only white urbanites and suburbanites are considered, white Catholics have been somewhat more liberal on such issues than white Protestants. Nor did the proclivities of most Catholic whites for the Democratic Party, compared with the Republican sympathies of most white Protestants, account for more than part of the interreligious attitudinal differences of the 1960's. White Catholic Republicans were more favorable to liberal foreign policies than white Protestant Republicans, white Catholic Democrats than white Protestant Democrats.

Catholic whites during these three decades have been consistently more inclined than white Protestants to consider themselves liberals and to favor more liberal policies on such domestic issues as race relations, social welfare, and transfers of wealth and services from the more affluent to the less. Among both Christian groups, racial equalitarians have been significantly more supportive than segregationists and racial conservatives of economic aid, liberalization of relations with communist countries, and other multilateral cooperation. When reactions to civil rights are held constant, differences of opinion between Catholics and Protestants on international issues have been noticeably reduced, if not eliminated. Approval of expanding the federal aid to education, which is wider among Catholics than among Protestants, has been likewise (to a lesser extent) related to the more liberal views of Catholics in international matters. Fiscal conservatives who favor cutting the federal budget, reducing taxes, and lowering the national debt through paring general expenditures have been somewhat less enthusiastic than fiscal liberals among both Catholics and Protestants about nonmilitary expenditures abroad.

Except for these limited linkages, the liberalism in domestic views of Catholics, greater generally than that of Protestants, has had little bearing on the recently more liberal views of Catholics in foreign policy. Policy preferences in such issues as Medicare, Social Security, unemployment compensation, aid to dependent children, and other transfers of wealth and services from the prosperous to the poor have had little connection with preferences in foreign policy. Support for liberal domestic programs, more widespread among Catholics than among Protestants, long antedates the development of more multilateralist foreign-policy thinking among Catholics.

At least in recent years, the clergymen of most non-fundamentalist Christian denominations harbor more liberal internationalist or multilateralist views than do their laities. The more conservative a clergyman's theological orientation, or the more he emphasizes individual salvation and conversion, the more conservative his international views are. Correlations have been consistent—theological conservatives prefer tough postures toward communist governments, assign high priority to military reactions to communist challenges, and so on, while theological liberals or *persuadés* of the social gospel place more emphasis on nonmilitary means.

Such associations between theological and international preferences were apparent in the 1960's among rank-and-file parishioners, but were less pronounced than among theologically trained professionals. Protestants from denominations with more liberal theological traditions have recently put forward international opinions that are on the whole more liberal or multilateralist than are those of compatriots affiliated with the Southern Baptists, the Missouri Synod Lutherans, and fundamentalist sects. However, these differences in attitudes on international questions seem to be due as much to the higher level of education among Episcopalians, Congregationalists, Presbyterians, and suchlike, when compared with fundamentalist groups, as to their divergent theological proclivities.

There is a small minority of laymen who show the greatest interest in the substantive content of their religion, and these may harbor views on foreign affairs that are more congruent with views expressed by the Vatican and by the leaderships of the N.C.C. and the major non-fundamentalist denominations. The data which came to our attention neither prove nor disprove this conjecture. However, Protestants who attend church regularly or who say they feel more than average devotion to their denomination have not differed on world affairs from less active Protestants or Protestants who show less psychological identification with their church. Among Catholics, the more devout laymen have been slightly more favorable than the less devout toward economic aid for less-developed countries and the like. On the whole, Christian churches in the United States seem to have little direct impact on the thinking of their parishioners on world affairs, even in such ethical issues as foreign aid.

In Part IV, Chapter 10 offers explanations and interpretations of the findings in the pages that precede it. Since virtually no systematic research has been devoted to the flow of information and ideas in this field in American churches, these impressions will be largely suggestive and hypothetical. Chapter 11 speculates about possible general approaches through which the churches might gradually improve understanding among their members of the ethical dimensions of international affairs and U.S. foreign policy. The recommendations advanced are derived mainly from observations made of Protestant bodies, though the more valid of them may well apply with some amendment to Catholic institutions and perhaps to Jewish institutions as well.

Percentages and other figures are cited in the text chiefly for illustration. Detailed documentation for the generalizations may be consulted in the tables that follow the Appendix. Surveys within each table are put in chronological order.

PART I. BEFORE PEARL HARBOR

CHAPTER 1. ISOLATIONIST PRELUDE

Prior to U.S. entry into the Second World War, Catholics were less informed and somewhat less inclined to express views on most aspects of foreign policy than were Protestants, especially when Negroes and Southerners—mostly Protestants—are eliminated from consideration. Jews then as now were more generally aware of international developments and more apt to hold opinions than were either Catholics, Protestants, or non-church-members. Insofar as they entertained opinions, Jews were the most favorably inclined of the religious groups toward more active U.S. commitments abroad. Catholics were the least likely to approve of a more active or less isolationist policy with respect to most international issues of the period. However, differences in prevailing views were usually larger between Jews and either of the two major Christian groups or non-church-members than they were among the three latter.

CATHOLICS AS LEAST INTERVENTIONIST

Thus, in early 1939, shortly before Hitler's Germany absorbed what was left of Czechoslovakia, only among Catholics did a majority feel it had been a mistake for the United States to enter the First World War. The number among all religious groups who thought U.S. participation in that war an error declined somewhat with the defeat of France in 1940, the Battle of Britain, and Axis occupation of most of Europe. Nevertheless, as late as January 1941 Catholics remained the only major religious group within which more considered our entry a mistake than considered it not a mistake (Table 1–1).

There was more isolationist thinking among Catholics than among other Americans with respect to the League of Nations and international commerce as well. In September 1938, during the Munich crisis, Catholics were less likely than Protestants or especially Jews to think that "America's failure to join the League of Nations was partly responsible for the present trouble in Europe" (Table 1–2). Catholics were likewise the least favorable to expansion of reciprocal trade, though differences between the two Christian groups were quite small.

Fascism, Communism, and Franco

Equally consistent differences in attitude showed up among the religious groups with respect to the advent of the fascist and Nazi menaces in Europe and what should be done about them. Jews, not surprisingly, were most opposed to compromises with the authoritarian Spanish, Italian, and German regimes and most apt to favor active measures to limit their power and influence. Roman Catholics were the least so, and Protestants in between.

Thus, asked in early 1939 whether they would prefer communism or fascism if they had to choose, two out of three Catholics venturing opinions preferred fascism, contrasted with only two out of five Protestants and a slightly smaller fraction of Jews (Table 1–3).[1] As might have been surmised, Catholics were also considerably more inclined than any other religious group to sympathize with the cause of Franco rather than the Loyalist cause in Spain, and to oppose liberalization of the features of the Neutrality Act which prohibited sales of munitions to either side in the Spanish Civil War (Table 1–3). Even when informed in February 1939 that "Franco is now obtaining war materials from Italy and Germany," only 20 percent of the Catholics who said they had followed events in the Civil War (compared with 41 percent of Protestants, 52 percent of Jews, and 39 percent of non-church-members) would permit the Loyalists to buy military supplies in the United States.[2] The supposedly pro-Church orientation of the Nationalists, and anti-Catholic or at least non-Catholic aspects of the Loyalists, as well as popular concern about the reported communist influence among the latter, probably accounted for much of the difference in sentiments between the two Christian groups.

Defense of the West

This special connotation for Catholics of the Spanish struggle helps to explain why differences in views between Catholics and Protestants were smaller with respect to the two major European Axis powers, especially Nazi Germany. Nevertheless, consistent—though smaller—differences of attitude in the same direction separated the religious groups so far as the Hitler and Mussolini regimes were concerned as well.

For example, immediately after the Munich debacle, slightly smaller majorities of Catholics than of other religious groups felt that "England and France made a mistake in agreeing to Germany's demands on

1. The difference between Jews and other Americans would probably have been larger had fascism been limited to nazism.

2. AIPO 147, 2–2–39. The sample included 547 Catholics, 1,613 Protestants, 107 Jews, and 802 non-church-members.

Czechoslovakia" (Table 1–4). Conversely, somewhat larger majorities of Catholics than of others felt that President Roosevelt should not "openly criticize Hitler and Mussolini for their warlike attitude." Several months later, a significantly larger minority of Catholics (20 percent) than of Protestants (14 percent), Jews (4 percent), or non-church-members (14 percent) believed that the colonies taken from Germany after the First World War should be returned to the Hitler regime.

Even after most of Europe fell to the Axis, Catholics were the least inclined of the religious groups to think that our vital interests were at stake in the war on the other side of the Atlantic. Although a majority of Catholics believed that they personally would be affected if "the United States does not go into the war, and Germany defeats England," that majority was distinctly smaller than the majority of like mind among other religious persuasions (Table 1–5). At the time of the heated debates of the Lend-Lease bill in Congress and the mass media, only among Catholics did fewer than half think that the Germans would bomb or otherwise attack the United States "if the British navy were defeated or surrendered." Jews were the most convinced of the dire consequences for the United States of a possible German-Italian victory.

In the light of these observations, it is not surprising that regardless of how the question was worded, Catholics were less enthusiastic than Protestants or particularly Jews about measures designed to help Britain and France contain Germany and Italy. Insofar as they held views on the subject, Catholics were without exception the most apt to favor maintaining intact the restrictive provisions of the Johnson Act of 1934 prohibiting further loans to governments which had not at least paid interest on their previous debts and the even more stringent prohibitions of the neutrality legislation of 1935, 1936, and 1937 (Table 1–6). For example, even before the opening of formal hostilities in Europe, as early as February 1939, Catholics somewhat more than Protestants and a good deal more than Jews would not have allowed the British and French to buy "warplanes manufactured in this country"; conversely, a larger minority of Catholics than of either of the others would have permitted Germany and Italy to do so. As the Nazi and Soviet armies were mopping up Poland, only 21 percent of Catholics versus 26 percent of Protestants, 31 percent of Jews, and 24 percent of non-church-members would change the neutrality law even so far as to enable Britain and France or any other belligerents to "buy war supplies here" on an equal basis. Those who would lend "money to England and France to buy war materials in this country" were still smaller minorities of all religious groups the following December, but smallest among Catholics. Only slightly more numerous minorities, even among Jews, would have lent the Allies "money to buy war supplies in this country" even if they satisfied the provisions of the Johnson Act by paying "something on the war debts they now owe us"; but again Catholics were the least willing to do so.

After the collapse of western Europe before the Nazi forces, the number favorable to expanded assistance to Britain grew among all groups, but Catholics remained the least supportive of such aid (Table 1–7). During the height of the Battle of Britain and just after the public announcement of the exchange of fifty "over-age" destroyers for bases on British dependencies in the Western Hemisphere, 53 percent of Catholics, compared with only 43 percent of Protestants, 32 percent of Jews, and 45 percent of non-church-members, felt it more important "to try to keep out of the war ourselves" than "to help England win, even at the risk of getting into the war." The proportions of this isolationist frame of mind declined during the following months as our actual assistance to Britain expanded, but invariably, Catholics were the most inclined to accord greater priority to staying out of the war than to helping the British. Whether or not the provisions of the Johnson or Neutrality Acts were spelled out to the respondents, Catholics remained the least inclined to favor changing them to permit loans or credits for purchases of weapons, or even food, by Britain in this country. Catholics were the only religious group which did not accord majority unqualified support to passage of the Lend-Lease bill in early 1941, and the most likely, as the Nazis invaded Russia and again the following fall, to believe that President Roosevelt had "gone too far in his policies of helping Britain."

The numbers favorable to revising the neutrality legislation radically, so as to permit transportation of war supplies to Britain in American merchant ships with American crews, convoyed by the American navy, were considerably smaller among all religious groups than those who supported Lend-Lease and other schemes under which such material was supplied by the United States but carried away in foreign ships under the protection, if any, of the British navy (Table 1–7). The minorities who would have had this country formally enter the war against Germany and Italy were smaller still. But again, Catholics were the least favorable to such nonneutral actions against the Axis (Table

1–7). Overwhelming majorities of all groups, but still proportionally fewer Catholics than Protestants or, especially, Jews, would have provided more help "if it appears that England will be defeated by Germany and Italy unless the United States supplies her with more food and war materials." Although only relatively small minorities of any group agreed "with Lindbergh's viewpoint on aid to Britain and foreign policy" after its defeatist and isolationist tone was explained, the ratio of those in agreement to those opposed was highest among Catholics and, of course, lowest among Jews.

Defense of Finland and the U.S.S.R.

Attitudinal differences between Catholics and other Americans were smaller with respect to most issues not so directly related to the Spanish Civil War, the ensuing Franco regime, and assistance to Britain against Germany and Italy. Nevertheless, some differences, in the direction of lesser Catholic support of wider international commitments, were apparent regardless of the particular foreign countries or controversies involved. For instance, the anticommunism which was more prevalent among Catholics than others was not sufficient to countervail the Catholics' more widespread general isolationism and did not generate as much approval among Catholics as Protestants and, particularly, Jews, for aid to Finland during the Soviet attack on that country in the winter of 1939–40. A significantly smaller majority of Catholics than of either of the others in January 1940 felt that Congress should pass the bill to lend $60,000,000 to Finland "to help her in her war against Russia" (Table 1–8). But Catholics were also slightly less inclined than others to extend the Lend-Lease provisions applicable to Britain to include the U.S.S.R. when the latter was invaded by the Nazis a year and a half later, as well as clearly less likely to prefer that the Soviets rather than the Nazis win that war.

The Far East

Although there was no difference in opinion between Catholics and Protestants in early 1939 on whether the Japanese or the Soviets would win if there was a war between them, Catholics more than any other religious group preferred that the Japanese win if such a war should develop (Table 1–9). As Japanese pressure against China grew with the Nazi victories in western Europe and the Luftwaffe attack on Britain, Catholics were somewhat more reluctant than other Americans to forbid sales of arms, aircraft, gasoline, or other war materials to Japan. They were also slightly more willing than others to "let Japan get control of China" rather than to "risk a war with Japan to keep the Japanese from controlling China."[3] As might have been anticipated, differences in thinking between Jews and other citizens were smaller on such issues in the Far East than differences on the containment and defeat of nazism and fascism in western Europe. Nevertheless, Jews were consistently more inclined than any other religious group to approve of expanded U.S. action to stop further Japanese aggression, as they were to support most other international commitments suggested by the President or his senior foreign-policy aides.

Relations with the Vatican

Catholics were, of course, sharply more favorable to the establishment of formal diplomatic relations with the Vatican than were Protestants, but only a few percentage points more favorable to this idea than were Jews. Asked in early 1940, when this suggestion was being publicly discussed, "Do you think the United States should send an ambassador to the court of Pope Pius in Rome, as it does to other foreign countries?", 64 percent of Catholics in comparison with 30 percent of Protestants, 53 percent of Jews, and 31 percent of non-church-members replied in the affirmative, while 22 percent of Catholics vs. 50, 36, and 48 percent, respectively, opposed. As one might have anticipated, most of the minority of Catholics who felt the American government should not establish formal diplomatic relations with the Vatican were general isolationists in that they also opposed any loan by the federal government to Finland to help her defend herself against the Soviet attack at the time; they said they had not "given any thought to what should be done to maintain world peace after the present European war is over"; they felt "the Constitution should be changed to require a national vote before Congress could draft men for war overseas"; and they either had never heard of reciprocal trade treaties or opposed them. On the other hand, a considerable, though smaller, fraction of Catholics who favored formal diplomatic relations with the papacy also advanced isolationist views on these other issues. For instance, 42 percent of the Catholics who favored sending an ambassador to the Vatican disapproved of our government lending Finland $60,000,000 even though she had serviced her debts from the First

3. Differences were too small for statistical significance at the 10 percent level.

World War, and only a small majority of 54 percent of these Catholics favorable to ambassadorial relations with the Church approved of such a loan to Finland.

No such clear correlation between views on establishing diplomatic relations with the Vatican and opinions on these other international issues appeared among Jews and Northern Protestants. In fact, Jews who favored diplomatic relations with the Vatican seemed somewhat less inclined to approve of a loan to Finland than Jews who opposed such formalized relations.[4] Among Protestants living outside the former Confederacy, those who approved the establishment of formal diplomatic relations with the court of Pope Pius XII were only very slightly, if at all, more favorable to aiding Finland in its defense than those who disapproved of such diplomatic contact.[5] Protestant and Jewish isolationists opposed sending an ambassador to the Vatican, but so did many Jews and Northern Protestants who favored other types of international involvement. Non-Catholics were more favorable than Catholics to most other forms of international cooperation, regardless of their views on the Vatican issue. Many otherwise relatively internationalist (or interventionist) non-Catholics apparently feared that formal relations with the papacy would undermine the balance of church-state relations in this country and perhaps have negative results abroad as well.

4. AIPO 181, 1–10–40. Among Jews who favored formal relations with the Vatican, 58 percent approved and 29 percent disapproved of a $60,000,000 loan to Finland; among Jews who opposed sending an ambassador to the Vatican, 67 percent approved and 28 percent disapproved of such a loan. However, the Jewish sample numbered only 41 persons.

5. Ibid. Non-Southern Protestants numbered 1,374. Among the 29 percent who approved of sending an ambassador to the Vatican, 57 percent approved of the proposed loan to Finland, 39 percent disapproved, and 4 percent expressed no view. Among the 51 percent who disapproved of establishing diplomatic relations with the papacy, 55 percent approved, 39 percent disapproved, and 6 percent ventured no opinion. Among the 20 percent who did not care whether such diplomatic ties were set up or not or who ventured no views on the matter, 58 percent approved of aiding the Finns, 33 percent disapproved, and 9 percent offered no opinion. Correlation between views on aiding Finland and those on sending an ambassador to the Vatican was not statistically significant, nor were correlations between views on establishing diplomatic relations and thinking about reciprocal trade, interest in and thought about international institutions to maintain peace after the war, and opinions toward possible requirement of a plebiscite before Congress could draft men to fight overseas.

PART II. THE POSTWAR WORLD

CHAPTER 2. KNOWLEDGE, INVOLVEMENT, AND GENERAL INTERNATIONAL COOPERATION

Support for a more active foreign policy grew considerably among all religious groups after U.S. entry into the Second World War. Nevertheless, even midway in the war Catholics were still the least enthusiastic about continuing Lend-Lease to allies, non-church-members next least favorably disposed, Protestants more inclined than either to continue this assistance, and Jews most enthusiastic of all.[1] Among Catholics the combination of more widespread hesitations about long-term cooperation with the Soviet Union (see below, p. 41) and of stronger reservations about helping the British continued during the war as before to limit their support for this important program.

INFORMATION, INTEREST, AND OPINIONS

Nevertheless, by the late 1940's Catholics had become only slightly less well-informed about most aspects of foreign relations than Protestants. Jews, as was the case previously and would remain thereafter, were normally more knowledgeable about most international developments than either. For example, as Table 2–1 demonstrates, the two principal Christian groups were equally likely in late April of 1948 to have heard of the Palestinian partition issue, to know that the UN and the U.S.S.R. favored partition, and to realize that the U.S. government had come to oppose it. The following summer Catholics were as apt as Protestants to know that the fighting had stopped, at least temporarily, in Palestine. Later that year similarly small minorities of both said they had heard something of the Bernadotte Plan for the solution of the Palestinian problem, and Catholics were significantly more inclined than Protestants to be able to recall correctly the name of Count Bernadotte, the UN mediator, as the "famous person assassinated recently in Palestine."

Equal minority fractions of both religious groups in April 1948 had heard of the recent defense agreement among the countries of continental western Europe (Table 2–1). Two years later only a somewhat smaller minority of Catholics—19 percent—than of Protestants—24

1. AIPO 287, 1-7-43. Seventy-six percent of Catholics, 81 percent of unaffiliated persons, 85 percent of Protestants, and 90 percent of Jews favored "continuing the Lend-Lease program"; 14, 10, 7, and 2 percent, respectively, would have terminated it. Catholics numbered 333, unaffiliated persons 492, Protestants 1,110, and Jews 61.

percent—had heard of Point Four technical assistance to "backward" countries suggested in President Truman's inaugural address a year or so earlier. During a period of accentuated tension in the Formosa Straits in the spring of 1955, there was no difference in the proportions of Catholics and Protestants who had heard or read of the problem, and Catholics were but slightly less likely than Protestants to know that the Nationalist Chinese controlled Quemoy and Matsu. And in April 1957 equally large majorities of both Christian groups were unable to mention correctly even one African country or dependent territory, while comparably small minorities of both could name as many as five.

By the mid-sixties, however, it appears that Catholics had become somewhat better informed about world developments than Protestants, particularly when Southerners and Negroes, mostly Protestants, are included in the comparison (below, pp. 85–87). In the fall of 1964, for instance, Catholics were somewhat more apt to know that mainland China was controlled by a communist regime and that it was not a member of the UN (Table 2–1). And although Catholics were consistently a bit less likely than Protestants to have heard or read anything of tariffs, international trade, GATT, or related subjects during the first ten years after the war, the reverse seemed to be the case by the end of the 1950's.

Among all religious groups, as with other segments of the population, interest in world affairs and importance accorded to them have been intimately connected with knowledge about that field. Thus, given the disappearance of the prewar information gap between Catholic and Protestant Christians, it is not surprising that the prewar lag of Catholics with respect to interest in and exposure to international relations disappeared as well.

By the fall of 1956, for example, the same small proportion of Catholics—9 percent—as of Protestants considered some aspects of foreign affairs or foreign policy generally to be the most important issue in the presidential campaign, and about a quarter of both religious groups felt that field to be of greater importance than domestic matters (Table 2–2). Asked several months later which of five fields would interest them the most if they had "time to spare," a slightly more minuscule minority—8 percent—of Protestants than of Catholics—12 percent—chose "world affairs, the UN," or related subjects. Nor was there any difference in the fall of 1956 in the roles of the major media of communication in informing members of the two Christian groups about foreign affairs. Even magazines, the source of information and interpretation of international developments most important to the more interested and better-informed minority, were equally likely to be cited by both religious groups as the media from which they derived "a great deal of information about world affairs."[2] Finally, by late 1964 Catholics had become somewhat less apt than Protestants, even when Negroes were not included, to say they were not interested enough to have any views on foreign aid, negotiations and trade with the communist world, and possible membership of Communist China in the UN (see below, Tables 3–19, 3–21, and 4–6).

This disappearance of the prewar tendency of Catholics to know somewhat less than Protestants about foreign affairs, to be less interested, and to pay less attention was associated with a gradual elimination of differences between the two Christian groups in their expression of any policy preferences or opinions and in their inclination to say they did not know. In fact, by the 1960's Catholics had become on the whole somewhat more inclined than Protestants (when Negroes were included) to hold opinions on most foreign-policy matters.

Support for an Active Foreign Policy

A year after V-J Day, a somewhat larger minority of Catholics—35 percent—than of Protestants—27 percent—and Jews—31 percent—agreed with the isolationist view that "we fought in World War II only because we were attacked at Pearl Harbor"; while a somewhat smaller majority of Catholics than of other citizens (50, 62, and 62 percent, respectively) believed "there were some other reasons why we fought" as well (Table 2–3). However, about equally large majorities of both Christian groups approved of a relatively active U.S. posture in international relations during most of the decade following the war. For instance, less than one out of ten of any religious group felt without qualification in the summer of 1946 that "our government should keep to itself and not have anything to do with the rest of the world"; while only another 7 percent of Catholics and 5 percent of Protestants agreed with specified reservations or qualifications.

In the summer of 1953 a smaller minority of Catholics—5 percent—

2. Catholics in the mid-fifties were as apt as Protestants, but not as likely as Jews, to read a daily newspaper. However, the disproportionate number of Southerners and Negroes among Protestants lowered the national Protestant average of newspaper readership. See *The Public Impact of Science in the Mass Media* (Ann Arbor: Survey Research Center, 1957), p. 19.

than of Protestants—18 percent—believed "we should have taken a larger part in world affairs" than we had since the war, and a slightly larger minority of Catholics—23 percent—than of Protestants—20 percent—that we "should have taken a definitely smaller part." However, this religious difference was explained by the larger majority of Catholics—67 percent—than Protestants—48 percent—who agreed that the part we had taken was "on the whole about right."

During the height of the public debate over the impending Bricker amendment in early 1954, only one American out of four had ever "heard or read anything" about it, and over half of even this minority were unwilling to express any opinions for or against it. But among the small minority who did offer views on this bill designed to restrict the treaty-making power of the President and shift the conduct of foreign policy from the Executive toward the Congress, as large a majority of Catholics as Protestants (though not as large as among Jews) disapproved. Then 2½ years later and again in early 1969 Jews continued to be less inclined than either Christian group to agree that the U.S. would be "better off if it just stayed home and did not concern itself with problems in other parts of the world." But Catholics were on both occasions at most but slightly more in agreement with this isolationist view than Protestants.[3]

Americans who have felt that their country should take an active role in international relations have not, of course, necessarily agreed on the nature of the foreign problems challenging the United States or on how best to deal with them. However, during most of the ten years just after the war, there was hardly any difference between Catholics' and Protestants' reactions to the general question of how well "the officials in Washington," "our government," the Secretary of State, or the like were handling our relations with other countries.

Typically, majorities of about the same proportions of both religious groups approved of the general conduct of foreign policy by our senior federal officials (Table 2–4). For instance, even during Catholic Senator Joseph McCarthy's initial claim in 1950 about communists in the Department of State, a slightly larger proportion of Catholics than Protestants or Jews felt Secretary Acheson was "in general" doing a "good job as Secretary of State in Washington." During the height of the attacks by the junior senator from Wisconsin on the Foreign Service

3. Catholic-Protestant differences were too small for statistical significance (Table 2–3).

and Department of State in 1953, 61 percent of both Catholics and Protestants approved of the general conduct of Secretary of State Dulles, and 73 percent of both approved of "the way the present officials in Washington are handling our foreign affairs." (See also pp. 45–46, for the relative popularity and influence of Senator Joseph McCarthy among the religious groups.)

THE UNITED NATIONS

Unfortunately, similar general questions about active international commitments have not been posed since the mid-fifties. However, comparative surveys of attitudes toward the UN—closely associated statistically with general internationalism or approval of multilateral cooperation versus isolationism or ultranationalism—are available over the entire period since the Second World War.

The Late Forties and the Fifties

Although Catholics had been less enthusiastic than other religious groups about U.S. membership in the League of Nations, or collaboration with it, the differences between the two Christian groups with respect to U.S. policies toward the UN for some fifteen years after the war were in most cases neither statistically significant nor consistent. Jews, as might have been supposed, were normally more favorably disposed than either Christian group toward the world body.

Thus in the fall of 1946, when 80 percent of Jews thought that "making the UN strong" would be more likely to "give us the best chance of keeping peace in the world" than "trying to keep ahead of other powers ourselves," 64 percent of Catholics and 67 percent of Protestants agreed (Table 2–5). In the spring of 1948, during the period of accelerating tension with the Soviet Union which was shortly to culminate in the Berlin blockade, Catholics were as likely as Protestants (though not as Jews) to feel that the UN was "important to world peace" and that whatever weaknesses it had were due more to "the way its members act" than to "the way it is set up." Only relatively small minorities of either Catholics, Protestants, or Jews disagreed with these views. In the spring of 1950 as large a minority of Catholics (37 percent) as of Protestants (33 percent) in proportion to their numbers favored channeling at least some technical assistance to underdeveloped countries through the UN.

During the Korean War, in October 1952, a larger majority of Jews (89 percent) than of other Americans felt it "very important that the United States try to make the United Nations a success," but there was no significant difference between the two Christian groups—76 percent of Catholics and 77 percent of Protestants agreed (Table 2–5). When the same query was posed in late November 1956, shortly after the Suez and Hungarian crises, no difference appeared in the reactions of the three religious groups. Apparently, the role of the UN vis-à-vis Israel in the Suez controversy reduced American Jewish support for the international organization sufficiently to eliminate the typical divergence between Jews and other citizens with regard to greater approval of the UN. At that time in fact a larger minority (40 percent) of Jews than Christians felt the world body was "doing a poor job." Whereas small majorities of Catholics (51 percent) and Protestants (52 percent) thought the UN was "doing a good job," only a minority (31 percent) of Jews agreed.

Thus, during the first decade or so following the war, Catholics were as favorably disposed as Protestants toward active U.S. participation in the UN and as inclined to consider it important—to peace, to the national interest, and the like[4]—as they were to approve of most active foreign programs or policies more generally pursued or suggested by our President and his senior foreign-affairs aides. However, Catholics were less likely than either Protestants or Jews to advocate still wider commitments for the government than those executed or suggested by leading federal Executive officials, to feel that the United States should have taken an even more active part in international relations than it actually had (see above, p. 34), to prefer policies to the left of those of the President, or to approve of more or less utopian propositions, such as unilateral disarmament, pacifism, and world government.

These proclivities are reflected in comparative Catholic and Protestant attitudes toward the UN during this period. In 1948, for example, only 14 percent of Catholics versus 22 percent of Protestants and 71 percent of Jews felt the United States should have done more than it had "to make the United Nations successful" (Table 2–5).

---

4. For a similar conclusion that Protestants and Catholics harbored like attitudes toward the UN during the period 1945–54, see William A. Scott and Stephan B. Withey, *The United States and the United Nations: The Public View* (New York: Manhattan Publishing Co., 1958), pp. 134, 135, 140, 147, 212–13, and 228.

A slightly smaller fraction of Catholics (35 percent) than of Protestants (38 percent) and a much smaller proportion than of Jews (60 percent) at that time agreed the UN "should be made into a government of the entire world, with power to control the armed forces of all nations, including the United States." In the summer of 1953, Catholics were no more inclined than Protestants to agree that "we shouldn't get tied up in any more alliances or joint commitments with other countries and we should aim at getting out of as many as we can as soon as we can," and they were at least as willing as the latter to "continue to work along with the United Nations just about as we have been, gradually trying to make it better as time goes on." However, Catholics were less disposed than either Protestants or Jews to "get behind strengthening the United Nations and do everything necessary to give it more power and authority than it has—enough to actually keep even a strong nation from starting a war," to stay in the UN but also form a single government with "friendly democratic countries," or to "start now working toward transforming the United Nations into a real world government of *all* nations of the world, in which every nation would in effect become a state, somewhat like the different states in this country."

The Sixties and Beyond

Equally minuscule minorities—about one individual in twelve—of both Christian groups in the early sixties would have had the United States withdraw from the world organization (Table 2–5). Similarly, large majorities—four persons out of five—of both considered it "very important that we try to make the United Nations a success." As late as the summer of 1960, during the early days of the Congo crisis, Catholics seemed slightly less inclined than Protestants and considerably less than Jews to approve of building up a "United Nations Emergency Force to a size great enough to deal with 'brush fire' wars."

However, as early as 1957 a significantly larger proportion of Catholics—48 percent—than of Protestants—39 percent—had come to feel that "as things stand today, the chances of the United Nations keeping the peace in the world are good"; only 14 percent of Catholics, contrasted with 23 percent of Protestants, considered them "poor" (Table 2–6). In early 1962, again six months later, and still a third time in late 1963, Catholics were more inclined than Protestant Christians to agree that the UN was "doing a good job in trying to solve the problems it has had to face"; conversely on all three occasions Protestants were the more apt to feel the world body was "doing a poor job." By 1965 Catholics more than Protestants or even Jews believed "if the United Nations had not been in existence . . . there would likely have been another world war."

By April 1964 the former tendency of Catholics to be less enthusiastic about a UN peacekeeping force than Protestants had become reversed—almost as large a majority of Catholics as of Jews, and a clearly larger majority of both than of Protestants, favored building up a standing UN Emergency Force (Table 2–5). Three months later a larger majority of Catholics—77 percent—than of either Jews— 70 percent—or Protestants—63 percent—approved of this idea. At the latter time only 55 percent of Protestants compared with 67 percent of Catholics and a like percentage of Jews approved of the proposal that "a UN Army deal with the problems of Southeast Asia and Vietnam." In August 1965, only 71 percent of Protestants contrasted with 79 percent of Catholics and 94 percent of Jews approved of asking "the United Nations to try to work out its own formula for peace in Vietnam." Similar interreligious differences in reactions to the same query were apparent again in February 1966. Moreover, a smaller minority of Protestants—19 percent—than of either Catholics—25 percent—or Jews—27 percent—thought in February 1966 that the UN would be able to succeed in such an endeavor. At the end of 1965 and again in August 1966 both Catholics and Jews were significantly more disposed than Protestants "to submit the case of what to do about Vietnam to the United Nations and the World Court and agree to accept the decision, whatever it happens to be." Then in the fall of 1967, 63 percent of Catholics contrasted with but 58 percent of Protestants approved of the suggestion that the "entire problem of Vietnam" be turned "over to the United Nations" and that the world organization be asked to find a solution, both sides agreeing in advance to accept the decision (even if it called for withdrawal of U.S. troops) and to empower the UN to police the border between North and South Vietnam during the interim.

Although many Catholics had voted against the Unitarian, divorced, "Ivy League," though Democratic Adlai Stevenson in 1952 and 1956, they were sharply more inclined than Protestants (though less so than Jews) to "approve of the way Adlai Stevenson is handling his job as Ambassador to the United Nations" in late 1962 (Table 2–5).[5] Finally, as we shall demonstrate in Chapter 3 (pp. 51–52), by the mid-sixties both Catholics and Jews were consistently more inclined than Protestants to agree that Communist China should become a member of the UN and to feel that we should "go along" and not withdraw from the organization if a majority of the General Assembly voted to admit it.

Thus Jews have remained consistently better informed about world affairs and more enthusiastic about active U.S. involvement in international relations than either Catholics or Protestants throughout the decades since at least as long ago as the mid-1930's. Although less knowledgeable in that field than Protestants before the Japanese attack on Pearl Harbor, by the late 1960's Catholics were at least as well informed as Protestants. Moreover, whereas Catholics were less inclined than Protestants to support expansion of U.S. commitments abroad during the interwar period, by the 1960's they had become at least as favorably disposed toward active U.S. participation as their Protestant compatriots. Indeed, Catholics of the mid and late 1960's had somewhat more affirmative images of the UN and were willing to ascribe to it somewhat more important roles in world affairs in general and in U.S. foreign policy in particular than Protestants.

5. Even when party identification is held constant, Catholic Republicans were more likely than Protestant Republicans to approve of Ambassador Stevenson's performance and Catholic Democrats were more inclined to do so than Protestant Democrats.

CHAPTER 3. RELATIONS WITH THE COMMUNIST WORLD

The shift in comparative Catholic-Protestant opinion following the mid-fifties was similarly apparent in respect of perceptions of the nature of the communist challenge and of how the United States and the non-communist world could best deal with it. Jews remained clearly less pessimistic than either Christian group about the long-run possibilities of avoidance of war and reduction of tensions with the communist powers and more favorable than either to expanded negotiation and compromise to achieve these ends. However, American Catholics changed gradually from being more opposed than Protestants to concessions to the U.S.S.R. and other communist regimes, and from being more inclined toward hard-line policies toward them in the 1940's, to according more importance than their Protestant compatriots in the 1960's to negotiation and other nonmilitary means. Moreover, these small, though consistent, differences in recent years have been somewhat larger between white Americans in the two major Christian groups than when nonwhites, mainly Protestants, have been included in the statistics (see below, pp. 101–5).

FROM THE WAR INTO THE MID-FIFTIES

Perception of the U.S.S.R.

Thus, during the Second World War and the first year or so thereafter Catholic Americans were significantly more pessimistic (and, as it turned out, more realistic) than Protestants about our future relations with the Soviet Union (Table 3–1). Jews were, of course, considerably more optimistic than either in 1943 that the U.S.S.R. could "be trusted to cooperate with us when the war is over" and that we could "count on the Russian government being friendly with us" in June 1946, but in each instance Catholics were the most pessimistic of the three major religious groups. By the end of the summer of 1946, the number who felt that the Soviet regime could be trusted to cooperate had fallen to quite limited minorities of all religious groups, but Catholics seemed to remain more negatively inclined than other Americans,[1] while Jewish opinion continued to be more optimistic than that prevailing among

1. This difference between Catholics and Protestants was not statistically significant at the 10 percent level of confidence.

either Christian group. Similarly, in the fall of 1946 Catholics were the most likely and Jews the least likely to feel that the newspapers they read "generally make Russia look better than she really is" and that the Soviet Union was "entirely to blame" for the disagreements between the two countries.

It is thus understandable that Catholics during the first few years following the war were more inclined than Protestants (and Jews less than either) to expect another world war, this time with the U.S.S.R., with or without her allies. As early as the fall of 1946, for example, approximately one Catholic out of four, contrasted with less than one Protestant out of six and one Jew out of eight, considered "the present disagreements between Russia and the United States . . . serious enough to consider going to war about" (Table 3–1). At that time 67, 63, and 45 percent, respectively, expected "the United States to fight another war within the next twenty-five years."[2]

Preferred Policies Toward Communist States

The view, more prevalent among Catholics than other Americans, that the Soviet bloc was or would be a major threat to our country was reflected in policy preferences toward that country. Particularly when Southerners were excepted (see below, p. 134), but also to some extent when they were not, Catholics were more inclined than others toward a tougher and less compromising American stance vis-à-vis the communist countries. In the spring of 1948, shortly before the Berlin blockade, for instance, Catholics were the most and Jews the least likely to feel that "we should be even firmer than we are today"; conversely, Catholics were the least apt to agree that "the United States should be more willing to compromise with Russia" (Table 3–2). Two years later a considerably larger majority of Catholics than other Americans believed it "very important for the United States to stop the spread of Communism in the world"; conversely, Catholics were less apt than either Protestants or Jews to feel it "only fairly important" to do so.

These differences were associated with a greater emphasis on military means in our relations with the communist world among Catholics than Protestants and, especially, Jews. In mid-1946, a somewhat larger minority of Catholics than of others agreed (in some cases with qualifications) that "we should use our army and navy to make other

2. However, no such difference between Catholics and Protestants was apparent four years later, in 1950 (Table 3–1).

countries do what we think they should" (Table 3–2). Several months prior to the Korean War, Catholics were significantly more inclined than either of the other two religious groups to feel that "U.S. government spending should be increased . . . on . . . national defense." In the summer of 1953 a somewhat larger minority of Catholics than of Protestants and Jews favored preventive war or primary reliance on military means in our relations with the Soviet Union. Related to these differences was the more prevalent support among Catholics than others early in the first Eisenhower administration for the idea of "rolling back" communist control of eastern Europe. In the spring of 1953, Catholics were probably slightly more opposed than Protestants and definitely more opposed than Jews to international control of atomic energy and weapons, including international inspection in both the U.S. and the U.S.S.R.[3] As late as the fall of 1956, 57 percent of Catholics, contrasted with but 51 percent of Protestants, agreed "strongly" that the best way to deal with the Soviet Union and Communist China would be "to act as tough as they do."

Conversely, during the early postwar years Catholics were the least and Jews the most enthusiastic about diplomatic negotiations, conciliation, and compromise as means of lessening our disagreements with the communist countries (Table 3–3). In April 1948, during a period of increasing tension with the U.S.S.R. which would shortly result in the blockade of Berlin, only a minority of Catholics, compared with small majorities of Protestants and Jews, approved of the suggestion that President Truman go "to Europe to talk with Stalin, to try to settle the differences between the United States and Russia." Catholics were also somewhat more apt than either of the other two religious groups to argue that the Soviet government could not be trusted to live up to any agreements made there and to feel that such a summit meeting would show American weakness and encourage further Soviet pressures or aggressions. Catholics during this period were similarly the most likely of the three religious groups to feel that the United Nations should be reorganized without the communist states and that "we would be more likely to have world peace . . . if Russia were not a member of the United Nations." Even as late as the spring of 1957, a slightly larger minority of Catholics than of Protestants and a considerably larger

3. Differences between Catholics and Protestants were too small for statistical significance at the 10 percent level of confidence.

minority of Catholics than of Jews felt we should "break off all dip-lomatic relations with Russia."

However, these religious differences were usually smaller than most of those before the war, except in cases where ethnic identifications with the "old country" were salient, such as the relative importance accorded to liberating eastern Europe. Moreover, by the 1950's there were no consistent differences between the two major Christian groups in their respective views about our Presidents taking the lead in arranging sum-mit meetings with communist leaders to try to settle cold-war differences or inviting them to visit the United States (Table 3–4), or about allow-ing communist journalists to report to their media from the United States and U.S. journalists to do likewise from communist societies. In fact, by 1957 Catholics were significantly more favorably disposed than Protestants to exchanges of musicians and athletes (and probably other rather apolitical types as well) with the U.S.S.R. (Table 3–4).

Nor did the two Christian groups differ in their sentiments about collective security and actual military action against communist aggres-sion. In the spring of 1948, shortly after the negotiation of the defensive alliance among the western Europeans but before the announcement of American intentions of allying the United States formally with these countries, at least as large a proportion of Catholics (43 percent) as of Protestants (40 percent) agreed that "we should promise to go to war on their side if the western European countries are attacked" (Table 3–5). Equally large majorities of both in the following fall favored negotiation of "a permanent military alliance" with these countries whereby all would "agree to come to each other's defense immediately if any of them is attacked." Catholics were at least as willing as Prot-estants, and somewhat more willing than non-Southern white Protes-tants, to "give money and send troops to help Europe build up a defense against Russia." Moreover, Catholics were on the whole somewhat more disposed than Protestants to send military supplies at U.S. expense to European (and other) allies (see below, pp. 57–58).

During the year or so before and the year following the ratification of the North Atlantic Pact, Jews were typically less inclined than either Christian group to approve of the alliance and of its implementation through the sending of military assistance. They tended more than Christians to accord priority to such nonmilitary means as negotiation and economic aid under the European Recovery Program (see below, pp. 55–56) in the endeavor to limit communist expansion.

This difference between Jews and the others was also reflected in the greater emphasis among the former on negotiation rather than military escalation to end the fighting in Korea, even though Jews were more likely than either Christian group to regard that war as "worth fighting" (Table 3–5). However, Catholics and Protestants did not differ in their sentiments about the importance of this war in the containment of communist expansionism or about how best to terminate it successfully.

By the spring of 1957 Jews were at least as inclined as Christians to consider it "essential that we get . . . [the NATO] alliance fixed up" after the disarray entailed by friction between the U.S. and its French and British allies over the Suez question (Table 3–5). Catholics were at most very slightly less apt than Protestants to ascribe importance to that objective. Similarly, Jews were at least as likely as either Christian group to carry out the recently enunciated Eisenhower Doctrine, to come to the aid of Middle Eastern countries with U.S. armed forces to repel communist aggression should it come. Catholics were at most only slightly less willing than Protestants to do so.[4]

Communist China and Yugoslavia

These two communist countries have constituted special cases for American public opinion, as they have for federal policy. In the mid-fifties Catholics were significantly less favorably inclined than others toward liberalization of nonstrategic trade with Mainland China; more Catholics disapproved than approved "of Americans carrying on trade with Communist China, if this trade did not include war materials," whereas the reverse was the case among Protestants and, particularly, Jews (Table 3–6). Although only one out of four Catholics felt the U.S. should withdraw from the UN if the Peking government were to become a member, Catholics were somewhat more disposed toward this view than either of the other two religious groups. On the other hand, during a period of accentuated tension between the two Chinas over Quemoy and Matsu, three-quarters of both Christian groups approved of the suggestion that the United States invite "Russia, Communist China, and all other interested nations to meet together to see if a peaceful solution can be worked out"; there was no significant difference between the two

4. None of these Catholic-Protestant differences were individually statistically significant at the 10 percent level, though they were all in the same direction, indicating probably a slight real difference between the two groups toward lesser support for these collective security measures among Catholics.

on this issue, though Jews, as has usually been the case with respect to negotiations with unfriendly states, were more favorably disposed than either.

Comparisons between the two major Christian groups in respect of their views on U.S. relations with Yugoslavia were equivocal. They did not differ in early 1951 in their willingness to send military equipment, or for that matter American military forces, to help defend that communist country if it were attacked by its communist neighbors (Table 3–7). Although in early 1957 a slightly larger minority of Catholics than of Protestants opposed the proposed invitation to Marshal Tito to visit this country, Catholics at the time were somewhat more likely than Protestants to feel that we could "count on Yugoslavia to cooperate with us."

Communist Influence at Home

Catholics were no more prone than Protestants to consider domestic communists in our federal government, including the Department of State, or in nongovernmental institutions a major menace to our national security. In April 1948 both Catholics and Protestants were sharply more opposed than Jews to allowing communists to speak on the radio or to permitting criticism of "our form of government" in the press (Table 3–8), but no significant differences appeared between the two Christian groups on these questions.

Senator Joseph R. McCarthy, a Roman Catholic of Irish and German ancestry, was consistently more popular personally among Catholics than among other Americans (Table 3–9). But this apparent ethnic and religious affinity for the junior senator from Wisconsin among many Catholics did not seem to generate any more widespread acceptance of his message about a supposed major internal communist threat among them than among Protestant Americans (Table 3–8). At the beginning of the senator's campaign in the spring of 1950, approximately the same proportion of both Christian groups—about half—felt his claims about communists in the Department of State were "true," sharply more than among Jews; approximately a sixth of each Christian group agreed to some extent with the senator, most of them with the reservation that he overestimated the number of subversives in the Department or that there was only some truth in his accusations, and the same proportion of both, 28 percent, thought his claims "just a case of politics." Several weeks later Catholics were at least as likely as other Christians (though not as likely as Jews) to feel that "all the people who work in the State Department in Washington are probably loyal to the United States." Nor did any larger minority of Catholics than of Protestants feel communists who might be in the Department were doing "a great deal of harm to our country's interests"; conversely, as large a majority of Catholics as of other citizens held a basically "favorable impression about the type of officials working in the State Department in Washington."

In the late summer and fall of 1952 the two Christian groups were equally inclined to consider "keeping Communists out of government . . . one of the two or three most important [things] for the next administration to do" (Table 3–8). The following spring a significantly larger minority of Catholics—27 percent—than Protestants—20 percent—thought "former members of the Communist Party who have resigned from the Party should be allowed to teach in colleges and universities," while a smaller minority of the former than the latter believed there was "a need for a Congressional investigation of Communism in our churches." Several months later equally large majorities of both believed "the State Department in Washington is now doing all it can to keep disloyal people out of the Department." Finally, in late 1954 the same proportion of both, 37 percent, considered American communists a "great danger to our country," while 15 percent of Catholics contrasted with 13 percent of Protestants and 31 percent of Jews said they were of "practically no danger."

MORE RECENT TRENDS

Use of Military Means

As recently as 1965, Catholics remained at least as inclined as Protestants to maintain a strong defense establishment and effective collective security arrangements with our allies and to resist any communist attack by military force, even at the risk of world nuclear war. However, by the end of the sixties Catholic Americans had become distinctly less supportive than their Protestant compatriots of large defense budgets, the prevailing magnitude of U.S. military forces, and military means generally as a central instrument in U.S. relations with its communist antagonists.

Thus, in early 1960 both Catholics and Jews were somewhat more likely than Protestants to feel that our federal government was spending

either "too little" or "about the right amount . . . for national defense"
(Table 3–10). Shortly before the inauguration of President Kennedy,
somewhat larger minorities of both Catholics and Jews than of Protestants felt the "new President and new Congress should . . . spend more
money to strengthen national defense." In February 1965 the three
religious groups were about equally "satisfied with America's military
strength." Several months later, during the rapid buildup of American
forces in Vietnam, at least as large a majority of Catholics as of others
thought "every able-bodied American boy 18 years old . . . should . . .
be required to go into the armed forces for one year." Nor has there
been any difference between the two Christian groups in anxieties that
reductions in American armaments or expanded international arms
control would result in serious domestic economic difficulties: in 1964
similar minorities of both felt that "drastic" reductions in military expenditures would bring on a "serious depression," while about half of
both believed "the money now spent on armaments and the armed forces
would be used for other things and there would be no serious depression."

During the 1961 Berlin crisis, shortly after the communists closed
the border between the two Berlins, a somewhat larger majority of
Catholics, 85 percent, than of either Protestants or Jews would have
favored "fighting an all-out nuclear war" over "living under communist
rule" if necessary to avoid war (Table 3–11). Similarly, Catholics
somewhat more than the other two religious groups thought "the United
States and its allies should try to fight their way into Berlin . . . if
Communist East Germany closes all roads to Berlin and does not permit planes to land in Berlin." Several weeks earlier, a larger majority
of Catholics than of either of the others felt "we should keep American
forces in Berlin—along with British and French forces—even at the
risk of war."

Catholics were likewise as favorably disposed as other citizens to
military intervention in Cuba and the Dominican Republic in the early
and mid-1960's. During the propaganda campaign of Fidel Castro
against the U.S. base at Guantanamo in early 1961, equally large
majorities of both Christian groups felt "the United States should fight
to keep it . . . if Castro should attempt to take over this base by force"
(Table 3–12). In 1962, again in 1963, and once more in 1965, similar
minorities of all three religious groups believed we should invade Cuba
and overthrow the Castro regime. Catholics and Protestants in 1963
were equally apt to think that "the Cuban situation is a serious threat

to world peace." In late 1965, a significantly larger majority of Catholics (57 percent) than of Protestants (51 percent) or Jews (44 percent) agreed that "the United States did the right thing in deciding to send troops into Santo Domingo" the April before.

However, by mid-1969, a significantly larger proportion of Catholics (56 percent) than of Protestants (48 percent) had become convinced that their federal government was "spending too much . . . money . . . for national defense and military purposes." Conversely, only 35 percent of Protestants contrasted with 43 percent of Catholics felt that U.S. military expenditures were either at about the right level or that they should be increased (Table 3–10). An apparent reversal had taken place in the comparative thinking of the two Christian groups on this matter within less than a decade.[5]

Probability of War with Communist Regimes

Since as early as 1957 Catholics as well as Jews have been distinctly more optimistic than Protestants about avoiding another war and reaching peaceful settlements of disputes with communist powers short of military action. The relative views on this important question of the two Christian groups prevailing during the early 1950's and before had likewise become reversed.

Thus in the spring of 1957 only 13 percent of Catholics and 7 percent of Jews, contrasted with 19 percent of Protestants, expected a major war within two years. Catholics and, especially, Jews at the time were also less inclined than Protestants to anticipate war "eventually" (Table 3–13). Protestants were clearly less optimistic than either about avoiding war entirely. A year and a half later a larger majority of Jews than of Catholics venturing opinions believed "the Western countries can continue to live peacefully with the Russians," but Protestants were more prone to feel there was "bound to be a major war sooner or later" than to think it could be avoided. Twenty-one percent of Protestants at that time felt we were "likely to get into another world war in the next five years" while only 16 percent of Catholics and 10 percent of Jews agreed.

The numbers who anticipated major war with the Soviet Union, Communist China, their allies, or some combination of them fluctuated

5. Similarly in July 1970 a smaller minority of Catholics (24 percent) than of Protestants (34 percent) said they accorded a "highly favorable" rating to the Pentagon; conversely, 6 percent of Catholics contrasted with only 3 percent of Protestants gave the Pentagon a "highly unfavorable" rating (Table 3–10).

with international events among all religious groups. When tensions were more evident, as shortly after the U-2 crisis and the collapse of the Paris summit conference in mid-1960 and again during the Berlin crisis in the late summer and fall of 1961, all three became less hopeful about avoiding major war. But this pessimism declined whenever relations grew less overtly acrimonious. However, regardless of such fluctuations and of how questions were worded, Protestants since the late 1950's have consistently been the most inclined at any given moment to anticipate war rather than peaceful negotiation of disagreements with communist adversaries, Catholics less so, and Jews least of all (Table 3–13).[6]

Negotiations with Communist Regimes

Prior to the early sixties Catholics were certainly no more favorable than Protestants to arms control negotiations, summit meetings, and bilateral or multilateral discussions generally to alleviate both overall tensions and particular disputes with the communist powers. Catholic-Protestant differences in respect of these issues were small, but more often than not Catholics tended to be the somewhat more conservative of the two.

The more widespread opposition among Catholics than others to summit discussions with Soviet leaders noted earlier persisted into the late fifties. For example, at the end of 1956, 54 percent of Catholics, contrasted with 57 percent of Protestants and 76 percent of Jews, thought "it would be a good idea for President Eisenhower to invite Russia's top leaders to come and visit America" (Table 3–14). Several months later only 49 percent of Catholics versus 59 percent of Protestants and 61 percent of Jews favored President Eisenhower inviting Marshal Tito to this country. Shortly before Premier Khrushchev's visit here in 1959, only 62 percent of Catholics, contrasted with 66 percent of Protestants and 76 percent of Jews, approved. Catholics were similarly least inclined to regard favorably President Eisenhower's projected reciprocal visit to the Soviet Union.

In the spring of 1957 there were no significant differences between the two Christian groups in sentiments about further negotiations for arms control with international safeguards (Table 3–15). Some 2½ years later, three-quarters of both Christian groups and seven-eighths of Jews favored extending the U.S.-Soviet agreement to stop testing

6. By the end of 1966 Catholics were similarly more likely than Protestants to feel the war in Vietnam would probably be settled within a year (Table 3–13).

H-bombs beyond the end of 1959. In the early fall of 1960 the ratio of those who thought "if Russia agrees to disarm under careful inspection by the UN . . . the United States should agree to disarm to the same extent" to those who felt the U.S. should not was the highest among Jews, but there was no difference whatsoever between Catholic and Protestant Christians. Indeed, as late as March 1962 a somewhat larger majority of Catholics (73 percent) than of Protestants (65 percent) or Jews (71 percent) believed that our government "should resume nuclear bomb tests in the atmosphere."

However, shortly before the inauguration of President Kennedy, a significantly larger minority of Catholics (46 percent) than of Protestants (37 percent) agreed that the new administration and Congress should "find a new way to deal with the U.S.S.R." (Table 3–16). By the late summer of 1963 Catholics were clearly more apt than Protestants to have heard of "the agreement with Russia to have a partial ban on testing of nuclear weapons" and to agree that "the Senate should vote approval of this ban." Catholics were also patently more inclined than Protestants to feel "the United States should agree to make further agreements with Russia to reduce armaments and armed forces . . . if Russia agrees to reduce their armaments and armed forces." Although the two Christian groups did not differ with respect to trading with the U.S.S.R. in early 1954—Jews were more favorably disposed than either—by late 1964 both Catholics and Jews were more likely to approve of letting U.S. businessmen, farmers, and others trade in non-military goods with communist countries than were Protestants. Similarly by the fall of 1964 Jews and Catholics were somewhat more inclined than Protestants to say that they had made up their minds that it would be a good idea for our leaders to meet with leaders of the communist regimes to try to work out our differences.

The People's Republic of China

Comparable shifts were apparent in Catholic as contrasted with Protestant views with respect to U.S. relations with the regime in Peking. Until the early 1960's most Americans regarded the Soviet Union as a greater long-range threat to world peace and to our national interests than any other country, including the People's Republic of China. However, starting in the late fifties public opinion gradually shifted as the Soviet regime seemed to become more moderate and the Chinese regime more stridently anti-Western. By the spring of 1964 a clear majority of 56 percent of the public felt that by 1970 the People's Republic of China rather than the U.S.S.R. would constitute "the greater threat to world peace"; only 27 percent believed that the Soviet Union would.[7] The more educated and better-informed minority was the most likely to have changed its opinion during this period. By the late 1960's the poorly educated and little informed constituted most of the minority who still viewed the Soviets as the more threatening in the long run.

Even though Catholics were no better educated (see below, p. 127), they nevertheless were clearly more inclined than Protestants by 1964 to perceive the Peking regime as the worse long-run menace (Table 3–17). Undoubtedly this difference helped to account for the greater willingness of Catholics than Protestants of the sixties to negotiate and compromise with the Soviets and their East European allies. It also probably in part explained the fact that by 1965 Catholics were significantly more inclined than Protestants to feel the West could "continue to live peacefully with the Russians," but only slightly more disposed to think it could "live peacefully" with the Chinese communists (Table 3–13).

Nonetheless, the relative thinking of the two Christian religious groups with respect to U.S. policy toward Mainland China changed significantly during the early sixties. Whereas as late as March 1961 there was no difference between these two groups in their sentiments about admitting the People's Republic of China as a member of the United Nations, by the mid-sixties and increasingly thereafter, Catholics, like Jews, were consistently more favorable than Protestants to admitting that state (Table 3–17).

Throughout the period since the retreat of the Nationalists from the mainland in 1949, much larger numbers—typically a majority of those venturing opinions—of all religious groups have agreed that we should remain in the UN and go along in the event of a majority General Assembly vote to admit Peking (Table 3–17). Up until early 1961 Catholics more than either Protestants or Jews felt our government should not go along with such a majority decision. However, as in the case of Communist Chinese entry per se, the proportion of Protestants who thought we should go along with the majority remained relatively static during the 1960's, while Catholics became more inclined to go along. By the mid-sixties both Catholics and Jews were clearly more apt

7. AIPO 689, 4-22-64.

than Protestants to go along and less disposed to withdraw from the world body if the Peking regime were voted in by the General Assembly.

Finally, by the fall of 1966 majorities of all three major religious groups favored Chinese Communist membership in the United Nations "if it would improve U.S.–Communist China relations." But once again Catholics, though not as inclined to agree as Jews, were more favorably disposed than Protestants: 60 percent of Catholics and 79 percent of Jews, contrasted with only 53 percent of Protestants, would have supported Peking's membership under such conditions.

Domestic Communism

The perceived danger to our security of communism within this country declined among all groups after the McCarthy period. However, the decline was more marked among Catholics than Protestants, such that by February 1965 smaller minorities of both Catholics—31 percent—and Jews—19 percent—than of Protestants—36 percent—believed that "left-wing groups, such as the Communist Party, here in America, are at the present time . . . a very great deal . . . of danger to our country."[8]

The War in Vietnam

This shift in Catholic opinion, as contrasted with Protestant opinion, relative to how the United States should handle the communist challenge was reflected in the comparative reactions of the two Christian groups to American policy in Southeast Asia during the latter half of the sixties (Table 3–18).

As might be assumed, Jews remained consistently more opposed to U.S. military intervention and more inclined to favor deescalation over escalation and to support cooperation with international bodies to resolve the Vietnam issue than either Christian group. For two years or so after active intervention by U.S. combat troops in the spring of 1965, Catholics were at least as supportive as Protestants of U.S. military intervention and as apt to feel that it had not been a "mistake,"[9] that it was morally justified, that the U.S. should maintain forces there

8. POS 655, 2-15-65. Thirty-five percent of Catholics, 32 percent of Protestants, and 21 percent of Jews considered them a "considerable danger"; 24, 24, and 42 percent, respectively, "not very much danger"; and 4, 3, and 9 percent "no danger at all." Catholics numbered 359, Protestants 1,152, and Jews 46.

9. As late as the beginning of 1970, Catholics remained as inclined as Protestants to feel that the U.S. military intervention had not been a mistake.

until a "reasonable" settlement had been achieved (even at the risk of nuclear war), and that the U.S. government should be willing to intervene militarily again should a similar situation develop elsewhere. The two major groups did not differ in early 1966, for instance, in regard to the proposed extension of the bombing to North Vietnamese cities and particularly to oil dumps and other strategic targets in Hanoi and Haiphong, or to the arguments of the "hawks" for stepping up the fighting generally.[10]

However, by the spring of 1967 significant differences toward more conciliatory views among Catholics than Protestants began to appear, differences which would persist (or expand) thereafter. Thus 69 percent of Catholics contrasted with but 62 percent of Protestants in May of that year rejected the view that the U.S. should "go all out to win a military victory" in Southeast Asia, employing nuclear weapons if necessary to achieve this objective. The following July only 36 percent of Catholics versus 42 percent of Protestants favored increasing the 460,000 U.S. troops in Vietnam by another 100,000. The next October Catholics were somewhat less inclined than Protestants toward general expansion of the war by letting U.S. military leaders run it as they saw fit, including expanded bombing of the North, use of nuclear weapons, and giving them whatever military resources they said they needed to "win." Similar differences toward lesser Catholic than Protestant approval for extension of the fighting were apparent in March 1968. In May 1970 Catholics were less supportive than Protestants of sending American troops into Cambodia and of dispatching arms and other materials to the new government of that country and less apt to believe that the U.S. would avoid major extension of the war and military involvement in Cambodia through such action. Consistently from early 1968 into 1970 Catholics were less apt than Protestants to consider themselves "hawks" and to advocate stepping up the military effort.

Conversely, shortly after President Johnson announced that he would terminate most bombing of North Vietnam to bring its government to the negotiating table, 69 percent of Catholics, contrasted with but 61 percent of Protestants, approved of this decision. Catholics

10. Catholics were somewhat more inclined than Protestants to say they approved of President Johnson's policies in Vietnam throughout his Presidency (Table 3–18). However, this phenomenon was undoubtedly more attributable to the more widespread Democratic partisan affinities of Catholics than to any significant divergence in thinking among the two Christian groups on the Vietnam issue itself. Thus Catholics were less inclined than Protestants to approve in May 1970 of Republican President Nixon's handling of the situations in Vietnam and Cambodia (Table 3–18).

had been slightly more favorable than their Protestant compatriots to negotiation and compromise to achieve peace in Southeast Asia even before the major buildup of U.S. combat forces there in 1965 (Table 3–18). As we noted earlier (pp. 38–39), they were likewise more willing to search for a solution through multilateral means, particularly the United Nations. It is thus understandable that once the Paris peace talks were initiated, Catholics more than Protestants favored their continuation regardless of their apparent lack of success. In January 1969, 64 percent of Catholics versus only 53 percent of Protestants felt the number of U.S. troops in Vietnam should be reduced "month by month." The following October, 50 percent versus 40 percent thought "the U.S. should withdraw troops at a faster rate" than was then the case. In June 1969, the following October, and again in March 1970 Catholics were consistently more favorable than Protestants to immediate withdrawal of all U.S. combat forces from Vietnam. Equally consistently after early 1968, Catholics more than Protestants considered themselves "doves" insofar as that term connoted reduction of U.S. military involvement.[11]

11. A national survey of a representative sample of college campuses in November 1969 likewise determined that 69 percent of Catholic, contrasted with but 62 percent of Protestant students, considered themselves "doves," while, conversely, 19 percent versus 27 percent viewed themselves as "hawks" (*Gallup Opinion Index*, Jan. 1970).

CHAPTER 4. FOREIGN AID AND TRADE

On no international issue has the relative thinking of Catholics and Protestants changed more markedly than on foreign aid. Significantly less favorably disposed than both Protestants and Jews to aiding the enemies of the Axis before and during the war, Catholics were consistently more supportive than Protestant Christians of the major economic, technical, and other nonmilitary aid programs of the 1960's.

EARLIER POSTWAR PROGRAMS

Few of the rather considerable differences in opinion between the two Christian groups with respect to foreign aid prior to and during the Second World War were apparent in regard to early postwar aid programs. There was no difference in the magnitude of the majorities of Catholics and Protestants who approved of the large shipments of food and other emergency relief to war-torn areas shortly after the war. Jews were the most favorable to such short-term assistance,[1] as they would be thereafter to virtually all types of nonmilitary aid (Tables 4–1, 4–3, 4–4, 4–5, and 4–6). The large loan to Britain in 1946 was slightly less popular among Catholics than Protestants,[2] but the difference was smaller than it had been with respect to aiding Britain before our entry into war. The prewar anglophobia of many Irish-American Catholics had apparently abated (see below, p. 116), and Catholics of German and Italian origins had no particular reason to oppose such assistance as they had when Britain was at war with the lands of their ancestors.

The Truman Doctrine and the Marshall Plan

Aid to Greece and Turkey under the Truman Doctrine—some of it economic, some military—was intimately associated in the minds of all religious groups with containing communism. Therefore it should not be surprising that Catholics were at least as inclined as Protestants to approve such assistance. A week or so after President Truman's announcement of 12 March 1947 and request for the necessary funds, 49 percent of Catholics, 47 percent of Protestants, and 55 percent of Jews approved "of the United States lending Greece 250 million dollars."[3]

1. NORC 210, Jan. '43; NORC 223, Feb. '44; AIPO 361, 12-5-45; AIPO 368, 3-27-46; Roper 53, April '46; and AIPO 373, 6-12-46.
2. AIPO 360, 11-21-45.
3. AIPO 392, 3-12-47. Catholics numbered 488, Protestants 1,619, and Jews 65.

Catholics were less likely to have heard or read about the Marshall Plan or to know much about it than were Protestants and, especially, Jews (Table 4–1), but among those who were aware of this program, Catholics were approximately as likely as Protestants to harbor favorable impressions of it. Throughout the period of the European Recovery Program, that is, 1947–52, Catholics and Protestants were equally supportive of capital assistance to help western Europe recover economically from the effects of war, of continuing it for four years, and of appropriating the sums requested by the President from Congress to implement it, and they were equally inclined to ascribe major importance to it. Catholic ethnic associations were at least as likely as Protestant ones to encourage favorable sentiments toward economic aid to western Europe. Jews were, of course, better informed and more favorably disposed than either Christian group.[4]

By the mid-fifties economic assistance to western Europe had about terminated; most material aid to NATO allies other than Greece and Turkey was by then military in nature. However, when it was suggested in some quarters in late 1956 that we give economic aid to Britain and France to help them meet the difficulties caused by the closing of the Suez Canal shortly after the crisis over Anglo-French-Israeli military intervention against the Nasser regime in Egypt, a sharply larger majority of Jews (88 percent) than of other religious groups approved of such aid, while only 10 percent of Jews disapproved. But no significant difference between Catholics and Protestants was evident: 56 percent of the former versus 55 percent of the latter approved of such assistance, while 40 percent and 38 percent disapproved.[5]

Military Assistance

Except for a part of Truman Doctrine aid to Greece and Turkey and assistance to Nationalist China, relatively little of U.S. aid during the first four years or so after the war was military in nature. Military matériel became a major aspect of aid to western Europe in the implementation of the Atlantic Pact, especially after the communist attack on South Korea in 1950.

Apart from a very limited period in 1950 when many Americans

4. See Louis Harris, *Is There a Republican Majority* (New York: Harper, 1954), pp. 161-63, for further data documenting more widespread support for the Marshall Plan among the Jews than among other religious and ethnic groups.

5. NORC 401, 12-28-56. The sample consisted of 279 Catholics, 870 Protestants, and 42 Jews.

feared a communist military assault on little-armed western Europe, military aid has been significantly less popular with the public than economic and technical assistance and the shipment of food and other emergency assistance abroad. Although Catholics were less enthusiastic than other Americans about sending military aid to Britain, France, Finland, and the U.S.S.R. before U.S. entry into World War II and about continuing Lend-Lease during the war, in the late forties and the early fifties military assistance to allies and "friendly countries" was somewhat more popular among Catholics than Protestants, particularly Protestants outside the South.

Thus even prior to the North Atlantic Pact, in the spring of 1948, 58 percent of Catholics, contrasted with but 51 percent of Protestants and 49 percent of Jews, were willing to send "military supplies to these [western European] countries . . . now, in order to strengthen them against any future attack" (Table 4–2). As the North Atlantic Pact was being negotiated in late 1948, 35 percent of Catholics, contrasted with 32 percent of Protestants and 25 percent of Jews, favored "the United States spending two billion dollars in the next year to help Western European countries rearm." During the summer of 1949, after the Senate had ratified the NATO Pact but before Congress had enacted President Truman's request for military aid to its members, 59 percent of Catholics versus 58 percent of Protestants and 31 percent of Jews who had heard of the pact approved sending them "arms and war materials" at our expense. In the summer of 1952, during the Korean War, 31 percent of Catholics, 26 percent of Protestants, and 41 percent of Jews thought our government should "keep on building the armed strength of Western Europe like we've been doing." Similar interreligious differences appeared again in reply to the same query just before the 1952 national election.

Catholics were likewise somewhat more favorably disposed than Protestants toward sending military supplies to Latin America and Asia. In early 1948, 49 percent of Catholics, contrasted with but 46 percent of Protestants and 42 percent of Jews, agreed that "strengthening military defenses in our part of the world by sending arms to South American countries" would be "a good thing" (Table 4–2). At the same time 38 percent of Catholics versus 32 percent of Protestants and 33 percent of Jews favored sending military supplies to the Chinese Nationalist regime, led by Methodist Chiang Kai-shek. Several months later, after the Nationalist cause had worsened considerably, 62 percent of Catholics contrasted with 55 percent of Protestants and 48 percent of Jews approved of "our sending military supplies to help the Chinese government against the Communists." In the fall of 1952, 72 percent of Catholics compared with only 69 percent of Protestants and a like proportion of Jews favored "the U.S. training a South Korean army of . . . about 2 million men" to help fight the war against the communists.

These small differences between the two Christian groups[6] were associated with the tendency somewhat more prevalent among Catholics than Protestants of the period to anticipate war with the U.S.S.R. and to prefer a less compromising, more militarily based posture vis-à-vis that country. Conversely, the greater reluctance among Jews than others prior to the Korean War to send military supplies was related to their more widespread optimism about avoiding war with the Soviet bloc, their more marked emphasis on economic and technical assistance to noncommunist countries, and their proclivity toward negotiation and other nonmilitary relationships with the communist world. However, as fears of communist attacks on their noncommunist neighbors grew with the assault on South Korea, Jews became more favorably inclined toward military assistance than either Christian group.

THE SHIFT OF AID TO LESS-DEVELOPED COUNTRIES

From 1949 to 1957

Most U.S. foreign aid was directed to noncommunist Europe, Turkey, Japan, Nationalist China, and Korea until well into the fifties. Except for a relatively minor technical-aid endeavor in Latin America before the Second World War and some assistance to Greece, Turkey, Nationalist China, and Korea in the early postwar period, aid for development purposes for unindustrialized societies began with the modest technical-assistance program suggested as Point Four in President Truman's inaugural address of January 1949. This program, originally focused primarily on noncommunist Asia, was launched with rather naively optimistic arguments, based on the implied assumption that transfer of modern technology to these agrarian societies and the elimination of economic underdevelopment could be accomplished through technical help without major injections of capital from the governments of the industrialized world. Capital assistance to these

6. Differences were larger than above indicated outside the South between Catholics and Protestants (see below, p. 124).

countries would not become of significant magnitude until the mid-fifties.

During the early 1950's Catholics were somewhat less inclined to have heard of these programs or to know much about them than were Protestants (Table 4–3). However, among those Americans who ventured any views, there were few consistent differences between the two major Christian groups before the late 1950's on aid to less-developed countries as a general idea. Nor did Catholics and Protestants differ on aiding countries allied to the United States or at least apparently friendly to it. Jews were typically the most favorably disposed toward aiding less-developed societies, virtually regardless of their posture in the cold war. Jews even appeared somewhat more inclined than either Christian group to send both military and economic assistance to the Arab Middle East under the Eisenhower Doctrine.

On the one hand, slightly larger majorities of Catholics than Protestants in April 1950 considered it "a good policy for the United States to try to help backward countries . . . raise their standard of living" and felt such assistance would "really help the United States" (Table 4–3). It was noted above (p. 35) that Catholics at that time were as inclined as Protestants to channel at least part of our aid to less-developed societies through the United Nations. Again in December 1956–January 1957 a larger majority of Catholics than Protestants felt "the aid we're sending to various foreign countries helps the United States."

On the other hand, the ratio of those in favor to those opposed to sending "less economic and military aid to Western European countries and . . . more aid to our allies in Asia" while the Korean War was still going on in the spring of 1953 was the same among both Christian groups. Nor was there any difference between them two years later with respect to sending "aid to non-communist countries in Asia" similar to that given earlier to western Europe under the ERP. Both were equally likely to agree, and to disagree, in the fall of 1956 with the idea of the United States giving economic help to the poorer countries of the world "even if they can't pay for it." In January 1957 similar majorities of Catholics and Protestants approved of sending economic and military assistance to "friendly countries" in the Middle East under the recently announced Eisenhower Doctrine. Several weeks later there was no difference in norms of opinion between the two with respect to the prevailing order of magnitude of economic and of military aid to underdeveloped countries generally; they were equally apt to favor increasing, maintaining, or reducing the levels of each type of assistance, or stopping it entirely. Again the following spring, Catholics were about as likely as Protestants to support President Eisenhower's request for approximately $4 billion "for all foreign aid next year—both military and economic . . . roughly the same as we spent this past year."

Small differences between Catholics and Protestants were apparent with regard to the priority accorded to military assistance over economic assistance and the importance ascribed to anticommunist objectives in foreign aid. These differences were apparently associated with the tendency, somewhat more widespread among Catholics than Protestants, to prefer a harder line toward the communist world.

For instance, in the spring of 1953 Catholics were distinctly less enthusiastic than either Protestants or, especially, Jews about using any part of the funds then devoted to defense "to help needy countries" even if the defense budget could "safely be cut" and other industrialized countries also shifted some resources from defense to foreign nonmilitary aid (Table 4–4). Although Catholics were at least as favorably disposed as Protestants to continuing "to send economic aid—like machinery and supplies—to countries that have agreed to stand with us against communist aggression" in April 1957, a significantly smaller majority of the former than the latter considered "it was more important to send our allies economic aid . . . than military aid, like tanks and guns." Shortly before, 31 percent of Catholics, contrasted with only 26 percent of Protestants and 23 percent of Jews, suggested that economic aid be reduced or terminated entirely, but that military aid be increased or kept at the current level.

This proclivity, somewhat more marked among Catholics than Protestants, toward emphasizing national defense and military aid over economic assistance was also apparently linked with a tendency slightly more widespread among Catholics than Protestants to consider aid in terms of stopping the spread of communism. Thus, even though Catholics were no more inclined to approve of the prevailing magnitude of aid and of the sums requested of Congress by the President when the communist issue was not mentioned (Table 4–3), Catholics in late 1956 were significantly more favorable than Protestants to Congress's appropriating $4 billion for the next fiscal year "to help prevent . . . other countries . . . from going communistic" (Table 4–5). As late as April 1957 Catholics were also slightly more critical than Protestants of such neutralist regimes as that in India which did not formally ally themselves with the West against the communist bloc.

However, Catholics were not consistently less enthusiastic than Protestants about sending economic assistance to such nonaligned countries, or even to communist Yugoslavia and Poland. It is true that Catholics in the fall of 1956 were slightly more apt than Protestants to disagree with the suggestion that the United States give "help to foreign countries even if they are not as much against communism as we are" (Table 4–5), and those Catholics who felt "closer to other Catholics than . . . to other people" were more strongly opposed to this proposition than other Catholics who did not.[7] On the other hand, Catholics and Jews were both more disposed than Protestants in late 1956 and again the following spring to continuing "economic aid . . . to countries like India, which have not joined us against the Communists" (Table 4–5). However, as was observed earlier, Catholics were about as disposed as Protestants in 1951 to send military supplies to Yugoslavia (p. 45). Furthermore, in April 1957, several months after the anti-Stalinist rumblings in eastern Europe, Catholics were more rather than less favorable than Protestants to sending "economic aid to . . . Communist countries like Poland, which have rebelled against Russian control."

The Late Fifties and Beyond

By 1958 material aid to western Europe and Japan had virtually ceased and almost all assistance, both economic and military, was focused on the underdeveloped world. Since roughly that date Catholics, like Jews, have been consistently more favorable to aiding those countries than Protestants. Furthermore, differences in attitudes toward at least some aspects of foreign aid between Catholics and Protestants, and particularly between whites of these two Christian persuasions, seemed to widen between the late fifties and the mid-sixties.

Catholics in the spring of 1958 were not yet any better informed than Protestants about foreign aid. Only 6 percent of each of the two Christian groups, contrasted with 13 percent of Jews, estimated the amount of aid requested of the Congress by President Eisenhower for the forthcoming fiscal year within a billion dollars of the correct figure of approximately $4 billion. When asked for what purposes foreign aid was spent, only 10 percent of Catholics, 11 percent of Protestants, and

7. V. O. Key, Jr., *Public Opinion and Democracy* (New York: Knopf, 1963), p. 222.

36 percent of Jews mentioned the general objectives of both economic and military assistance (Table 4–6).

Nevertheless, a distinctly larger majority of Catholics (58 percent), as well as of Jews (65 percent), than of Protestants (48 percent) at that time said they were "in general for foreign aid" (Table 4–6). Although there had been no difference between the two Christian groups with respect to "helping poorer countries" two years before, 53 percent of Catholics and 61 percent of Jews versus 49 percent of Protestants in the fall of 1958 favored this idea, and by the autumn of 1960 the respective figures were 56 and 63 versus 50 percent. Furthermore, even though there had been no observable differences between Catholic and Protestant thinking on financing relief and rehabilitation in war-torn areas in the late forties, by the summer of 1959 a slightly larger majority of Catholics than Protestants favored "having Congress set aside the money . . . to take some unused Navy ships and fit them out as hospital ships, food supply ships, training schools, and the like" and sending them "any place in the world where needed."

Catholics consistently more often than Protestants were "in general for foreign aid" in early 1963, again in early 1965, and also in early 1966 (Table 4–6). By late 1964, 51 percent of Catholics and 56 percent of Jews versus only 43 percent of Protestants were definitely in favor of giving "aid to other countries if they need help"; conversely, only 15 percent of Catholics and 9 percent of Jews versus 20 percent of Protestants felt "each country should make its own way as best it can." The following February, 56 percent of Catholics and 60 percent of Jews, contrasted with only 45 percent of Protestants, felt the United States had "an obligation to help the poorer nations of the world." Moreover, both Catholics and Jews who favored aid for the less-developed world were more apt by the 1960's than Protestants to approve without major qualifications or reservations—"if they pay us back," "if they support us in Vietnam" (or elsewhere), "if the communists don't get any," and the like.

Both Catholics and Jews in recent years have also been consistently more inclined than Protestants to increase foreign aid or, at a minimum, to maintain it at its current level. Informed of the sum requested by President Eisenhower for fiscal year 1959, Catholics and Jews somewhat more than Protestants in March 1958 felt Congress should authorize at least as much as he asked. In May 1961 both were significantly more willing than Protestants to make personal "sacrifices, even if it meant increasing your own taxes" for foreign aid. A month later 68 percent of Catholics, contrasted with but 58 percent of Protestants and 51 percent of Jews, thought that "communism would be in a greater position of world power today" if Congress had not appropriated "three to four billion dollars each year . . . during recent years . . . for countries in other parts of the world."

The following November, 16 percent of Catholics and 42 percent of Jews, compared with only 13 percent of Protestants, felt "America and the West are not doing as much as they should do to help under-developed countries with financial and technical aid." At that time 55 percent of Catholics versus 49 percent of Protestants and 44 percent of Jews agreed that "the interests of the United States have actually been helped by the U.S. foreign aid program during the last five years." In October 1963, only 37 percent of Catholics, contrasted with 42 percent of both Protestants and Jews, mentioned foreign aid when asked if they could "think of anything which the government spends too much money on." Two months later, as the President's annual foreign-aid request was undergoing especially vigorous attack in Congress, which would soon cut it by over a third—more than ever before—38 percent of Catholics and 62 percent of Jews versus only 30 percent of Protestants among a national sample which excluded self-declared Democrats agreed that "the U.S. government's program of foreign economic aid to assist other nations should be kept at the present level at least." Told in early 1965 that "each year the federal government provides about $1.00 in aid to foreign countries for every $200 in goods and services produced in the United States," Catholics and Jews were significantly more likely than Prot-estants to feel it should be continued at that or a higher level. At about the same time Catholics and Jews were once again more inclined than Protestants to support the amount proposed by the President rather than the cuts later made by Congress (or even greater reductions). Again in May 1967, 44 percent of Catholics versus only 35 percent of Protestants said they would like to see the amount of aid requested by the President, "$3.1 billion or 2 percent of the U.S. budget," either kept the same or increased; conversely only 46 percent versus 52 percent wanted it de-creased or terminated (Table 4–6).

Catholics of the 1960's were, of course, less enthusiastic than Prot-estants and, particularly, Jews about inclusion of population-control programs within foreign aid (Table 4–6). However, Catholics did not diverge as much from Protestants on this issue as might be supposed.

As late as February 1966, only 31 percent of Catholics, contrasted with 48 percent of Protestants and 63 percent of Jews, would provide birth-control information to less-developed countries under the foreign-aid program. But by August 1968, shortly after Pope Paul VI's encyclical on the subject, 65 percent of Catholics versus 70 percent of Protestants favored the U.S. government helping nations which requested aid in birth control—a Catholic-Protestant difference of only five percentage points.[8]

Moreover, Catholics were at least somewhat more favorable to virtually every other type of aid, regardless of the political complexion or cold-war posture of the recipients, than were Protestants.

Such was the case, for example, with the major types of technical assistance. In January 1961 Catholics and Jews more than Protestants favored the proposal that a Peace Corps should "send qualified young men, at government expense, to underdeveloped nations around the world to give technical assistance in such fields as agriculture, medicine, and engineering" and said they would like to have any son of theirs "who was qualified . . . participate in such a program" (Table 4–6). After the program had been in operation for almost two years, Catholics and Jews were both more inclined to approve of its performance than were Protestants. Similarly, in the summer of 1961 larger majorities of both Catholics and Jews than of Protestants approved of the suggestion that "the United States take the lead in establishing" a university in both Africa and Southeast Asia "open to all qualified students" in those parts of the world and that our government should be willing to supply most of the teachers. By February 1965 Catholics more than Protestants favored inclusion of the training of teachers, building of schools, construction of hospitals, training of nurses and physicians, provision of medicines, sending of surplus foods, helping in industrial development, and assisting in the construction of basic means of transportation in our aid programs. Only 14 percent of Protestants, contrasted with 18 percent of Catholics and 28 percent of Jews, approved of all these types of aid.

8. By that time at least as large a percentage of Catholics—76 percent—as of Protestants—75 percent—agreed that "birth control information should be available to anybody who wants it" (AIPO release, 9-1-68). In March 1970, 48 percent of Catholics versus 53 percent of Protestants favored making birth-control pills "available free to all women on relief of child-bearing age"; 15 percent versus 17 percent, respectively, would make them "available to teenage girls"; and 32 percent versus 40 percent would recommend them "to a woman who does not want more children" (*Gallup Opinion Index*, March 1970).

Aid to nonaligned and communist regimes has been approved by sharply fewer Americans of all religious persuasions than has the general idea of foreign aid and assistance to allies or "friendly" countries—as was the case in the earlier postwar period as well. However, by the 1960's Catholics were no longer more critical of neutralism than Protestants,[9] and Catholics as well as Jews were consistently more favorable to aid to both nonaligned and communist governments than were Protestants. Differences between the two Christian groups were not always large enough for statistical significance, but they were, without exception, in the same direction—Protestants were the least inclined of the three groups to favor aid to such regimes.

In February 1966, for example, only 14 percent of Protestants, contrasted with 17 percent of Catholics and a like percentage of Jews, felt the United States should "continue giving aid . . . to [a] country which . . . fails to support the U.S. in a major foreign policy decision such as Vietnam"; Protestants were the most likely to feel that aid to such countries should be stopped entirely (Table 4–6). Among those who said they had "heard or read anything about the fighting between India and Red China" in the fall of 1962, only 61 percent of Protestants as compared with 72 percent of Catholics and 70 percent of Jews agreed that the United States should do something "to help India in this connection." During one of the periodic attacks in Congress against aid to Yugoslavia in the spring of 1962, when only approximately one out of four American adults sided with the program against its critics, only 24 percent of Protestants versus 27 percent of Catholics and 39 percent of Jews did.

Food and emergency relief to victims of war and natural catastrophes have always been more popular than capital or military assistance to the same society, be it communist, neutralist, or aligned with the West. However, by the sixties Catholics were more favorable to such assistance, even to the most anti-American of communist regimes, than were Protestants. Informed of the "severe food famine in Communist China" in

9. Although Catholics in April 1957 had been less apt than Protestants to feel the U.S. could "count on India to cooperate with us in world affairs" (see above, p. 60), by 1961 there were no differences between the reactions of the two to the query, "Which two of these nations can be depended upon as being the most friendly to the United States?" so far as neutralist India and Indonesia were concerned. Twelve percent of both chose India, and 3 percent of Catholics and 2 percent of Protestants chose Indonesia from among seven countries including, in addition, Japan, Pakistan, South Korea, Thailand, and the Philippines (AIPO 650, 9–19–61; Catholics numbered 341, Protestants 1,011).

mid-1962, only 46 percent of Protestants, compared with 50 percent of Catholics and 69 percent of Jews, thought the "United States should send food to that country . . . if Communist China's government requests it" (Table 4–6). Similarly, but 64 percent of Protestants, contrasted with 68 percent of Catholics and 84 percent of Jews, at the time would have liked "to see the United Nations Organization try to solve the problem of feeding and resettling refugees from Communist China."

As during most of the initial dozen or so years after the war, Americans of all three religious traditions continued to regard economic aid as more important on the whole than military aid, except for particular countries actually undergoing communist attack such as India in 1962 and South Vietnam several years later. However, the relative increase in popularity of nonmilitary assistance among Catholics compared with Protestants in the late fifties and sixties was not accompanied by any change in the earlier-noted tendency of Catholics more than Protestants to support military assistance. In early 1966, 22 percent of Catholics versus only 17 percent of Protestants favored foreign aid "to help build up military strength abroad." Jews, on the other hand, were less inclined than either to approve of such aid—by 1966 they were sharply more likely than Christians to emphasize economic and technical assistance over the sending of military equipment and the training of armed forces in the less-developed world.

By the sixties, aid to Latin America was more popular by a wide margin among all religious groups (other than Negro Protestants; see below, p. 96) than similar assistance to either Asia or Africa. Even a considerable number of neo-isolationists who disapproved of most U.S. commitments outside the Western Hemisphere did not oppose the Alliance for Progress and other aid to the south.[10] However, if Negroes are eliminated from Catholic-Protestant comparisons, white Catholics were significantly, but certainly not sharply, more inclined than white Protestants to assign priority in our aid effort to predominantly Catholic Latin America over Asia and Africa. Religion of the recipients has not been an irrelevant consideration in Catholic support for aid, but recently Catholics have been at least slightly more favorably disposed toward aid than Protestants regardless of the predominant faith of the country to

10. This has been no new phenomenon. Even prior to the attack on Pearl Harbor many isolationists who opposed intervention against the Axis in Europe and Asia favored vigorous U.S. action against possible Axis penetration or influence in Latin America. Their isolationism did not apply to the Western Hemisphere.

receive it—communist Yugoslavia and China, Hindu India, or Catholic Latin America (Table 4–6).

Catholics and Jews have also differed in recent years from Protestants in their perception of the underdeveloped world and of the basic purposes of our aid there. Since opponents of aid and those who would reduce it substantially have tended to feel that the poorer countries remain in their underdeveloped state owing primarily to their own laziness, indifference, and unwillingness to help themselves, it is interesting to observe that both Catholics and Jews have been more apt than Protestants—especially white Protestants—to feel that underdevelopment has been more due to circumstances beyond these countries' control than to lack of effort by their respective peoples and leaders. The greater prevalence of the Calvinist ethic of hard work and rugged individualism among Protestants (especially white Protestants) and the wider emphasis on charity among Catholics may help to account for the more favorable disposition of Catholics toward transfers of wealth from the prosperous to the underpriviledged both at home (see below, pp. 144–46) and abroad.

Even among those who opposed foreign aid in general or felt it should be reduced, Catholics were more inclined to argue that these resources could be better expended to alleviate unemployment, to expand social welfare, and otherwise to improve the lot of the underprivileged at home, whereas Protestants were more apt to feel they should not be spent at all and taxes and/or the national debt reduced instead (Table 4–6). This more widespread identification of Catholics than Protestants with charity for the underdog has also helped to account for the more favorable disposition of Catholics toward emergency relief abroad, shipment of food and medicines, training of medical personnel, and the like.

Nevertheless, Catholics of the sixties were also more likely than Protestants to view the raising of living standards and basic economic growth as the most important purpose of our foreign-aid endeavor (Table 4–6) and, as we have observed, to favor expenditure of aid funds on industrialization, improvement of communications, education, and other programs designed to assist in more long-term social and economic change. By the mid-sixties Catholics and Jews were both significantly more "satisfied with America's help to poor nations" generally than were Protestants (Table 4–6).

INTERNATIONAL TRADE

The American public, regardless of religion, has been less aware of the issues of tariffs, quotas, and other aspects of world commerce than it has of most of the major foreign-policy questions discussed so far. Less than half the public has known what tariffs or quotas are, and not very many more have even so much as heard or read anything about them (see above, Table 2–1).

The distribution of expressed opinions on whether our government should take action to liberalize trade through lowering import barriers or other means or should discourage imports by raising them has varied during the postwar decades with the particular measure in question and the amount of public debate devoted to it at the moment (Table 4–7). During most of this period more Americans have favored reducing imports through increased tariffs, more restrictive quotas, or other means than have wished import barriers lowered. Moreover, considerably larger numbers of all religious persuasions have expressed approval of expanded trade as a general idea than have favored reduction of tariffs or other import restrictions on most particular products—textiles, oil, automobiles, steel, or whatever.

Differences in thinking on trade matters among the religious groups have been smaller and less consistent than on some of the other aspects of our foreign relations. United States restrictions on imports seem to be perceived more in terms of domestic politics and economics than as aspects of American foreign policy.

Jews have on the whole been at least somewhat more liberal than Christians on these issues, but, except for being better informed, their views have typically differed less from those of Catholics and Protestants on this subject than on most other aspects of foreign relations—foreign aid, relations with the communists and "third" worlds, the Middle East, the United Nations, intercultural relations, and immigration. Moreover, although Catholics recently have been somewhat more aware of trade issues and more inclined to express opinions about them than have Protestants, especially when nonwhites are included—a reversal of the lesser familiarity among Catholics than Protestants as late as the mid-fifties—they have not been any more enthusiastic about freer trade (Table 4–7).

No consistent differences between the two Christian groups were apparent for a dozen years or so after V-J Day with respect to whether the general level of U.S.-imposed trade restrictions should be raised, lowered, or maintained at prevailing levels (Table 4–7). In fact tariffs, quotas, and other barriers were liberalized considerably under the Reciprocal Trade Agreements Act of the period. In 1959 a significantly larger fraction of Catholics than of either Jews or Protestants favored higher tariffs, but two years later no difference was apparent between the two Christian groups on this issue; Jews were more willing to lower tariffs than either. In February 1962, during active discussion of the impending trade-expansion bill, Catholics more than Protestants would have put on more import restrictions on textiles, oil, automobiles, steel, and foreign goods generally. But a month later there was no difference in the distribution of views on the general level of tariffs in the two groups.

CHAPTER 5. THE VATICAN, FRANCO, ISRAEL, FOREIGNERS, AND THE FUTURE

Some international issues have particular saliency for one religious group or another, so that attitudes among its members are clearly divergent from those prevailing among Americans of other faiths. Thus, as we have observed, Catholics, on the whole more favorable than Protestants in the sixties to foreign aid generally, have been less enthusiastic about including population-control projects in our technical-assistance programs.

We noted that prior to Pearl Harbor, U.S. relations with the Vatican, with the Franco group in Spain, and with several belligerents in the Second World War—particularly Britain, Germany, and Italy—evoked considerably different attitudes among Catholics than other Americans. To what extent have these differences persisted after the war? How different have been the views of the religious groups, especially of Jews, with respect to the new Jewish state in the Middle East? And to what extent have the three groups diverged consistently from one another in their views on other major postwar issues as yet unexamined, to wit, the dependability of our allies in the cold war, intercultural exchanges, and immigration?

Finally, how have the religious groups differed recently in their fears and hopes for the future with regard to America's role in the world and in their thinking about how their country might achieve those hopes?

THE HOLY SEE

The relationships of the federal government with the Vatican have remained the one international issue on which Catholic and Protestant Americans have continued to diverge sharply from one another. In fact, differences between the two major Christian groups seemed to widen after the war, when Protestants apparently considered establishment of diplomatic relations less important than during active hostilities in Europe. This was also one of the few questions on which Catholics of the first postwar decade were clearly more inclined than Protestants to have heard or read anything and to harbor clear-cut views.

Thus in 1951 three out of four Catholics who had opinions on the matter, contrasted with but slightly more than one out of four Protestants holding views, thought "the U.S. Senate should approve of the appointment of an Ambassador to the Vatican" as proposed by President Truman (Table 5–1). Even after the election of the first Catholic American President, in the spring of 1961 only 23 percent of Protestants contrasted with 68 percent of Catholics said they would "like to have our present administration send an American representative to the Vatican."

As was the case before American entry into World War II, Jews were considerably more favorably disposed toward establishment of diplomatic relations with the Holy See than were Protestants, though less so than Catholics. However, as late as 1951 more Jews opposed than favored establishment of diplomatic relations through an ambassador, and even after the election of President Kennedy only a slightly larger number of Jews approved than disapproved of "sending an American representative to the Vatican."

RELATIONS WITH FALANGIST SPAIN

The more prevalent prewar affinities for the Franco regime among Catholics than Protestants persisted to some extent thereafter, but postwar interreligious differences in opinion on this issue have been sharply smaller than those with respect to relations with the Vatican. World War II and the sympathies of the Madrid regime for the Americans' enemies in that struggle soured most Catholics as it did other Americans on the Franco government. The minority of Catholics sympathetic with the Spanish government and its policies remained somewhat larger than among Protestants, but interreligious differences had declined significantly since before the war.

Thus in May 1946 only 14 percent of Catholics, 6 percent of Protestants, and 2 percent of Jews said they had "a favorable impression of the present government in Spain, headed by General Franco" (Table 5–2). Even among Catholics unfavorable impressions outnumbered favorable ones by over three to one. Only 31 percent of Catholics versus 38 percent of Protestants and 47 percent of Jews considered "the Franco government in Spain . . . a threat to international peace," but about equally small minorities of all three—7, 6, and 8 percent—would have the United Nations break off diplomatic relations, but go no further, and 2 percent of all three would have the United Nations take further action, but not at the risk of another civil war in Spain. However, 22 percent of Jews and 17 percent of Protestants, contrasted with only 8 percent of Catholics, would have had the UN risk civil war again in taking further measures to eliminate the Franco regime.

A larger minority of Catholics (32 percent) than of Protestants (24 percent) or Jews (22 percent) favored extension of the Marshall Plan to include Spain, but even so, more Catholics opposed than favored this suggestion in November 1948 (Table 5–2). Moreover, Catholics who approved were no more inclined to feel strongly about this question than Protestants who approved; nor did the larger number of Catholics who disapproved than approved feel any less strongly opposed than Protestants.

With the communist coup in Czechoslovakia in 1948, the Berlin blockade, and generally accentuated tensions with the Soviet bloc, the number who approved of rapprochement with the Spanish government increased among all religious groups, though somewhat more among Catholics and less among Jews than among Protestants. Among those who could identify Francisco Franco in the spring of 1949, 47 percent of Catholics, contrasted with but 30 percent of Protestants and 23 percent of Jews, agreed that Spain should be invited to become a member of the UN. Three years later, during the Korean War and the rapid rearmament of western Europe, a larger majority of Catholics than of Protestants harboring views, contrasted with only a minority of Jews, thought "the United States should join with Spain in a mutual defense agreement, that is, agree to come to each other's defense immediately if either one is attacked."

Nevertheless, Protestants and even Jews were almost as disposed as Catholics to send military or economic aid to Spain. Several weeks after Stalin's death, but before the armistice in Korea, but 57 percent of Catholics, compared with 53 percent of Protestants and 50 percent of Jews, approved "of the United States sending military supplies to the Franco government in Spain, to help strengthen the defenses of Western Europe" (Table 5–2). Informed in late 1953 that the United States had recently agreed to send military and economic aid to Spain in return for air and naval bases there, 81 percent of Catholics approved. But so did 77 percent of Protestants and 75 percent of Jews.

No nationwide surveys of opinion regarding Spain since the end of 1953 have included questions about respondents' religious preferences, so we are unable to trace interreligious differences more recently. Pending further empirical study, a reasonable hypothesis seems that by the mid-sixties Catholic Americans were probably no more, or only very little more, sympathetic to the Franco regime than Protestants. As memories of the clerical versus anticlerical overtones of the Spanish Civil War receded into history, the harsher aspects of the dictatorship in Madrid moderated, liberal Catholics both outside and within Spain became increasingly critical of the practices of the Franco government, and American Catholic opinion gradually became more favorable to most aspects of multilateral collaboration, small Catholic-Protestant differences of 1953 should have declined further—they may even have virtually disappeared.

FOREIGN "FRIENDS," INTERCULTURAL RELATIONS, AND IMMIGRATION

Dependability of "Friends"

The more prevalent suspicions or even antagonisms toward the largely Protestant British and their government among Catholics than Protestants of the prewar period had virtually disappeared by the late 1950's (Table 5–3). Equally overwhelming majorities of both Christian groups in the spring of 1957 felt we could "count on England to cooperate with us in world affairs." Six years later 63 percent of both agreed "Great Britain is a dependable ally [friend] of the United States." Only Jews among the major religious groups were more inclined than Catholics to go along with these pro-British views.

More Catholics regarded Britain as a reliable friend of the United States than so considered any other country, with the possible exception of Canada. However, in relative terms Catholics have been somewhat more favorably inclined toward most other noncommunist foreigners and their governments than have Protestants (Table 5–3), whereas they have been only about as positively oriented as Protestants toward Britain.

As early as the summer of 1949 Catholics, probably slightly more than Protestants[1] and, as might have been anticipated, much more than Jews, felt "that Germany, on the whole, has been punished enough for its part in World War II." The following spring a significantly larger minority of Catholics felt that the United States could trust the Germans than did Protestants and, especially, Jews. And in 1963 Catholics were clearly more apt to regard the German Federal Republic as a dependable

1. Differences between the two Christian groups were not statistically significant at the 10 percent level of confidence.

ally of the United States than were either of the other two religious groups.

It is notable that the rather large differences between the Jewish and Christian sentiments about the West Germans and their political leaders apparent shortly after the Second World War had dissipated considerably by the 1960's. By 1963 more Jews regarded West Germany as a relatively reliable friend of the United States than felt her undependable. Moreover, Jews, like other Americans, by 1963 considered the Germans more dependable allies than the French. In fact, Jews were less inclined than Christians to so consider the French, perhaps because of Jews' wider familiarity with the foreign policies of President De Gaulle and with his criticisms of the United States.

The somewhat more marked affinity of Catholics than Protestants for the West Germans was perhaps due in some degree to the former's slightly stronger feeling that Germany was needed in the North Atlantic alliance to prevent Soviet-bloc expansion westward and, maybe, to some small residue of ethnic attractions to the land of their forefathers among Catholics of German extraction. Lutherans, many of them of German background, have been even more inclined to trust the Germans than have Catholic Americans (see below, p. 177). However, German-Americans have been a rather small fraction of American Catholics, and they have had but a very limited influence on the norms of overall postwar Catholic opinion.

Fewer among all religious groups during the later years of General De Gaulle's presidency regarded France as a dependable friend or ally of this country than was the case even earlier in the 1960's, but Catholics apparently remained slightly more inclined to so consider her than did others, including Jews. As may be partly the case with respect to Germans and their Christian Democratic regimes of 1949–69, the few Catholics of French origins or the probably larger number of Catholics who have continued to consider the French basically Catholic may have raised somewhat the Catholic average favorable to France.

However, these possible religious and ethnic affinities seem rather minor factors. Since at least as long ago as 1956 Catholic Americans have also been more favorably disposed toward Japan and its mostly non-Christian people and to regard them as reliable allies than have Protestants, although few of either Christian group have had any ethnic or religious connections with that society. Furthermore, Catholics were as likely as Protestants in 1961 to consider non-Catholic Japan, South Korea,

India, Pakistan, Thailand, and Indonesia to be more dependable, or as dependable, friends of the United States as the more heavily Catholic Philippines. In fact, Catholics appeared somewhat less inclined than Jews to view the Philippines as being one of the two "most friendly to the United States" of these seven Asian countries. Rather, Catholics more than Jews seemed to so regard less Catholic Japan and India.[2]

Intercultural Exchanges

We do not have empirical data of a comparative nature on the reactions of the major religious groups toward other countries, governments, or peoples, but the evidence mentioned so far leads to the hypothesis that by the 1960's Catholics were probably more favorably inclined toward and more likely to rely upon the cooperation of most foreign peoples and governments than were Protestants, though less than were Jews. This supposition is also supported by the observation that Catholics in recent years have been significantly more apt than Protestants to approve of intercultural exchanges, virtually regardless of the foreign country concerned. For example, when asked in the summer of 1960, "To increase good will and our understanding of world problems, it has been suggested that all U.S. school teachers who so desire be sent at government expense to various nations during their summer vacations to study and to write about these nations. Does this sound like a good idea or a poor one?" considerably larger proportions of Catholics (70 percent) and Jews (74 percent) than of Protestants (58 percent) thought it a "good idea."[3] As we observed above (p. 43), Catholics of the sixties were even more favorably disposed than Protestants to international exchanges of persons with the Soviet Union.

Immigration

Only among Jews have more approved than opposed most proposed liberalizations of U.S. immigration policies. However, the Catholic minorities who have approved have been consistently larger in proportion to the number of Catholics in the country than the comparable Protestant minorities. Only in part could the more liberal Catholic than Protestant sentiments about the admission of foreigners to the United States be ex-

2. Differences between Catholics and Jews were not large enough for statistical significance at the 10 percent level.

3. AIPO 630, 6-28-60. Percentages were based on weighted samples of 820 Catholics, 119 Jews, and 2,187 Protestants.

plained by the greater recency, on the whole, of the Catholics' foreign origins and their possible interest in migration of relatives from the "old country" to the New World. Catholics have also been more willing than Protestants to expand admission of non-Christians to the United States.

For instance, during the war 81 percent of Catholics, contrasted with 73 percent of Protestants, felt that "the Jews should have the same chance as other people to settle in all other countries after the war" (Table 5–4). Some non-Jewish Americans changed their reactions when queried further whether "Jews of other countries should have the same chance as non-Jews of other countries to settle in America after the war." Nonetheless, a larger majority of Catholics than Protestants—66 percent versus 57 percent—replied in the affirmative. Virtually all American Jews approved of both these suggestions.

After the war, in 1946, significantly larger minorities of Catholics than Protestants agreed that we should let some of the "over 800,000 homeless people in Europe [many of them Jews] . . . come here now"— particularly "if other countries agreed to take some of them too" (Table 5–4). Two years later 44 percent of Catholics and 85 percent of Jews contrasted with only 36 percent of Protestants approved of the plan then before Congress to let 200,000 displaced persons from communist-controlled eastern Europe "come . . . to the United States . . . during the next two years to live in this country." Shortly after the Soviet suppression of the Hungarian revolution, 37 percent of Protestants versus but 30 percent of Catholics and 5 percent of Jews felt "the United States is letting in too many refugees from Hungary"; conversely, only 9 percent of Protestants compared with 13 percent and 26 percent, respectively, thought we were not letting in enough, and but 46 percent of Protestants vis-à-vis 51 percent of Catholics and 67 percent of Jews believed we were admitting about the right number. Although fear that a number of Hungarian immigrants might be communist spies and subversives was a major source of public opposition to their coming to the United States, Catholics were nevertheless clearly more favorably disposed than Protestants to admit them.

On two occasions in the mid-sixties Catholics were distinctly more disposed than Protestants to increase the number of foreigners permitted to immigrate to this country, while Jews were more willing to expand immigration than either. Conversely, Protestants were the most and Jews the least inclined to reduce the number then being admitted (Table 5–4). Informed in June 1965 that the President had proposed basing future quotas on individual skills rather than national origins as was then the case, 51 percent of Catholics and 75 percent of Jews, contrasted with but 48 percent of Protestants, approved.

ISRAEL VERSUS THE ARABS

Although Catholics in recent years have been somewhat less inclined to harbor anti-Semitic sentiments than Protestants as a group,[4] the two major Christian groups did not differ in any consistent way in their thinking about Israel and related aspects of Middle Eastern affairs from World War II through the six-day war of June 1967 (Table 5–5).[5]

Thus similar proportions of the two groups, 36 percent of Catholics and 34 percent of Protestants, agreed in 1944 that a Jewish state should be established in Palestine after the war, and 20 percent and 18 percent felt our government "should officially demand that Palestine be made into a Jewish state." In early 1948 proportional numbers of both approved partition of Palestine into two states, one Jewish, the other Arab, and the ratio of those sympathizing with the Jews to those sympathizing with the Arabs in the conflict was roughly two to one among both. Overwhelming majorities of both wanted the arms embargo continued; only 2 percent of each would have ended it and sold arms only to the Jews. Protestants were slightly more inclined to send U.S. troops as part of a UN force to keep the peace in Palestine, if they were requested, but Catholics were slightly the more favorable to sending U.S. troops even if no UN force were sent.

As the Israeli-Arab conflict continued into the fifties, the distribution of sympathies for the Israelis versus those for the Arabs and those for

4. The incidence of anti-Semitism among Protestants has been positively correlated with religious orthodoxy and fundamentalist theological beliefs. Thus members of pentecostal sects, the Southern Baptist Convention, and other more fundamentalist denominations have on the whole been more anti-Semitic than Protestants affiliated with theologically more liberal denominations. See, for instance, Charles Y. Glock and Rodney Stark, *Christian Beliefs and Anti-Semitism* (New York: Harper and Row, 1966), pp. 62, 75, 110, 113, 117, 129, 142–46, 150, and 158.

5. Although correlations between attitudes toward Israel and reactions to Jews in the United States and Jews more generally were positive, they were not particularly high. British Foreign Minister Ernest Bevin's comment to the effect that American support for the establishment of a Jewish state in Palestine was related to reluctance to let more Jews into the United States seems to have had some basis in fact. A considerable number of American anti-Semites went along with the idea of a Jewish homeland in the Middle East.

neither remained approximately equivalent among both Christian groups. More sympathized primarily with the Israelis than with the Arabs, more thought relatively well of Israel than did not, and only small minorities considered it "not so important to cooperate with Israel," even after the Sinai war of 1956, among both Catholics and Protestants. However, only equally small minorities, 17 percent and 16 percent respectively, would have supplied arms to Israel several months before the open hostilities in the fall of 1956 between Israel and Egypt.

The continuing crisis in Israeli-Arab relations following the brief war in June 1967 resulted in declining sympathies for the Israelis over the Arabs among both Christian groups, but more markedly so among Catholics than Protestants.[6] A year after the six-day war only 21 percent of Catholics contrasted with 23 percent of Protestants would supply arms to the Israelis (only 5 percent and 8 percent would send troops to aid them) in case of a future "full-scale" war in the area (Table 5–5). At the beginning of 1969, 44 percent of Catholics, contrasted with 50 percent of Protestants, said they sympathized more with the Israelis than with the Arabs, while 7 percent and 4 percent, respectively, sympathized more with the Arabs. By March 1970 these differences between the two Christian groups had widened further; only 34 percent of Catholics versus 45 percent of Protestants sympathized more with Israelis, while 6 percent and 2 percent, respectively, sympathized more with the Arabs.

American Jews were, of course, much more pro-Israel than either Christian group. Overwhelming majorities favored active U.S. governmental support of the Zionist cause, sympathized with their coreligionists against the Arabs, approved of sending U.S. troops if requested, opposed the change of official U.S. policy in March 1948 from support of the UN partition plan to opposition to it, and favored the U.S. supplying arms to Israel before it became a state and thereafter. Nevertheless, it is notable that over half of the Jews interviewed in late 1953 also considered it "very important to cooperate closely with the Arab states" and sizable minorities considered it "only fairly important to cooperate closely with Israel," believed both Israel and the Arab states or neither were mainly to blame for the continuing conflict, and, after the Sinai invasion, disapproved of at least some of the actions of the Israeli government.

6. The more widespread proclivity among Catholics than Protestants to approve of the way President Johnson dealt with the June 1967 crisis in the Middle East (Table 5–5) can be largely explained by the more Democratic proclivities of the former. See n. 10 in Chapter 3, p. 53, above, and pp. 133–37 below.

THE FUTURE

By the 1960's Catholics had become at least somewhat more optimistic than Protestants about most public issues—more apt, for instance, to anticipate for the future domestic economic growth and prosperity, full employment, lessened tension between management and labor, and even lower taxes (Table 5–6).

This general sentiment about internal problems has been paralleled by similarly more prevalent optimism among Catholic than Protestant Christians about the course of international affairs and America's role in the world. As we have observed, Catholics have been the more disposed to feel that our differences with other countries, including even the People's Republic of China, could be worked out short of major war, that the causes of turbulence, violence, and hostility to the West in much of the less-developed world could in the long run be remedied, and that the world generally could be encouraged to become a more peaceful and less threatening place. In 1965 a larger majority of Catholics—59 percent—than of Protestants—49 percent—or even Jews—52 percent—believed that "United States influence in the world will increase twenty years from now" (Table 5–6). At the end of 1966 Catholics were the more likely to feel that relative "American power" would "increase in the world" and, conversely, that Communist Chinese and Soviet power would probably decline during even so brief a period as the following year. By the end of the 1960's Catholic Americans were somewhat more inclined than their Protestant counterparts to believe that by 1990 Soviet communism would either have disappeared or changed so fundamentally that the U.S.S.R. and the West would be "living together peacefully," that production of atomic weapons would have ceased, that passports would no longer be necessary for world travel, and that human beings would be living on the moon (Table 5–6).

Among no religious group did many feel such a less dangerous, less anti-American, and more peaceful world would just come about by itself, regardless of U.S. policies in the interim. Catholics and Protestants were equally apt to regard a strong military defense, buttressed with collective-security alliances, as vital to our national welfare. They did not differ in their willingness to use our military power if necessary to resist military or paramilitary adventures by hostile regimes. Neither seemed to consider liberalized world trade as a significant means of achieving the long-range international objectives of the United States.

However, by the 1960's Catholics—more than Protestants—felt that expanded negotiations of disagreements and widened diplomatic, cultural, and economic relations with the communist countries, including Mainland China, should be major means in achieving this hoped-for more stable, less warlike world in which American standing would be enhanced. Catholics were more inclined than Protestant Christians to consider economic aid and technical assistance for less-developed countries a significant instrument in bringing about this kind of future international environment. Finally, Catholics more than Protestants viewed cooperation with the United Nations, even if it included the People's Republic of China, as an important way of furthering this objective.

Jews more than either Christian group have emphasized more vigorous efforts to alleviate tensions with the communist powers, expanded development assistance and other accommodations with countries in Asia, Africa, and Latin America—regardless of their postures in the cold war—and broadened cooperation with multilateral institutions, especially the United Nations. More than Christians of either persuasion, Jews would deemphasize military means in U.S. foreign policy, including further compromises to reduce U.S. and other defense establishments and to curtail nuclear proliferation, a shift of effort from military to economic assistance, and greater hesitancy to intervene militarily abroad. Also somewhat more than Christians, they have considered freer trade to be a desirable and integral part of long-range foreign policy.

PART III. CHRISTIAN DIVERSITIES

CHAPTER 6. NEGRO AND WHITE CHRISTIANS

Nonwhite Americans, all except a small minority of them Negroes, have differed in some respects from whites in their reactions to international affairs. Although the number of Negro Catholic converts has grown in recent years, Negroes constituted only some 600,000 of nearly 50,000,000 American Catholics in the later 1960's. Thus, their removal from survey samples has seldom resulted in any significant modification in the norms of international views apparent among white as contrasted with all Catholics. However, overall Protestant norms have usually been influenced considerably because of the vast majority of American Negroes that have been included within them—almost one Protestant out of six has been nonwhite.

Negro Catholics, Muslims, individuals of no religious preference, and other non-Protestants have been so few that it is impossible to compare them statistically with one another or with other groups. Since Negro Catholics have on the whole been better educated, less lower-class, and more urban than Protestant Negroes, they have probably been more cosmopolitan in their international orientations. However, Catholic and other non-Protestant Negroes have been so few among national Negro samples that norms of international behavior of nonwhite Protestants have usually deviated no more than a percentage point or two from those of all nonwhites taken together.

Therefore the discussion following will focus primarily on the comparative international thinking of the two races among Protestants. Since the race and the religion of the respondent have not both been simultaneously available on surveys of a number of international issues prior to the late 1950's, comparisons of white and Negro Protestants will be supplemented with some of Negroes with whites generally,[1] especially on issues on which the two major Christian groups have not differed significantly.

Several methodological limitations pertinent to the validity of the generalizations to follow should be mentioned. Although most surveys have grouped Negroes together with other nonwhites, we shall use the terms Negro and nonwhite as though they were synonymous.[2] Moreover,

1. For a systematic comparison of international behavior of whites in general with Negroes in general, see Alfred O. Hero, Jr., "American Negroes and U.S. Foreign Policy: 1937–1967," *Journal of Conflict Resolution* 13, no. 2 (June 1969), pp. 220–51.

2. Non-Negro groups have normally numbered less than 5 percent of total nonwhite samples.

the drawing of earlier AIPO samples from voters in the previous election rather than from the total adult population resulted in severe under-representation of Negroes, especially of educationally, economically, and socially underprivileged Negroes in the rural and small-town South. The number of Southern Negroes in most AIPO samples prior to the fifties was usually considerably smaller than that of Northern Negroes, though the reverse was then the case among the actual Negro population. Fur-thermore, since interest, knowledge, and more cosmopolitan opinions in foreign affairs have been more prevalent among better educated than more culturally deprived Negroes, and among those in the urban North than those in the rural and small-town South, these surveys probably overestimated the actual levels of concern, understanding, and liberal views among Negroes. Thus, the shift among Negroes toward greater interest, knowledge, and support in respect of multilateral involvements was probably more marked than the data cited below tended to suggest. AIPO surveys in more recent years, though based on the total adult pop-ulation, have likewise included proportionally fewer lower-class, poorly educated Negroes than the population generally. However, during the 1960's these samples have been weighted to compensate for this under-representation of culturally deprived groups.

In addition, most of the prewar and early postwar interviews of Negroes were conducted by white interviewers, while most of the more recent ones have been conducted by interviewers of the same race as the respondent. Other evidence suggests that a significant fraction of Negroes have tended to provide different replies to the same questions, particular-ly those related to race relations, to Negro interviewers than to white ones. Expressed views on the foreign programs of the U.S. prior to ap-proximately 1950 were probably somewhat more favorable than the private views of Negro respondents, whereas those advanced more re-cently, to Negro interviewers, were perhaps closer to actual opinions.[3] The probable effects of the use of white interviewers were thus in the same direction as those of underrepresentation of more ignorant, apa-thetic, and isolationist Negroes before approximately 1950; in general, therefore, the relative shifts in actual Negro international opinions vis-à-vis those of whites have probably been more marked than the surveys mentioned below suggest.

3. See also Alfred O. Hero, Jr., *The Southerner and World Affairs* (Baton Rouge: Louisiana State Univ. Press, 1965), pp. 507–8.

EXTENT OF INTEREST AND KNOWLEDGE

Given the relatively low average education of Negroes, it is not surprising that they have been considerably less well-informed about most international issues, less interested in them, less apt to ascribe importance to them, and less inclined to hold opinions on them than have whites, regardless of religion. The less generally known a world phenomenon or a proposal or program of the United States, the smaller the proportion of Negroes among the informed. These racial differences have narrowed over the years as the educational level of Negroes gradually approached that of whites, but Negroes still clearly lagged behind whites by considerable margins in these regards in the mid-sixties.

Even among the Negro voters interviewed in the years just after the war—on the average better informed than the nonvoters, who were excluded—the general level of awareness was distinctly lower than among whites (Table 6–1). For instance, a month and a half after Secretary Marshall's Harvard commencement address in 1947, only 48 percent of Negroes, contrasted with 62 percent of whites, had heard or read of the proposed Marshall Plan, and only 2 percent of Negroes versus 7 percent of whites could describe it correctly as U.S. economic assistance to war-torn Europe to help it rehabilitate its economies, or words to that effect. Only 44 percent of Southern Negroes, contrasted with 49 percent of Northern Negroes, had heard of the Marshall Plan, and but 1 percent of those in the South versus 5 percent in the North could describe it at all accurately. Similar differences persisted as the European Recovery Program became more widely known during the ensuing two years. In the fall of 1947 only 4 percent of Negroes, contrasted with 14 percent of whites, considered "helping European countries to recover" to be among the most important of nine "things" for the federal government "to try to do." In the late summer and autumn of 1953 only 3 percent of Protestant Negroes (and of all Negroes), contrasted with 9 percent of white Protestants and 8 percent of white Catholics, agreed that "continuing our policy of aiding Western Europe" was among the most important issues to them in the election campaign then in progress; similar percentages of Negroes, as contrasted with whites that August, regarded such assistance as one of the "most important policies" among ten mentioned for the next national administration to continue.

A sharply smaller minority of Negroes than whites considered "strengthening the United Nations" to be among the "two [of nine] things . . . which [they would] like most to see the government try to do" in November 1947 (Table 6–1). During a major British economic crisis in the summer of 1949, a smaller majority of Negroes than of whites felt it made much difference to the United States whether Britain remained a strong power or not, and a distinctly smaller proportion of Negroes than of whites had heard anything of her financial problems. Negroes were patently less aware than whites, regardless of religion, of the General Agreement on Tariffs and Trade shortly after it was signed with considerable fanfare in 1947, of the projected Atlantic Security Pact when it was being negotiated in early 1949, and of the Point Four program over a year after its initial mention in President Truman's inaugural address. In April 1950 only 1 percent of Negroes, contrasted with 5 percent of whites, could describe the general purpose or content of Point Four.

In the summer of 1953 only one-fifth of adult Negroes, contrasted with one-third of whites, said they read regularly any newspaper columnist writing on national or international affairs (Table 6–1). During the accentuated tensions over Quemoy and Matsu in the spring of 1955, only 33 percent of Negro Protestants, compared with 47 percent of their white coreligionists, knew that these islands were in noncommunist hands, and only 65 percent versus 85 percent had heard or read of any "trouble in the Formosa area." Three out of eight of the former, contrasted with only one out of five of the latter, could locate neither France, England, Spain, Poland, Austria, Rumania, nor Bulgaria on a map of Europe. Only one out of six Negroes, vis-à-vis one out of two whites, had heard of "the recent French elections" in early 1956, a less generally familiar bit of information.

Negroes lagged behind whites, regardless of religion, to a similar extent in respect of awareness of any public discussion of tariffs and/or trade in the fall of 1954. Even as late as the end of 1961, during the height of the debate over the proposed Trade Expansion Act of 1962, only 23 percent of Negroes (and of Protestant Negroes) had recently heard or read of any discussion whatsoever of "tariffs and trade," contrasted with 55 percent of whites, 54 percent of white Protestants, and 56 percent of white Catholics (Table 6–1).

Negroes have not even been nearly as familiar as whites of either religious persuasion with black Africa. In 1957, for instance, only 1 percent of Negroes (and of Negro Protestants) contrasted with 6 percent of whites (6 percent of Protestant and 5 percent of Catholic whites) could name as many as five countries, colonies, or other territories on the African continent; 70 percent of Negroes versus only 55 percent of whites could not name any at all (Table 6–1).

RACE AND DIRECTIONS OF OPINION:
BEFORE PEARL HARBOR

The proportions of Negroes who have been unwilling to express any opinions on major foreign-policy questions have been so much larger than those among whites that it is often difficult to interpret interracial differences in views expressed. Negro Protestants have often been less apt either to approve or to disapprove of particular policies than have Protestant whites.

Perhaps the most meaningful comparisons are those of the distributions of opinions within the two racial groups among only those who expressed opinions, or of the ratios of those favorable to those unfavorable to the pertinent policy or line of action. However, the less interested or informed an individual American, regardless of race, has been, or the less inclined he has been to venture any view, the more isolationist or neo-isolationist has he been on the average in his general sentiments or vague leanings in world affairs. Thus, more among Negroes than whites does elimination of the "no opinion" group probably lead to overestimates of the ratio of so-called "enlightened," liberal, or multilateralist international opinion to isolationist, neo-isolationist, strongly nationalist, or unilateralist thinking. The tables documenting the observations below will therefore present the distributions of both opinions and nonopinions among the racial and religious groups.

Since economic and, particularly, educational underprivilege has been associated among all groups with more isolationist, neo-isolationist, or unilateralist opinions, it might be supposed that Negro Protestants— especially some years ago—were a good deal more inclined to such frames of mind than were their white coreligionists. Negro Protestants who expressed opinions in the South were in fact less inclined than white Protestant Southerners to approve of U.S. cooperation with the League of Nations, liberalization of the Johnson and Neutrality Acts, Lend-Lease, other assistance to the enemies of the Axis, the initial postwar loan to

Britain, Truman Doctrine aid to Greece and Turkey, the Marshall Plan, NATO, the UN, and most other bilateral or multilateral commitments of the U.S. government prior to the late 1950's.[4]

However, Southern Negro Protestants were usually less favorable to these programs than Protestant Negroes in the North. The latter diverged only to a more limited degree from Northern white Protestants, insofar as they expressed opinions, on most foreign questions. Thus, attitudinal differences between Negro and white Protestants expressing views in the country as a whole, though for the most part in the direction of less cosmopolitan thinking among the Negroes, were on the whole smaller than educational and other demographic differences between them might have led one to suppose.[5]

For instance, Negro Protestants and Negroes generally in the prewar years were more inclined than their white counterparts to prefer that Japan win in any war that might develop between her and the Soviet Union (Table 6–2). Negro Protestants were also less favorable than whites regardless of religion to embargoing arms to Japan. However, racial differences were quite small, suggesting that Negro identification with the yellow Japanese accompanied by comparable white affinities for the Caucasian Russians was probably a relevant factor, but not a particularly strong one.

Moreover, Negroes were more disposed than whites to let yellow Japan take over equally nonwhite China rather than risk war to prevent it—apparently part of a generally more isolationist stance among Negroes than other Americans during that period (Table 6–2). Furthermore, Negroes were in general less willing than whites, regardless of religion, to draft men for any war overseas. Negroes were likewise less willing than whites of either Christian persuasion to lend money to Finland to purchase military and other supplies here to defend itself against the U.S.S.R. in the winter war of 1939–40, less inclined to let Britain purchase similar supplies here on credit and to modify the Johnson Act to permit her to do so, and less approving of the leasing of destroyers to the British and the passage of the Lend-Lease bill by Congress.

However, when "no opinions" were eliminated these differences

4. See Hero, *Southerner*, Chap. 14.
5. Given the underrepresentation of educationally and socially underprivileged, especially Southern rural Negroes, in these surveys, actual Negro-white differences in the country may have been larger than the data cited here suggest.

were relatively modest ones. Moreover, among people expressing views, there were no differences between Negroes and Negro Protestants on the one hand and whites and white Protestants on the other with respect to extending Lend-Lease to the U.S.S.R. after the Nazis attacked that country. Furthermore, Negroes were clearly more rather than less favorable to the lowering of tariffs and reciprocal trade than whites (though not than Southern whites—see below, p. 119). Thus, although Negroes were on the whole more isolationist and less willing to involve the country in foreign affairs than whites of either Christian religion, the Southern background of most Negroes (including most in the North) seemed more important in shaping their views on international commerce[6] than was the general isolationism associated with their cultural and educational underprivilege.

THE POSTWAR PERIOD: FOREIGN AID

Negro Protestants continued to be at least somewhat less enthusiastic about most of the major international commitments of the federal government during the first ten years after the war than whites of either Protestant or Catholic religious preferences.[7] Such seemed to be the case even when such crucial factors as level of formal education were held constant. Thus in 1948 Negro Protestant college graduates held more conservative or isolationist opinions than did either Catholic or Protestant whites on six major issues of the day—whether to strengthen the UN to permit it to make decisions binding on its members, whether liberalized immigration would "lower our standard of culture," whether lower tariffs and expanded foreign imports would "lower our standard of living," whether we should try to make the standards of living abroad rise more rapidly than our own, whether ideological differences between such countries as the U.S.S.R. and the United States were "irreconcilable,"

6. For documentation of the greater prevalence during this period of liberal trade attitudes in the South than elsewhere, see Hero, *Southerner* pp. 139–47.

7. For example, as late as the fall of 1956, 35 percent of Negro Protestants, contrasted with 24 percent of white Protestants and 23 percent of white Catholics, agreed "this country would be better off if we just stayed home and did not concern ourselves with problems in other parts of the world." Conversely, only 33 percent versus 60 percent and 56 percent disagreed with this isolationist view; while 5, 5, and 6 percent were undecided, replying, "it depends" or words to that effect, and 27, 11, and 15 percent replied that they had no opinions on this matter. Negro Protestants numbered 125, white Protestants 1,151, and white Catholics 364 (SRC 417, Sept.–Oct. 1956).

and whether the U.S. must be stronger than all other countries "to have lasting peace."[8]

These observations were patently applicable to most of the foreign aid of the period, particularly that going to Europe and other largely Caucasian societies—as most of it did.

Aid to Europe

Thus a significantly smaller majority of Negroes than whites expressing opinions a few months before the end of World War II thought the United States would "have the best chance of having prosperity in this country after the war . . . by helping other countries . . . get back on their feet" whereas a larger minority of Negroes than whites agreed we would be better off if we did not, or that it would make no difference either way (Table 6–3). Negroes were likewise less willing than whites regardless of religion to go back to rationing after the war "if necessary to feed the hungry in Europe" and to aid either Greece or Turkey under the Truman Doctrine.[9] Throughout the Marshall Plan, Negroes were less inclined than whites to favor it as a general idea, to approve of the amount of funds devoted to it, to be willing to pay taxes to support it, or to consider economic aid to Europe a relatively important endeavor for the American people and its federal government. During the British economic crisis in the late summer of 1949, Negroes who had heard of these financial difficulties less than whites believed the United Kingdom would "have to have more money from the U.S. than Congress is providing under the Marshall Plan" and favored "the U.S. making a new loan to England of a billion or two billion dollars."

Negroes generally were likewise less supportive of military assistance to the NATO countries of western Europe than were whites regardless of their religion (Table 6–3). In March 1949, as the North Atlantic Pact was being negotiated, a distinctly smaller majority of Negroes than whites felt "the U.S. should . . . supply arms and war materials to the Western European nations if they agree to provide us with air bases and any other help which they may be able to give." Three years later, during the height of the military buildup of NATO, Negroes

8. From retabulations of a study of a national sample of 9,064 college graduates for *Time* magazine by the Bureau of Applied Social Research. Thirty-seven percent of Negro Protestants versus 18 percent of Protestant whites and 20 percent of Catholic whites opted for relatively isolationist positions on a composite of these six issues.

9. However, when "no opinions" were eliminated, Negroes were no more opposed than whites to channeling aid to Greece and Turkey through the UN (Table 6–3).

were less willing than whites to continue giving "money and military equipment to Western European countries to help them build up an army for defense against the communists." A larger majority of Negroes than whites felt at the time that the $8 billion estimated from the United States during the next fiscal year for this purpose was "too much." The following late summer and fall, only 18 percent of Negro Protestants, contrasted with 28 percent of white Protestants, thought we should "keep on trying to build up the armed strength of the countries of Western Europe to resist Communism like we've been doing"; only 37 percent of the former, compared with 46 percent of the latter, would give some, but less, military aid, and 27 percent versus 14 percent agreed with the isolationist alternative, that we should "get out of European affairs and let them build up their own defenses against the Communists if they really want to."

Aid to Colored and Less-Developed Countries: 1949–1956

These rather consistent racial differences were to some extent related to the white race of the western European recipients and the ethnic and cultural ties of white Americans of all three religious groups with them. The divergence in thinking between the races was larger for aid to Greece than for aid to less apparently white Turkey in 1947 (Table 6–3). Although Negroes were less favorable than whites to providing either technical or capital assistance to predominantly white South America and Central America in the mid-fifties, they appeared about as disposed as whites to have "the United States . . . do more to help [nonwhite] Japan get back on her feet" in March 1949, to give grain to famine-plagued dark-skinned Indians two years later, to shift our aid emphasis from western Europe "to our allies in Asia" in the spring of 1953, and to send aid two years later such as that extended previously to western Europe "to non-communist countries in Asia." Negroes were likewise at least as apt as whites in early 1956 to feel that "our government should try harder to win the friendship of [colored] countries like India, Egypt, and Burma."

Nevertheless, prior to the late fifties, Negro Protestants and Negroes generally were on the whole somewhat less supportive than whites, regardless of religion, of nonmilitary aid to most less-developed recipients,[10]

10. Few differences were large enough for statistical difference, owing to the limited sizes of Negro samples. However, the consistency of these differences leads to the conclusion that Negroes and Negro Protestants were both less favorable and more opposed to most types of nonmilitary aid to underdeveloped countries (other than in Africa

at that time mainly in Asia. When those who said in early 1956 that the U.S. government should try harder to win the friendship of the three neutralist countries mentioned above were asked what it should do, Negroes were less inclined than whites to suggest expanded or liberalized foreign aid or the like and, for that matter, to make any suggestions whatsoever. Even though Negroes seemed at least as favorably disposed as whites to sending military supplies to colored South Korea during the war there and to the Arab Middle East under the Eisenhower Doctrine in January 1957, the Negroes appeared the less enthusiastic about according economic assistance to either (Table 6–4). In fact, throughout this period Negroes were consistently less likely than whites to assign relative importance to economic vis-à-vis military aid; Negroes were distinctly underrepresented among the majority of Americans who considered capital and technical assistance of greater long-run importance in the underdeveloped world than the sending of military supplies and the training of troops. Related to this observation was another, that Negroes were less willing than white Americans to approve of President Eisenhower's unsuccessful proposal in 1956 that at least part of our economic aid to less-developed countries be placed on a longer-term, more continuing basis than was permitted by one-year congressional authorizations.

When no nonwhite recipient country or region was specifically mentioned, Negroes were rather consistently less favorable than whites toward aid to the underdeveloped world from its beginnings in 1949 into early 1956. Fifteen months after President Truman's inaugural address, only 47 percent of Negroes, compared with 64 percent of whites, thought it "a good policy for the United States to try to help backward countries to raise their standard of living"; conversely, 34 percent of Negroes versus 30 percent of whites considered this of "no concern to our government" (Table 6–4). Among the small minority who had heard of Point Four, Negroes were patently less inclined than whites to approve of it in April 1950, as they were six years later to consider it a "good idea for our government to spend money on technical assistance to backward countries." In the spring of 1953, near the end of the Korean War, only 53 percent of Negro Protestants, contrasted with 68 percent of their white coreligionists, agreed that "if defense spending can safely be cut . . . the United States, along with

south of the Sahara) than were either Protestant, Catholic, or Jewish whites or all whites considered together.

other nations, [should] use part of the money they would save to help the needy countries of the world." During the congressional debate in the summer of 1953 of the bill which would become P.L. 480, only 53 percent of Negroes versus 71 percent of whites replied in the affirmative to the query, "President Eisenhower has asked the right to give or lend government-owned surplus (extra) grain to nations faced with famine (food shortage). Should Congress give Eisenhower this power or not?"

In the mid-fifties Negroes were somewhat less willing to send economic or even military aid to unnamed "allies," "friendly countries," "countries that have agreed to stand with us against communist aggression," or the like. Although Negroes were no more hostile than whites to neutralism in the cold war on the part of Asian and African countries, they were nevertheless less inclined in 1956–57 to continue economic aid to countries "like India, which have not joined us as allies against the Communists." In late December 1954 and early January 1955, only 13 percent of Negroes, contrasted with 19 percent of whites, felt "the U.S. should not withdraw aid to nations which refuse to cooperate with us." In the late fall of 1956 and again in the spring of 1957, Negroes were less favorably disposed than white Americans to sending economic aid "to countries like Poland, which have rebelled against Russian control." On three occasions from the beginning of 1956 into the spring of 1957, Negroes were less supportive than whites regardless of religion of aid at then prevailing magnitudes.[11]

The Underdeveloped World: Late Fifties and Sixties

By the second Eisenhower administration, most attitudinal differences between Negroes and whites, and between Protestants of the two races, with respect to aid to less-developed countries (other than in information and expression of any opinion) had disappeared. From late 1956 until roughly 1961, Negroes were slightly less supportive than whites of some aspects of aid, about as approving of others, and somewhat more favorable to still others, depending on the type of assistance at issue, the recipient mentioned, the wording of the question, and other factors. As most of

11. A survey of a representative sample of adults in the Detroit area in 1957–58 found Protestant Negroes less supportive than white Protestants of foreign aid even when such relevant variables as education and socio-economic status were held constant. See Gerhard Lenski, *The Religious Factor* (Garden City, N.Y.: Doubleday Anchor Books, 1963), pp. 210–11. See also p. 89 above for similar findings among a national sample of college graduates a decade earlier.

Africa south of the Sahara became independent and requested aid from the United States, the relative position of the two races with respect to assistance which had been apparent when most aid went to western Europe gradually reversed. By the time of the Kennedy administration Negro Protestants and Negroes generally who ventured any views were typically somewhat more favorably disposed than white Protestants and, in some instances, than white Catholics, to most types of foreign aid. Negroes of the sixties tended to raise the Protestant average of support for aid rather than to reduce it. Typically, differences between Catholics and Protestants toward lesser support of foreign aid increased among Protestants during recent years when Negroes were excluded from the statistics.

In the fall of 1956, for instance, the ratio of those who agreed to those who disagreed that "the United States should give economic help to the poorer countries of the world even if they can't pay for it" was somewhat higher among Negroes than either white Protestants or white Catholics (Table 6–5). Such was also the case with regard to giving "help to foreign countries even if they are not as much against communism as we are." The little aid that went to Africa in the late 50's was, of course, more enthusiastically received among Negroes than whites, be they Protestants or Catholics. Negroes were significantly more apt to consider it "very important to help Africa improve its living standards" in the spring of 1957, though the differences between Negro and white Protestants were not as large as one might suppose. Protestant Negroes and all Negroes considered together were also somewhat more inclined than whites and white Protestants to increase "economic aid to Asia and Africa" around the same time, and conversely, less apt to feel it should be cut. Almost a year later Negroes were similarly less inclined than whites to reduce and more disposed to expand "economic aid to underdeveloped Asia and Africa," and more willing to have their own "income taxes raised to meet Soviet economic competition and promises of economic aid to Africa and Asia."

However, black Africa received only a very small fraction of U.S. aid in 1957–60, and when it was not specifically mentioned, Negroes were not any more favorable to economic assistance to less-developed countries generally than whites of either of the two major Christian groups. Among those citizens expressing views, Negroes were about as inclined as whites to be "in general for foreign aid" and to approve of the general level of aid expenditures. In the summer of 1959 Negroes were less likely than whites to approve of equipping hospital, food, training, or other ships for service in underdeveloped areas at U.S. governmental expense. As late as the end of 1960 the two races, regardless of religion (Jews excluded), were about as inclined to feel that the Kennedy administration and the new Congress should increase, or decrease, foreign aid. Even as recently as May 1961 Negroes, and Negro Protestants, were less willing than whites of either Christian persuasion to make "personal sacrifices, including higher taxes, for foreign economic aid," although Negroes and the Protestant majority among them did not differ from white Protestants or whites generally in their willingness to pay for military assistance. Even by November 1961 there was no difference between the races among Protestants, insofar as they expressed any views, in their feelings about whether or not foreign-aid expenditures during the preceding five years had advanced our national interests.

However, by the beginning of the Kennedy administration and, particularly, by the mid-sixties, Negro Americans expressing opinions—including the Protestants among them—were on the average somewhat more favorable to foreign aid than white Protestants. On some aspects of aid (or wordings of questions posed to them) there were no differences between the races among Protestants, but on more than not, Negro Protestants, insofar as they advanced views, were more supportive, and on very few were they less so than Protestant whites.[12] Whites regardless of religion remained more apt than Negroes to express opinions on these matters, but even differences in this respect between the races had declined significantly since the Second World War.

Thus at the beginning of the Kennedy administration 78 percent of Negro Protestants approved and only 6 percent disapproved of the proposed Peace Corps for technical assistance to the less-developed world, while but 69 percent of their white coreligionists approved and 22 percent disapproved (Table 6–5). Almost two years later the ratio of those who approved to those who disapproved "of the job the Peace Corps is doing" among Americans who had heard of this program was somewhat higher among Negro than white Protestants. In late 1961, only 51 percent of Negroes versus 71 percent of whites among Protestants felt that "the U.S. and the West" had been doing enough for less developed countries; 18 percent versus 13 percent thought they had not. During the widely publicized famine in Communist China in early

---

12. Differences on individual surveys were, however, often too small for statistical significance at the 10 percent level of confidence.

1961, and again in the spring of 1962, Negroes (and Negro Protestants)[13] among citizens offering views were somewhat the more inclined to send surplus U.S. food to that country. Thirty-three percent of Protestant Negroes, contrasted with only 22 percent of white Protestants, approved of continuing both economic and military aid to Yugoslavia in April 1962; only 24 percent versus 44 percent opposed this line of action.

Although the proportion of Negroes who were "in general for foreign aid" was about the same in early 1963 as that among whites when individuals expressing no opinions on the matter were eliminated from consideration, two years and again three years later Negro Protestants were distinctly more apt to be "for" aid than their white coreligionists (Table 6–5). In October 1963, only 27 percent of Negro Protestants, contrasted with 45 percent of white ones, mentioned foreign aid or some aspect thereof as something on which their federal government spent too much money. Thirty-three percent versus only 13 percent at the time said they had "a very great deal of trust in the way President Kennedy and his administration are handling foreign aid."[14] Whereas Negro Protestants in April 1957 had been about as inclined as whites to cut or eliminate foreign aid, in late 1963 and on two occasions in 1965 Protestant Negroes were consistently more likely than white Protestants to feel the general magnitude of aid should be increased and distinctly less apt to suggest that it be reduced. Although Negro Protestants remained more inclined than Protestant whites to assign priority to our aid programs to Africa over those to Asia and Latin America, by the mid-sixties they appeared somewhat more likely to feel we had some obligation to help underdeveloped countries in general, to be relatively satisfied with our efforts to do so, to consider circumstances beyond their control rather than lack of effort the primary cause of their low standards of living, and to favor continuing aid even "to countries which fail to support the United States in major foreign policy decisions, such as Vietnam."

However, this wider support for economic assistance for underdeveloped, including neutralist, countries among Negro than white Protestants did not imply any lesser approval of military aid to these countries, as one might perhaps have supposed from some of the attacks on U.S. military intervention abroad heard from the left or more radical wing of Negro civil-rights leadership. In fact, the greater importance ascribed

13. Religion was asked on only one of these surveys (see Table 6–5).
14. Undoubtedly the disproportionately large number of self-perceived Democrats and voters for Kennedy among Negroes accounted in part for this difference.

to military vis-à-vis economic aid among Negro than white Protestants apparent earlier persisted at least as late as 1966. Negro Protestants of the late fifties and sixties who harbored any views were usually more favorably disposed toward military aid than were whites of either Christian group.[15]

For instance, in April 1957 Negroes were somewhat more inclined than whites to increase military aid and less disposed to reduce it. Although in the late spring of 1961 they seemed somewhat less willing than Protestant whites to make sacrifices, including increased personal taxes, for foreign economic aid, they appeared at least as willing as white Protestants to make such sacrifices for military aid. Among those who had "heard or read anything about the fighting between India and Red China" in late 1962, Negro and white Protestants were about equally apt to favor, and to oppose, doing "anything to help India in this connection." In early 1966, 27 percent of Negro Protestants, contrasted with only 16 percent of their white coreligionists, were favorably disposed to "help build up military strength abroad."

TARIFFS AND TRADE

Such small minorities of Negroes have understood what a tariff or quota is or heard of the general arguments for or against freer trade that it is difficult to compare their views with those among whites of either Christian persuasion. During the initial decade after the war the distributions of views on trade among those Negroes, Negro Protestants, whites, white Protestants, and white Catholics who held any were about the same (Table 6–6).

Negro Protestants of the sixties remained distinctly less inclined than whites of either Christian faith to ascribe importance to increasing the general level of American purchases and sales abroad (Table 6–6). However, by the end of the fifties, or at least the early sixties, Negroes who harbored views on these issues had become more liberal than either Catholic or Protestant whites. When Americans who had never heard of any discussion of tariffs or trade or held no opinions on them are eliminated from consideration, Negroes more than whites of either Christian faith favored lower tariffs and expanded imports of foreign goods into this country. Negroes seemed more favorable to freer trade virtually

15. Differences, particularly with respect to military aid, were too small for statistical significance.

regardless of the items in question—textiles, oil, automotive equipment, or steel.

INTERCULTURAL EXCHANGE AND IMMIGRATION

Negro Protestants by the 1960's had likewise become more favorably disposed than their white coreligionists to exchanges of persons with other countries, even when Africa was not mentioned. In the summer of 1960, for example, 75 percent of Protestant Negroes, contrasted with only 56 percent of their white counterparts, favored sending U.S. school teachers abroad at federal expense during their summer vacations; 59 percent versus 49 percent considered bringing foreign teachers to this country "at our expense in order to get a better understanding of this country . . . a good idea" (Table 6–7). Conversely, significantly larger minorities of white than Negro Protestants opposed both these suggestions.

Americans of relatively limited education and lower socioeconomic position, largely in jobs for which little-skilled immigrants would be likely to compete, have traditionally been more generally nativist and antagonistic to liberalized immigration than their more privileged compatriots. Negroes have, of course, been concentrated in the less economically secure roles in their country.

Nevertheless, by the mid-sixties Negro Protestants were clearly more liberal in their thinking about immigration than white Protestants. In June 1965, 8 percent of Negro versus 5 percent of white Protestants felt the number of foreigners allowed to enter the country and settle here should be "increased" while only 23 percent of the Negro, in contrast with 39 percent of white Protestants, would have "decreased" the rate of flow of immigrants to America (Table 6–7). Informed that the then current immigration practice—"called the quota system"—restricted "the number of persons coming from some countries more than others," 56 percent of Negro versus 48 percent of white Protestants favored, while 20 percent versus 36 percent opposed, "changing this law so that people would be admitted on the basis of their occupational skills rather than . . . of the country they came from."

THE UNITED NATIONS

To what extent has the influx of black African member states into the United Nations affected relative sentiments about the world body among the two races? Attitudinal differences between Negro and white Christians with respect to the UN have been small and less consistent than those pertinent to foreign aid, international exchanges, and immigration. On the whole, it appears that Protestant Negroes—insofar as they have harbored any views—have shifted from slightly lesser support than among their white coreligionists in the early and mid-fifties to slightly greater approval of the international institution and of active U.S. cooperation with it in the mid-sixties. However, interracial differences among Protestants have remained small.

In the spring of 1950 fewer Negroes felt at least part of our aid to "backward countries" should be channeled through the UN than preferred that all of it be "handled entirely by our own government," whereas the reverse was the case among whites (Table 6–8). In early 1955 only 67 percent of Negroes contrasted with 73 percent of whites felt "the United States should give strong support . . . to the UN," while 17 percent versus 16 percent believed our government should give "only a little" or no support to it. As late as the summer of 1960 Negro Protestants and Negroes generally were less inclined than either Protestant or Catholic whites to approve of the suggestion that a standing UN emergency force capable of dealing with limited or "brush fire" wars be organized.

However, when the same query was posed four years later, in July 1964, Negro Protestants were more inclined than their white coreligionists to consider such a standing force "a good idea" and less apt to regard it as a poor one (Table 6–8). Equally small minorities of both in early 1962 and again almost two years later thought the United States should give up its membership in the world body. In late 1963 a somewhat larger majority of Negro than white Protestants thought the UN was doing at least "a fair job in trying to solve the problems it has had to face" and considered it at least "fairly important . . . to try to make the United Nations a success." Negro Protestants were about as inclined as their white counterparts at the end of 1965 and again in August 1966 to "ask the United Nations to try to work out its own formula for peace in Vietnam" or "to submit the case of what to do about Vietnam to the United Nations or the World Court and agree to accept the decision." They were at least as favorably disposed—those with views on the matter probably more so—to sending an international military force under UN control into that area to deal with the problems there. And although Protestant Negroes continued to be more pessimistic than whites regardless of religion about the likelihood of another world war, by 1965 they were at least as apt as white Protestants to feel "there would likely have been another world war . . . if the United Nations had not been in existence."

COMMUNISM, NATIONAL DEFENSE, AND COLLECTIVE SECURITY

Negroes have been and remain more likely to expect another world war than whites regardless of their religion (Table 6–9). It is therefore understandable that Negro Americans have been at least as favorable as whites of either Christian persuasion to prevailing or higher defense budgets, to maintaining or expanding the number of men in uniform, and to UMT, military conscription, and military service generally. Contrary to the utterances of some of the leaders on the left of the civil-rights movement in the mid and late sixties, the military and military service have had at least as favorable an image among Negroes and Negro Protestants as among whites of either Protestant or Catholic persuasion.

Nor have Negro Protestants been any more willing than their white counterparts for their government to take part in reciprocal arms-reduction programs, even under effective international inspection (Table 6–10). When those expressing no opinions are eliminated, Protestant Negroes were about as likely to agree as white Protestants in 1960 that "the United States [should] agree to disarm to the same extent . . . [if] Russia agrees to disarm under careful inspection by the United Nations." Three years later Protestant Negroes who had heard of the recently signed nuclear-test-ban treaty were approximately as inclined as their white coreligionists to feel that the Senate should ratify it. In May 1964, a larger minority of Negro (37 percent) than of white (27 percent) Protestants felt "there would be a serious depression . . . if the U.S. were to reduce drastically its spending on armaments and the armed forces"; only 32 percent, contrasted with 51 percent, agreed "that the money now spent on armaments and the armed forces would be used for other things and there would be no serious depression." It is clear that support for further compromises and a generally more flexible U.S. negotiating posture to achieve wider arms-control agreements has not been particularly strong among either Negro Americans generally or their Protestant majority.

This more marked pessimism about the likelihood of another major war and somewhat lesser enthusiasm for arms-control schemes among Negroes than whites were at least in part associated with the lower average education and predominantly Southern rural backgrounds of American Negroes.[16] They were not, however, linked with any more negative perceptions of the behavior and intentions of the communist world or any more belligerent attitudes toward it.

The Containment of Communism

Thus several months after Stalin's death in 1953 a smaller majority of Negroes (53 percent) than of whites (79 percent) thought "Russia is trying to build herself up to be THE ruling power in the world," while 14 percent of the Negroes contrasted with but 5 percent of the whites, felt "Russia is just building up protection against being attacked in another war" (Table 6–11). By the summer of 1963 Protestant Negroes, insofar as they ventured any views on the subject, were more apt to consider it "possible to reach a peaceful settlement of differences with Russia," whereas almost as many white Protestants felt this "impossible" as believed it "possible"; for every three Protestant Negroes who considered it "impossible," five regarded it as "possible." However, equally large majorities of both in early 1965 felt we could not in the long run "live peacefully" with Communist China.

During the Joseph R. McCarthy period, Negro Protestants who had any opinions about the senator and about his views were no more inclined than their white coreligionists to agree that communist infiltration constituted a major threat to our national security. Interracial differences among Protestants on the issue of internal communism were small, statistically insignificant, and inconsistent. At the beginning of the Wisconsin senator's campaign in early 1950, a slightly larger fraction of Negro than white Protestants harboring views felt his claims were mainly politics or otherwise either untrue or exaggerated. However, a month or so later, only 18 percent of Negroes, compared with 31 percent of whites, believed Senator McCarthy was doing more harm than good to his country through his allegations about communists in high places; the two groups were about equally likely to feel he was doing more good than harm. In November 1954 Negro Protestants were less apt than either white Protestants or, especially, white Catholics to have a generally favorable impression of Senator McCarthy, but

16. See Hero, *Southerner*, p. 504.

they were at least as inclined to consider American communists "a great danger" to this country. In January 1955 Negroes seemed slightly less inclined than whites to feel there were "any Communists now in the government in Washington," but about the same minority fractions of those offering impressions among the two races thought there were "a great number" of them in the federal government. When the larger number of those with no opinions among Negroes are eliminated from consideration, Negroes may have been slightly less inclined to disapprove of the Senate's censure of the Wisconsin senator than whites, but the difference was too small for statistical significance.

However, by early 1965 Negro Protestants were significantly less inclined than their white coreligionists to consider "left wing groups, such as the Communist Party, here in America . . . a very great danger" or even a "considerable danger . . . to our country . . . at the present time" (Table 6–11). Whereas 47 percent of Negro Protestants viewed them as at least "a considerable danger," 68 percent of Protestant whites were of this opinion; conversely, 36 percent versus only 25 percent considered domestic communists "not very much of a danger, or no danger at all." In part the emergence of these interracial differences has been related to the tendency of segregationist whites to perceive civil-rights agitation as communist-inspired, but it also probably has been connected with the rather general shift of Negro international attitudes in a liberal direction in relation to those prevailing among white Protestants.

Except for the somewhat more prevalent general isolationism and especially the more marked paucity of information and opinions among Negroes, no consistent differences in thinking on how the federal government should best deal with the communist challenge were apparent between the races among Protestants for ten years or so after World War II. For instance, equally large majorities of those Negroes and whites who ventured opinions agreed in March 1949 that "the U.S. and the Western European nations participating in (receiving aid from) the Marshall Plan should join together in a mutual defense pact—that is, agree to come to each other's defense immediately if any of them it attacked" (Table 6–12). Negroes were more inclined than white Protestants or white Catholics in the summer of 1952 to either pull out of Korea or press forward with negotiations with the North Korean and Communist Chinese regimes, and conversely, less inclined to carry the Korean War further—probably more a reflection of Negroes' more isolationist proclivities than of any greater support for more flexible practices and policies in our endeavor to contain communism. Negroes harboring views on the matter were no more apt than whites with opinions to favor a summit meeting of "the leaders of the Western allies . . . with the leaders of Russia to try to settle world differences" in mid-1953. They may have been somewhat more disposed than whites of either Christian affiliation toward "a business arrangement to buy and sell goods" with the Soviet Union, but the difference was too small to be significant in early 1954. However, the two races were equally inclined (or disinclined) to blockade the coast of Communist China in January 1955, during a period of accentuated tension over Quemoy and Matsu and the Formosa Straits.

Nor did any consistent differences between Negro Americans and either Protestant or Catholic whites develop later with respect to resisting apparent communist aggression by military force if necessary. The race of the communist attacker seemed quite irrelevant to Negro thinking on the matter.[17] A somewhat smaller majority of Negroes than whites of either Christian persuasion felt "we should keep American forces in Berlin—along with British and French forces—even at the risk of war" during the Berlin crisis of 1961, but equally large majorities of Negro and white Christians offering views thought "the U.S. and its allies should try to fight their way into Berlin . . . if Communist East Germany closes all roads to Berlin and does not permit planes to land in Berlin" (Table 6–12). Similar minorities of Negroes, Negro Protestants, whites, white Protestants, and white Catholics expressing opinions in 1963 and again in February 1965 favored armed invasion of Cuba by U.S. military forces to overthrow the Castro regime. In late 1965 approximately three Negroes (and Negro Protestants) approved of the U.S. military intervention in Santo Domingo to each one who opposed it, a slightly larger proportion than favored it among whites generally, white Protestants or white Catholics.

A somewhat larger majority of Negroes than of whites expressing views approved of President Johnson's general handling of the Vietnam

17. Nor has the racial composition of allied or other friendly countries—except perhaps for black Africa—had much apparent impact on American Negroes' impressions of their reliability as "friends" or allies. In late 1965, for instance, whites regardless of their religion were sharply more inclined than nonwhites to regard nonwhite Japan as "a dependable ally (or friend) of the United States"—only 16 percent of Negroes contrasted with 44 percent of whites, 44 percent of white Protestants, and 45 percent of white Catholics so considered Japan, while 26, 36, 36, and 38 percent, regarded her as "undependable" (AIPO 723, 12-29-65).

question in the fall of 1966, a difference probably due largely to more widespread Democratic preferences among the former (Table 6–13).[18] However, other than the residue of somewhat greater isolationism among Negroes which was reflected in the slightly larger minority of them than of whites who would have withdrawn from Vietnam (as they felt earlier about Korea), few differences appeared between the races about prosecution of the war after the rapid build up of U.S. forces there in the mid-sixties. Insofar as they held opinions, Negro and white Protestants were about equally inclined to feel we should have become involved with our armed forces in Southeast Asia, that it had not been a mistake to enter the actual fighting with our own combat troops, that we should not escalate the bombing of the North to include the major cities, and that we should not continue the war alone if a "South Vietnam government decides to end the war and stop fighting."

However, Negro Protestants were somewhat more opposed than white correligionists to expanding the war in Vietnam beyond the announced policies of the President (Table 6–13). In the autumn of 1965, for instance, Negro Protestants more than whites of either Christian persuasion said they would be less inclined to vote for a congressional candidate who "advocated sending a great deal more men to Vietnam" than for another who did not, other factors being equal. Rather, Protestant Negroes felt more attracted than either Protestant or Catholic whites to candidates for Congress who "said we should try harder to reach a compromise peace settlement in Vietnam."[19]

In fact, although Negroes were about as willing as whites of either Christian persuasion to use military force against communist aggression if deemed necessary by their Democratic President, by the mid-sixties they seemed generally a bit more disposed toward negotiation and other nonmilitary intercourse with communist states than did Protestant whites. In late 1964, for example, Negro Protestants who

18. Fifty-three percent of self-identified Democrats versus 34 percent of Republicans approved of President Johnson's handling of Vietnam (Gallup release, 9-21-66).

19. A national NORC survey devoted to public attitudes toward the Vietnam War in February-March 1966 found Negroes significantly more opposed than whites to escalation and more willing to support deescalation. Interracial differences were larger when education and level of information were held constant. (See Sidney Verba et al, "Public Opinion and the War in Vietnam," *American Political Science Review* 61, no. 2 (June 1967), p. 331; and John P. Robinson and Solomon G. Jacobson, "American Public Opinion About Vietnam," unpublished paper (University of Michigan, 1968), pp. 3–4.

offered views were slightly less opposed than white Protestants to negotiations with communist leaders to reduce tensions and to permitting American business and agricultural interests to expand trade with their countries (Table 6–12). Although as apt as white Protestants to consider war with Mainland China relatively likely, Negro Protestants of the mid-sixties were also somewhat less opposed to admission of Mainland China to the United Nations (Table 6–14).

RELATIONS WITH THE VATICAN

Fundamentalist Protestants, especially those of rural backgrounds, have been more anti-Catholic in most respects than Protestants of more liberal theological bent, and Negro Americans have been more fundamentalist and rural than white Protestants. Nevertheless, Protestant Negroes have been consistently less antagonistic to diplomatic relations with the papacy than their white coreligionists.

In early 1940, for instance, 30 percent of Negro Protestants favored and only 31 percent opposed sending an official ambassador to the court of Pope Pius XII, contrasted with 29 percent and 51 percent of Protestant whites in the North and 31 percent and 41 percent of Protestant white Southerners (Table 6–15). The considerable interracial differences could be partly explained by the largely Southern heritage of the Negroes,[20] but Protestant Negroes residing in the North at the time who expressed opinions on the matter were also somewhat less inclined to oppose formal diplomatic relations than Southern white Protestants.

Moreover, Negroes were at least as much more inclined than their white counterparts to formalize our relations with the Holy See in the 1950's and 1960's, when Southerners were no longer any more favorable than other Americans to most international commitments, as prior to Pearl Harbor (Table 6–15). In mid-1950, for instance, Negroes were more inclined than whites in general, including Catholics, to feel it had been a "good idea" for Presidents Roosevelt and Truman to have "a personal representative at the Vatican" and that our federal government should "send an American representative to the Vatican in the future." A year and a half later, Negro Protestants were patently less likely to

20. All of the 100 Negroes in this sample were residing in the North at the time. Those in the South were perhaps even less inclined to oppose establishment of formal diplomatic relations with the Vatican.

have "heard or read anything about the naming of an American ambassador to the Vatican in Rome" than whites of Protestant persuasion, but a majority of those Negroes who had heard anything felt "the U.S. Senate should approve the appointment" of such an ambassador, whereas only minorities of white Protestants, whether Southern or non-Southern, agreed. In the spring of 1961 two Negro Protestants out of three with opinions on the question, contrasted with less than one out of three white Protestants in the North and three out of eight in the South, favored the suggestion that "our present administration send an American representative to the Vatican." Apparently the fears and arguments advanced by many white Protestant leaders that diplomatic relations would upset the separation of church and state and result in undue influence of the Catholic Church in the United States, although convincing to most white Protestants, either failed to reach or did not persuade most Protestant Negroes.

AN INTERPRETATION

Thus, Negro Protestants did not differ consistently from whites—Protestants or Catholics—during the 1960's in respect of resisting communist aggression by force if deemed necessary by the President, regardless of the race of the antagonists. Nor have Negroes differed significantly from Protestant or Catholic whites in their recent sentiments about military service and the cost of armaments. Protestant Negroes in recent years have been at most only slightly more supportive of the UN than their white coreligionists. However, Negro Protestants were more favorably inclined than white Protestants by the mid-1960's to foreign aid, negotiation, and compromise to alleviate tensions with the communist world, admission of the People's Republic of China to the UN, intercultural exchanges, and liberalized trade and immigration.

Therefore Negroes tended to raise the average level of Protestant support for nonmilitary multilateral cooperation during the 1960's. When white Protestants and white Catholics alone were compared, differences toward more prevalent approval among the Catholics of foreign economic and technical aid, the United Nations, expanded immigration and intercultural exchanges, diplomatic relations with the Holy See, and liberalized trade and other cooperation with the communist world—including UN membership for the People's Republic of China—were normally somewhat larger than those between the two major Christian groups when Negroes were included. By the mid-1960's white Protestants constituted the most internationally conservative ethno-religious group in the country.

What developments brought about this shift of Negro Protestants from relative isolationism prior to the fifties to relative liberalism with respect to foreign policy in the sixties? The gradual narrowing of the gaps between the races in respect of urbanization, socioeconomic status, political participation, and particularly education has been one important factor.

Negro Protestant samples on individual national surveys have seldom been large enough to permit reliable comparisons of Negroes of different demographic and social characteristics with one another, or with whites in similar categories. However, results derived from combining Negro samples in several surveys in which the same or similar questions were posed suggest that international attitudes among them have been related to the same individual and social variables as among whites (see below, Chapter 7). Thus, better-educated middle-class urban Negroes have been more favorably disposed toward developmental assistance, liberalized trade, and admission of the People's Republic of China into the UN than have educationally and economically underprivileged Negroes and those living in the country or in small towns. Southern Negroes, like Southern whites, have been less supportive of such policies than non-Southerners of the same race. The shift of Negroes out of the rural South into the urban North and the increasing proportions of them who have become economically comfortable and exposed to secondary and, particularly, higher education thus help to explain the more liberal attitudes and more widespread information on world affairs among them in the sixties than a generation earlier.

However, Protestant Negroes of the mid-sixties were still considerably less educated, less affluent and middle-class, less urban, and less non-Southern than Protestant whites, while their international views on a number of issues were more liberal. In fact, when Negroes have been contrasted with only those Protestant whites of similar education, income, and urban-versus-rural residence, differences toward more liberal foreign-policy views among Negroes have typically been larger than the above figures suggest. At each level of education and income Protestant Negroes of the 1960's were more favorable to foreign aid and Communist Chinese membership in the UN than Protestant whites of similar education and income. Rural Negroes were more liberal than rural Protestant whites, urban Negroes than urban and suburban Protestant whites.

The slow increase in knowledge of, interest in, and firm opinions on international issues and the development of more liberal opinions in that field are also traceable to some degree to the growth in Negro voting and political participation more generally. Negro voters, like white ones, have been more interested, better informed, and more supportive of international collaboration than nonvoters. However, Negroes of the mid-sixties were still considerably less likely than whites to vote. Moreover, Negro voters held more liberal views than white Protestant voters, Negro nonvoters than nonvoting Protestant whites.

Another significant factor has been the more Democratic partisan identification and greater preference for Democratic over Republican presidential and congressional candidates among Protestant Negroes than Protestant whites. As among Americans generally, Democrats and voters for Presidents Kennedy and Johnson have been more inclined to support their foreign policies and programs than Republicans and voters for the Republican candidates opposing these two men. Thus Negro Protestant Democrats and Kennedy and Johnson voters have differed less from white Protestant Democrats and white Protestant voters for these candidates in their thinking about international affairs than have Negro and white Protestants in general from one another.

Nevertheless, Negro Protestant Republicans of the 1960's were somewhat more favorable to foreign aid and membership in the UN for Mainland China than white Protestant Republicans, Negro Protestant independents than white Protestant independents, and Negro Protestant Nixon voters (1960) than white Protestant Nixon voters. Furthermore, Protestant Negroes were also more Democratic than Protestant whites in their partisan preferences during the second and third F. D. Roosevelt administrations (when few of them voted), but at that time they were more isolationist than white fellow-Protestant Democrats.

These demographic, social, and political factors combined seem to account for a considerable part of the relative shift of Negro as compared with white Protestant international attitudes. Changes in the substance of U.S. relations with the rest of the world, the divergent connotations of those changes among the two races, and the differential significance of the domestic race issue for the two groups probably together explain most of the rest.

The transfer of most U.S. aid from white Europe since Lend-Lease and the Marshall Plan to the largely colored less-developed world, and the general rise in importance in U.S. foreign policy of Asia and, particularly, Africa, have been received at least somewhat more favorably among Negroes than whites. It is true that American Negro Protestant affinities with black Africa have not been nearly as marked as some observers have argued. Negro attitudes on issues involving Africa have not, for example, diverged as much from those among white Protestants or Catholics as have views of Jews in regard to questions pertinent to Israel. Nevertheless, although Negro Americans have been less emotionally, culturally, and intellectually identified with black Africa than Jewish Americans with Israel, racial phenomena, particularly those involving blacks, in world affairs have at least in part accounted for the relative shift in Negro thinking on related international issues.

Coupled with the growing role of color on the world scene has been the divergent significance of the civil-rights movement in the United States. As it developed momentum following the Supreme Court school desegregation decision of 1954, the civil-rights movement tended to awaken the sensitivities of many Negroes to both domestic and foreign phenomena in which race has been an apparent element. Negro leaders, organizations, and communication media have increasingly brought racial connotations of international issues, especially in Asia and Africa, to the attention of American Negroes and have linked the domestic civil-rights campaign to occurrences in the formerly colonial territories, especially in Africa. Conversely, racially conservative Protestant whites, especially in the South, have tended to be more hesitant about cooperation with colored Africa and, in lesser measure, Asia than they were previously about collaboration with western Europe. They, too, have perceived connections between decolonization and its aftermaths abroad and domestic race relations, but these perceptions have led them to adopt opposite attitudes from Negroes on foreign policy.

Although views on most domestic welfare and economic issues have continued to manifest but little connection with opinions on most aspects of foreign policy among either Negroes or whites, those on race relations have changed from only minor correlations with international opinions in the thirties and forties to considerable ones in the sixties. (pp. 153–57). Among both races those harboring more conservative views of race relations—opponents of desegregation and racial change generally among whites and acceptors of the racial status quo among Negroes—have been clearly less favorably disposed to negotiation and accommodation with the communist powers and non-military aid for Asia, Africa, and Latin America than have racial liberals or equalitarians. Indeed, the white Protestant minority who have approved of the new civil-rights legislation of the 1960's and have felt that desegregation of schools, jobs, and housing should be speeded up have been as liberal in their international attitudes as Negroes of like mind, or more liberal.

CHAPTER 7. WHITE CHRISTIANS: SOCIAL AND PARTISAN DIFFERENCES

NATIONAL ORIGINS

Ethnic considerations have been closely associated with religious preferences. The national backgrounds of white Catholics as contrasted with white Protestants are crucial to an understanding of differences in international views between the two major Christian groups prior to the entry of the United States into the Second World War—much more so than was to be the case thirty years later.

Before Pearl Harbor

Aside from diplomatic relations with the Vatican and perhaps a very few other issues with connotations peculiar to Catholics or Italians, Americans of Italian extraction were typically the least inclined of the white ethnic groups to favor international commitments; German-Americans were almost as isolationist as Italian-Americans; and Irish-Americans were only somewhat more favorably disposed than their compatriots of German origin. Citizens of remote or, especially, more recent British or white British Commonwealth ancestry[1] were usually more enthusiastic than any of these three national groups about active foreign involvements, especially with respect to aiding the Western Allies against Germany and Italy. So were Scandinavian-Americans, Russian-Americans, and persons whose parents or grandparents were natives of countries occupied by the Nazi and Fascist armies (Table 7–1).

Thus, in early 1939, before hostilities began in Europe, Americans of German, particularly Italian, and to a lesser extent Irish origins were patently less enthusiastic than other white Americans about helping Britain and France short of entering the war ourselves if they were attacked by the Axis—even about selling them either food or war materials for cash. Differences were equally wide with respect to sending our armed forces to assist in resisting possible Axis aggression. Moreover, whereas a majority of other white Americans believed Germany and Italy would "start a war against the United States . . . if [they] defeat England and France in a war," only 14 percent of Italian-, 34 percent of German-, and 41 percent of Irish-Americans thought so.

1. With the probable exception of those of French-Canadian origins.

These ethnic differences narrowed somewhat with the actual Nazi attack on Poland. However, Italian-, German-, and to a lesser extent Irish-Americans during September 1939 remained less inclined than most other white Americans to favor liberalization of the Neutrality Act to permit the British, French, and others to buy munitions in this country, to declare war and send American troops to aid the allies, or even to defend the Caribbean and Central America should it be invaded by the Axis. More than other whites, these ethnic groups were inclined to regard the war in Europe as "just another struggle between the European nations for power and wealth" rather than as "a struggle of democracy against the spread of dictatorship." During the Battle of Britain they were less willing to expand aid to that country even if it appeared she would be defeated otherwise. Throughout the period between the fall of France and our formal entry into the war, these three groups were the most inclined among white Americans to emphasize staying out of war ourselves rather than helping Britain to defeat the Axis. They were likewise least apt to think the United States would, in fact, enter the war, or that Britain would win. During the congressional debate of the pending Lend-Lease bill in early 1941, Italian-, German-, and in lesser measure Irish-Americans were less likely than others to feel that Congress should enact this legislation. Shortly after the Nazi attack on the Soviet Union, considerably smaller percentages of them than of others approved of the convoying of supplies to Britain by the U.S. Navy (Table 7–1).

In most cases Americans of British extraction were among the most favorably disposed to American intervention on the side of Britain against the Axis. Citizens of Polish national backgrounds and those from other parts of Axis-invaded Europe were likewise typically among the more inclined to approve. Apparently many Americans of Italian and German background felt differently from their compatriots about helping to defeat, or at least to contain, the lands of their ancestors. Irish-Americans, though for the most part harboring no special sympathies for the Axis countries, seemed hesitant about assisting the British, although they were not as inhibited about doing so as their compatriots of Italian or German ancestry. Starting at least with the invasion of their ancestral land, Polish-Americans were among the more enthusiastic about U.S. involvements in efforts to contain and finally defeat the Germans, as seemed to be the case as well among other ethnic groups as the Axis overran their "old countries" (Table 7–1).

The impact of ethnic connections on international thinking was further demonstrated by the rather different patterning of views on extending Lend-Lease to the Soviets after they were attacked by Hitler's forces. Italian-Americans continued to be the most opposed group, with German-Americans somewhat less disapproving. But Irish-Americans did not differ from American whites generally, from people of British origins, or from persons of older-stock American (largely Anglo-Saxon) heritage. Whereas Americans of British ancestry were consistently among the most favorably disposed toward assisting Great Britain against the Axis in the West, those of Russian forebears were so disposed toward sending similar help to the Soviet Union, although few of the latter cared much for communism or the Stalin regime (Table 7–1).

Religion and national origins were not often asked on the same surveys. Moreover, even when they were, samples were frequently too small to permit systematic comparisons of the international attitudes of Protestants and Catholics with their national origins held constant— Catholic Italians with Protestant Italians, Catholic Britishers with Protestant Britishers, etc. However, Italian- and Irish-Americans were in the vast majority Catholics, whereas Anglo-Saxon Americans were predominantly Protestants. German immigrants and their immediate progeny were distributed about equally between Protestant and Catholic adherence. Among the predominantly Catholic ethnic groups, only the Poles and the small percentage of French and certain other East Europeans were among the more inclined to approve of intervention against the Axis. Although the presence of a number of Jews among Americans of Russian or Polish parentage tended to raise the level of interventionism among those two national groups, the non-Jews among the two groups were also more enthusiastic about measures to stop the Axis than were Germans or Italians, be they Catholics or, in much lesser number, Protestants.

Ethnic ties alone did not account for all of the prewar differences between the two major Christian groups, even on such issues as aid to Britain against Germany and Italy, and they were responsible to only a relatively minor degree for interreligious differences with respect to international trade, the League of Nations, and Japanese aggression. But national origins were more important than Catholic or Protestant religious preferences in determining views on Germany and Italy and the various measures suggested to assist in their defeat.

The Fifties and Beyond

Changes in prewar attitudinal differences between Catholic and Protestant whites can be at least partly explained by the attenuation of ethnic differences among non-Jewish white Americans. Few of the important questions of foreign policy since the war have had the ethnic overtones of the central issue of the several years prior to the attack on Pearl Harbor, whether to aid Britain against Germany and Italy. Moreover, the generation born in the "old country" was gradually replaced in the body politic by its children and grandchildren, who were for the most part substantially less emotionally attached to the lands of their ancestors and more inclined to perceive U.S. policies pertinent to these countries in terms similar to those of other Americans.[2]

Catholics have, of course, remained chronologically closer to immigrant origins than Protestants, even when Negroes have been excluded from consideration. As late as the mid-sixties 44 percent of white Catholics, contrasted with but 17 percent of white Protestants, had at least one foreign-born parent, living or dead.[3] However, by even as early as 1952 recent immigrant origins had lost their earlier connotations for most international attitudes. The impression of some observers that children and grandchildren of immigrants are more prone to xenophobia, isolationism, ultranationalism, unilateral military intervention, and the like has not been supported by available empirical evidence.

Thus, in the late summer and fall of 1952 a slightly larger percentage of descendants of one or more foreign-born grandparents (31 percent) than of Americans all four of whose grandparents were natives of the U.S. (27 percent) felt "we should keep on trying to build up the armed strength of the countries of Western Europe to resist communism, like we've been doing." The same percentages of both (43 percent) would have cut the amount of military aid going to Europe; and only 16 percent of both preferred the isolationist suggestion, to "get out of European affairs and let them build up their own defenses against the Communists if they really want to." With respect to Korea, grandchildren of one or more foreign natives were four percentage points more likely than older-stock Americans to feel we should "keep trying

2. For a discussion of the assimilation of ethnic groups in Ameria, see Will Herberg, *Protestant–Catholic–Jew: An Essay in American Religious Sociology* (Garden City, N.Y.: Doubleday Anchor Books, 1960), esp. chap. 2.

3. SRC 473, Sept.–Oct. 1964.

to find a way to stop the fighting," two percentage points less inclined to think "we should stop fooling around and do whatever is necessary to knock the Communists out of Korea once and for all even at the risk of starting World War III," and equally apt to agree we should "pull out of Korea right away." Proximity of immigrant ancestry had no relationship whatsoever to the relative priority ascribed to continuing economic aid to western Europe, to ending the Korean War quickly, or to "keeping Communists out of government jobs."[4]

Four years later these two groups did not differ at all in their attitudes toward either "economic help to poorer countries . . . even if they can't pay for it," "help to foreign countries even if they are not as much against communism as we are," keeping U.S. "soldiers overseas where they can help countries that are against communism," going "more than halfway in being friendly with the other countries of the world," or our overall stance toward "Russia and Communist China."[5] In the fall of 1960, only 16 percent of the American adults with one or more foreign-born parents versus 17 percent of those both of whose parents were natives of the U.S. agreed that "this country would be better off if we just stayed home and did not concern ourselves with problems in other parts of the world," while 70 and 67 percent disagreed with this isolationist view.[6] At that time 54 percent of those of more recent foreign origins, contrasted wih 53 percent of older-stock Americans, agreed we should "give economic help to the poorer countries of the world," while conversely, 17 versus 22 percent opposed this proposition. By the fall of 1964 offspring of one or two foreign-born parents were somewhat more favorable toward economic aid for less-developed countries and toward negotiations with leaders of communist countries than were Americans of the fourth and later generations.[7]

The disproportionately large number of Jews among Americans of more recent foreign origins and of Negroes among old-stock citizens

4. From the combined results of two Roper surveys, in August and October 1952. Descendants of one or more foreign-born grandparents numbered 3,197, older-stock Americans 4,610.

5. SRC 417, Sept.–Oct. 1956. Descendants of at least one foreign-born grandparent numbered 779, persons of older U.S. stock 901.

6. SRC 440, Sept.–Nov. 1960. Those with one or more foreign-born parents numbered 229, third and later-generation Americans 1,214.

7. SRC 473, Sept.–Nov. 1964. Offspring of at least one foreign-born parent numbered 290, those both of whose parents were natives of the U.S. 1,033. Sixty percent versus 50 percent respectively favored foreign economic aid, 74 versus 69 percent agreed we should continue to negotiate.

has distorted the attitudinal norms of the two groups somewhat, but even when Jews and Negroes are eliminated, the attitudes of Americans of more recent foreign ancestry differed little, if any, in the 1950's from those of Americans all of whose ancestors had been in this country for three or more generations. By the mid-1960's, white non-Jewish Americans who were born abroad or who had one or two foreign-born parents were slightly more inclined to favor aid to less-developed countries than those who were more remote from origins abroad. By then, white Catholics both of whose parents were natives of the U.S. were more supportive of such aid and of liberalizing of relations with communist regimes than white Protestants of equally remote foreign ancestry. Proximity of foreign antecedents thus had no apparent bearing on tendencies of white Catholics toward greater liberalism than white Protestants in the mid-sixties.

With the formal entry of the U.S. into World War II, mdst Irish-Americans, German-Americans, and even Italian-Americans rallied behind the war effort as did other national groups. Among these three ethnic groups, opposition to the war and to continued material aid to our allies was almost as limited as that among Americans of British extraction. Moreover, Americans of Irish, German, and Italian backgrounds, regardless of religion, did not differ significantly from other citizens in their sentiments about most governmental policies after the war had been won. In late 1943, for instance, 65, 67, and 63 percent, respectively, contrasted with 69 percent of British-Americans and 65 percent of all other non-Jewish whites, preferred that in the 1944 electoral campaigns both the Republican and the Democratic Parties adopt stands "for an active part in world affairs after the war." Sixty-four, 65, and 63 percent versus 66 and 64 percent said they would be willing "to continue to put up with shortages of butter, sugar, meat, and other rationed food products for a year or two after the war . . . in order to give food to people who need it in Europe" (Table 7–2).

Nor did non-Jewish white ethnic groups differ consistently from one another during the 1950's with respect to the Marshall Plan, military aid to western Europe, the Korean War, the preferred general policies vis-à-vis the communist world, the importance of the domestic communist threat, the United Nations, how best to preserve world peace, or economic aid to less-developed countries (Table 7–2). Even though the junior senator from Wisconsin was an Irish Catholic, Irish Catholic Americans in 1952 were no more likely than other non-Jewish citizens to consider keeping "Communists out of government jobs" one of "the two or three most important [things] for the next Administration to do." Non-Jewish Americans whose forebears came from Poland or elsewhere in eastern Europe tended less to ascribe importance to this objective and more to favor continued negotiations in Korea than most other non-Jewish white groups, be they predominantly Catholic or Protestant. Americans whose antecedents came from western Europe were neither more nor less favorably inclined toward either military or economic aid for that area than were compatriots of Scandinavian, eastern European, or older-stock American backgrounds. Italian-Americans may have been somewhat less favorably disposed than other white ethnic groups— predominantly Catholic or Protestant—to aiding nonaligned regimes, and perhaps somewhat more conservative on several other issues as well, but these differences were usually too small to be statistically significant— considerably smaller than those between Italian-Americans and most other non-Jewish whites in respect of aiding Britain and France prior to our entry into the war. Whites, all four of whose grandparents were born in the U.S., and compatriots of English, Scotch, Welsh, and Scotch-Irish origins—largely Protestants—were no more favorably disposed toward any of these programs or policies than Catholics of Irish, western European, Polish, or other eastern European antecedents.

By 1960–65 segments of non-Jewish Americans of relatively recent Irish, western European, Polish, and other eastern European origins— predominantly Catholics—each seemed somewhat more favorable to foreign aid and negotiations with the leaders of the communist world than largely Protestant compatriots of either British, Scandinavian, or older U.S. stock. Italian-Americans appeared somewhat less willing to trade with eastern Europe than most other groups—Protestant or Catholic—including non-Jews from eastern European backgrounds. The latter, in fact, were on the average somewhat more willing to liberalize U.S. relations with the communist regimes in the homelands of their parents or grandparents than were all other non-Jewish whites taken together.[8] The impression among some observers that Polish-Americans

8. Such differences between Italian-Americans and other Catholic ethnic groups may have been due as much or more to their lower average educational and socioeconomic-occupational status than to ethnic factors per se. Among Catholics of the mid-sixties, those of Italian and Polish origins were least successful in these regards, while Irish were most so. Germans were next most successful to the Irish and French-Canadians, between them and Italian- and Polish-Americans. See Andrew M. Greeley, "Ethnicity as an Influence on Behavior" (unpublished paper presented at the National Consultation on Ethnic Behavior sponsored by the American Jewish Committee at Fordham

have been more conservative about such foreign-policy issues than most of their compatriots is not supported by the empirical evidence.[9] Moreover, all of the predominantly Catholic ethnic groups—Irish, Polish, other eastern European, and even Italian—have been more favorably disposed to liberalized immigration policies than primarily Protestant British-Americans or older-stock white citizens.

The foregoing generalizations apply whether or not Protestants are eliminated from the Irish, Italian, and Polish groups or Catholics are removed from the British, Scandinavian, and old-stock American categories. In both the 1960 and 1964 surveys, for example, Catholic Irish-Americans were more favorably disposed to foreign economic aid to less-developed countries than either white Protestants in general or British Protestants, Scandinavian Protestants, German Protestants, other western European Protestants, eastern European Protestants, Protestants all of whose grandparents were born in the U.S., or even than other Irish-Americans of Protestant persuasions. In 1964 Irish Catholics were more likely than any of these Protestant ethnic groups to approve of further negotiations with communist leaders, trade with communist countries, and admission of Mainland China into the UN. Similarly disposed with respect to foreign aid, negotiations and trade with communists, and Communist China were German Catholics, eastern European Catholics, and Catholics of fourth-generation or earlier foreign origins. Italian Catholics, on the other hand, were more conservative than most of these groups—Catholic or Protestant—on at least foreign aid and negotiations with communist leaders.

Even within the same ethnic group, Catholics in the mid-sixties seemed to be somewhat more liberal than Protestants on aid and relations with the communist world—Irish Catholics were more liberal than Irish Protestants, western European (other than Italian) Catholics than western European Protestants, and Catholics all four of whose grandparents were born in the U.S. than Protestants of similarly remote foreign ancestry. Whereas ethnic background was more pertinent than religious preference—Catholic versus Protestant—to views on what to do about the Axis prior to the attack on Pearl Harbor, by the sixties

University, 20 June 1968). These results were derived from national survey samples of 370 Italian-, 180 Polish-, 328 Irish-, 361 German-, and 177 French- (mostly Canadian) Americans.

9. However, Polish-American Catholics were apparently more anti-Semitic and anti-Negro than most other Catholic ethnic groups, particularly than German- and Irish-American coreligionists, as late as 1966–68. See Greeley, "Ethnicity."

this religious distinction had, with some exceptions, become a more important factor in most international attitudes than ethnic origins.

REGIONAL FACTORS

The geographical distribution of Catholic whites compared with that of white Protestants within the United States likewise explains in part the differences in foreign-policy preferences apparent between them, especially prior to 7 December 1941.

The Prewar Period

Differences between Catholic and Protestant whites on most prewar issues paralleled those between whites in the South (the former Confederacy) and non-Southern whites. Southern whites, like white Protestants compared with white Catholics in the country generally, were more favorably disposed than white non-Southerners to expanded international trade, the League of Nations, aid to Finland, and most of the measures proposed by President Roosevelt to limit aggressions by the Axis—particularly aid to Britain. Differences in thinking between the white South and North were widest on virtually the same international issues as those in regard to which Catholic and Protestant whites diverged the most. Ethnic factors are, of course, a significant source of these interregional differences—except for southern Louisiana and a handful of less populous places on the coasts, the Southern white population was with few exceptions of Anglo-Saxon, largely British ancestry, and virtually devoid of Italians, Germans, Irish, or other ethnic groups among the less enthusiastic about the major international involvements of the prewar period. Moreover, the Southern military tradition, the region's vested interest in freer trade, and several other factors unrelated to either ethnicity or religion also encouraged support of the activist policy alternatives of the thirties and early forties.[10]

The South was also predominantly Protestant, again with the exception of southern Louisiana and a handful of smaller areas. Southern white Protestants were more favorable than their Northern coreligionists to most of the international commitments suggested by the "internationalists" of the era (Table 7–3). For example, prior to the war in Europe, Southern white Protestants were more inclined than their non-Southern

10. For a detailed discussion of comparative international behavior of the South during this period, see Alfred O. Hero, Jr., *The Southerner and World Affairs* (Baton Rouge: Louisiana State Univ. Press, 1965), chaps. 2–6.

coreligionists to opt for communism over fascism, to oppose appeasement of the Nazis and fascists through reversing the Versailles Treaty with respect to former German colonies or accession to their demands at Munich, to feel that America's failure to join the League of Nations was at least partly responsible for the "troubles in Europe" and that President Roosevelt should openly criticize Hitler and Mussolini for their "warlike attitude," and to prefer that the Soviet Union defeat Japan if a war developed between them. During the Soviet attack on Finland in late 1939 and early 1940, Southern Protestant whites were more inclined than either white Northern Protestants or Catholics to lend money to Finland to purchase arms in America. In the following fall, white Southerners of Protestant affiliations were less opposed than either white Northern Protestants or Catholics to risking war to prevent Japan from getting control of China, and more inclined to approve of an embargo on selling further strategic goods to Japan. White Southern Protestants were similarly more favorably disposed than white Northerners of either major Christian persuasion to lending money to Britain to purchase weapons here to fight the Axis and to liberalizing the Johnson Act to allow her to do so, more inclined to feel that President Roosevelt had not gone far enough in assisting Britain and that it was more important to help her defeat the Axis than to stay out of war ourselves, and more likely to support extension of Lend-Lease to the U.S.S.R. on the same basis as to Britain after the invasion of Russia by the Wehrmacht. Southern white Protestants accounted for a significant portion of the average attitudinal differences beween Catholics and Protestants in the country as a whole, especially on matters related to assisting Britain against Germany and Italy.

The greater relevance of Southern residence than religious preference to thinking on most aspects of prewar foreign policy was dramatically illustrated by the comparative reactions of white Protestants in the South and outside to the suggestion that a U.S. ambassador be sent to the Vatican. Southern Protestants—more fundamentalist and isolated from any direct experience with Catholics than Protestants elsewhere—had long been more anti-Catholic and suspicious of the presumed interest of the Vatican in influencing American Society and politics. The Ku Klux Klan, evangelist preachers, and other Southern Protestant groups had been known for their anti-Catholic utterances. Southern Protestants had been more inclined than their Northern coreligionists to say they would not vote for a Catholic for public office, even if he were otherwise qualified from their point of view.[11] The leadership of Southern Protestantism—particularly of the largest denomination in the region, the Southern Baptists—was articulately opposed to establishing formal diplomatic relations with the court of the pope.[12]

Nevertheless, Southern white Protestants were more rather than less favorably disposed to diplomatic relations than were Northern white Protestants (Table 7–3). Whereas Northern white Protestants opposed to this idea outnumbered those in favor by almost two to one, their Southern counterparts were almost as inclined to approve as to disapprove.

Views on this issue were virtually independent of most Northern white Protestants' thinking on most other aspects of foreign policy, but in the South, approval of such a step tended to form part of a pattern of thinking favorable to active international involvements generally. For instance, among Southern white Protestants who approved of diplomatic recognition of the Vatican in January 1941, only 19 percent disapproved of our government lending $60 million to Finland, while 32 percent of those who opposed establishment of diplomatic relations with the papacy and 37 percent of others with no views on the latter subject disapproved of lending this money. Similarly, whereas a majority of the Southern Protestant whites who favored recognition of the Vatican opposed the suggestion that "the Constitution be changed to require a national vote before Congress could draft men for war overseas," a majority of those who disapproved of sending an ambassador to the pope favored this proposal. Likewise, more than not of those favorable to Vatican relations who offered views on reciprocal trade felt "Congress should give Secretary Hull the power to make more such treaties" whereas most of those opposed to such diplomatic recognition who expressed views on this trade question opposed such further liberalization of world trade.[13] Thus, the considerably greater approval of international involvements generally in the white South rather than in

11. AIPO 67, 2–1–37 (2,970), and AIPO 188, 3–26–40 (3,266).
12. Eldon Waldo Bailey, "Southern Baptist Reactions to Diplomatic Relations with the Vatican, 1939–1953" (Fort Worth, Texas: Th.D. dissertation, Southwestern Baptist Theological Seminary, 1955). See also Edward E. Joiner, "Southern Baptists and Church State Relations, 1845–1954" (Louisville, Ky.: Th.D. dissertation, Southern Baptist Theological Seminary, 1959), pp. 233–35, and Rogers M. Smith, "A Study of Southern Baptists and the Relationship of Church and State, 1918–1952" (Fort Worth, Texas: Th.D. dissertation, Southwestern Baptist Theological Seminary, 1953), esp. chap. 4.
13. AIPO 181, 1-10-40.

the North more than countervailed the effects of widespread Southern Protestant suspicions of the Catholic Church to produce a relatively favorable reception for the proposal that diplomatic relations with the Church be established.

Samples of Southern white Catholics were too small for statistical analysis, but leaving aside such issues as relations with the Vatican, it seems unlikely that their thinking on world affairs diverged much from that among other Southern whites.[14] They were thus probably more favorable to most international involvements of the period than their non-Southern coreligionists. Since the predominantly non-Catholic Southern population tended to raise the national Protestant interventionist average more than it did the Catholic one, removal of all Southerners from national statistics typically indicated narrower differences in international opinion between the two religious groups in the non-South than in the whole country taken together.

Midwesterners, including people in the Great Plains, were more isolationist on most of these issues than inhabitants of any other major region, particularly than residents of the South and, next, the Northeast (Table 7–3). Differences in international opinions were smaller for the most part, however, between the three major non-Southern regions than between each of them and the South. Catholic samples in the West, including the Rocky Mountain region, were too small for statistical comparisons, but the popular impression that Westerners, regardless of religion, were more inclined to involve their country in the problems of the Far East—especially that of containing Japan—and less in those of Europe than were Americans to the east of them seemed valid. However, the regional differences outside the South even on Far Eastern problems were quite small, whether or not religion is held constant. Midwestern Protestants were clearly less enthusiastic than their coreligionists elsewhere about policies which they feared might involve us more deeply in Europe, but there were hardly any observable differences between them and Northeastern Protestants so far as Japan and China were concerned.

Regional differences among Protestants and among non-church-members were for the most part more marked than those among Catholics. Whereas Northeastern Protestants and unaffiliated persons were clearly more inclined to risk war if necessary to help contain the Axis in

14. Comparative international opinions of Southern Catholics vs. Southern Protestants are discussed in greater detail in Hero, *Southerner*, chap. 12.

Europe than were their counterparts in the Midwest, there was virtually no difference between Catholics in the two regions in this respect. It follows that attitudinal differences between Catholics on the one hand and Protestants and the non-churched on the other tended to be wider in the Northeast than in the Midwest, and probably elsewhere as well. Whereas Northeastern Protestants and non-church-members were significantly more favorable to active intervention in Europe, especially in the form of helping Britain against the Axis, than Catholics in that region, Midwestern Protestants and unaffiliated persons were almost as isolationist on these issues as were their Catholic neighbors (Table 7–3).

The Postwar Era

Southern Protestants, both white and black, remained less well informed than their non-Southern coreligionists about most aspects of world affairs well into the 1960's (Table 7–4). White Protestants in the Northeast, Midwest (including the Plains States), and Far West during the initial postwar decade were on the average somewhat better informed on foreign-policy questions than white Catholics in the same geographical regions. However, by the mid-1960's these religious differences among whites had virtually disappeared outside the South, at least at the relatively low levels of knowledge probed by national surveys.[15]

Southern white Catholics, on the other hand, seemed on the whole somewhat better informed than Protestant whites in the same region— understandably so in the light of their higher average education and disproportionately urban residence.[16] Moreover, whereas Southern

15. Catholics outside the South remained in the 1960's disproportionately few among the most internationally sophisticated 1 percent or so of the population. However, such Catholic-Protestant differences near the top of the knowledge continuum have likewise declined gradually since the Second World War.

16. The proportion of Catholics in the South has gradually risen, mainly through immigration from other regions of the U.S. since the Second World War. Nonetheless, as late as 1968 only 9 percent of American Catholics, contrasted with 34 percent of Protestants, resided in the South. However, 24 percent of Southern Catholics versus only 18 percent of Southern Protestants at that time had been to college, while, conversely, 26 versus 35 percent had not gone beyond grade school. Twenty-four percent of Southern Catholics, contrasted with but 19 percent of Protestants in the region, were of professional or business-managerial occupational status; 25 compared with 19 percent enjoyed family incomes in excess of $10,000 during the preceding year. Conversely, only 30 percent of Southern Catholics versus 44 percent of Southern Protestants lived on family incomes smaller than $5,000 in 1967. Whereas 65 percent of Catholic Southerners lived in urban communities of 50,000 or more inhabitants, only 35 percent of Protestants in the South did. Conversely, although 45 percent of Southern

Protestant whites have been rather consistently less knowledgeable about foreign affairs than their coreligionists in the other three major geographical regions, Southern white Catholics have been for the most part about as well informed on such matters as Catholic whites elsewhere. Contrary to the impressions of some observers, white Protestants in the Northeast have not been on the average any more knowledgeable about international affairs than their coreligionists in the Midwest and, particularly, the Far West—at least not at the mass level. In fact, those on the Pacific Coast—better educated on the average than their counterparts in the rest of the country—have probably been somewhat better informed than white Protestants in each of the other major regions. Catholic whites in the Northeast have apparently been somewhat more ignorant of international developments than their coreligionists in the Midwest and West, perhaps owing to their more recent immigrant past and their on the average somewhat more limited educational backgrounds.

Postwar interregional attitudinal trends have only partially paralleled these informational differences among the regions. Southern white Protestants, on the whole more favorable than other Protestants to most of the international commitments of their federal government in the several years immediately prior to our entry into World War II, differed hardly at all from the latter on the major issues of the late forties and early fifties—except for their continued tendency to be less apt to express any views at all. By the 1960's, however, white Protestants in the South had become less supportive than their non-Southern counterparts of most aspects of nonmilitary aid to less-developed countries, less willing to admit Mainland China to the UN, less favorable to liberalization of U.S. relations with eastern Europe and the U.S.S.R., and somewhat less favorably inclined to liberalized U.S. barriers to world trade (Table 7–4). The combination of the decline of cotton raising and the expansion of import-vulnerable low-technology industries in the South, the exacerbation of the Southern race issue, and the shift of emphasis of U.S. foreign relations from western Europe to the underdeveloped world largely account for these shifts in Southern as compared with non-Southern white Protestant thinking.[17]

Protestants resided in rural areas or in villages of less than 2,500 people, only 20 percent of Catholic Southerners did. *Gallup Opinion Index*, Special Report on Religion, Feb. 1969. The above percentages were derived from a composite national sample of 10,665 U.S. adults replying to AIPO surveys during 1968.

17. See also Hero, *Southerner*, chaps. 4, 5, 12, and 15.

These developments appear to have made less impact on Catholic whites in the South than on their Protestant associates. Southern white Catholic samples have been too small for definitive comparisons, but during the mid-sixties they appeared more liberal on most international issues than white Protestants in the South, and more nearly like their non-Southern coreligionists than was the case of Southern Protestant whites in comparison with Northern Protestant whites. Thus, whereas the paucity of Catholics in the South helped to account for the statistically more widespread support by that region than others for international commitments prior to Pearl Harbor, by the 1960's the reverse had become the case—the relative lack of Catholics (and of Jews) there had contributed to its lesser approval of economic aid, liberalization of U.S. relations with communist regimes, and perhaps other international programs as well.[18]

White Catholics in the West, like those in the South, have typically been too few for statistically significant comparisons of their international attitudes with those of other Americans. However, no consistent differences appeared before the 1960's between white Catholics in the Northeast and those in the Midwest, nor between Northeastern as contrasted with Midwestern and Western white Catholics combined, nor between Midwestern white Catholics and their coreligionists in the Northeast and West combined. Nor did white Catholics differ in any consistent fashion from Protestant whites in their same regions so far as their opinions on most international issues were concerned during the first decade and a half following V-J Day (Table 7–4).

However, by the mid-sixties white Catholics in the Midwest and in the Midwest and West combined, as in the South, were consistently more liberal than their Protestant white neighbors in the same regions on foreign aid, negotiations and trade with the communist powers, and admission of Mainland China into the UN (Table 7–4). Only in the Northeast was such not consistently the case. Whereas white Protestants in the Northeast in the 1960's, as earlier, were more liberal on most international issues than their coreligionists in each of the other major geographical areas, Northeastern Catholic whites were not more liberal than their counterparts in the Midwest and the Midwest and West combined. In fact, Midwestern white Catholics may have become

18. The lesser support by the South than other regions for such programs in the 1960's has also been in part attributable to the fact that Southern Negroes have been less favorably disposed toward them than Negroes outside that part of the country (see above, pp. 87–88).

somewhat more liberal on several international issues than their co-religionists in the Northeast.

Moreover, although Western white Catholic samples were not large enough to permit reliable comparisons, they did not seem any more conservative on foreign policy than whites of the same religion in the Northeast. The supposed influence of such conservative Western prelates as Cardinal McIntyre notwithstanding, the Western Catholic rank and file may even have become by 1964 somewhat more liberal than their coreligionists in the Northeast on several foreign-policy questions.

EDUCATION AND SOCIOECONOMIC STATUS

Before the War

Differences in social status and, particularly, in education between white Catholics and white Protestants of the prewar years also partly accounted for the more widespread isolationism among the former. Relatively fewer white Catholics than white Protestants or, especially, Jews had been to college or had completed high school or were associated with high-income, complex occupations and social roles, factors positively correlated with support for more active American policies abroad. Thus, among whites differences between Catholics who had gone no further than grade school or were in the lower socioeconomic levels and Protestants and non-church-members of equally low education and social and economic standing were typically smaller than those between all Catholics taken together and all non-Catholics, be they Protestants or unaffiliated persons (Table 7–5).

However, educational and economic factors do not alone account for prewar differences in international attitudes between Catholics and other non-Jewish Americans. On the crucial question of aiding Britain in her war against the Axis, considerable differences toward greater Catholic isolationism remained even when such factors as educational attainment and standard of living were held constant (Table 7–5). Moreover, attitudinal differences among white Catholics of different educational experience were smaller than they were among white Protestants and non-church people—there was less difference in thinking between college-educated and grade-school-educated white Catholics with respect to aiding Britain at the risk of being drawn into the war than there was between the same two educational groups among white

Protestants and unaffiliated people. The same generalization applied to white Catholics of upper versus those of lower income as contrasted with their respective Protestant and unaffiliated economic counterparts. Whereas non-Catholic white Americans who had been to college were considerably more favorable to aiding Britain than their poorly educated coreligionists, there was relatively little difference between college-educated and grade-school-educated white Catholics on this issue. Among the lower social and educational orders white Catholics, Protestants, and unaffiliated persons thought more or less alike, but among the college-educated and better off, the white Catholics were considerably less inclined than others to approve of expanded American efforts to aid Britain against Germany and Italy. In fact, differences were somewhat larger between white Catholic and non-Catholic college-educated citizens after the Nazi invasion of the Soviet Union than before (Table 7–5).

Furthermore, churchless compatriots, though somewhat less well off and less well educated than Catholics, were on the whole at least slightly more favorable to more active American participation in the effort to stop the Axis. Southern white Protestants and unaffiliated persons, considerably less privileged both educationally and economically than Catholics on the average, were clearly more favorably inclined toward virtually all types of expanded international involvements and commitments suggested by the Roosevelt administration prior to our entry into the Second World War (see above, pp. 119–22).

Decline of Educational and Economic Differences
Between Catholics and Protestants

The gap in education between white Catholics and white Protestants in this country has gradually narrowed over the last three decades. Thus as late as 1946 only 17 percent of white adult Catholics, contrasted with 23 percent of white Protestants, had experienced at least some college, while 35 percent versus 28 percent had no more than grade-school educations. However, by the mid-sixties the ratios of college to grade-school educated among these two white religious groups did not differ so significantly. White Catholics were somewhat less apt than Protestant whites to have gone to college, but they were also somewhat less likely to have failed to get as far as high school.[19]

19. Seventeen percent of Catholics versus 18 percent of Protestants in 1967 had experienced some college, 56 versus 50 percent had not gone to college but had completed at least some high school, and 27 versus 32 percent had gone no further than

Similar changes took place in the relative occupational characteristics and standards of living of the two major religious groups. By 1967 the proportion of white Catholic families in the business and professional group, 23 percent, was only one percentage point less than that among white Protestants. Thirteen percent versus 12 percent respectively were in white-collar jobs. White Catholics were more apt than white Protestants to hold blue-collar or manual jobs in urban places, but the latter were much more apt to work on farms—the most internationally conservative of the major occupational groups. Although Catholics were still disproportionately few among the policy-making and senior executive groups in large-scale industry, commerce, and finance and among the most affluent 2 percent or so of the population, by 1967 they were as apt as white Protestants to receive comfortable annual family incomes larger than $7,000 and only two percentage points (16 versus 18 percent) less likely to make more than $10,000 annually.[20]

The gradual disappearance of educational and, to a lesser degree, of occupational and income differences between the two major Christian groups to some extent accounts for the relative shift of white Catholics toward support for multilateral international commitments. Level of education has been closely associated with most liberal international thinking during the postwar decades, as was the case earlier. Income and, especially, occupation have also been correlated with such attitudes, though not as much so as education. However, the combination of college education, professional occupation, and comfortable standards of living has been more intimately connected with approval of expanded economic aid, liberalization of relations with communist regimes, and the like than any other major social or demographic factor.[21]

---

grade school. *Gallup Opinion Index*, Special Report on Religion, 1967, based on a composite national sample of approximately 40,000. Similar small differences were apparent in composite survey results in 1968. *Gallup Opinion Index*, Special Report on Religion, Feb. 1969. When Negroes—mostly Protestants—were included, the average level of education of Catholics in 1967 was slightly higher than that of Protestants.

20. The relatively low average money incomes of white Protestant farmers and rural dwellers and of Southern white Protestants together accounted primarily for this small difference. Table 7–6, derived from SRC 473, Sept.–Nov. 1964, documents this observation.

21. See, for example, the following by Alfred O. Hero, Jr.: *Americans in World Affairs* (Boston: World Peace Foundation, 1959), pp. 21–29; *The Southerner and World Affairs*, chap. 7; and "Public Reactions to Government Policy," in John P. Robinson, Jerrol G. Rusk, and Kendra B. Head, eds., *Measures of Political Attitudes* (Ann Arbor, Mich.: Institute for Social Research, 1968), pp. 38–50.

These variables have been similarly linked with more liberal foreign-policy views among both Catholics and Protestants (Table 7–7). However, white Catholics of the mid-sixties were no better educated, more professional in occupation, or more affluent than white Protestants, as would necessarily be the case if these factors alone accounted for the more generally liberal international views of the former.

Moreover, even when education has been held constant, white Catholics of the middle sixties have been more apt than white Protestants of equal education to favor such policies (Table 7–7). Whereas Catholic college graduates as late as 1948 tended to hold slightly less liberal or internationalist views on such issues as international trade, the UN, immigration, foreign aid, and the ideological struggle with the Soviet Union than did their Protestant counterparts,[22] by the 1960's college-educated white Catholics had become somewhat more favorable to foreign aid, trade and negotiations with communist countries, admission of Mainland China into the UN, and probably other multilateral cooperation as well, than college-educated white Protestants. So had high-school-educated Catholic whites than high-school-educated Protestant whites, and grade-school-educated Catholic whites than equally educationally deprived Protestant whites. Similarly, well-to-do Catholic whites in business and professional roles have been more liberal on these issues in recent years than equally affluent and occupationally privileged white Protestants, as has likewise been the case among the least prosperous third or so and least occupationally skilled of these two religious groups.

Furthermore the differences between the two religious groups were of about equal magnitudes at all educational, occupational, and income levels. Whatever forces have brought about these interreligious attitudinal differences apparently have operated more or less equally at all such levels within the Catholic, the Protestant, or both religious communities, rather than primarily among particular segments—such as the college educated and economically privileged—of one or the other.

RURAL-URBAN CONSIDERATIONS

Rural Americans have been less well-informed and less inclined to express views about most international issues than their urban and,

22. See Ernest Havemann and Patricia Salter West, *They Went to College* (New York: Harcourt, Brace, 1952), p. 193.

especially, suburban compatriots throughout the period since the mid-thirties. However, insofar as they advanced any opinions, attitudinal differences between country and city people prior to the Japanese attack on Hawaii were either very small or nonexistent. Although rural and small-town folk in the Midwest and Great Plains included dispro-portionately large numbers of isolationists, the predominantly rural and small-town South was more supportive of an active international stance than any other major region.

However, the Protestant traditions of most rural and small-town Americans[23] have had some bearing on the international attitudinal differences observed more recently between the two Christian groups. People living in such environments, regardless of their religious pref-erences, have on the average tended to harbor somewhat more con-servative or hard-line views on most international questions than in-habitants of medium-sized and larger urban places. Urban white Protestants have expressed views more nearly like those of Catholics (all except a small minority of them urban) than have rural Protestant whites.[24]

Nevertheless, usually consistent (though small) differences toward more widespread support for multilateral cooperation among white Catholics than white Protestants appeared in the mid-sixties even when rural people were eliminated and only urban and suburban dwellers were compared. Thus in the fall of 1964, for instance, 58 percent of urban white Catholics versus but 53 percent of urban white Protestants favored giving economic aid, 30 versus 26 percent felt farmers and businessmen should be allowed to do business in nonmilitary goods with communist countries, and 18 versus only 14 percent thought the People's Republic of China should be admitted to the UN.[25] The fol-lowing February, 57 percent of urban and suburban Catholic whites, contrasted with but 48 percent of Protestant whites in similar locales, felt the U.S. had an "obligation to help poorer nations," and 53 percent, contrasted with only 46 percent, were either "extremely" or "consider-

23. In 1967, 37 percent of Protestants, contrasted with but 14 percent of Catholics, lived either in rural sections or in towns of populations less than 2,500. *Gallup Opinion Index*, Special Report on Religion, 1967, based on a national sample of some 40,000.

24. Rural and small-town white Catholics have typically been too few in national-survey samples to permit their statistical comparison with Protestant whites in similar surroundings.

25. SRC 473, Sept.–Oct. '64. White urban Catholics numbered 281, white urban Protestants 709. All built-up places of greater than 2,500 population were considered urban.

ably well satisfied" with the concept of aiding such countries.[26] At about the same time, 47 percent of white Catholics in communities of greater population than 2,500, contrasted with but 40 percent of their Protestant white neighbors, agreed that Congress should appropriate either the $3.4 billion for foreign aid requested by President Johnson or a larger figure; conversely 41 versus 48 percent would have decreased or eliminated aid.[27]

GENERATIONAL DIFFERENCES

Young Americans in their twenties have been no more attentive to world affairs or better informed about international developments than their seniors. Although on the whole better educated than their elders, prior to our entry into the war Americans in their twenties were not consistently more liberal, internationalist, or interventionist in their foreign-policy thinking than their older compatriots. In fact, on some issues like aid to the opponents of the Axis, draft-age youth tended to take a somewhat more conservative or isolationist stance than compatriots in their forties and older. Doubtless the younger group was more concerned that such action might involve this country in war, one in which they would be obliged to fight.

However, in recent years younger citizens of both Christian groups have on the whole been more liberal or multilateralist in their foreign-policy preferences than their seniors—more inclined, for example, to emphasize development assistance, negotiation, trade, intercultural exchange, and other nonmilitary means of dealing with our foreign problems. Citizens in later middle age, and especially in their sixties and older, on the other hand, have been more favorably disposed than their juniors to isolationist or neo-isolationist ideas, unilateral interventions, military means, and generally less conciliatory policies toward communist and other regimes which oppose the perceived national interests of the United States. These attitudinal differences between the generations have been attributable in considerable measure to the higher average education of younger people, but even when education is held constant, by the 1960's they were on the average somewhat more liberal in their foreign-policy preferences than compatriots in their

26. POS 655, 2–15–65. Urban white Catholics numbered 287, urban white Protestants 701.

27. AIPO 706, 2-17-65. Urban white Catholics numbered 269, urban white Protestants 689.

thirties and forties, and clearly more so than the oldest third of the national population.

As a result of their higher birth rate (as well, perhaps, of other factors), the average age of white Catholics has been significantly lower than that of white Protestants. In the fall of 1964, for example, 21 percent of white Catholic adults versus only 17 percent of their white Protestant counterparts were in their twenties, 23 percent versus 18 percent in their thirties, 23 versus 21 percent in their forties, 15 versus 20 percent in their fifties, and 18 versus 24 percent sixty or over.[28] To what extent have such age differences accounted for the international attitudinal differences of the 1960's between Catholic and Protestant whites?

Differential age has had some limited connection with these inter-religious differences, but on the whole it has been less important than education.[29] The more youthful composition of the white Catholic than

28. SRC 473, Sept.–Nov. 1964. In a Feb. 1965 survey (POS 655), 24 percent of Catholic contrasted with 19 percent of Protestant white adults were in their twenties, 43 versus 39 percent in their thirties and forties, and 33 versus 41 percent were fifty or more years old. Even when nonwhites were included, Catholics of the mid-sixties have been on the average significantly younger than Protestants. In 1968, for instance, 20 percent of Catholics, contrasted with but 16 percent of Protestants, were in their twenties, 43 versus 35 percent in their thirties or forties, and 35 versus 43 percent in their fifties or older. *Gallup Opinion Index*, Special Report on Religion, Feb. 1969. Percentages were derived from a composite sample of 10,655.

29. Differences in international interests, knowledge, and attitudes between the age groups among Christian laymen have been smaller than those among their clergymen. Younger ministers and priests have held distinctly more liberal views on international affairs than older ones, have been more inclined to feel that the churches should be active in this field, and have generally been more interested in the ethical implications of foreign policy. For example, in a survey of 4,031 ministers of eight denominations affiliated with the N.C.C. in 1960, 66 percent of the 1,228 less than thirty-five years of age contrasted with but 52 percent of the 1,221 fifty and older said they were "very interested in national and international affairs," 62 versus 48 percent "strongly" approved of the purposes of the UN, 61 versus 39 percent "strongly" approved of the purposes of the World Council of Churches, 61 versus 47 percent would "like very much to see a church-sponsored examination of the major ethical issues in American life," 85 versus 60 percent said they "frequently" or "occasionally" included "currently controversial topics in sermons," 76 versus 57 percent agreed with the N.C.C.'s "goals in international affairs and peace," 73 versus 46 percent disagreed that the N.C.C. was "too concerned with national and international social problems," 38 versus 23 percent agreed that the N.C.C. should issue "pronouncements for its member denominations," 9 versus 21 percent considered N.C.C. pronouncements "far to the left," 69 versus 48 percent said most utterances by the N.C.C. were "in agreement with my own views" to a "considerable" or "great" extent, and 52 versus 44 percent knew of the N.C.C.'s declared position on the UN and the People's Republic of China. From a national study for the N.C.C. by the Bureau of Applied Social Research of Columbia University in early 1960. A national survey of 2,183 Roman Catholic priests and 2,216 active laymen in the early sixties similarly discovered wider differences in international attitudes between younger and older priests than between younger and older active parishioners. Thus

of the white Protestant population was as apparent in the 1930's, the 1940's, and the 1950's as it has been more recently. But prior to the Japanese attack on Pearl Harbor white Catholics at each age level were less supportive of such policies as aid to Britain and France and Lend-Lease than were white Protestants in the same age bracket. Differences declined in the early postwar years, but on some issues younger Catholics still seemed slightly less inclined toward liberal policies than younger white Protestants, and older Catholics than older Protestant whites as well.

Nor did international attitudinal differences between whites of the two major Christian persuasions in the mid-1960's disappear when age was held constant (Table 7–8). They were typically smaller between Catholic and Protestant whites of the same age than between the two religious groups as wholes, but they were nonetheless consistent. At each age level, white Catholics were at least somewhat more approving than white Protestants of economic aid, negotiations and trade with the communists, and admission of Mainland China into the UN. Catholic-Protestant differences were of roughly similar magnitudes at each age level. Nor can the more widespread support for these policies among Catholics be explained by any greater differences between a younger, better-educated "new breed" of Catholics and their seniors than those separating equally young, better-educated Protestants from their seniors.

IMPACTS OF PARTISAN AFFILIATIONS

Differences between Catholics and Protestants have also been in part related to the disproportionately Democratic preferences of the former in contrast with the more Republican inclinations of the latter. In every presidential election except in 1964 and 1972 during at least the three and a half decades since 1936, Catholic white majorities have voted for the Democratic alternatives, whereas Protestant white majorities voted for the Republican candidates. Particularly among whites outside

---

53 percent of the 404 priests less than thirty years of age versus only 28 percent of the 129 priests sixty and older would expand foreign economic aid, while the respective figures among the 246 laymen less than thirty versus the 130 laymen in their sixties and older were 44 and 30 percent. Although the priests as a group were more inclined to increase aid than their active parishioners, the difference was accounted for primarily by the more liberal views of younger priests as contrasted with laymen of the same age. No significant differences appeared between clergy and active parishioners sixty and older—both were equally conservative about foreign aid. See Joseph H. Fichter, *Priest and People* (New York: Sheed and Ward, 1965), p. 101.

the South have Catholics been sharply more inclined than Protestants to favor Democratic over Republican candidates and to consider themselves Democrats rather than Republicans.

These partisan differences have declined somewhat in recent years as the average family incomes of Catholics rose relative to those of Protestants and prosperous descendants of Catholic immigrants moved to the suburbs and gradually replaced the Democratic traditions of their parents with the predominantly Republican preferences of their neighbors.

Nevertheless, as late as the 1964 election 31 percent of white Catholics considered themselves "strong" Democrats and another 29 percent "not so strong" Democrats, contrasted with 23 and 25 percent respectively of white Protestants (and only 19 and 21 percent of white Protestants outside the South); conversely only 9 percent of white Catholics viewed themselves as "strong" Republicans and 8 percent "not so strong" Republicans versus 14 and 17 percent respectively of white Protestants (17 and 20 percent of them outside the South).[30] Even when Negroes—largely Protestant Democrats—were included, only 15 percent of all Catholics, contrasted with 33 percent of all Protestants, in 1967 perceived themselves as Republicans, while 54 versus 37 percent viewed themselves as Democrats.[31] Moreover, Catholics at all economic and educational levels in the mid and late sixties continued to be more inclined to perceive themselves as Democrats and to vote for Democrats than Protestants at the same economic levels—well-to-do, college-educated Catholics more than well-to-do, college educated Protestants, middle-income Catholics than middle-income Protestants, and even poor, little-educated Catholics than Protestants of comparable status.[32]

Rank-and-file Republicans or voters for Republican candidates have not differed as much on foreign policy from their Democratic equivalents as have the professional politicians of the two parties. Re-

30. SRC 473, Sept.–Nov. 1964.

31. *Gallup Opinion Index*, Nov. 1967. Although Jews have been the most affluent ethnic and religious group in America, they have also been the most Democratic. In 1967 only 9 percent of them considered themselves Republicans while 64 percent perceived themselves as Democrats. *Gallup Opinion Index*, Special Report on Religion, 1967.

32. This generalization is also highly likely to prevail in the coming generation of college-educated middle class Americans. In November 1969, only 12 percent of Catholic, contrasted with 33 percent of Protestant, college students considered themselves Republicans, while 33 versus 23 percent viewed themselves as Democrats. *Gallup Opinion Index*, Jan. 1970.

publicans have on the average probably been somewhat more conservative than Democrats on most international questions, but such attitudinal differences have varied significantly depending on which party has controlled the White House at the time.

During the Roosevelt years Republicans and Landon or Wilkie voters were 3 to 15 percentage points more apt than their Democratic counterparts to feel our entry into the First World War had been a mistake and, after the invasion of Poland, about as much less willing to aid the allies against the Axis.

Except when partisan aspects were involved in the wording of the question—such as support for President Truman's proposals to which his name was patently attached—partisan differences on most international issues seemed somewhat smaller in 1945–52 than before 1942. However, Republicans and Dewey voters were a dozen or so percentage points more inclined than their Democratic equivalents to feel the U.S. had "gone too far" since the war (under President Truman) in concerning itself with world affairs and 2 to 11 percentage points less favorable to the initial postwar loan to Britain, food shipments to war-torn areas, Truman Doctrine aid to Greece and Turkey, Marshall Plan and military aid to western Europe, aid to Yugoslavia, and U.S. membership in NATO.

But with the advent of the Eisenhower administration, relative attitudes of the two partisan groups slowly shifted. By the end of President Eisenhower's first term, virtually no partisan differences were left in respect of most international issues—except that Democrats remained less well informed and less apt to express any opinions, as they had in the past, largely because of their lower average education than that of Republicans. By the last two years of the second Eisenhower administration, Republicans and people who voted for President Eisenhower had actually become somewhat more favorable to most types of foreign aid, active participation in NATO, and some other policies of their federal government than Democrats and Stevenson voters.

However, with the advent of the Kennedy and Johnson administrations, the relative positions of the partisan groups reversed once again. By the mid-sixties Democrats and Kennedy voters were 2 to 13 percentage points more favorable to most nonmilitary aid than Republicans and Nixon voters. Between early 1961 and the end of 1968 Democrats were 4 to 5 percentage points more supportive than Republicans of a UN emergency force and 1 to 6 percentage points more willing to admit Peking to the UN and to "go along" with a General Assembly majority on this matter. Attitudinal differences between Johnson and Goldwater voters on most international issues have been substantially larger than those between Democrats and Republicans, or between Kennedy and Nixon voters.

It is thus not surprising that differences between Catholic and Protestant white Democrats, or F.D.R. voters, were larger than those between the two religious groups as wholes, including Republicans and Independents, with respect to most of the more crucial prewar foreign policy issues. Southern white Anglo-Saxon Protestant Democrats and F.D.R. voters were the second most willing ethnic and religious group (after Jews) to aid Britain, even to the point of entering the war in late 1939, while Catholic Italian, German, and Irish Democrats were at least as much opposed as were Protestant (and other) Republicans. Similarly during the Truman administration Catholic Democrats tended to be slightly less supportive of some international commitments of the period than white Protestant Democrats, even in the cases where Catholics as a whole did not differ from Protestants as a group.

However, these religious differences among the same partisan groups seemed to disappear during President Eisenhower's incumbency, as did differences between Democrats and Republicans in general.

The advent of a Catholic Democratic President doubtless had somewhat greater impact on Catholic than on Protestant Democrats toward congruence with his foreign programs (see below, pp. 208–9). By early 1963 white Catholics who considered themselves Democrats were on the average somewhat more approving of his major foreign commitments—foreign aid, the Peace Corps, the Trade Expansion Act, summit meetings with communist leaders, and so forth—than white Protestant Democrats. But the difference was in part due to the gradual shift of Southern white Protestant Democrats away from support of such programs, a trend which began during the first Eisenhower administration but continued under his Democratic successor. Moreover, the international attitudinal differences between white Catholic and white Protestant Democrats continued under the Johnson administration; in fact, they seemed slowly to widen after President Kennedy's assassination. The election of John F. Kennedy may have contributed to the gradual liberalization of American Catholic international opinion, but it was at most only one of several significant factors which brought about this trend (see below, pp. 208–9).

In any event, white Catholic Democrats under President Johnson were more liberal in regard to development assistance, foreign aid in general, trade and negotiations with communist states, and admission of Mainland China into the UN than white Protestants of the same partisan preferences (Table 7–9). White Republicans of both religious orientations were typically more opposed to these programs and policy alternatives than white Democrats of the same religion, but among Republicans Catholic whites were more apt to approve of them than their white Protestant Republican colleagues. In fact, on some of these issues Catholic white Republicans seemed somewhat more liberal than Protestant white Democrats, though Republicans as a group were more conservative than Democrats.

Thus even when such relevant demographic factors as ethnic background, geographical region, education, socioeconomic status, occupation, rural versus urban or suburban residence, age, and partisan preferences are held constant, white Catholic Americans have recently manifested somewhat greater approval of foreign aid, admission of Mainland China to the UN, and probably multilateral cooperation generally than have their Protestant compatriots. Perhaps these Catholic-Protestant differences would be smaller still if all these variables could be controlled simultaneously. However, some differences would undoubtedly remain even if large enough samples were available for such multiple controls. These findings, together with those discussed in the next two chapters, strongly suggest that active Catholic as contrasted with Protestant affiliations per se have contributed to interreligious differences in views on these international issues during the sixties.

This relatively recent phenomenon has not been limited to international affairs. Catholic Republicans have also been more liberal in their views on most domestic economic, welfare, and other internal issues than their white Protestant Republican compatriots; Catholic Democrats more than their Protestant Democratic counterparts. Educated Catholics have been more liberal on such internal questions than educated white Protestants, well-to-do Catholics than equally prosperous white Protestants, urban Catholics than urban white Protestants, old Catholics than white Protestants of the same age, and so on. To the impacts of such domestic public attitudes on foreign-policy opinions among the religious groups we now turn our attention.

CHAPTER 8. DOMESTIC ISSUES VERSUS FOREIGN POLICY

To what extent can the differences between the religious groups in respect of foreign policy be traced to parallel differences in general political ideology and in attitudes toward major domestic issues? Have Jews been consistently more liberal than Christians on domestic affairs as they have been on foreign affairs? Were Catholics more conservative than Protestants on controversial internal questions prior to the Second World War, later more or less indistinguishable from Protestants, and during the last few years more liberal than the latter? To what degree have the prevailing international attitudes of the three major religious groups been reflections of or associated with such more general ideologies and reactions to issues nearer to home?

CONSERVATISM VERSUS LIBERALISM

Jews since at least the 1930's have been much more inclined than either Christian group to consider themselves liberals rather than conservatives and to say they would prefer a more liberal party or candidate over more conservative ones (Table 8–1). Catholics have been more nearly like Protestants than like Jews in their general political ideology in the liberal-conservative spectrum. However, Catholic citizens have been consistently at least somewhat more inclined to verbalized or abstract declared liberalism than Protestants, even during the earlier period when they were the less supportive of certain important international commitments.

These Catholic-Protestant differences have apparently widened somewhat since the 1950's, that is, since the advent of Pope John XXIII and the Second Vatican Council. Although the wider conservatism among Protestants than Catholics has been to some extent attributable to the more conservative tendencies among white Protestant Southerners than among their Northern coreligionists, Northern white Catholics have also been at least somewhat more liberal (or less conservative) than Protestant whites in the same part of the country (Table 8–1).

Negro Americans, mostly Protestants, have been considerably less apt than whites, regardless of their religion, to understand the connotations of such terms as liberal and conservative (Table 8–1). However, among those who have expressed either preference, Negroes have been more liberal over these three decades than either white Christian group, though not so liberal as Jews. As has been the case in world affairs as well, Southern Negroes have been consistently more conservative than Northern ones. However, Negroes as a group were less inclined than whites toward an active foreign policy in the earlier period, when they were nevertheless more apt than whites to think of themselves as liberals.

Thus the difference toward greater liberalism among Catholics than Protestants has been slightly wider when Negroes have been excluded than when they have been included. The degree of expressed liberalism of Southern Protestants has been especially reduced when Negroes have been eliminated and Southern white Protestants alone considered. However, Southern white Protestants have not always been more inclined than their Northern coreligionists to consider themselves conservatives, as they did during the late 1950's and 1960's, since the region has experienced more forceful pressures to desegregate racially (Table 8–1). During the New Deal they were slightly more inclined than their Northern counterparts to consider themselves liberals and to say they preferred a liberal over a conservative party or candidate.[1]

Self-perception as liberal or conservative and expressed preference for a more conservative party or candidate have been linked with Democratic and Republican partisan preferences respectively—though not so closely as some might suppose. During the Eisenhower administration, in 1954, 42 percent of self-identified Republicans considered themselves liberals and 33 percent thought of themselves as conservatives while the respective figures among Democrats were 41 versus 24 percent.[2] Partisan differences have been wider, but still not large, during the Kennedy, Johnson, and Nixon administrations. In 1966 20 percent of Republicans versus 26 percent of Democrats considered themselves liberals and 40 versus 29 percent conservatives;[3] in March 1970 18 percent of Republicans, contrasted with 33 percent of Democrats, classified themselves as liberals, 62 and 35 percent as conservatives.[4] Southern whites in recent years have tended to raise the conservative and lower the liberal averages among self-identified Democrats, but even when they have been omitted, Democrats have been less apt than Republicans to

1. See Alfred O. Hero, Jr., *The Southerner and World Affairs*, pp. 365–73, for a more detailed discussion of this phenomenon in the South.
2. AIPO 541, 12-29-54.
3. National Analysts, Inc., survey of April 1966.
4. *Gallup Opinion Index*, April 1970.

understand the meaning of these terms and only a third or less more inclined than Republicans to consider themselves liberals rather than conservatives.

The labels "liberal" and "conservative" have had varying issue connotations at different times (and among different groups within the public at the same time).[5] "Liberal" and "conservative"—like the labels "Democrat" and "Republican"—have been more intimately associated with certain domestic attitudes than with policy preferences on most aspects of international relations. When asked to define "liberal" and "conservative," many Americans have mentioned only internal issues, and most of the remainder have emphasized domestic over international questions. Only limited minorities have accorded equal prominence to both, and only minuscule ones have assigned greater priority to foreign than to domestic questions or have mentioned only the former.

Self-identified liberals prior to the Second World War were sharply more inclined to favor most of the measures of the domestic New Deal than were conservatives. These differences narrowed somewhat during the Eisenhower administration as a number of relatively conservative Republicans came to support such programs as social security, federal aid to education and housing, public works, graduated income taxes, and federal interventions in the economy generally. However, even during President Eisenhower's second term, self-perceived conservatives remained clearly less supportive of expansion of social-welfare programs and of governmental economic and social responsibility in general. Moreover, by the mid-sixties conservatives were still fifteen or (often) more percentage points less favorably disposed to most such domestic programs than liberals.

Differences in international attitudes between liberals and conservatives have been smaller—on some issues and during certain periods virtually nil.[6] Among neither Catholics nor Protestants did such terms have much bearing on prewar international opinions. For example, among both Christian groups, whites who preferred that the Roosevelt administration become more liberal or continue along its "present lines" in the fall of 1938 were only slightly more inclined than coreligionists

5. Linkages between self-identification as a liberal or a conservative and policy preferences on domestic and international questions among the U.S. population in general are discussed further in Alfred O. Hero, Jr., "Liberalism-Conservatism Revisited: Foreign vs. Domestic Federal Policies—1937–67," *Public Opinion Quarterly* 33, no. 3 (Fall 1969), pp. 399–408.
   6. Ibid.

who preferred that it become more conservative to feel that "America's failure to join the League of Nations was partly responsible for the ... troubles in Europe" and that "England and France made a mistake in agreeing to Germany's demands on Czechoslovakia" and to say that they would "like to see President Roosevelt openly criticize Hitler and Mussolini for their war-like attitude" and that they would "join a movement in this country to stop buying goods from Germany" (Table 8–2). International attitudinal differences between liberals and conservatives so defined were too small for the disproportionate numbers of liberals among Catholics and of conservatives among Protestants to countervail the lesser support for intervention against the Axis among Catholic Americans.

Correlations of liberalism-conservatism with international attitudes rose somewhat with more active U.S. participation in world affairs following the Second World War. However, they depended on the particular international issue in question and the party in control of the White House (Table 8–2). A considerable number of working-class citizens of both Christian persuasions who have regarded themselves as liberals have continued to constitute a substantial fraction of the remaining postwar isolationist and neo-isolationist minority.

During the Truman years self-identified liberals—like self-identified Democrats, which most of them were—provided more support than conservatives for foreign economic aid and other nonmilitary programs requiring relatively large expenditures of federal funds. Thus among both white Christian groups, liberals were significantly more likely than conservatives to feel that Marshall Plan aid should be increased and less apt to want it decreased (Table 8–2). However, several months before the communist attack on South Korea, liberal white Catholics and Protestants did not differ at all from their conservative coreligionists in their reactions to the suggestion that President Truman take the lead in arranging a summit meeting with Stalin and the chiefs of state of other major powers to try to alleviate cold-war disagreements.

By the second Eisenhower administration even these rather small differences of opinion on foreign aid between liberals and conservatives had virtually disappeared as a number of relatively conservative voters for Eisenhower came to accept his international programs and some liberals who had voted for Adlai Stevenson became disaffected with the foreign policies of the Republican administration. Thus in early 1957 among neither Catholic nor Protestant whites did self-identified liberals diverge from conservatives in their views on either the likelihood of the UN preventing another major war, economic and financial assistance to the Middle East, or the sending of military supplies to "friendly" regimes in that area of the world to help strengthen their armed forces (Table 8–2).

Small differences in views on international affairs seemed to develop once again between self-identified liberals and conservatives in both religious groups after the election of President Kennedy. Within five months after he assumed office, Catholics who preferred that he "go more to the left by following more the views of labor and other liberal groups" were several percentage points more inclined to feel that "communism would be in a greater position of world power today" if Congress had not "appropriated from three to four billion dollars each year . . during recent years" for foreign aid than were Catholics who preferred that he "go more to the right by following more the views of business and conservative groups." Similar differences were apparent among Protestants (Table 8–2).[7]

In the autumn of 1964 both Catholic and Protestant whites who held favorable feelings toward liberals were six to fifteen percentage points more likely than coreligionists who felt unfavorably toward liberals to approve of foreign economic aid, negotiations with communist leaders, trade in nonmilitary goods with communist countries, and admission of Mainland China into the UN. However, though these attitudinal differences were consistent, they were relatively small. Moreover, those who harbored favorable impressions of conservatives did not diverge as much, or even as consistently, with respect to these foreign-policy questions from coreligionists who felt unfavorably toward conservatives (Table 8–2).

Thus by the mid-sixties the more prevalent general liberalism among white Catholics than white Protestants had some small bearing on the greater support among the former for multilateral international cooperation and liberalization of relations with the communist powers. Nevertheless, liberal white Catholics were slightly more supportive of such international actions than were even liberal white Protestants. Conservative white Catholics were likewise slightly more favorably disposed to such policies than their conservative white Protestant fellow

7. However, among both religious groups people who preferred that he "follow a policy halfway between the two" were more inclined to feel that foreign aid had helped limit the spread of communism than either those who wanted him to move to the left or others who wished him to shift to the right (Table 8–2).

Americans. This disproportionate number of self-perceived liberals among Catholics and conservatives among Protestants was thus only one of at least several factors which accounted for the greater Catholic support for liberal international programs during the Johnson administration.

DOMESTIC ECONOMIC, LABOR, AND WELFARE QUESTIONS

Jews have consistently been more favorably disposed than either Catholics or Protestants to expansion of federal responsibilities, services, and expenditures for the less privileged in this country—"relief," old age pensions, medical care, unemployment compensation, aid to education, slum clearance and new housing, higher minimum wages, public works and social welfare programs, and transfers of wealth from the haves to have-nots generally (Table 8–3). Jews more than either Christian group have approved of a strong, relatively expensive federal government, active in the economy and society generally. Moreover, they have been more willing than either to pay increased taxes if necessary to support such activities.

These consistent tendencies of Jews vis-à-vis both Catholics and Protestants are particularly interesting in the light of the economic status of most Jews. Jews for a number of years have enjoyed higher average family incomes than either Christian group and than any major Protestant denominational group, even Episcopalians and Presbyterians. However, within the general American population the higher the income, the less the support for federal expenditures for which the prosperous pay a disproportionately large share of the taxes to receive a much smaller part of the expenditures. Among ethnic and religious groups only Negroes have closely approached Jews in their level of approval for such expensive activities, but Negroes, being for the most part relatively poor, have had much personally to gain and little to lose in supporting them. When such factors as income, socioeconomic status, occupation, and education have been held constant, differences between Jews and Christians toward more liberal domestic views among the former have been considerably larger than those between Jews and Christians in general (Table 8–3).[8]

8. For example, a national survey of 9,064 college graduates for *Time* magazine by the Bureau of Applied Social Research of Columbia University in 1948 discovered that 66 percent of Jews versus only 39 percent of Catholics and 34 percent of Protestants who had received college degrees expressed generally favorable attitudes

Catholics, though not so favorable to liberal economic and welfare programs as Jews, have been consistently more approving than Protestants of most of them since the late 1930's (Table 8–3). The more favorable reactions by Catholics to trade unions, the union shop, the guaranteed annual wage, and the like could be in part explained by the relatively fewer Protestant than Catholic union members. On the other hand, few Catholics have been engaged in agriculture, so it is not surprising that expensive federal farm programs have constituted one of the few types of federal interventions into the economy and society which Catholics have supported to no greater extent than Protestants. The lower average incomes of white Catholics than white Protestants in the prewar years probably in part explain the former's greater approval of federal spending on "medical care for those unable to pay for it" in 1938, of expansion of old-age pensions and unemployment compensation to poor citizens as yet uncovered, and of increased expenditures on "relief," pensions, and social services generally in 1939.

However, at least as early as 1948 even college-graduated, relatively prosperous Catholics were significantly more favorably disposed toward most of the domestic programs and of the New Deal and the Fair Deal than were Protestants with equal advantages in education and economic position.[9] Moreover, by the 1960's Catholics enjoyed slightly higher average incomes than Protestants as a whole, and about the same average ones as white Protestants (see above, p. 128). Nevertheless, Catholics remained more favorable than Protestants to expansions of federal expenditures on education (although Catholic schools would receive little), public health, medical care, low-cost housing, prevention and

---

toward the domestic New Deal and Fair Deal programs of Presidents Roosevelt and Truman, respectively. Ernest Havemann and Patricia Salter West, *They Went to College* (New York: Harcourt, Brace, 1952), p. 193. From a secondary analysis of other surveys since the late thirties and a new survey of his own in a heavily Jewish ward of Boston (Ward 14), Fuchs concluded that Jews had been the only major ethnic or religious group in the country in which the more affluent, socioeconomically and occupationally privileged, and college-educated had not been more conservative than their less privileged coreligionists on most domestic economic and welfare issues and more inclined to prefer Republican Presidential candidates over Democratic ones. Lawrence H. Fuchs, *The Political Behavior of American Jews* (Glencoe, Ill.: The Free Press, 1956), pp. 84–85, 87, 90–107. For similar findings, see Wesley and Beverly Allinsmith, "Religious Affiliation and Politico-Economic Attitudes," *Public Opinion Quarterly* 12 (Fall 1948), pp. 379–85; S. J. Korchin, "Psychological Variables in the Behavior of Voting" (Ph.D. dissertation, Harvard University, 1946), pp. 93 and 194 ff.; and Robert T. Bower, "Voting Behavior of American Ethnic Groups, 1936–1944" (unpublished paper, Bureau of Applied Social Research, Columbia University, 1944).

9. Havemann and West, p. 193.

alleviation of unemployment, and welfare programs as a whole. Catholics also remained more approving of federal price and inflation control and a strong central government active in the economy of the country. The differences between the two Christian groups were as large or larger in the 1960's, when Catholics were as affluent on the average as Protestants, as they had been two to three decades before when they were not.

Moreover, since Negroes—the vast majority of them Protestants—have been more supportive of such federal programs than most non-Jewish whites, differences between white Catholics and white Protestants have usually been larger than those between the two Christian groups when Negroes are included (Table 8–3). Although Southern Protestant whites in the New Deal years were at least as enthusiastic about most of these domestic programs as Northern Protestant whites, in recent years the former have been somewhat less supportive than the latter of "big federal government" active in these areas. Meanwhile, Catholic whites have been more favorably disposed toward most of these governmental interventions into the society and the lives of individual citizens than even white Protestants outside the South.

These interreligious differences have been associated with comparable ones in respect of the so-called Protestant (mostly Calvinist) ethic of laissez-faire free enterprise, rugged economic individualism, and the self-made man. Although these values have affected many American Catholics as well as Protestants, they have been more apparent among Protestant whites than among Catholics of the same race (Table 8–3). Thus the former more than the latter have tended to attribute poverty mainly to lack of individual effort rather than circumstances beyond the control of the poor person, to feel "not at all satisfied with the opportunity for the individual to get ahead" rather than "well satisfied," and to believe the federal government does "too much for people" in this country rather than "not enough." During the Johnson administration white Catholics more than white Protestants thus held favorable views of the Anti-Poverty Program, advocated that "despite the cost of the war in Vietnam, the Administration should continue its programs of federal aid to education, medical care, cleaning up water pollution, the war against poverty, and other Great Society programs . . . here at home," and approved of the idea of a minimum income guaranteed to every individual and family by the federal government. The more prevalent tendency of Catholics to approve of trade unions and of the arguments of their leaders in disputes with management vis-à-vis the more widespread popularity of the arguments of business and finance among white Protestants has also been related to these phenomena.

However, support for liberalized social welfare, Medicare and Medicaid, public works, and like federal expenditures at home has been at most only loosely linked with approval of federal expenditures abroad or active multilateral involvements in general. Correlations of international attitudes with views on such internal issues have been no higher for the most part than those with self-identification as a liberal or a conservative, for basically the same reasons.

Approval of active, financially expensive policies both at home and abroad has been apparent in the thought patterns of a minority composed of liberal intellectuals, ideologues, and other well-educated citizens atypically interested in public affairs at the national and international levels. Even among college-educated Americans generally, however, correlations between international and domestic economic and welfare attitudes have been only somewhat higher than among the public as a whole.[10]

Among American adults generally—be they Catholic or Protestant—approval of multilateral cooperation, particularly in nonmilitary fields, has been closely associated with relatively high, especially college, education. But since the better educated have been on the average more prosperous, international liberals have on the whole been more affluent than international conservatives and, particularly, than isolationists and neo-isolationists. The reverse, however, has been the case for support for trade unions, federally financed welfare programs, Medicare, and the like at home—economically less privileged persons, the more likely to benefit directly from such spending, have been more approving than the better-off (and for the most part better-educated) minority, who would pay disproportionately large shares of the taxes but receive disproportionately small benefits from the programs on which they would be expended.

10. Correlations between domestic economic and welfare attitudes and views on multilateral cooperation have also been more apparent among the more prosperous economic groups than among the public generally. Even during the second Eisenhower administration (see above, pp. 135–36), the minority among the most affluent quarter or so of the population who favored increased federal spending on medical care for the less prosperous, low-cost housing, and other transfers of wealth from people like themselves to the less privileged were significantly more supportive of economic aid to neutralist regimes, negotiations and trade with communist countries, etc., than were the majority of their economic peers who opposed such expansion of the welfare state.

It is thus understandable that American adults who have been less enthusiastic about social welfare and related programs at home—on the whole better educated—have typically been somewhat more aware of international developments and better informed about them than compatriots who have favored such domestic activities.

Reactions to the domestic New Deal, balancing the budget, and trade unions had no connection whatsoever with sentiments about lending money to Finland when she was attacked by the Soviet Union. Americans who favored governmental ownership of public utilities and opposed turning the TVA over to private operation were actually somewhat less willing to aid Finland than compatriots who felt all such industries should be under private enterprise (Table 8–4). Nor did views on these controversial domestic issues have any consistent bearing on attitudes toward reciprocal trade agreements, tariffs, or intervention to assist the allies against the Axis. Americans who opposed high income taxes on the rich, approved of Henry Ford's refusal to recognize unions in his plants, and believed employers should have the right to refuse jobs to union members did not feel any differently about Lend-Lease and other aid to Britain than compatriots who disagreed with them on these domestic matters.

Weak connections developed between some domestic economic attitudes and views on certain fields of foreign affairs during the Truman administration as Democrats who agreed with him on domestic issues came to accept his foreign policies. Thus those who favored more governmental control or ownership of utilities were significantly more willing to expand shipments of food and other supplies to war-torn Europe in 1947 than were other Americans who disagreed with them about public utilities (Table 8–4). People who considered their own income taxes "too high" were less favorably disposed to sending economic aid to Japan and western Europe than others who considered them "about right" or "too low." Those who would expand federal spending on social welfare, health, social security, housing, and public works were somewhat more supportive of the ERP at prevailing or higher levels than others who opposed expansions of federal action in these domestic issues.

However, these differences were quite small. Moreover, views on some Truman domestic policies had no connection at all with attitudes toward certain international questions of the period. Thus, people who sided with management did not differ from those who sided with unions in disputes between the two on the Marshall Plan (Table 8–4). Nor did opinions on the minimum wage and on whether high wages or high profits were mainly to blame for inflation have any bearing on lending to Britain. Support for NATO seemed entirely unrelated to thinking on trade unions, the Taft-Hartley Act, or progressive taxation. Those who favored federally subsidized low-cost housing were neither more nor less supportive of the Marshall Plan than compatriots who opposed it.

Moreover, most of even the loose linkages between international and domestic economic and welfare attitudes apparent during the early years after World War II largely disappeared by the end of the first Eisenhower administration. People who approved of liberal domestic policies on bread-and-butter issues were on the whole slightly more favorably disposed to foreign economic aid and to helping even neutralist regimes than those who opposed such internal policies, but few of these differences exceeded half a dozen percentage points (Table 8–4).

Moreover, those who felt the federal government should be responsible for full employment and should help people get medical care at low cost were actually slightly less inclined to send aid to neutrals in late 1956 than others who opposed both. At the beginning of the second Eisenhower administration people who approved of unions were slightly more willing to send economic help to the Middle East than those who disapproved of labor organizations, but feelings about raising the minimum wage had no such bearing on views about aid to this area.[11]

With the advent of another Democratic administration in 196. correlations between such domestic views and those on world affairs increased somewhat once again (Table 8–4). Thus shortly after President Kennedy took office, 75 percent of Americans who approved of unions, contrasted with but 66 percent of those who disapproved favored the proposed Peace Corps. Fifty-six percent of those who felt

11. A survey of Greater Detroit during the second Eisenhower administration likewise discovered little or no correlation between views on domestic welfare and related issues on the one hand and those on world affairs, civil liberties, and civil rights on the other. As we determined from national surveys, liberals on civil liberties and/or civil rights tended to be relative liberals on international affairs, and conservatives on civil liberties and civil rights to be conservatives on international affairs (see below pp. 153–57). But liberals on domestic welfare expenditures were often conservatives on civil liberties, civil rights, and foreign economic aid. The Detroit study also concluded that liberalism on welfare, primarily found among the working or economically underprivileged classes, was essentially a matter of perceived economic self-interest. See Gerhard Lenski, *The Religious Factor* (Garden City, N.Y.: Doubleday Anchor Books, 1963), p. 209.

their income tax "about right" versus 50 percent who considered it "too high" favored sending food to Communist China if she requested it. Near the end of 1961, 21 percent of those who felt federal funds going into welfare programs were insufficient, contrasted with 11 percent of others who considered them excessive, thought the "U.S. and the West are not doing enough to help less developed countries with financial and technical assistance," while 54 versus 47 percent believed that U.S. interests had been helped by foreign-aid programs in the preceding five years. In 1963 people who approved of unions, who felt that strikes should be permitted in communications industries and who believed that taxes should be cut, federal aid to depressed areas should be increased, and Medicare should be passed were six or more percentage points more favorably disposed toward foreign aid at prevailing or higher magnitudes than those who felt the reverse about these domestic questions. Similar correlations between thinking on economic aid and that on trade unions, Medicare, federal responsibility for full employment and fair living standards, big business versus big labor versus big government, how much the federal government ought to do for individuals, and the overall size and power of central government were apparent in late 1964 and early 1965.

Federal expenditures on public works and on aid to education, especially the latter, have been partial exceptions to some of these observations. The well-to-do and the well-educated have been as supportive of expenditures on highways, dams, flood control, and other public works as the economically and educationally underprivileged, whereas the higher the income and education, the greater the opposition to most of the rest of the New Deal, aid to dependent children, Medicare, progressive income taxes, etc. Moreover, support for federal aid to education has had somewhat the reverse relationship with income and education: the higher-income and, especially, better-educated groups have been for the most part somewhat more supportive of aid to education than have the lower economic and educational segments of the population.

Therefore approval of public works has had a rather consistent, though low, positive correlation with approval of multilateral cooperation, at least since World War II. Supporters of expanded aid to education—including higher taxes if needed for this—have been clearly more favorably disposed to the Marshall Plan, economic aid to the Middle East under the Eisenhower Doctrine, the prevailing or a higher magnitiude of nonmilitary aid to less-developed areas, and the like than have opponents of more active assistance to American education throughout the postwar period (Table 8–4).

Views on overall federal spending and fiscal policy have also had some connections with opinions about foreign aid. Thus those who would cut significantly the overall federal budget, governmental expenditures generally, the general tax level, or (to a lesser degree) the national debt "even if it means putting off important things that need to be done" have been consistently less supportive of foreign aid, especially economic aid, throughout all administrations, than have fiscal liberals on such issues. However, even these differences seldom exceeded fifteen percentage points, and they were typically less. Furthermore, attitudes toward general budgetary policy, taxes, and the like had virtually no connection with opinions on most other foreign policy matters (Table 8–4).

These generalizations—little or no connection between most domestic and most international attitudes during the New Deal, a slight increase in correlation under President Truman, followed by disappearance of most of this weak association under President Eisenhower, in turn succeeded by a reappearance of linkages during the Kennedy and Johnson years, and a positive connection of support for aid to education with approval of international cooperation—apply equally to Catholics and Protestants. Thus in the mid-sixties Catholics and Protestants who favored Medicare, federal responsibility for jobs and living standards, trade unions, federal aid to education, and a strong central government active in the society and economy generally were typically somewhat more favorable to foreign developmental assistance, negotiations and trade with communist countries, and membership of Mainland China in the UN than were their respective coreligionists who opposed these domestic policies and programs (Table 8–5).[12]

12. Table 8–5 and the discussion here below include only white Christian groups. Negroes, consistently more liberal than whites on domestic welfare, economic, and, of course, racial issues, have not been any more favorable than whites to multilateral cooperation until relatively recently. Nonetheless, most of the generalizations to follow apply to Negro as well as to white Christians. Views on most international questions had very little connection with those on most domestic questions among Negroes until the 1960's. During the Kennedy and Johnson administrations the minority of Negroes who opposed Medicare, antipoverty programs, public works, federal aid to housing and education, and, especially, desegregation were on the average more conservative than the Negro majority which favored these programs about foreign policy as well—more isolationist, more inclined to emphasize military means and hard-line policies vis-à-vis communist powers, and less supportive of foreign economic aid.

However, even by the mid-sixties international attitudinal differences between supporters and opponents of federal interventions in the economy and society among both Christian groups were quite limited. Moreover, even when such domestic attitudes are held constant, Catholics were somewhat more liberal on these international issues than Protestants. For example, Catholics who favored Medicare and felt the federal government was not too powerful were more inclined to approve of economic aid, trade with communist countries, and membership in the UN for the People's Republic of China than Protestants who likewise favored Medicare and thought the government not too powerful.

Thus the consistently more liberal Catholic than Protestant thinking on such domestic issues had little or no bearing on international attitudinal differences between the two Christian groups before the late 1950's. The more widespread domestic liberalism of Catholics than Protestants in the sixties accounted in part for the more prevalent Catholic support for multilateral collaboration, but certainly not for all, or even most, of these international attitudinal differences.

CIVIL RIGHTS

Jews have likewise been consistently more equalitarian about the Negro in American society than either of the two major Christian groups since the early national surveys on the subject before Pearl Harbor. Catholics have been less racist or segregationist than Protestants, even when Negroes—mostly Protestants—have been included in the Protestant statistics (Table 8–6).

The higher average level of education prevailing among Jews than Christians and the disproportionately large number of Protestants residing in the South account only for a limited part of these interreligious differences in attitudes toward Negroes. Even when such factors have been controlled, Jews have been more equalitarian and liberal in their racial thinking than white Catholics, and they in turn than white Protestants. Thus college-graduated Jews have harbored more liberal opinions about Negroes (and other minorities) than college-educated Catholics. The latter, although more like Protestants who finished college than like equally educated Jews in their racial views, have been more supportive than their Protestant educational peers of civil rights, desegregation, and the

like.[13] Southern white Protestants have been markedly more conservative in this field than Northern white Protestants, Northern white Catholics, or even Southern white Catholics. Nevertheless, white Catholics
in each of the four major geographical regions have been more liberal
about desegregation than white Protestants in the same region.[14]

These observations apparently apply over virtually the entire range
of race relations and the controversial actions and proposals for action
by the federal government since 1937—the barring of a former Ku
Klux Klan member from serving on the Supreme Court; a possible
antilynching law; desegregation of buses, trains, and other interstate
transportation; the 1954 Supreme Court school desegregation decision;
equal job opportunities; open housing; sit-ins, freedom rides, and other
Negro demonstrations; federal intervention to enforce desegregation in
the South and elsewhere; the opening of hotels, restaurants, and other
public accommodations to Negroes; the right of Negroes to vote; the
successive civil rights laws; and willingness to elect competent Negroes
to important public offices (Table 8–6).

Views on race relations during most of the period since 1936 have
had little or no connection with reactions to expanded federal intervention in the economy and society—social security, old age benefits,
medical care, public works, progressive income taxation, and so on.
Only approval of more aid to education has been more or less consistently positively correlated with racial liberalism—understandably
so, since both have been associated with higher education. Seldom
have white supporters of transfers of wealth from the haves to the have-
nots at home been significantly more equalitarian about Negroes than
opponents of such economic programs. In fact, so-called liberalism on
such matters has in some instances been negatively related to racial
equalitarianism among white Americans.

The principal explanation of this phenomenon has likewise been
the differential relationships of these two syndromes of attitudes with
socioeconomic status and, particularly, education. Whereas the potential
recipients of transfers of wealth and services—mostly poorly educated
as well as economically deprived—have been the more apt to favor

13. For instance, a national study of 9,064 college graduates in 1948 by the
Bureau of Applied Social Research of Columbia University discovered that 75 percent
of Jewish college graduates, contrasted with but 42 percent of their Catholic and 35
percent of their Protestant counterparts, held basically tolerant, equalitarian, or
liberal views on Negroes and other minorities. Havemann and West, p. 193.

14. For further analysis of this phenomenon in the South, see Hero, *Southerner*,
pp. 453–54 and 459–60.

such transfers, the educationally privileged—largely also more prosperous—have harbored the more liberal views on most aspects of race relations.[15]

It is therefore not surprising that racial liberals have on the average been somewhat more interested in, aware of, and informed about world affairs than segregationists, whereas liberals on most domestic economic and social issues have been slightly less attentive to and knowledgeable about this field than conservatives on the same questions. Moreover, it is comprehensible that liberalism on race—concentrated among more or less the same white demographic groups as liberalism on foreign policy—has been more closely linked with international liberalism than has liberalism on most other domestic issues.

Correlations between racial and international attitudes have been somewhat higher in the white South than outside that region, a phenomenon perhaps due mainly to two factors: (1) The race issue has been more directly pressing in the South, and racial attitudes there have been more conservative and probably more strongly and emotionally held. (2) Particularly in areas of plantation traditions and large ratios of Negroes to whites, liberalism on race has been not only more atypical, or more extreme, among whites than in the white North, but also more limited to the better-educated and socially privileged.

In fact, racial views had little, if any, connection with international opinions outside the South before U.S. entry into the Second World War (Table 8–7). In January 1940, for instance, Northern whites who favored passage of a federal antilynching law did not differ from their neighbors who opposed it in their sentiments about lending money to Finland to help her defend herself against the U.S.S.R., extension of the Reciprocal Trade Agreements Act, and whether the U.S. Constitution should be amended "to require a national vote before Congress could draft men for war overseas." But among white Southerners 74 percent of the minority who favored an antilynching law contrasted with but 65 percent of the majority who opposed it would have lent to Finland, 28 versus 23 percent thought Congress should give Secretary Hull the power to make more reciprocal trade treaties, and, conversely, 52 versus 59 percent favored such a Constitutional amendment.

15. Such was apparently also the case in Greater Detroit among whites in the late fifties. Lenski, p. 209, found that respondents who were liberal on domestic welfare were often conservative on civil rights and civil liberties. The working class was more liberal than the middle class on welfare, but more conservative on civil rights and civil liberties.

However, as pressures for desegregation mounted after the war, and especially following the Supreme Court school desegregation decision of 17 May 1954, linkages between racial and international attitudes gradually became more pronounced in both the North and the South. Segregationists became consistently less enthusiastic than integrationists and racial equalitarians about foreign economic aid and other non-military multilateral cooperation and less optimistic about our ability to avoid major war and to reach peaceful settlements of disagreements with the communist powers. Racial conservatives more than racial liberals or "moderates" came to harbor isolationist or neo-isolationist thinking and to emphasize military over diplomatic, economic, or other means of achieving basic foreign-policy objectives—through either unilateral intervention by the U.S. defense establishment or collective-security arrangements with "reliable" allies.

Thus, white segregationists have been about as supportive as integrationists, in both the North and the South, of U.S. participation in NATO, the stationing of U.S. armed forces abroad, military aid for U.S. allies, and an expensive national defense establishment (Table 8–7). However, as early as 1949 whites who approved of a federal antilynching law, felt that poll taxes should be abolished, and agreed that interstate transportation should be desegregated were consistently more favorably inclined to the Marshall Plan and to expanding assistance to Japan than were compatriots who disagreed with them on these racial questions. Seven months after the Supreme Court school-desegregation decision, significantly larger proportions of the whites in both regions who approved of that ruling than of compatriots who disapproved would continue economic aid to neutralist countries and agreed that the U.S. should "give strong support" to the UN. Conversely, the segregationists were somewhat more apt to anticipate another world war, this time with the communists, within five years, to favor the suggested blockade of Communist China, and to approve of the proposed Bricker amendment "to curb the treaty-making power of the President."

During the late fifties and sixties, whites in both the North and the South who favored desegregation of schools, jobs, housing, transportation, hotels, etc., who felt the federal government should do more to help Negroes and that Negroes should have more "power" in the country than they had, or who approved of the civil rights acts that were before the Congress or had just been passed were consistently more liberal about nonmilitary aid than were racial conservatives—readier to feel that the U.S. "should help poorer countries," including even those "less against communism than we," to be "in general for foreign aid," to approve of it at prevailing magnitudes or higher levels, and to be willing to pay higher taxes for economic assistance. Although even racial liberals were more inclined to emphasize Latin America than either Asia or Africa in our aid programs, the white minorities who would give these two predominantly nonwhite continents equal priority or precedence to that accorded to Latin America were distinctly larger among the racial liberals and moderates than among the segregationists (Table 8–7).

These differences in international perspectives between segregationist and equalitarian whites help considerably to account for the divergence of the white South from the rest of the country, particularly since the mid-fifties, toward lesser support for development assistance, liberalization of relations with communist countries, and the like. The white integrationist minority in the South has harbored international views for the most part indistinguishable from those of Northern white racial liberals. Moreover, Northern white segregationists have held foreign-policy preferences very similar to those of racially conservative Southern whites (Table 8–7). North-South differences on world issues have thus been closely connected with the greater prevalence of segregationist sentiment in the South.

Interreligious differences with respect to foreign policy have likewise been increasingly connected with differential racial attitudes. Prior to Pearl Harbor, Southern white Protestants who favored the proposed federal antilynching legislation were several percentage points more likely to approve of lending money to Finland and extending the Reciprocal Trade Agreements Act and to oppose the suggested Constitutional amendment requiring a plebiscite before draftees could be sent overseas than were their Southern coreligionists who disapproved of such a federal law. However, differences were small enough to be due primarily to educational factors rather than to any causal or ideological linkages of racial and international attitudes. Moreover, views on antilynching legislation had virtually no statistical connection with opinions on these foreign-policy matters among either white Catholics or white Protestants outside the South. Furthermore, Southern white Protestants were at least somewhat more favorable to international involvements in these fields than were either white Catholics or white Protestants outside the South regardless of their respective racial views. Thus, even

Southern white Protestant opponents of antilynching legislation were somewhat more favorable to these international involvements than Northern Protestant or, especially, Catholic whites who supported it.

By the mid-fifties, however, racial liberals among Catholic, Northern Protestant, and Southern Protestant whites alike had become at least somewhat more supportive of economic aid to the less-developed world, including aid to nonaligned countries, than segregationists and racial conservatives (Table 8–8). Such differences seem to have widened further during the ensuing five to ten years among all three religious groups. By the 1960's integrationists were consistently and clearly more favorably disposed than segregationists to foreign economic aid as a general proposition, to maintaining prevailing aid budgets or increasing them, even if such increases would entail higher personal taxes for them, to expanded trade with the Soviet Union and eastern Europe, and to UN membership for Mainland China. Racial liberals within each religious group had also become more inclined to consider helping the less-developed world to be an obligation for wealthier countries and less apt to be basically dissatisfied with the principle of aiding such countries economically (Table 8–8).

In fact, Catholic, Northern Protestant, and Southern Protestant white racial liberals differed hardly at all from one another in their international thinking; each group of them was more liberal in international thinking than racial conservatives, regardless of the latter's religious preference or region of residence (Table 8–8). Likewise, racial conservatives seem to have harbored similar international opinions, again regardless of their religion. Thus Southern white Protestant racial liberals, like other Protestant or Catholic integrationists, were more favorable to liberalization of relations with the communists, including those in Peking, than were either Northern white Protestant, Southern white Protestant, or even Catholic racial conservatives. When racial views were similar, religious preferences had no connection with international attitudes. The more liberal foreign-policy preferences among Catholics than white Protestants—even than Northern white Protestants—in the sixties were thus closely connected with the less widespread racism among the Catholic population.

Thus the generally more liberal views of Catholic than Protestant whites on most domestic economic, welfare, and related issues have had little connection with the former's more liberal international thinking in recent years. On the other hand, the more equalitarian racial sentiments prevailing among white Catholics have been rather closely associated with their more widespread support for foreign economic aid, expanded negotiation and other nonmilitary efforts to lessen tensions with communist regimes, and more liberal foreign policies and programs in general.

CHAPTER 9. CLERGY, THE DENOMINATIONS, THEOLOGY, AND CHURCH INVOLVEMENT

Minorities among the leaderships of the Roman Catholic Church, the National Council of Churches (N.C.C.) and its predecessor, the Federal Council of Churches (F.C.C.), and the major Protestant denominations affiliated with them disapprove of the uttering of pronouncements by these bodies in support of particular policy alternatives toward such controversial issues as foreign aid, arms control, relations with the communist world, and membership of the Peking regime in the UN.[1] Others who do not oppose such public statements in principle disagree with the policies recommended by them. Some well-informed churchmen in foreign affairs have criticized some of the utterances by Protestant agencies as utopian, morally absolutist, pacifist, or otherwise politically naive or unrealistic.[2]

Nevertheless, Protestant religious institutions in the United States have together since the mid-1930's devoted more resolutions, proclamations, policy statements, background papers, and other public utterances to international affairs, peace, and American foreign policy than to any other area of public policy.[3] Particularly since the Second World War have the F.C.C., the N.C.C., and the main-line Protestant denominations publicly advanced opinions about most of the more important issues of American foreign policy of the time. Although their views expressed to their own members, to the federal Executive

1. E.g., Paul Ramsey, *Who Speaks for the Church?* (New York: Abingdon Press, 1967). For a discussion of the range of disagreement with the thesis that the churches should express themselves on such issues, see Ralph B. Potter, "The Structure of Certain American Christian Responses to the Nuclear Dilemma, 1958–1963" (Th.D. dissertation, Harvard University Divinity School, 1965), pp. 432 ff.

2. E.g., Ernest W. Lefever, "Protestants and United States Foreign Policy, 1925–54: A Study of the Response" (Ph.D. dissertation, Yale University, 1954), and Donald T. Sparks, "The Influence of Official Protestant Church Groups on the Formulation and Conduct of American Foreign Policy" (Ph.D. dissertation, University of Chicago, 1954), pp. 71–91. This criticism has been less frequent (and less justified) in more recent years, at least on the part of specialists in international affairs.

3. With the possible exception among denominations of strong Calvinist traditions of attention to alcoholic prohibition, gambling, and other aspects of personal behavior. The discussion of public stances of the churches below (pp. 159–65) is derived from the results of a systematic inventory of research, published materials, and unpublished theses and other documents performed under the direction of the author in 1969. Abstracts of relevant materials, together with a critical analysis of their content, are available in Alfred O. Hero, Jr., "Communication of World Affairs Within and By American Churches: Bibliography and Extracts," mimeographed (Boston, Mass.: World Peace Foundation, 1969), 234 pp.

and Congress, and to the American public generally have not been homogeneous, their overall tone has been clear enough to those who have paid attention to these utterances.

During the great debate following the First World War over ratification of the Versailles Treaty, U.S. participation in the League of Nations, and more active involvement of the country in international affairs generally, the F.C.C., its major member churches, and the non-fundamentalist religious press were actively identified with the internationalists.[4] However, by the mid and late 1930's they tended in varying degrees toward neutrality and pacifism. Though they deplored successive Axis aggressions and trends toward World War II and argued for U.S. participation in international agencies for the peaceful settlement of controversies between nations, they opposed U.S. involvement insofar as it might draw the country into military action. They echoed the concerns of the Nye committee that the munitions industry and high finance might lead this country into another unnecessary war and in general reflected the prevailing secular view that America should stay out of disputes beyond the Western Hemisphere. The Society of Friends, the Church of the Brethren, the Mennonites, and (to a lesser extent) the Methodists were the most unreservedly pacifist, but other denominations also reflected their sentiments to varying degrees.[5] The

4. James L. Lancaster, "The Protestant Churches and the Fight for Ratification of the Versailles Treaty," *Public Opinion Quarterly* 31, no. 4 (Winter 1967–68), pp. 597–619; Dormier A. Lund, "The Peace Movement Among the Major Protestant Churches" (Ph.D. dissertation, University of Nebraska, 1956), pp. 6–22; and Robert Moats Miller, "An Inquiry into the Social Attitudes of American Protestantism, 1919–1939" (Ph.D. dissertation, Northwestern University, 1955), pp. 712–72.

5. For the pre-Pearl Harbor stances of the F.C.C. and its member churches, see Lefever, chap. 3; Sparks, pp. 71–91; Lund, pp. 22–219; Miller, pp. 726–63; John P. Hummon, "Protestants and Point Four: The Churches' Response to U.S. Programs of Aid to the Less Developed Countries" (Ph.D. dissertation, University of Michigan, 1958), pp. 28–31; Lucian C. Marquis, "Political Thought of Protestant Churches and Sects in the United States, 1928–1953" (Ph.D. dissertation, University of California, Los Angeles, 1959), pp. 71 ff.; and Elsie Harper, "The Churches and Foreign Policy," *Social Action* 23, no. 8 (April 1957), pp. 8 ff. For comparative content of the Protestant, Catholic, and Jewish presses on the rise of the Nazis, see Frederick Kohlman Wentz, "The Reaction of the Religious Press in America to the Emergence of Nazism" (Ph.D. dissertation, Yale University, 1954). Ronald E. Magden, "Attitudes of the American Religious Press Toward Soviet Russia" (Ph.D. dissertation, University of Washington, 1964), provides a content analysis of forty-seven Protestant, Catholic, and Jewish periodicals with respect to the Soviet Union during this period.— The postures of the Presbyterian Church, U.S.A., are examined in Gordon L. Shull, "The Presbyterian Church in American Politics" (Ph.D. dissertation, University of Illinois, 1955), pp. 13–24, and Edward E. Brewster, "Patterns of Social Concern in Four American Protestant Denominations" (Ph.D. dissertation, Boston University, 1952), esp. pp. 421–79. The public stances of the Methodists, among the

Episcopalians were a partial exception; apparently they felt that the moral issues were not evident enough to warrant many clear-cut positions by their denomination on complex international issues.[6] Though the Southern Baptist Convention and its state-level counterparts for the most part continued to support the League of Nations, U.S. adherence to the Permanent Court of International Justice, American rearmament, and assistance to the opponents of the Axis short of war, and eschewed pacifist arguments, even their stances were not entirely immune to neutralist thinking.[7]

---

most active denominations in this field, are discussed in Brewster, pp. 421–79; Sparks, p. 91; E. Franklin Carwithen, "The Attitudes of the Methodist Episcopal Church Toward Peace and War" (Th.D. dissertation, Temple University School of Theology, 1944), chap. 7; Robert P. Lisensky, "Methodism as an Initiator of Social Thought and Action in the Area of World Peace, 1900–1956" (Ph.D. dissertation, Boston University, 1960), pp. 50–60 and 92–98; Jack E. Corbett, "The Peace Education and Action Program of the Methodist Church" (Ph.D. dissertation, The American University, 1967), pp. 4 ff.; Walter G. Muelder, *Methodism and Society in the 20th Century* (New York: Abingdon Press, 1961), esp. pp. 42–43, 79–83, and 148–52; James W. Gladden, "The Methodist Church and the Problem of War and Peace: An Analysis in Social Understanding" (Ph.D. dissertation, University of Pittsburgh, 1945), pp. 1–132; John H. Huber, Jr., "A History of the Methodist Federation for Social Action" (Ph.D. dissertation, Boston University, 1949), pp. 120–231; Frank J. Mitchell, "The Virginia Methodist Conference and Social Issues in the Twentieth Century" (Ph.D. dissertation, Duke University, 1962), pp. 238–62. Comparable analysis of the international orientations of the Congregationalists may be found in Cyrus R. Pangborn, "Free Churches and Social Change: A Critical Study of the Council for Social Action of the Congregational Christian Churches of the United States" (Ph.D. dissertation, Columbia University, 1951), pp. 33–62, and Brewster, pp. 421–79. For the stances of the Northern Baptist Convention, see Brewster, pp. 421–79, and Lund, pp. 136 ff. Harold Haas, "The Social Thinking of the United Lutheran Church in America, 1918–1948" (Ph.D. dissertation, Drew University, 1953), pp. 177–208, considers the stances of the United Lutherans and the theological bases underlying them. Henry Lewis Brumbaugh, "Changing Patterns of the Church of the Brethren Toward Certain Social Problems" (Ph.D. dissertation, University of Pittsburgh, 1945), pp. 136–38 and 178–201, considers the international stances of the Brethren during this period. For discussion of the Society of Friends vis-à-vis U.S. foreign policy between the two world wars, see William Darwin Swanson White, "Quaker Pacifism in the United States, 1919–42, with Special Reference to Its Relation to Isolationism and Internationalism" (Ph.D. dissertation, Columbia University, 1954).

6. Lund, pp. 140 ff., and M. Moran Weston, "Social Policy of the Episcopal Church in the Twentieth Century" (Ph.D. dissertation, Columbia University, 1954), pp. 3, 97, 283–84, 326–35, 447–500, 513–22 and 533–73.

7. John Lee Eighmy, "The Social Conscience of Southern Baptists from 1900 to the Present as Reflected in Their Organized Life" (Ph.D. dissertation, University of Missouri, 1959), pp. 59–62 and 97–100; Stanley Owen White, "Southern Baptists' Attitudes on War and Peace" (Fort Worth, Texas: Th.D. dissertation, Southwestern Baptist Theological Seminary, 1965), pp. 4–83; George D. Kelsey, "The Social Thought of Contemporary Southern Baptists" (Ph.D. dissertation, Yale University, 1946), pp. 23–104; Edward Earl Joiner, "Southern Baptists and Church-State Relations, 1945–1954" (Louisville, Ky.: Th.D. dissertation, Southern Baptist Theological Seminary, 1959), pp. 268–70; and Lund, pp. 132 ff.

The F.C.C. and its successor, the N.C.C., most major Protestant denominations—including the Southern Baptist Convention—and most of the Protestant press rejected isolationism during the Second World War and have since continued to argue for active U.S. participation in world affairs. With few exceptions, the F.C.C., the N.C.C., their affiliated denominations, and most national Protestant or ecumenical periodicals have generally advocated multilateral, internationalist, or liberal post-war foreign policies.[8] They actively supported U.S. membership in the United Nations in 1945 and thereafter favored close American co-operation with the world body and continued American efforts to strengthen it. They were vociferous supporters of emergency relief to war-torn areas and, shortly thereafter, the Marshall Plan and other assistance to economic reconstruction. Although their prewar pacifism and alleged moral absolutism—even that of the Methodists—became tempered by "realism" and they have not been of one mind on issues such as arms control, disarmament, and nuclear weapons, they have generally argued for deemphasizing military means in American foreign

8. For the postwar stances of the F.C.C. and N.C.C., see Lefever, chaps. 4 and 5; Sparks, pp. 92–102; Harper; Marquis, pp. 116 ff.; and Kenneth Nelson Vines, "The Role of the Federal Council of Churches of Christ in America in the Formation of American National Policy" (Ph.D. dissertation, University of Minnesota, 1953), pp. 135–58. Methodist positions are described in Sparks, pp. 71–91; Corbett, pp. 4 ff.; Muelder, pp. 177–95, 244–48, 300–306, and 368–80; Huber, pp. 278–81; Lisensky, pp. 71 ff.; and Mitchell, pp. 279–91. Sparks also examines the postures of the Presbyterians, U.S.A., the Episcopalians, and the American Baptists through 1950, while John R. Warner, Jr., "Religious Affiliation as a Factor in Voting Records of Members of the 89th Congress" (Ph.D. dissertation, Boston University, 1968), pp. 96–123 and 159–60, considers the themes of pronouncements between 1960 and 1965 by the N.C.C., the United Presbyterians, the Episcopalians, the United Church of Christ, the Methodists, and the American Baptists. For the stances of the Presbyterian Church, U.S.A., see also Shull, pp. 24–117. For the public orientations of the Congregationalists, the Episcopalians, and the United Lutherans in the early postwar period, see, respectively, Pangborn, pp. 64–69; Weston, pp. 327–65, 503–12, and 523–73; and Haas, pp. 211–20. —Robert C. Batchelder, *The Irreversible Decision, 1939–1950* (Boston: Houghton Mifflin, 1962), discusses the range of opinion among the intellectual and organizational leaders of the main-line Protestant denominations and of the Catholic Church on nuclear energy and weapons through 1950, and Potter continues this discussion into the early 1960's. Hummon examines the postures of the F.C.C., the N.C.C., eight of their major affiliated denominations, and of the Friends' Committee on National Legislation on assistance to the underdeveloped world, through 1957. For a discussion of the behavior of religious groups, including the Roman Catholics, with respect to the proposed Peace Corps in the early 1960's, see George R. La Noue, "Church-State Relations in the Federal Policy Process" (Ph.D. dissertation, Yale University, 1966). The stances of the United Presbyterian Church and its predecessors on foreign aid are examined in *A Survey of Attitudes on Foreign Aid* (Philadelphia: Office of Church and Society, Board of Christian Education, United Presbyterians Church, U.S.A., 1968), pp. 3 and 29–39.

policy, for peaceful solutions to violent and potentially violent situations, and for more vigorous efforts by the U.S. government to achieve international agreements to limit, if not eliminate, armaments. Influential elements among the national church leadership have demanded outlawry of the use of nuclear armaments, especially against civilians, and some, such as the Methodists, have accorded disarmament and peace a priority emphasis in social action.

The major Protestant denominations and their ecumenical bodies welcomed decolonization and argued for more active cooperation with the resulting newly independent, largely nonaligned regimes in the less-developed world. They advocated expanded nonmilitary aid, greater emphasis on humanitarian and developmental objectives of such aid and its divorce from short-term U.S. political and security interests, and more aid through multilateral institutions. They publicly favored broadened negotiations with communist governments, admission of Mainland China into the UN, and liberalized trade, immigration, and intercultural policies.

Although the Protestant national elite was not united on U.S. Vietnam policy in the mid and late 1960's, open public supporters of the gradual escalation of the war during the Johnson administration, particularly the bombing of North Vietnam, were very few. Most publicized statements urged greater emphasis on negotiation and less on military action, while active, articulate minorities of the Protestant leadership—such as those active in Clergy and Laymen Concerned About Vietnam—advocated U.S. withdrawal.

A minority of vocal Christian "realists," led originally by Reinhold Niebuhr, have accorded more importance to the imperfectibility of sinful man and have expressed views generally less optimistic, "utopian," and pacifist with respect to the communist world, less enthusiastic about and less convinced of the feasibility of achieving world government and more supportive of a significant role for U.S. military power and collective security than the N.C.C., F.C.C., and most of their affiliated denominations.[9] However, they too have approved of foreign policies at least as liberal as those advocated by the President and his senior foreign-policy advisors. Moreover, they also pressed for deescalation

9. See, for instance, Reinhold Niebuhr, *Christian Realism and Political Problems* (New York: Scribner's, 1953), esp. chaps. 1 and 2; Lefever, chaps. 6 and 7; Brunner, pp. 191–305; Lund, pp. 119 ff.; and Walter E. Hudgins, "The Changing Conception of Pacifism in American Protestantism of the 20th Century with Special Reference to the Critique of Reinhold Niebuhr" (Ph.D. dissertation, Duke University, 1957).

of American military involvement in Vietnam in the mid and late 1960's.

The Catholic Church began to articulate forceful positions on most of these controversial issues later than its Protestant counterparts. Its pronouncements have typically been less specific about U.S. policies and programs than most Protestant ones. However, like the Protestant utterances of the period, leading Catholic sources either questioned the use of atomic bombs on Japan or condemned it outright,[10] and continued thereafter to oppose future use of strategic nuclear weapons which would kill or harm large numbers of civilians.[11] By the late fifties the traditional Catholic approval of the just war had become severely attenuated, especially insofar as it might include use of strategic nuclear weapons. Moreover, since that time successive papal encyclicals and statements by the pope, senior Vatican officials, and influential American Catholic leaders have repeatedly voiced support for the UN, peace, expanded assistance to underdeveloped areas, and other aspects of world cooperation. At least implied criticism of U.S. military involvement in Vietnam was apparent by the late 1960's among a number of popularly visible Catholic figures, including the pope himself.

The principle exceptions have been the Missouri and Wisconsin Synods of the Lutherans,[12] the Southern Baptists, and, particularly, a number of relatively small fundamentalist sects. These groups have stressed the saving of individual souls, evangelism and conversion, revivalism, and literal interpretation of the Bible rather than the social implications of the gospel. In general, they have rejected both ecumenicism and modern theological liberalism. For the most part they have not advanced many public statements on foreign-policy issues.

However, a number of fundamentalist spokesmen have publicly differed from the expressed views of the F.C.C., the N.C.C., and their affiliated denominations with respect to international affairs throughout

10. Batchelder, pp. 113–15.
11. Ibid., pp. 170–71, 241, 249, and Potter, pp. 11 ff.
12. Different from most other religious groups which have eschewed the social-gospel movement and ecumenicism, however, these theologically conservative Lutheran denominations have not been fundamentalists or Biblical literalists in the meaning prevalent among fundamentalist sects and the Southern Baptists. They never supported revivalism, alcoholic prohibitionism, blue laws, or attacks on such worldly amusements as gambling, dancing, and moderate consumption of alcohol. See Ralph Luther Moellering, "The Missouri Synod and Social Problems: A Theological and Sociological Analysis of Reactions to War, Industrial Tensions, and Race Relations" (Ph.D. dissertation, Harvard University, 1964).

both the interwar and the postwar periods.[13] They criticized the proposed League of Nations during the 1919–20 debate as a delusion, opposed U.S. adherence to the Permanent Court of International Justice, argued for even more stringent limitations on immigration than those in force since the mid 1920's, and disagreed with the pacifist overtones of the F.C.C., the Methodists, and other main-line Protestant denominations. Prominent fundamentalist clergymen and the leadership of such fundamentalist groups as the National Association of Evangelicals, the American Council of Christian Churches, and the Christian Crusade during the years since 1945 have argued against surrenders of U.S. sovereignty to "world government," advocated generally conservative, unilateralist, or hard-line policies vis-à-vis the U.S.S.R., Mainland China, and "atheistic communism" generally, opposed aid to nonaligned governments, favored closer cooperation with Nationalist China and other conservative regimes in Asia, Africa, and Latin America, and disagreed with F.C.C. and N.C.C. international stances on most issues other than diplomatic relations with the Vatican (which they all opposed).

Moreover, although some fundamentalist groups publicly supported only certain of these views while they moderated or even eschewed others,[14] most religious spokesmen who have advocated such policies

13. John H. Redekop, *The American Far Right: A Case Study of Billy James Hargis and the Christian Crusade* (Grand Rapids, Mich.: Eerdmans, 1968), pp. 20–26, 51–73 and 145–51; Sparks, pp. 282–83; Lancaster, pp. 599–600, 603; Lund, p. 132; Moellering, pp. 136–38; William G. McLaughlin, "Piety and the American Character," *American Quarterly* 17, no. 2 (Summer 1965), pp. 171–77; and the *New York Times*, 26 Jan. 1969. La Noue, pp. 238–40, noted that the National Association of Evangelicals, consisting of some forty small, largely fundamentalist denominations with some 2,000,000 members, was among the few religious groups highly skeptical of the Peace Corps when that proposal was being discussed in 1961.

14. Thus the Southern Baptist Convention itself or the reports of its Social Service Commission (since 1947, Christian Life Commission) supported U.S. membership in the League of Nations during the public debate of 1919–20, in the Permanent Court of International Justice in the 1920's and 1930's, and in the United Nations in 1945; approved the Kellogg-Briand Pact in 1928–29; and opposed the proposed Universal Military Training Act in the early postwar period. Official Southern Baptist statements since the Second World War have supported active U.S. participation in international institutions; negotiations to reduce armaments, eliminate nuclear weapons, and lessen tensions rather than primary reliance on military means in meeting threats of international communism; and economic aid to less-developed countries since President Truman's Point Four proposal. Moreover, minorities became increasingly articulate within the Southern Baptist Convention in arguing for more active and liberal stances after the Second World War and especially during the 1960's. See Eighmy, p. 174 ff.; Joiner, pp. 269–70; White, pp. 70–83 and 213 ff.; Rogers M. Smith, "A Study of Southern Baptists and the Relationship of Church and State, 1918–1952" (Fort Worth, Texas: Th.D. dissertation, Southern Baptist Theological Seminary, 1953), pp. 120–32; and the report by George Dugan on the annual meeting of the Southern Baptist Convention in Houston in 1968 in the *New York Times*, 5 June 1968.

have been associated with theologically conservative or fundamentalist bodies. At least among the articulate leadership, theological conservatism has frequently been associated with international conservatism, theological liberalism and interest in the social implications of the gospel with approval of international accommodation and cooperation.

To what extent have these relationships between theological orientations and international attitudes prevailed among clergymen and laymen at the local level? Have local priests and ministers and rank-and-file church members of the religious denominations which have taken active public positions supportive of multilateral cooperation differed significantly in their own views from adherents of other denominations or sects whose leaders have either taken no stands on these issues, or have expressed more conservative foreign-policy preferences? How have clergymen differed in their international opinions from laymen in their own denomination? What effects have the official pronouncements of the churches and the attitudes of local priests and ministers had on their members in these fields, particularly on their more active members, who have gone to church regularly or frequently and who have been relatively closely identified with their churches and clergy? To these questions we now direct our attention.

NATIONAL CHURCH LEADERS, CLERGY, AND LAYMEN

Non-Fundamentalist Clergy Considerably More Liberal Than Parishioners

Ordained clergymen within the denominations affiliated with the N.C.C. have consistently been more interested and better informed in world affairs, more aware of the pronouncements of their denominations and of the N.C.C. in that field, more inclined to agree with the policies advocated by those utterances, and generally more liberal or multilateralist in their views than have their parishioners. In general, the more elevated the level of their ecclesiastical positions within their denominational structures, the more knowledgeable, interested, and liberal their international inclinations. Nevertheless, differences in international behavior between parish clergy and laity have been greater than those between parish ministers and clergymen further up in their denominational hierarchies.

During most of the period since the 1930's the Protestant Episcopal Church has on the whole been more cautious or moderate (or less radical) in the tone of its public statements on world affairs than the F.C.C., the N.C.C., and such denominations as the Presbyterians, U.S.A., the Methodists, and the Congregationalists and, later, the merged United Church of Christ. Moreover, the Episcopalians have been less inclined to advocate particular policies on such issues as disarmament, foreign aid, international trade, and relations with communist countries.[15]

Nevertheless, whether or not their church had taken any positions on the issue in question, Episcopal bishops of the early fifties were somewhat more liberal than their parish priests on foreign aid, conscientious objection, immigration, the long-term desirability of world government, and the UN. (Table 9–1).[16] Moreover, both bishops and parish clergy were sharply more inclined than their rank-and-file laymen to agree that (1) the UN had been worth the money the U.S. had spent on it, (2) it would be all right for U.S. troops to serve under officers of another country appointed by the UN, (3) it would be good if the UN were someday replaced by some kind of world government, (4) the U.S. had not admitted too many refugees since World War II, (5) the immigration quota system should be liberalized, (6) the U.S. should help India, Britain, West Germany, Iran, Japan, and African areas to get on their feet economically, (7) the U.S. should spend money to help underdeveloped countries to raise living standards, and (8) Episcopalians should recognize the right of conscientious objectors to refuse to bear arms and had a moral obligation to give them financial and other assistance (Table 9–1). Both bishops and priests were much more aware than parishioners of the official stands of the Protestant Episcopal Church and the N.C.C. and considerably more inclined to agree with them.

By the mid-sixties the United Presbyterian Church and its predecessors had over two decades repeatedly expressed concern about the problems of the less-developed world and its need for larger-scale assistance, generally liberalized terms of aid, and trade policies more favorable

15. Sparks, p. 91, and Warner, pp. 108–9 and 160. Doubtless related to this phenomenon has been the more widespread sentiment among Episcopal clergymen than those of other major denominations affiliated with the N.C.C. that their denomination and its leaders have been too conservative in public affairs and social action. "The Clergy Views the National Council of Churches" (Report of the Bureau of Applied Social Research, Columbia University, 1960), pp. 111–19.

16. The Episcopal Church had enunciated an official stance supportive of the UN in 1949 and another, stronger one, shortly before the survey. See Charles Y. Glock, Benjamin B. Ringer, and Earl R. Babbie, *To Comfort and To Challenge* (Berkeley: Univ. of California Press, 1967), pp. 143–44. However, at that time it had not recently taken comparable stands on the other international issues included in the survey.

to it on the part of industrial countries. Its General Assembly reaffirmed in 1965 strong endorsement for expanded economic aid, progressive increase in the use of multinational channels, emphasis on economic development rather than on short-term U.S. political or strategic interests, longer-term authorizations, more grants rather than loans, and more programs of study and education to help Presbyterians understand such matters.[17] Nevertheless, parish ministers of the denomination were clearly both better informed and more liberal in their thinking about virtually all aspects of aid in 1966–67 than were even their active lay elders who attended presbytery meetings (Table 9–2). Such was the case whether or not their denomination had spoken out on the particular feature of aid in question.

Thus, 61 percent of Presbyterian clergy contrasted with but 39 percent of their elders were "in general for foreign aid"; 33 versus 24 percent felt it had been "on the whole successful"; 83 versus but 69 percent considered economic growth one of its important purposes while, conversely, 27 versus 46 percent so considered deterrence of "communist aggression." Whereas but 11 percent of clergymen would give aid "only to countries that agree to stand with us against communism," 30 percent of elders were like-minded. Conversely, 58 versus 44 percent would "continue aid to some countries like India that have not joined us as allies against communism," 43 versus 25 percent would "offer help to countries in need regardless of their stand on communism," and 37 versus 26 percent would "offer help to some communist countries like Yugoslavia and Romania that indicate political independence." Ministers were markedly more supportive of nonmilitary aid to each of fifteen specified underdeveloped countries, ranging in political ideology from Paraguay and Haiti on the right to North Vietnam and Communist China on the left.

Presbyterian clergymen considerably more than their elders favored increasing the magnitude of aid, even if higher taxes were required to do so; channeling more aid through multilateral institutions; and putting more of it on a long-term basis (Table 9–2). Clergy were more inclined to believe that economic aid is more important than military aid; that the growing gap in living standards between the industrialized and less-developed countries should be a matter of great practical and moral

17. Warner, p. 119, and "A Survey of Attitudes on Foreign Aid" (Philadelphia: Office of Church and Society, Board of Christian Education of the United Presbyterian Church, U.S.A., 1968), pp. 3 and 38–39.

concern to Americans; that the U.S. should help such countries raise their economic levels; and that capital aid, technical assistance, the Peace Corps, gifts and sales for local currencies of agricultural products, help in population control, and other forms of aid are "good ideas." The clergymen were likewise more apt to reject the view that the U.S. should spend less on foreign aid in order to have more resources for domestic programs. They were also better informed about aid and the behavior of their own congressmen and senators toward it. Finally, the clergy more than their active elders felt that the less-developed world and U.S. policies and programs pertinent to it should be of major concern to their denomination, that the Presbyterian Church should take public positions on such issues with moral or ethical connotations, and that it should seek to educate its members about such ethical implications.

These generalizations have apparently applied as well in other N.C.C.-affiliated denominations, even when the crucial factor of education is held constant. Thus in 1948, ministers along with teachers and journalists were more liberal than other Protestant college graduates on tariffs and trade, immigration, foreign aid, the UN, and the long-run possibility of negotiating differences with countries whose ideologies are very different from our own.[18] Interviews with ministers and lay people in a number of Southern communities in 1960–62 revealed that these parish clergy were on the average more favorable to developmental and other nonmilitary assistance, reciprocal trade, liberalization of relations with communist powers, and other multinational cooperation than were members of their own congregations, including those of comparable educational and social status.[19] In 1963 and again in 1966, delegates to the Triennial Assembly of the N.C.C. were clearly more approving than average members of their churches of the UN, arms control, loans and grants to underdeveloped nations, and trade with the U.S.S.R. in nonstrategic goods; and in 1966 these delegates were patently more opposed to escalation of U.S. military operations in Vietnam.[20]

18. From retabulations of a survey of 9,064 college graduates for *Time* magazine by the Bureau of Applied Social Research of Columbia University. A study conducted in 1960 by the Bureau of Applied Social Research of a national sample of clergymen in denominations affiliated with the N.C.C. found that 63 percent felt they generally agreed with views expressed in most N.C.C. pronouncements and regarded them as challenging to at least "a fairly considerable extent," presumably including those dealing with world affairs. "The Clergy Views the National Council of Churches," Tables V–5 and VI–2.

19. Hero, *The Southerner and World Affairs*, chap. 12.

20. Surveys reported in *Information Service*, biweekly publication of the Depart-

A survey of readers of Protestant denominational magazines in early 1968 discovered that 57 percent of ministers versus only 28 percent of laymen favored prompt, unconditional termination of the bombing of North Vietnam. Conversely, while only 30 percent of the clergy favored a military push for victory, 60 percent of laymen were of that mind.[21]

Within N.C.C.-affiliated denominations, younger ministers have tended to hold more cosmopolitan or liberal views on world affairs than their elders, particularly those trained prior to the Second World War. Moreover, it appears that the generation in seminaries in the mid and late 1960's will be more internationally liberal or radical than those who graduated a decade before. However, older clergymen who graduated from more liberal, intellectually sophisticated seminaries have held less conservative international views than those prevailing among most of their age group. Differences in international thinking among younger clergymen have on the whole been smaller than among their seniors. Although parish ministers have been less liberal on the average than college and university chaplains, seminary teachers, and, to a lesser extent, clergymen in other roles outside local congregations, at all levels and in all religious callings clergymen have held less conservative opinions on world affairs than even college-educated laymen of comparable age.[22]

Differences in international opinions between priests and laymen in the Roman Catholic Church have perhaps been smaller than among non-fundamentalist Protestants—especially prior to approximately the

---

ment of Research, National Council of Churches of Christ in the U.S.A., vol. 46, no. 9, 6 May 1967, and the correction which appeared in the following issue. In 1966 and 1963, respectively, only 0 percent and 1 percent of Assembly delegates opposed "continued U.S. support of the UN," 4 percent and 2 percent "steps toward disarmament with international control," 5 percent and 2 percent "conclusion of a [the] treaty banning nuclear testing in air, space, and water," 2 percent and 2 percent "loans and grants by the U.S.A. to underdeveloped countries," 3 percent and 4 percent an "increase in U.S. trade with Russia in non-strategic goods." In 1966 52 percent of delegates felt that the U.S. should "begin to withdraw its troops from the war in Vietnam," 24 percent that "the U.S. should carry on its present level of fighting," and only 13 percent that it "should increase the strength of its attacks on North Vietnam." These replies may be compared with responses to similar queries by Protestants generally in tables of Chapters 2 to 4 above and with those of members of denominations affiliated with the N.C.C. in Table 9–5 below.

21. Reported in the *New York Times*, 16 March 1968.

22. Bureau of Applied Social Research survey of clergymen in N.C.C.-affiliated denominations in 1960 referred to above; Jeffrey K. Hadden, *The Gathering Storm in the Churches* (Garden City, N.Y.: Doubleday, 1969), pp. 52, 194–206, and 219; and Keith Bedston and Dwight W. Culver, *Pre-Seminary Education* (Minneapolis: Augsburg, 1965), pp. 227 ff. Data presented by Hadden and the latter two authors indicate that these generalizations apply to such controversial domestic issues as race relations as well.

mid-fifties. However, limited data on clerical versus lay attitudes in the early 1960's in the Catholic Church suggest that parish priests have also been more supportive of multilateral cooperation than their parishioners. Such was the case in 1960–62 in the South.[23] A national survey of Catholic parish priests around the same time found that 40 percent of them would expand the U.S. foreign economic aid program, 24 percent would continue it at prevailing levels, and only 33 percent would reduce it[24]—more favorable views about aid than those among Roman Catholics in general throughout the country at the time (Table 4–6).

This more liberal outlook of the clergy than of the laity in the non-fundamentalist Christian churches has not been limited to world affairs. In the 1948 survey of college graduates mentioned above, ministers were more supportive of the basic ideas of the New and Fair Deals and more tolerant of minorities in this country than were other Protestant college men and women. In 1951–52 Episcopal bishops and priests were likewise distinctly more liberal than their parishioners on most controversial domestic issues as well—more desegregationist, more supportive of civil liberties, more favorable to organized labor and less attached to laissez-faire social, economic, and political ideology, and more willing generally for the federal government to intervene in the U.S. society and economy.[25] Presbyterian ministers in the fall of 1967 expressed consistently more liberal views about a number of aspects of race relations—"black power"; school, housing, and job desegregation; interracial marriage; etc.—than did Presbyterian elders. The elders were likewise significantly more conservative on domestic welfare and economic issues—the proposed guaranteed minimum wage, large-scale programs to remedy urban problems, expanded public housing, higher-quality schools in slums, and more help for Negro-owned small businesses and other Negro institutions.[26] Catholic parish priests were similarly more in favor of racial equality and other liberal domestic programs than the average among lay Catholics in the early 1960's.[27] Southern clergymen,

23. Hero, *Southerner*, pp. 467–73.
24. Joseph H. Fichter, *Priest and People* (New York: Sheed and Ward, 1965), p. 31.
25. Glock, Ringer, and Babbie, pp. 153–60.
26. "Attitudes on Civil Rights" (unpublished report of a survey of 4,394 ministers and 3,460 elders in 151 presbyteries, under the auspices of the Office of Church and Society, the Commission on Religion and Race, the Office of Social Education and Evangelism, and the Office on the Renewal and Extension of the Ministry of the United Presbyterian Church, U.S.A., 1967).
27. Fichter, pp. 31 ff. For comparative opinions of lay Catholics, see Tables 8–1, 8–3, and 8–5, below.

both Catholic and Protestant, were more liberal on race relations in the early sixties than most of their parishioners—including most who went to college.[28]

These clergy-laity attitudinal differences can be attributed partially to the more widespread awareness among the clergy than among lay persons of the public positions of their denominations, the National Council of Churches, and the Vatican. It is true that clergymen have favored multilateral cooperation more than laymen even in fields where their national and international religious leaders and institutions have either said nothing or advanced much qualified or even equivocal views. However, differences have been wider on the whole on issues on which their denominational pronouncements have clearly supported a more liberal policy or opposed a more conservative one. Some evidence indicates that the more definite and forceful the public stance of their national or international leaders, the less inclined are local clergymen to compromise with or reflect the views on the pews, the more congruent their own opinions are with those uttered from above, and the more willing they have been to express such opinions to their communicants.[29]

However, even ministers who have been unaware of their denomination's liberal statements of given issues have nevertheless held views closer to the contents of such utterances than have their communicants. Furthermore, awareness of the official positions of their denomination or of the N.C.C. has apparently had relatively little bearing on most parishioners' opinions. The minority of Episcopal parishioners who knew of their church's strong public pronouncements in support of the UN were not significantly more apt to support it themselves than the majority who did not know that the Episcopal Church had taken any position relative to the world organization.[30] There seems no reason to assume that the situation has been much different in most other denominations.

Thus it appears that vigorous, publicized support of liberal foreign-policy alternatives by the denominations and ecumenical institutions

28. Hero, *Southerner*, chap. 12. See also Hadden, *The Gathering Storm in the Churches*, chap. 4, for further documentation of the more equalitarian racial attitudes prevailing among clergy than among laity.

29. Such was apparently the case in a national survey of 1,530 Episcopal parishioners and 239 of their ministers in 1951–52 on both international and domestic questions. Charles Y. Glock and Benjamin B. Ringer, "Church Policy and the Attitudes of Ministers and Parishioners on Social Issues," *American Sociological Review* (April 1956) 21, no. 20, pp. 148–56.

30. Ibid., p. 162–67.

has exerted some effect on clergymen but relatively little, at least directly, on most laymen. Even in the absence of guidance from those higher up in religious structures, clergymen tend to hold more liberal international opinions than even the college-educated among their parishioners. Apparently, fundamental differences in personality, values, training, occupation, and/or life styles account for such divergences in views on world problems and what their government should do about them.

Contrasts with Fundamentalist Groups

Catholic priests and Protestant clergymen within N.C.C.-affiliated denominations have been considerably more liberal in their international thinking, as well as more interested and informed in that field, than ministers of Protestant groups of more fundamentalist traditions which have not been associated with the N.C.C.

In a national survey of Protestant clergymen in local parishes in 1960, for example, Missouri Synod Lutherans and Southern Baptists were patently less inclined than ministers in eight denominations affiliated with the N.C.C. to (1) say they were very interested in news of "national and international affairs," (2) strongly approve of the purposes of the UN, (3) agree with the goals of the N.C.C. in international affairs and peace, (4) disagree with the view that the N.C.C. is too concerned with such issues, and (5) agree with the policy alternatives suggested by the N.C.C.'s pronouncements (Table 9–3). Southern Baptist ministers and white clergymen with unaffiliated sects in the South were less inclined than Episcopal, Presbyterian, and Methodist ministers in the same communities in 1960–62 to favor foreign economic aid, further accommodation and compromise with the communist world, and other liberal policy positions.

Evidence on the comparative international views of clergy versus laymen in these non-N.C.C., theologically conservative Protestant groups is only suggestive. College- and seminary-trained Southern Baptist ministers in the early 1960's tended to be less conservative in their international views than most of their parishioners. Less academically trained clergymen of that denomination and those of pentecostal sects did not appear to differ much in their foreign-policy opinions from their flocks. Overall international attitudinal differences between clergy and laymen among Missouri Synod Lutherans, Southern Baptists, and the sects, if any, have very probably been smaller than within most N.C.C.-affiliated denominations.

DENOMINATIONAL DIFFERENCES

The hypothesis that the public stances and other efforts of national and international religious institutions in the field of international affairs have exerted little impact on their rank-and-file members is supported by comparative international opinions held by those affiliated with different denominations. Unfortunately a number of denominations and sects have been too small to provide large enough samples in national surveys to permit reliable statistical comparisons. However, where such comparisons have been feasible, little connection has been observable between the relative public postures of the larger denominations and the attitudes prevailing among their respective members.

It is true that in recent years Southern Baptists, Missouri Synod Lutherans, and members of pentecostal and revivalist sects have been on the whole more conservative in their international opinions than have those of N.C.C.-affiliated denominations. Samples of such non-trinitarian or liberal theological groups as the Quakers, Unitarians, and Universalists have been too small for definitive comparisons, but during most of the postwar period they have provided rather consistently more liberal views on foreign affairs than other Christian groups, including those connected with the F.C.C. and N.C.C. Thus differences in rank-and-file views in these three general categories of religious groups have more or less paralleled those between the public stances of their articulate leaderships.

However, even the differences between the members of more fundamentalist groups and those of the main-line F.C.C. and N.C.C. denominations have been considerably smaller than those between their respective national spokesmen. Even these rank-and-file differences were not apparent prior to the Second World War. Moreover, international attitudinal differences among memberships of F.C.C. and N.C.C. denominations have had very little, if any, association with differences in the public stances of their respective national headquarters. In some cases correlations may even have been negative.

Judging from the replies of several dozen Quakers, Unitarians, and Universalists during the period 1938–41, these religious groups tended to be more favorable than members of most other Protestant denominations to international cooperation other than that perceived as likely to draw the United States into war or as support of military action by

Britain, France, or China against Germany, Italy, or Japan.[31] Similarly after our entry into the war they seemed more inclined than most other non-Jewish religious groups to favor active involvement in world affairs, economic aid to less-developed countries, expanded negotiations and trade with communist countries, and perhaps other types of international cooperation as well (Table 9–5).[32]

Southern Baptists and members of fundamentalist sects were at least as favorably disposed as members of F.C.C.-affiliated denominations to assisting the Western democracies and the Chinese in their efforts to resist the aggressions of Nazism, Fascism, and militarist Japan, to rearming the United States after the war began in Europe, and to open criticism of Hitler's and Mussolini's "warlike attitudes" by the President of the United States (Table 9–4). In fact, these fundamentalist groups were more interventionist in these respects than most of the less fundamentalist, main-line Protestant denominations, in some respects than even the much better educated and more socially and economically privileged Episcopalians.

However, the reverse has been generally the case recently (Table 9–5). Members of the more fundamentalist groups have not only been less well informed and less likely to harbor opinions on foreign policy than those of denominations of more moderate or liberal theological bents. By the early 1950's the fundamentalists had also become distinctly less enthusiastic than the moderates about the Marshall Plan, Point Four aid to less-developed areas, and the channeling of at least some aid through multilateral institutions. In the 1960's Southern Baptists and other fundamentalist groups were patently the ones less favorable to multilateral cooperation outside the military sphere—economic aid; negotiations and trade with communist countries; membership of Mainland China in the UN; and negotiations with Asian communist leaders, including the Chinese, to end the war in Vietnam.

This shift in comparative differences may have been due in some (probably small) measure to comparable shifts in the public postures in the denominations concerned. However, the Southernness of most fundamentalist denominations and sects was clearly a more important

31. These non-trinitarian groups constitute a minority within the category "other non-fundamentalist denominations" in Table 9–4 and help to account for the somewhat more internationalist or interventionist posture of that group than of Protestants generally.

32. Samples of non-trinitarian groups were too small for statistical significance at the 10 percent level.

causative factor than arguments emanating from their national leaderships. The apparent reversal in international attitudes of rank-and-file Southern Baptists as contrasted with lay members of other denominations was approximately parallel to a similar reversal that set off the white South from the rest of the country during the same period.[33] Moreover, Methodists residing in the South in the late thirties and early forties —supposedly exposed to the same neutralist and pacifist ideas from national Methodist elites as Methodists outside the region—were at least somewhat more inclined to approve of U.S. intervention against the Axis than members of the same denomination in the North (Table 9–4). Although the public pronouncements of Methodist leaders and intellectuals were on the whole more unreservedly pacifist, opposed to military conscription, and supportive of the League of Nations than those of most other trinitarian denominations,[34] Methodists in the South were more inclined to aid the Chinese, the British, and the French against the Axis and to feel that the U.S. should have joined the League of Nations than members of most other primarily non-Southern denominations, while Methodists in the North approximated the Northern Protestant averages on such issues (Table 9–4).

Furthermore, prewar differences among white Episcopalians, Presbyterians, Congregationalists, Lutherans, and non-Southern Baptists manifested virtually no correlation with differences among the public stances of these denominations. Although the Protestant Episcopal Church said little or nothing about most prewar international issues, Episcopalians did not differ significantly in their views from Presbyterians, Congregationalists, or most other non-fundamentalist denom-

33. Hero, *Southerner*, esp. chaps. 2–5.
34. Muelder, pp. 148–51; Corbett, pp. 4 ff.; Huber, pp. 168–78 and 280–81; Gladden, pp. 27–132; and Sparks, pp. 71–91. Muelder cites surveys of large national samples of Methodist ministers and theological school students in 1931 which found that 62 percent of ministers versus 79 percent of students felt the churches should go on record as refusing to sanction any future war; 52 versus 72 percent said they themselves would refuse to sanction war; and only 45 versus 27 percent replied they could conscientiously serve as military chaplains in war time. Eighty percent of the 19,372 ministers in the sample favored U.S. arms reductions even if this country had to be the first to reduce arms and to make proportionately greater reductions than others were willing to make; only 13 percent approved of military training in colleges and universities; 62 percent held that the U.S. should abandon armed interventions to protect American lives and property in Latin America or elsewhere; and 66 percent favored immediate U.S. membership in the League of Nations. However, Muelder continued that most observers felt that Methodist laymen generally were less pacifist than ministers, though they were willing for their pastors to affirm positions which they themselves considered unrealistic.

inational groups whose leaderships advocated particular policies on the pertinent issues. Non-Southern Baptists and Lutherans—including the theologically relatively conservative Missouri Synod—were somewhat more isolationist than Congregationalists, Presbyterians, and Episcopalians, but these differences were probably primarily attributable to the lower average education of American Baptists, the large number of German-Americans among Lutherans, and the concentration of both in the Midwest and Great Plains, rather than to the stances of their national leaderships.

Nor have such utterances from the top seemed to exert much more impact at the local level since the Second World War (Table 9–5). Although their leadership remained more cautious (or less radical) than that of the other major affiliates of the F.C.C. and N.C.C. about taking forthright positions on controversial international issues,[35] Episcopalians during the second postwar decade were typically better informed about and more favorably disposed than members of most other Protestant denominations toward economic aid, negotiations and trade with communist countries, membership for Mainland China in the UN, and willingness to negotiate with Asian communist leaders (Table 9–5). Methodists, Presbyterians, and members of such other theologically relatively liberal or moderate groups as the United Church of Christ have been next most favorably disposed in these matters, Lutherans[36] and American Baptists less so, and Southern Baptists and fundamentalist sects, especially the latter, least of all. The pacifist strain and general international liberalism evident in Methodist public utterances and among a number of social and political activists of that denomination have not been sufficiently influential at the rank-and-file level to differentiate the latter's international views from those prevailing in most other Protestant denominations affiliated with the N.C.C.[37] In fact, lay Methodists seemed less favorable to most forms of multilateral cooperation than Episco-

35. Warner, pp. 96, 108–9, 116–17, and 160.
36. Survey replies did not permit separation of Missouri Synod Lutherans, some 30 percent of all American Lutherans, from the others.
37. Herbert E. Stotts and Paul Deats, Jr., *Methodism and Society: Guidelines for Strategy* (New York: Abingdon Press, 1962), pp. 278 and 333, also cites a 1956 survey of Methodist laymen wherein only 2.5 percent replied that they could "under no circumstances support or participate in war" and 88.5 percent endorsed views supportive of U.S. involvement in war, depending on the circumstances. The authors concluded from this and other evidence that during the postwar period most Methodists have seemed to feel that the U.S. "must maintain a nonpacifist posture." See also Muelder, pp. 245–46 and 379.

palians whose denominational statements were on the whole less supportive of such policies.[38]

White Roman Catholics of the pre–Pearl Harbor period were no more isolationist than Lutherans or Baptists of the same race outside the South; in fact, they seemed somewhat less so with respect to some aspects of policy (Table 9–4). However, white Catholics were typically less supportive of action directed against the Axis than were most other Protestant denominations. White Catholics of the 1960's, although more liberal on such issues as foreign aid, negotiation and trade with communist countries, and entry of Mainland China into the UN than white Protestants in general, and considerably more liberal than members of the more fundamentalist Protestant groups, appeared less liberal than Episcopalians. The international views of Catholics have approximated (or have been slightly more liberal than) those of Methodists, Presbyterians, members of the United Church of Christ, and other liberal or moderate Protestant denominations combined.

THEOLOGICAL PREFERENCES VERSUS FOREIGN POLICY

These differences in international attitudes among whites in the Protestant denominations during the late fifties and sixties have paralleled the relative proportions of theological liberals versus theological conservatives or fundamentalists within them. More liberal religious views have increased considerably relative to more conservative ones, particularly among clergy, in most denominations since the thirties.[39] However, with the possible exception of the Methodists,[40] the rank order of the denominations in terms of ratios of theological liberals to theological conservatives among their clergy and membership has remained approximately the same.

Thus the most internationally liberal or multilateralist group of the postwar period, the non-trinitarian Quakers, Unitarians, and Universalists, have contained few fundamentalists. Individuals of such conserva-

38. A survey of Midwestern corn-producing country in the early 1960's found no significant connection between the positions of the denominations on public and social issues generally and the attitudes of their respective members. Victor Obenhaus, *The Church and Faith in Mid-America* (Philadelphia: Westminster Press, 1963), pp. 117–18.

39. See, for example, Hadden and Rodney Stark and Charles Y. Glock, *American Piety: The Nature of Religious Commitment* (Berkeley: Univ. of California Press, 1968), pp. 213 ff.

40. Methodist ministers seemed to shift more sharply than Protestant clergymen generally from a relatively revivalist, individual salvationist tradition in the thirties—especially in the South—to relatively liberal theological orientations in the sixties.

tive theological orientations have in recent years constituted only relatively limited minorities within the Congregational Church, the later merged United Church of Christ, the Protestant Episcopal Church, and—by the 1960's—the Methodist Church. They have constituted somewhat larger proportions in the (Northern) Presbyterian Church, U.S.A., and its successor, the merged United Presbyterian Church; still larger fractions within the (Southern) Presbyterian Church, U.S., the American Lutheran Church, the Lutheran Church in America, the United Lutheran Church, and the (Northern) American Baptist Convention; majorities in the Missouri Synod of the Lutheran Church and the Southern Baptist Convention; and even larger majorities among such revivalist or pentecostal sects as the Primitive Baptists, the Free Will Baptists, the Free Methodists, the Church of God and Christ, the Church of the Nazarene, and the Plymouth Brethren.[41]

To what extent have these theological differences been associated with divergent international opinions and accounted for such divergences apparent among the denominations?

Clergy

Unfortunately no reliable data are available on interconnections of theological and international orientations among clergy of the interwar period. In the light of the paucity of correlation among the general population affiliated with churches during those years (see below, p. 181), one might hypothesize relatively little association among clergymen between theological beliefs and thinking on world affairs before Pearl Harbor.

However, by the 1960's theological preferences were patently associated with international attitudes among clergymen. Theological conservatives of the sixties tended toward international conservatism, theological liberals toward international liberalism or multilateralism.

Thus among a national sample of 4,031 ministers of eight denominations in the N.C.C. in 1960, those who believed the Bible to be "an

41. For empirical evidence on the distribution of theological views among ministers of Protestant denominations, see Hadden, pp. 39–49; "The Clergy Views the National Council of Churches," pp. I–18 and I–19; and Jeffrey K. Hadden, "A Protestant Paradox," *Information Service*, biweekly of the Department of Research of the National Council of Churches of Christ in the U.S.A., 46, no. 13 (16 Sept. 1967), pp. 1–7. Similar data on the theological orientations of laymen in the various denominations are available in Charles Y. Glock and Rodney Stark, *Religion and Society in Tension* (Chicago: Rand McNally, 1965), chap. 5; Glock and Stark, *Christian Beliefs and Anti-Semitism*, chaps. 1 and 2; and Stark and Glock, *American Piety*, pp. 70–75.

infallible revelation of God's will," rarely questioned traditional interpretations of doctrine or creed, and frequently emphasized a biblically
conservative Christianity were much less likely to approve of the purposes of the UN and of the National and World Councils of Churches
in international matters and to be very interested in national and international affairs than were those with more liberal views of these theological questions (Table 9–6). The latter were likewise much more
apt to feel that the National Council had the right to issue pronouncements on world affairs, to recall the content of statements uttered, and
to agree with the views expressed in them on such matters as Communist Chinese membership in the UN. The more conservative their
theological preferences, the more these clergymen felt that the National
Council's pronouncements on both national and international affairs
had been "too far to the left." Clergymen who were more ecumenically
minded in 1960, who approved of the purposes of the National and
World Councils of Churches, were likewise more liberal in their international opinions than were those who disapproved of such ecumenical
endeavors. Conversely, ministers who agreed that the N.C.C. was "too
liberal in its theological interpretations" were sharply more likely than
those who disagreed to feel both that the N.C.C. was too concerned
with international and national problems and that its pronouncements
in such fields had been "too far to the left."

These correlations between theological and international thinking
were likewise apparent within each denominational group. Thus, among
ministers of each of the eight denominations, the more liberal the
theology, the more liberal their views on the UN, the role of the churches
in world affairs, and the international issues dealt with by N.C.C.
pronouncements. Thus theological liberals among Congregational ministers were on the average more apt to agree with the international pronouncements of their denominations and the N.C.C. and to be liberal
about foreign affairs generally than theologically more conservative
Congregational clergymen, theologically liberal Methodist ministers
than theologically more conservative ones, and so on.[42]

Much of the difference in international views among ministers of
different denominations was largely explained by the varying proportions
of theological liberals versus theological conservatives from one denomination to the next. Theological orientation was a more crucial

42. "The Clergy Views the National Council of Churches," p. IV–11. See also Hero,
Southerner, pp. 446–51.

factor than denomination. Baptist theological liberals harbored inter-national opinions more like those of Episcopalian and Congregational-ist theological liberals than like those of theologically conservative Baptists. Although some differences in thinking on world affairs remained between Baptist clergymen on the one hand and Episcopalian and Congregationalist clergymen on the other even when they held like theological beliefs, such differences were sharply smaller than between the two groups in general.[43]

The Laity, Theology, and Foreign Policy

Most of the theological differences on which clergymen have been divided have been apparent in only much diluted and more amorphous form among laymen.[44] The latter, of course, have known much less about theology and have been much less aware of theological con-troversies and traditions. Whereas most clergymen have held relatively consistent theological views, most laymen have been either quite vague in this area or have harbored mixtures of theologically relatively con-servative and relatively liberal preferences.

Relatively few surveys have posed queries about both theological preferences and foreign policy. Analysis of relationships between theo-logical orientations and international opinions must therefore be based to a considerable extent on rather indirect indicators of theological bents. However, these imperfect reflections of theological tone lead to the tenta-tive conclusion that the discernible association between conservative, fun-damentalist, and evangelical religious emphases and conservative think-ing among Church laymen on the international issues of the 1960's was feebler, if not almost insignificant, before our entry into the war (Table 9–7). At least among Protestants, frequent Bible reading and prohibi-tionism with respect to alcoholic beverages have traditionally been asso-ciated with religious fundamentalism and theological conservatism. The large fraction of white Protestants and the smaller minority of Catholics who had read the Bible during the last month were somewhat more hesitant about selling military equipment to the British and French and more inclined to favor a Japanese victory in case of war with the Soviet Union than were their respective coreligionists who had not

43. "The Clergy Views the National Council of Churches," p. IV–11, and retabula-tions of the survey reported there.

44. See also Hadden, *The Gathering Storm in the Churches*, p. 99, and Stark and Glock, *American Piety*, pp. 141–62.

"Drys" among both major Christian groups were likewise somewhat more isolationist than "wets"—less inclined to lend money for war supplies to either Finland or Britain and France, for example.

However, more nearly direct correlates of theological liberalism-conservatism had virtually no connection with such prewar foreign-policy attitudes. Neither white Protestants nor Catholics who preferred the Old Testament over the New were any more opposed to selling military equipment to Britain and France, any more willing to sell it to the Axis, or any more inclined to side with the Japanese in case they went to war with the Soviet communists, than were others of their respective faiths who preferred the New or liked both equally. Nor were those Catholics or Protestants who agreed with the proponents of the social gospel in November 1941 that clergymen should discuss from the pulpit such issues as American participation in the war any more willing to help Britain at the risk of involving ourselves in the war than their coreligionists who felt preachers and priests should stay out of such matters as international affairs.

Although relationships between theological and international orientations have been closer among clergymen than among laity, by the 1950's some correlation had become apparent in the same direction among the latter as the former. For example, in the fall of 1964 both white Protestants and Catholics who felt that "the Bible is God's word and all it says is true" were 3 to 18 percentage points less favorable to expanded trade with communist countries, membership of Mainland China in the UN, and the U.S. remaining in the world body if Peking were admitted, than were coreligionists who thought that "the Bible was written by men inspired by God, but it contains some human error" (Table 9–8).[45] White Protestants who viewed the Bible as literally accurate in every detail were also somewhat less supportive of foreign aid than those with less dogmatic views of the Scriptures.

However, differences on negotiations with communist governments between these theological groups were too small for statistical significance; only approximately one out of ten of even the theological conservatives opposed this idea. Moreover, Catholic theological conserva-

45. Respondents who replied, "The Bible is a good book because it was written by wise men but God had nothing to do with it" or "The Bible was written by men who lived so long ago that it is worth very little today," even when combined, were too few for statistically significant comparisons among either Catholic or Protestant whites (see Table 9–8).

tives were by 1964 as supportive of aid as coreligionists of less conservative Biblical sentiments; indeed, they were more supportive than Protestant whites regardless of their feelings about literal accuracy of the Scriptures. On the whole, theological orientations among lay Catholics seem to have had less connection with thinking about foreign affairs in the 1960's than was the case among white lay Protestants.[46]

Approval of ecumenical endeavors has been associated statistically with more liberal theological views among laymen—though again to a lesser degree than among clergymen. In 1950 white Protestants who favored the idea of "all Protestant Churches in this country [joining] to form a single Protestant church" were somewhat more inclined than coreligionists who opposed it to increase or at least to keep at current levels the funds devoted to the Marshall Plan (Table 9–6). Similarly, during the sixties Catholic and Protestant whites who harbored favorable feelings toward Jews[47] were several percentage points more favorably disposed toward economic aid, negotiations and trade with communist regimes, and membership for Mainland China in the UN than coreligionists who had unfavorable impressions of them. Similarly Protestant whites who regarded Catholics favorably and Catholic whites who similarly viewed Protestants were more inclined to approve of these policy alternatives than coreligionists who perceived the other major Christian group in a negative light (Table 9–9).

Neither Biblical literalism, opposition to cooperation with other religious denominations, nor negative feelings about religious groups different from one's own have alone been highly valid indications of theological fundamentalism among rank-and-file parishioners. Correlations of conservative international attitudes with a combination of such views associated with fundamentalism, including emphasis on individual conversion and salvation and opposition to church involvement in social and public issues, might of course be significantly higher than those apparent in Tables 9–8 and 9–9.

46. Stark and Glock, *American Piety*, p. 75, likewise found that the negative relationship of orthodox religious beliefs with concern for social ethics and liberal social attitudes generally apparent among Protestants was both weaker and in some cases slightly reversed among Catholics.

47. For correlations of anti-Semitism with theological conservatism, fundamentalism, and dogmatism, see Glock and Stark, *Christian Beliefs and Anti-Semitism*, chaps. 4, 11, and 12. Although few differences between Catholic versus Protestant attitudes toward Jews appeared in the national surveys of the 1930's and 1940's, by the 1960's expressed attitudes of Catholics seemed consistently somewhat less anti-Semitic than those of Protestants. See ibid., chap. 2, and *Gallup Opinion Index*, April 1969.

Theology and Denominational Adherence
as Determinants of World Views

Thus denominational affiliations, except for Jews, and theological orientations seem to have played at most only relatively minor roles in the determination of public reactions to major foreign-policy issues of the pre–Pearl Harbor period. Such factors as education, socio-economic status, and, especially, national origin and geographical and cultural region—each systematically associated with denominational and theological considerations—were clearly more influential.

By the 1960's theological orientations per se were undoubtedly linked logically and ideologically with thinking on a number of inter-national issues among theologically trained people. Their denomina-tional identifications and the stances of their respective denominations on international issues had less relevance than their theological beliefs for their views on foreign affairs.

Denominational affiliations and even theological preferences seemed substantially less important factors in thinking about world affairs among laymen than clergymen of the 1960's.[48] They probably form part of a congeries of interrelated and mutually reinforcing influences which together help to determine foreign-policy attitudes. Demographic fac-tors—especially education—associated with theological and, especially, denominational differences may have been as important or more im-portant determinants of international differences noted among the laities than these religious variables themselves. Denominations whose members have been more supportive of multilateral cooperation have been dispro-portionately composed of more highly educated, more prosperous, more urban people, in more complex walks of life, while pentecostal sects and, to a lesser degree, Southern Baptists have been made up in large measure of the less privileged, less urban, and more Southern elements of the U.S. population—those least supportive of such foreign policies (Table 9–10).[49] These same demographic variables related to international

48. For the much lower correlations among laymen than clergymen of theological preferences with views on such controversial domestic issues as race relations and federal government intervention in social and economic life, see Hadden, *The Gathering Storm in the Churches*, pp. 90–98.

49. The source of Table 9–10 is the combined AIPO (Gallup) surveys in 1966–67 (Special Report on Religion, *Gallup Opinion Index*, 1967). See also Hadden, *The Gathering Storm in the Churches*, p. 91, for the distribution of occupational groups among the denominations. For the increasingly middle-class composition of the Meth-odist Churches, see Stotts and Deats, pp. 227–29. However, Methodists of the 1960's re-mained less urban and more Southern than any major denomination other than the Baptists.

attitudes have been likewise associated—though to a lesser extent—with theological liberalism versus conservatism among rank-and-file laymen.

Samples of individual Protestant denominations or theologically oriented groups have unfortunately not been large enough to permit comparisons of their international views while such demographic variables are held constant. However, differences apparent between theological and denominational groups in Tables 9–5 and 9–8 and 9–9 would certainly be reduced thereby. International attitudinal differences between college-educated, prosperous, urban Southern Baptists and their Episcopal and United Church of Christ lay counterparts, for example, have almost certainly been considerably smaller than those between their respective general memberships.

PAUCITY OF EFFECTS OF CHURCHES ON LAYMEN'S WORLD VIEWS

People who attend church regularly or frequently should be more susceptible to the influences of their religious institutions than co-religionists who do not. So should those who feel relatively closely identified with their church as contrasted with others who are less interested or emotionally or otherwise involved.

However, insofar as surveys have measured such variables as church attendance and identification with one's church, denomination, or other religious institution, these factors seem to have had little connection with international attitudes among Protestants—even with respect to issues with rather obvious ethical implications, such as nonmilitary aid. Regular churchgoing Catholics and Catholics otherwise more involved in their church, on the other hand, had by the mid-1960's become somewhat more liberal in their international opinions than nominal Catholics.

Churchgoing and Church Identification Among Protestants

Regular or frequent churchgoers among both Protestants and Catholics have been on the average more highly educated and more successful economically than less frequent attenders and non-attenders of religious

50. In the fall of 1964, for example, 27 percent of white Protestants who attended church "regularly" or "often" had been to college, 52 percent had not, but had been to high school, and 21 percent had been no further than grade school. Among those who went to church "seldom or never," the respective figures were 21, 50, and 27 percent. Among white Catholic regular or frequent churchgoers the respective percentages were 24, 59, and 17. Among Catholic whites who "seldom or never" attended

services.[50] It is thus understandable that more active Protestants and Catholics have on the whole been somewhat better informed about world affairs and the activities of their churches in that field than more nominal churchmen. However, these informational differences have been very small or virtually nonexistent when churchgoers have been compared only with non-churchgoers of equivalent education. Education has been clearly a much more important factor than any effects of church exposure on knowledge about world affairs among Protestants.

Moreover, even though on the average better educated, Protestant churchgoers have recently differed little if any from apathetic Protestants in their international attitudes, whether or not education is held constant.[51] Such seems to have been the case regardless of the average level of education and socioeconomic status of the denomination, and whether or not its leaders have taken any public position on the issue in question.

These observations have been patently valid among postwar Episcopal parishioners—a group more highly educated themselves, served by a more highly educated and internationally sophisticated clergy, and supposedly exposed to relatively liberal foreign-policy stances by their denominational and N.C.C. leaders. Episcopal laymen of the early fifties who went to church regularly or frequently, were active in church organizations or church-connected activities, read religious literature, turned to their church and clergy for advice or comfort, and perceived pastoral functions as relatively important differed very little or not at all from more indifferent or nominal Episcopalians in their attitudes toward the UN, immigration, foreign aid, conscientious objection, or such domestic issues as civil and human rights.[52] Although resources

church, figures were respectively 19, 53, and 27 percent. Similar differences in annual family income were likewise apparent in both Christian groups (SRC 473, Sept.–Nov., 1964). On a combination of seven AIPO surveys in 1968 (N = 10,665), 47 percent of college-educated, 43 percent of high-school-educated, and 41 percent of grade-school-educated said they had attended church during the last week. So did 45 percent of those with family incomes in excess of $7,000 during the last year, 41 percent of those with family incomes between $3,000 and $6,999, and 40 percent with incomes below $3,000. *Gallup Report*, 12–22–68. See also Andrew M. Greeley and Peter H. Rossi, *The Education of Catholic Americans* (Garden City, N.Y.: Doubleday, 1966), p. 79, and N.J. Demerath, III, *Social Class in American Protestantism* (Chicago: Rand McNally, 1965), pp. 10–15.

51. Protestant churchgoers may have been somewhat more conservative in their thinking about world affairs than non-churchgoing Protestants of equivalent education in recent years. However, differences have typically been too small for statistical significance at the 10 percent level.

52. Glock, Ringer, and Babbie, p. 165.

and energy had been devoted to trying to communicate the Episcopal Church's liberal views on the UN to its parishioners, and local clergy had been urged to include the church's position on the world organization in their sermons, discussion groups, and other parish programs, the more actively involved minority of parishioners was no more inclined to agree with that position than nominal Episcopalians who seldom went to church.[53] Neither degree of identification with nor involvement in their church, interest in religion, awareness of their denomination's stands on foreign policy, nor all these factors combined had much bearing on Episcopal parishioners' own thinking about these important issues.[54]

Moreover, the personal views of parish priests seemed to exert little or no effect on the opinions of most of their communicants. Parishioners —even relatively actively involved ones—of priests who held more liberal views on international relations were at most only slightly more liberal on these matters than parishioners of more conservative priests.[55] Even if priests and congregations of a feather have tended to flock together, the criteria of similarity and attraction were patently little related to foreign affairs at the time of the Korean War.

Results of a survey of a representative sample of Episcopal churchwomen in the diocese of California in 1965 suggest that much of this state of affairs has persisted.[56] The generalization seems warranted that even relatively active, aware Episcopalians have not accorded much importance to their church's or their own local clergy's advice (if any) in foreign affairs.

This situation has not been unique to Episcopalians. A survey in Greater Detroit in 1958 also determined that involvement in churches generally had little relationship to the amount of thought given to world problems or to attitudes toward foreign economic aid.[57] Table 9–11 suggests that with but minor amendment these observations have likewise applied to white Protestant Americans generally.[58]

53. Ibid., p. 135.
54. Ibid., p. 168.
55. Ibid., pp. 170–71.
56. Earl R. Babbie, "A Religious Profile of Episcopal Churchwomen," *Pacific Churchman*, 97, no. 1 (Jan. 1967), pp. 6–8 and 12.
57. Gerhard Lenski, *The Religious Factor* (Garden City, N.Y.: Doubleday, 1961), pp. 170–71.
58. National samples of individual Protestant denominations have been too small to permit comparisons of frequent with infrequent church attenders within each of them. However, the paucity of correlation between churchgoing and international

Thus white Protestants who had gone to church the preceding Sunday or who typically attended church at least once a week in early 1939 did not seem to differ in any consistent way from less frequent attenders in their views on permitting Britain and France to purchase warplanes here, on also letting Germany and Italy do so, or on whether they would prefer a Japanese or a Soviet victory in case of war between the two (Table 9–11).

White Protestants who went to church regularly in 1956, 1958, and 1960 were probably somewhat less inclined than those who went seldom or never to feel the U.S. would be better off if it "just stayed home" and did not concern itself with problems in other parts of the world, and somewhat more supportive of economic aid abroad (Table 9–11). In 1956 the former were slightly more apt than the latter to agree that the U.S. should aid nonaligned countries and to disagree with the argument that the best way for the U.S. to deal with the U.S.S.R. and Communist China would be to "get just as tough as they do." At the end of 1961 white Protestants who had attended church during the preceding week were slightly more aware than those who had not of the discussions of tariffs and trade in process at the time (in connection with the Trade Expansion bill) and somewhat more inclined to favor lower tariffs. In the fall of 1964 regular churchgoers were likewise somewhat better informed about Mainland China and more favorable to economic aid and negotiations with communist leaders to settle our differences.

However, by 1964 churchgoing had no bearing whatsoever on white Protestants' views on proposed expanded trade with communist countries in nonmilitary goods or on admission of the Peking regime to the UN (Table 9–11). Nor did it have any connection with U.S. involvement in the Vietnam War in 1966. Moreover, all of the differences in 1956, 1958, 1960, 1961, and 1964 noted above were so small that they could be attributed largely to the higher average education of churchgoers.

This virtual irrelevance of church involvement to international thinking among most white American Protestants has not been unique to foreign-policy attitudes. Paucity of differences between those active in churches and nonchurchgoers has been equally evident in the 1960's with respect to such controversial domestic issues as desegregation and

---

attitudes has been apparent whether or not Southern Baptists, fundamentalist sects, and other groups whose leadership has either remained silent or advanced more conservative views on world affairs have been omitted.

civil rights, the death penalty, military conscription, and the antipoverty program.[59]

Perhaps other aspects of religious behavior have been more closely associated with thinking about ethically relevant aspects of public affairs than have frequency of church attendance and self-expressed identification with one's church or denomination. These measures may be indications more of conformity with middle-class norms prevailing in one's social environment than of religious beliefs themselves. Many churchgoers are attracted primarily by the conventions or forms of their denomination or of their relatively homogeneous parish. They seek social acceptance, emotional support for their worldly insecurities and the mores of their social group, business contacts, professional clients or patients, or other objectives extrinsic to religion itself (see below, p. 225). The late Gordon W. Allport and some of his associates at Harvard discovered that the limited minority of devout, regular church-goers who are interested more in the basic values and substance of their faith, the intrinsically religious, were clearly more liberal about domestic race relations and generally less prejudiced about Jews, other religious and ethnic groups, and people different from themselves generally than the majority that were in churches for such mainly extrinsic motives.[60] Perhaps the intrinsically religious minority are also more likely than the extrinsically motivated majority to accord some attention to the implications of their faith for world affairs and to the ideas in this field emanating from religious institutions, to agree with the tone of most of these utterances, and to favor multilateral cooperation generally. Unfortunately, data pertinent to such hypotheses relative to international attitudes, derived from satisfactory samples, are not so far available.

Nevertheless, on the basis of empirical evidence at hand, it appears that successive liberal public pronouncements of the National Council of Churches, the major non-fundamentalist denominations, and leading Protestant churchmen combined with the similar views on foreign policy of much of the local clergy have exerted little influence on the

59. *Gallup Opinion Index*, Special Report on Religion, 1967.
60. Gordon W. Allport, *The Person in Psychology* (Boston: Beacon Press, 1968), pp. 55–59, 201, and 224–52; Allport, *Religion and Prejudice in Personality and Social Encounter* (Boston: Beacon Press, 1960), chap. 16; and Allport, "Behavioral Science, Religion, and Mental Health," *Journal of Religion and Health* 2, no. 3 (April 1963), pp. 187–97. See also M. Argyle, *Religious Behavior* (Glencoe, Ill: Free Press, 1959), pp. 84 ff., for development of the thesis that the conventionally religious rather than the genuinely devout tend to be prejudiced and ethnocentric.

thinking of most rank-and-file church members.[61] Even on topics such as the role of military force in U.S. policy and the importance of foreign economic aid, where ethical considerations should be particularly salient and where one might expect parishioners to seek some guidance from or accord some credence to their religious institutions, active Protestant churchmen's views have been determined almost exclusively by secular, pragmatic, or ideological considerations rather than by precepts of organized Protestantism. Few Protestant churchgoers perceive significant implications of their supposed Christian convictions for their views about international issues. Most have remained unaware of their church's positions on those questions, and most of the minority who know of them have been little, if at all, affected by them.

Slightly Greater Recent Impacts of the Catholic Church

Regular Catholic churchgoers in early 1939 were somewhat more anti-communist, that is, more inclined than the minority of less faithful Catholic church attenders to prefer that Japan rather than the Soviet Union win any war that might develop between them (Table 9–11). Faithful mass attenders were likewise somewhat more likely than more indifferent Catholics to favor permitting Germany and Italy to purchase warplanes in this country during the tense months between the Munich debacle and the Nazi invasion of Poland. However, among the Catholics who held any views on whether we should sell warplanes to Britain and France, there was no difference in opinion between regular participants in mass and other activities of the church and less faithful attenders.[62]

Although regular Protestant churchgoers were somewhat less isolationist and hard line with respect to the U.S.S.R. and Mainland China and somewhat more supportive of economic aid than indifferent Protestants in 1956, by that time church attendance had no apparent connection with such opinions among Catholics (Table 9–11).[63] However, by

61. It may even be that Protestant churches had slightly more effect on their parishioners in the initial decade or so after the war than during the 1960's (Table 9–11). At that time a number of denominations, including the Southern Baptist Convention, were more active than more recently in their support for the UN and technical assistance for the less developed world and their opposition to universal military training or other peacetime conscription.

62. Pro-Franco attitudes were probably more closely associated with degree of Catholic church involvement, but no comparable data are available on this issue prior to the Second World War.

63. Since only 56 white Catholics said they "seldom or never" attended church, differences would have necessarily been quite large to be statistically significant at the 10 percent level. Those who said they attended "often" (rather than "regularly") were even fewer, 47.

the fall of 1958 more active white Catholics had become somewhat less isolationist and more favorable to foreign economic aid than Catholics who seldom or never went to church, differences which persisted thereafter. Although church involvement seems to have had no connection with Catholic views on international trade or continuation of U.S. military involvement in Vietnam in the 1960's, more faithful Catholic churchgoers have consistently been at least somewhat more inclined than nominal Catholics to favor admission of Mainland China into the UN, trade with communist countries in nonmilitary goods, and aid to underdeveloped areas (Table 9–11).

These recent differences may have been due to some extent to the higher average education and socioeconomic status of regular mass attenders than of their more indifferent coreligionists. More regular church attendance by certain ethnic groups, such as the relatively more liberal Irish, than of the on the whole somewhat more internationally conservative Italians may also partially account for these recent differences.[64] Unfortunately Catholic samples, especially those of infrequent churchgoers, have been too small to determine correlations of international behavior with church attendance when education, social status, and national origins are held constant.

However, these educational, social, and cultural factors applied just as much in earlier years when attendance at mass had no connection with opinions on world affairs as they applied in the 1960's when consistent differences toward more support for multilateral cooperation appeared among regular Catholic churchgoers. Moreover, similar educational and socioeconomic differences between Protestant churchgoers and religious activists and more nominal Protestants have not resulted in similarly higher support for world cooperation among the more involved of them. Regular mass attenders among Catholics have been clearly more supportive of economic assistance than either active or inactive Protestants. The more involved the individuals are in their church, the wider the differences are between white Catholics and white Protestants with respect to this issue. Differences have been nonexistent, or at least smaller, between indifferent non-churchgoing Catholics and Protestants who either go to church or do not.

Other evidence substantiates the conclusion that by the 1960's active

64. See Andrew M. Greeley, "Ethnicity as an Influence on Behavior" (unpublished paper presented at the National Consultation on Ethnic Behavior sponsored by the American Jewish Committee at Fordham University, 20 June 1968), p. 91.

Catholics had become at least slightly more favorable to foreign economic aid (and perhaps other forms of international cooperation) than were the more indifferent or nominal members of their church, while degree of identification with Protestantism or a particular denomination within it had little or no connection with thinking on this ethically relevant issue. Thus in the fall of 1960, 59 percent of those who considered themselves "strong Catholics," contrasted with but 52 percent who said they were "not very strong" ones, agreed that the U.S. should "give economic help to poorer countries," while strength of identification with their religion among white Protestants had no bearing on their sentiments about this issue.[65] A study of over two thousand priests and a like number of active laymen in their parishes in the early sixties indicated that these nuclear parishioners were more favorable to foreign economic assistance than Catholics in general. Moreover, the closer friends of priests were not only somewhat more favorable to expanding or maintaining economic aid but also more interested in international affairs and more socially aware generally than were more distant acquaintances of priests in their parishes.[66]

Furthermore, adult Catholics who attended Catholic schools during most of their childhood and adolescence have held more liberal attitudes in public affairs, including foreign affairs, than coreligionists who experienced no or less Catholic-school education. For example, even when such factors as education and socioeconomic status are held constant,[67] Catholics of the mid-sixties whose formal education took place mainly in Catholic schools were better informed about their church's stances in such fields and somewhat more inclined than those with less or no Catholic education to agree that the Catholic Church "has the right to teach what stand members should take" on such issues as "whether the United States should recognize Communist China." Moreover, associations of Catholic education with more liberal opinion were most apparent among younger Catholics, those who attended school

65. SRC 440, Sept.–Nov. 1960. "Strong [white] Catholics" numbered 274; "not very strong" ones 74.

66. Fichter, p. 11. Sixty-one percent of the closer friends of priests contrasted with 57 percent of their more distant friends in the parish would either increase or maintain economic aid at prevailing levels.

67. For attitudes of Catholics in general on this issue, see Table 4–6. Catholic adults all or most of whose education took place in Catholic institutions were themselves of higher average education and socioeconomic status than those educated mainly in public schools. Their parents were as well. See Greeley and Rossi, pp. 41–44 and 50–53.

during the post–World War II era when the Church placed more emphasis than previously on social consciousness and the implications of the faith for public issues.[68]

SOME PRACTICAL POLITICAL IMPLICATIONS

A number of comparative trends noted in international thinking among American church people generally have been apparent within Congress as well.

The votes of Jewish congressmen have been sharply more favorable to most forms of multilateral cooperation than those of either their Catholic or Protestant colleagues since at least as long ago as the late 1930's. Catholic congressmen did not differ significantly from Protestant ones of the same political party in the 76th (1939–40), 80th (1947–48), 83rd (1953–54), 85th (1957–58), and 88th (1963–64) Congresses in their voting on tariffs and international trade. But although Catholics in 1939–40 were less inclined to vote for aid to Britain and France than Protestants in the same party, by 1953–54 and thereafter Catholic Democrats were more supportive of broad aid programs than Protestant Democrats, and Catholic Republicans than Protestant Republicans. These differences are apparent even when such factors as geographical region and level of urbanization of congressional districts are held constant.[69]

Thus, as was the case among rank-and-file laymen, Catholic federal legislators have differed little from Protestant ones on trade during these three decades; but on foreign aid, relative support among the former rose while that among the latter declined within both partisan groups. By the mid-fifties Catholics in Congress voted more nearly along the lines suggested by the N.C.C. and its affiliated denominations than did members of these denominations on Capitol Hill.[70]

Furthermore, even though the Episcopal Church had provided less guidance to its members in the way of official utterances on foreign aid than had the Methodists, the United Church of Christ, the United Presbyterians, and the American Baptist Convention, congressmen affiliated

68. Ibid., pp. 59, 66, 136–40 and 256.

69. Leroy N. Rieselbach, *The Roots of Isolationism* (Indianapolis: Bobbs-Merrill, 1966), pp. 62–67 and 196. For similar findings on the late 1950's, see John H. Fenton, *The Catholic Vote* (New Orleans: Hauser Press, 1969), p. 104–7. For continuation of such differences in 1965–66, see Warner, pp. 305 ff.

70. Warner, pp. 305 ff.

with the Episcopal Church manifested a more liberal voting record in 1965–66 on this issue than did any of the other Protestant groups. United Presbyterians, whose church had repeatedly spoken out for expanded aid, multilateral administration of aid, and the like, voted more conservatively on foreign aid than did either Catholics or most other Protestants. Unitarians, Universalists, and Quakers, whose denominations were not members of the N.C.C., cast votes closer to the N.C.C.'s policy recommendations than did members of denominations affiliated with it.[71]

Similar trends parallel to those apparent among churchmen generally have been evident in Congress on other issues as well. The proportion of hard line or anticommunist votes in the mid-sixties was smallest among Jewish congressmen, next smallest among Catholic ones, and largest among Protestants. As has been the case for foreign aid, no correlation has been evident between the policy recommendations of the Protestant denominations and the behavior of congressmen affiliated therewith on international (or domestic) affairs generally. In both houses of Congress members of non–N.C.C. religious groups—Catholics, Unitarians, Quakers, and, especially, Jews—have supported policies advocated by the N.C.C. and its affiliates more than have members of these affiliates.[72]

Moreover, level of activity by Christian religious groups in Washington, other than the Quakers, seems to have had little relationship with behavior with respect to most international issues of members of those religious groups in either house of Congress. The Catholic Church and unofficial groups of Catholic religious persuasion have until quite recently been less active in the field of international affairs in the capital than the N.C.C. or some of its denominations, particularly the Methodists, and some unofficial Protestant organizations. Nevertheless, Catholic congressmen have behaved more nearly along lines favored by agencies of the N.C.C. and its affiliates in Washington than have congressional members of N.C.C. denominations. Methodist congressmen, many of them from the South, in the mid-sixties were less inclined to behave in ways recommended by articulate Methodist groups in Washington than were congressmen of most other religious denominations.[73]

71. Warner, pp. 306, 353–56, and 363–70.
72. Ibid. The criterion for church membership was declared affiliation, not church attendance or other indications of active involvement.
73. For votes on foreign-policy issues by senators and members of the House of Representatives of different denominational affiliations in 1965–66, see Warner, pp. 305–6, 353–56, and 363–70. Activities related to foreign affairs by the

A systematic empirical study of the impacts of the churches on the foreign-policy-making process, including perceptive interviews and observation of congressmen, their staffs, and Department of State, Office of the President, and other pertinent Executive officials, could shed considerable light not only on the effectiveness of current church operations, but also on potentially fruitful programs for the future. Lacking the findings of such comprehensive research, existing indications suggest the hypothesis that the churches, both separately and together, exert relatively little influence on most aspects of foreign policy. The few exceptions have been the handful of issues on which religious groups have mounted major campaigns such as was the case of the proposed universal military training and of diplomatic recognition of the Vatican.[74] The reasons for this apparent slightness of influence are undoubtedly complex, including a number of factors in addition to the failure of communication on the part of national church elites to their supposed lay constituencies within the electorates of federal officeholders.

Many congressmen and Executive officials—perhaps most of them— have continued to feel that religious institutions should confine themselves to questions of general values and leave specific policies and actions abroad to knowledgeable people in and perhaps also out of the national government who are intimately familiar with the pertinent facts. Many individuals closely associated with U.S. foreign policy—including a number who feel they themselves are sensitive to its moral and ethical aspects—have regarded a number of the policies advocated by religious groups as unsound or as moral perfectionist absolutes so general or so divorced from the concrete problems faced by our government as to offer little practical guidance. Although some admit that the level of sophistication of foreign-policy recommendations emanating from churches has improved in recent years, many would undoubtedly still opine that the churches deal too often with non-issues, or they treat real issues in politically unreal terms.

To some extent such friction between the churches and foreign-policy

churches in Washington are examined in Corbett, pp. 4 ff.; E. Raymond Wilson, "Are We Serious About Social Action?" *Christian Century* (10 Feb. 1965) 82, no. 6; and James A. Nash, "Church Lobbying in the Federal Government: A Comparative Study of Four Church Agencies in Washington" (Ph.D. dissertation, Boston University, 1967).

74. See Luke E. Ebersole, *Church Lobbying in the Nation's Capital* (New York: Macmillan, 1951), pp. 138–45, and Shull, pp. 1 and 17 ff. Shull also argues that American Christian churches were likewise influential in modifying the Dumbarton Oaks proposals and in determining the U.S. position at San Francisco on the forthcoming UN system.

makers is inevitable, given basic differences in their respective emphases. Federal officials involved in foreign affairs tend to consider most thoroughly and seriously short-run, pragmatic developments and to approach them from the point of view of the supposed national interest. At best they pursue policies which are in the longer-range interest of the nation. Their effectiveness in pursuing the national interest is the criterion on which they will be attacked politically and promoted or discharged by their elected superiors or appointed senior officials. Perhaps the enlightened long-run interests of the U.S. often coincide with the morally attractive policies advocated by the Church, but religious institutions do not seem to have made this relationship, if it is valid, clear in Washington.

Associated with this problem of intellectual and pragmatic quality of policy recommendations by religious institutions has been the paucity (alleviated somewhat in the last few years) of specialists in foreign affairs on church staffs (see below, p. 216). The churches have also failed on the whole to make effective use of laymen who are professionals in foreign affairs to help collect and analyze the relevant facts in an ethical perspective and present the results effectively at crucial junctures in the policy-making process.[75]

Another related factor is the ambivalence of most religious institutions about lobbying and about admitting that they do in fact attempt to influence legislation. Church agencies in Washington stress their "educational" rather than lobbying character. Apparently most national religious bodies fear jeopardizing their tax-exempt status and their relative immunity from political criticism, are anxious about preserving church-state separation (at least in foreign-policy), are hesitant to press for policies which may later prove to be unwise or ineffective, are sensitive to the considerable disagreement with their own foreign-policy preferences among their own members, and are generally cautious about abandoning the residues of their individualist and pietistic traditions to become actively involved in political controversy. National church groups have thus circumscribed the efforts of their Washington representatives to influence Congress and, moreover, encumbered them with time-consuming and energy-consuming duties at best tangential to political effectiveness. As a result the efforts of most religious groups—

75. For further discussion of these problems, see below, pp. 252–54; Wilson; Nash; and Frank M. Coffin, "Foreign Aid: A Crisis for Church and Nation," *Christianity and Crisis* 27, no. 1 (6 Feb. 1967), pp. 10–11.

with the notable exception of the Friends' Committee on National Legislation (FCNL)—have been piecemeal, usually indirect, poorly focused, and little coordinated rather than systematic, forceful endeavors to orchestrate the diversity of influences on Executive action and legislation in foreign affairs potentially available to churches.[76]

Churches are, of course, only one set of a number of institutions that seek entree to and hearing by those who formulate foreign policy. Even should they significantly improve the quality of their arguments and the effectiveness with which they are presented in Washington, they cannot expect to have and probably should not have more than a limited influence on public policy. Moral aspects, even if ably analyzed, are only one segment of a number of factors which should be considered in the making of policy, and even in the moral sphere, religious institutions cannot hope to become the sole source of ethical perception and wisdom.

However, with better organization and improving quality of their recommendations, churches should be able to gain significantly more serious attention to their views in Washington. The potential influence of individual denominations working separately is undoubtedly very limited. But together, the Christian churches, in cooperation with secular groups whose objectives are similar on particular issues, may realistically aspire to be heard attentively. Where the balance between supporters and opponents in and out of the government is close, Christian churches may make the vital difference between pursuit of a more rather than a less ethically desirable line of action.

But improvement of the content of policy recommendations and of the sophistication and vigor with which they are brought to the attention of policy makers and those who exert relatively direct influence on them is not likely to have even this limited impact unless more interest in and support for such ideas are apparent beyond N.C.C., denominational, and national Catholic headquarters and the few intellectuals and other activists who now actively support the views of their religious leaders.

76. Nash, Wilson, and Hummon, pp. 66–68 and 164 ff. The FCNL, different from other religious agencies in Washington, has been a registered, self-admitted lobby. It has enjoyed additional advantages over other religious bodies as well. It has had a small staff selected for its knowledge of the political process and its effectiveness with Congressmen, their staffs, and pertinent Executive officials. The FCNL has enlisted the active assistance of specialists on the issues concerned in its conversations with policymakers. The Quaker tradition of social and political interest and action combined with at least tacit approval of most of its general policy recommendations by the majority of its constituents have likewise been important supports. As a result the FCNL has probably had more real influence on U.S. foreign-policy making than any other religious body.

Politicians and public officials accord considerable importance to policy statements of the churches concerning the issues on which they surmise that the churches' views are widely supported by their members—issues such as prayers in public schools, use of public funds by private church-controlled schools, divorce laws, birth control, medical ethics, and diplomatic relations with the papacy. But they believe, with considerable validity, that testimonies by church representatives before Congress, pronouncements by the N.C.C. and the denominations, and other statements of religious groups on most aspects of world affairs reflect the views and active concern of only small elites beyond those individuals publicly identified with them.

Legislators report receiving little mail or other advice from churchmen back home on such issues as arms control, foreign aid, or other relations with the communist or third worlds, and a considerable part of that is either ill informed or contrary to the policy recommendations of national religious leaders. Few of them are asked to discuss foreign affairs by local church groups. The small number of their constituents who do discuss world affairs with congressmen are seldom identifiable as churchmen. Moreover, few of these constituents who do talk about foreign policy with congressmen bring up ethical implications stressed by national religious headquarters.

The churches are likely to continue to exert but very limited influence on foreign-policy making, especially in Congress, until they are able to develop real interest and vitality in this field among at least an articulate, active minority of churchmen in congressional districts and demonstrate some capacity to arouse and sustain considerably greater concern and involvement over extended periods at the local level than are now apparent.

PART IV. THE PRESENT AND THE FUTURE

CHAPTER 10. SOME EXPLANATIONS AND INTERPRETATIONS

Given the many progressive policy statements and other utterances on international affairs by the National Council of Churches and its major affiliated Protestant denominations and the relatively widespread approval of most of the ideas there expressed among parish ministers, why have Protestant Americans been sharply less supportive of virtually all types of multilateral cooperation than Jews since the mid-thirties? Why have Protestants been less approving since the late 1950's of foreign nonmilitary aid and liberalization of relations with the communist world than Roman Catholics—whose church was less specific and less articulately liberal on such issues until a few years ago? Why have these repeated policy recommendations had so little impact on rank-and-file American churchgoers, especially white Protestants? Why have Christian churches largely failed to generate much interest in or understanding of the implications of their faith for such issues even among their active adherents?

Undoubtedly many factors account for the phenomena described in the preceding pages. Observations on their relative influence will remain largely impressionistic until empirical, systematic analyses are carefully applied to them. But since the design of more effective efforts to remedy the current situation will depend on valid hypotheses about its causes, some speculative interpretations seem in order.

JEWISH INTERNATIONAL LIBERALISM[1]

The higher average education and occupational and socioeconomic status and the more urban background of Jews than other religious and ethnic groups explain only in part the more liberal international opinions prevailing among them. Even when American Jews have been compared with equally educated, prosperous, and urban Catholics and Protestants, they have been significantly more liberal in their foreign-

1. For further discussion of sources of Jewish political liberalism, see Lawrence H. Fuchs, *The Political Behavior of American Jews* (Glencoe, Ill.: Free Press, 1956), esp. chap. 9; Milton Himmelfarb, "The Jews: How We Are," *Commentary* 39, no. 1 (Jan. 1965); Lucy S. Dawidowicz and Leon J. Goldstein, "The Jewish Liberal Tradition," in *Politics in a Pluralist Democracy* (New York: Institute of Human Relations Press, 1963), pp. 76–90; and Milton Himmelfarb, "Secular Society? A Jewish Perspective," *Daedalus* 96, no. 1 (Winter 1967), pp. 220–36.

policy preferences, as they have also been on domestic issues as well. In all major occupational, income, and other segments of American society, Jews have held generally more liberal views on virtually all international, national, state, and local issues than their Catholic or Protestant counterparts since at least as long ago as the initial national surveys in the mid-1930's.

The justified concern among American Jews about their relatives, friends, and coreligionists generally in Germany, eastern Europe, and elsewhere controlled or threatened by the Nazis was patently an important motivation for support of aid to Britain, France, and the Soviet Union and other programs or proposals designed to limit German aggressions prior to our entry into the war.[2] However, both then and since Jews have also manifested consistently more liberal views than Christians on most international (and domestic) issues little related to the Nazi problem and the well-being of Jews abroad.

The divergent historical experience of Jews, both abroad and in this country, their wider transnational dispersion, and their more intimate associations with non-Americans as contrasted with most American Christians have undoubtedly been major sources of Jewish cosmopolitan-

2. Nevertheless, though more supportive of such measures than Christians, Jews were not immune to the isolationist sentiment in the country even on sensitive questions related to what this country should do about Nazi aggressions. Jewish samples were relatively small within individual surveys, but the considerable fractions of them who consistently sided with the isolationists suggests that many American Jews grossly underestimated the lengths to which anti-Semitism would shortly be carried by the Nazis. Thus, only minorities of American Jews apparently sympathized with the Spanish Loyalists against the Nazi and fascist-aided Nationalists and favored liberalization of the Neutrality Acts to permit sales of munitions to either side in late 1938 (Table 1–3). Fewer than half felt President Roosevelt should have openly criticized Hitler and Mussolini for their aggressive attitudes shortly after Munich (Table 1–4); thought the Neutrality Acts should be changed to permit sales of munitions to belligerants in October 1939 (Table 1–6); approved of any loans to Britain and France at the end of 1939, even if they complied with the Johnson Act (Table 1–6); felt President Roosevelt had not gone far enough in aiding Britain as the Nazis invaded the Soviet Union (Table 1–7); agreed that American ships should transport military and other supplies to Britain in October 1940 (Table 1–7); favored our formal entry into the war against Germany shortly before; or wanted to send Lend-Lease supplies to the U.S.S.R. on the same basis as to Britain after the German invasion of Russia (Table 1–8). Sizable American Jewish minorities would have preferred to live under fascism rather than communism in early 1939 (Table 1–3); believed Chamberlain's and Daladier's appeasement of Hitler at Munich was not a mistake (Table 1–4); thought in early 1941 that Germany would not attack this country if Britain capitulated (Table 1–5); considered it more important to try to stay out of war than to help Britain throughout the period from the fall of France until the Japanese attack on Pearl Harbor (Table 1–7); opposed passage of the Lend-Lease bill (Table 1–7); and disapproved of the convoying of ships to Britain by the U.S. Navy as the Soviet armies were retreating in apparent disorder toward Moscow (Table 1–7).

ism and liberalism. American Jews or their recent ancestors have often migrated from country to country and have been obliged to develop sensitivities to cultural differences in order to make their way. Relatives have frequently stayed in the "old country" or migrated to some country outside the United States. Not only do individual American Jews know relatives in a wider diversity of foreign cultures than most other citizens, but more than most other American ethnic and religious groups, they maintain their concern for and emotional involvement with the security of their ethnic and religious counterparts abroad.

The chilly reception that so many Jews receive in most societies and their perceptions of actual or potential threats to their well-being (if not their lives) likewise encourage tolerance of diversity and of individuals and people different from themselves and identification with more rational, democratic, and liberal (or radical) elements about them. Anti-Semitism is often associated with conservatism, traditionalism, nationalism, militarism, and parochialism, whereas progressives, intellectuals, and cosmopolitan internationalists are typically defenders of Jews, allies, and sources of career opportunities. The experience and fear of anti-Semitism likewise incline Jews to identify with persecuted, underprivileged, or otherwise unfortunate people, both in their own country and elsewhere.

Anti-Semitism probably also reinforces the traditional Jewish emphasis on rational, analytical approaches to human problems, educational attainment, and intellectual pursuits generally to produce relatively liberal international thinking. Only the Chinese among major ethnic or religious groups in America seem to approach the Jews in their respect for the values of knowledge, scholarship, higher education, and intellectuality.

The traditional emphases of the Jewish religion on charity, social justice, and social action in this world contrasted with that of many Christian groups on faith, repentance, the basic sinfulness and imperfectibility of man, personal salvation in the next world, and saving individual souls through conversion to one's own denominational version of Christianity are probably linked as well with the divergent views of the two toward public, including foreign, policy. Whereas Jews have long accorded importance to the role of religion vis-à-vis society and its problems and institutions, the pietistic Christian tradition often argues for separation of religious faith from secular or temporal controversies. The evangelistic Christian orientation and the related linkages of foreign missions with the colonial experience, the "white man's burden," and the like may also be associated with Christian as contrasted with Jewish attitudes toward communism as an ideological threat, U.S. relations with the newly independent third world, and ethnocentric thinking generally.

RECENT CATHOLIC-PROTESTANT DIFFERENCES

Renewal of the Church

Protestantism in America has been undergoing a process of renewal for quite some time—well before that observable in the Catholic Church since the advent of Pope John XXIII—with but little visible impact on the ethical perceptions of most parishioners. Nevertheless, the *aggiornamento* probably accounts for a significant part of the shift in rank-and-file Catholic relative to Protestant international opinions which began around the same time, the late 1950's.

Whereas the national and international leadership of the non-fundamentalist Protestant churches has publicly advocated liberal policies with respect to most international issues since the interwar period, the Catholic church has made significant changes in the priority it assigns to international questions, the specificity of its policy arguments, and the types of policies and practices it has favored since as recently as the late 1950's. Pope Paul VI is perhaps in some respects more cautious, traditionalist, or conservative than was John XXIII, his immediate predecessor, on theological and personal matters (e.g., contraception), but since the late fifties the emphases of the leadership have gradually shifted from the forms of the Roman Church towards the substance of religion and its implications for social, political, and economic issues. In world affairs the Catholic Church slowly moved from quiet diplomacy toward active attempts to influence public opinion.

The thrust of Catholic exhortation to its adherents has shifted particularly on an international issue with respect to which rank-and-file comparative U.S. Catholic opinion has changed the most—relations with the less-developed world. Before the last years of Pius XII, the Catholic Church *qua* church said little about the third world and what was said dealt mainly with the rights and freedoms of its churches and clergy in that area. But by the late sixties the encyclicals *Mater et Magistra* and, especially, *Populorum Progressio*, pastoral letters, publicized discussions at the Second Vatican Council and other communications emanating from Rome and at least part of the U.S. hierarchy had repeatedly pressed for decolonization and expansion and general liberalization of assistance from wealthier to poor societies. Industrialized countries were urged to help less-developed ones to develop economically, socially, and politically as quickly as possible so that their peoples could live in conditions conducive to human dignity. Pope Paul VI proclaimed, "The new word for peace is development"; *Populorum Progressio* stressed not only Christian duties of universal charity but also popular support for more vigorous action by governments of richer nations; and Vatican statements argued that aid should be administered in such a way that the cultures and moral values of the recipients would be respected and economic and political domination by the donors would be prevented.

The Catholic Church's observable behavior and public utterances on other world issues have likewise undergone changes more or less parallel to gradual shifts in general Catholic opinion in this country. Whereas the Church previously projected an anticommunist image, in the sixties the Pope was receiving officials from communist states. He was stressing that although peoples and governments might disagree, it was their right and duty to live in communion with one another. He observed that disputes should be settled by negotiation in truth and reason and by equitable reconciliation, compromise, and cooperation rather than by "force, deceit, or treachery." The traditional Catholic doctrine of the just war had given way to the view that it would be difficult to imagine war, especially nuclear war, as an instrument of justice. The Vatican increasingly opposed nuclear tests and argued that nuclear weapons should be banned, stockpiles equally and simultaneously reduced, effective controls negotiated, and the resources thus saved shifted to reduction of human misery, to development, and the like.

By the 1960's the Church was reasoning publicly that national sovereignty should be increasingly limited, that powerful states should cease pursuing their "one-sided interests" at the expense of the weaker ones, and that world organization must be strengthened to advance the common good. Silent on the UN since its inception, the Church, in *Pacem in Terris* and later statements, stressed membership in the total human community and a stronger UN "more equal to the magnitude and nobility of its tasks." By the mid-sixties the Holy Father was speaking of the need of "establishing progressively a world authority capable of acting effectively in the juridical and political sectors"—in other words, world government.

Although most Catholics, particularly those of limited education, have not been accurately informed about the specific content of these pronouncements, it is probable that they are more generally aware of them than are most Protestants with respect to comparable declarations of the N.C.C. and their respective denominations.[3] The pope, the Vatican Council, and other Catholic leaders and bodies speak to their faithful with more authority than their Protestant counterparts. Catholic statements are accorded more widespread publicity in both the church and the general presses.

Moreover, the general tone of Vatican and other major official pronouncements seems to have been communicated in local parishes more effectively in Catholic than Protestant churches. Though the substance of such encyclicals as *Populorum Progressio* has been infrequently treated, and then superficially, in Catholic sermons or other parish activities, meanwhile utterances of the World and National Councils of Churches and of the Protestant denominations on similar issues have probably enjoyed even less adequate coverage from Protestant pulpits. Catholic priests, less inclined to emphasize the Bible per se in their sermons than Protestant ministers, are more likely to preach from encyclicals, pastoral letters, and other communications from higher ecclesiastical echelons—even when they themselves have not been particularly interested in such documents or informed about their content.

We noted earlier that Episcopalians (and probably Protestants generally) who are aware of the positions of their church on foreign affairs have not been significantly more inclined than unaware co-religionists to hold attitudes congruent with those positions. However, such has probably been less true among Catholics. The more hierarchical (or authoritarian) tradition of the Catholic Church has un-

3. Victor Obenhaus, *The Church and Faith in Mid-America* (Philadelphia: Westminster Press, 1963), pp. 117–18, reported that in his survey of a county in the Midwestern corn-producing region, 40 percent of Roman Catholics were aware of their denomination's general position on at least one public or social issue, contrasted with less than 25 percent of Protestants. Sixty percent of Catholics versus 100 percent of United Lutherans, 88 percent of Augustana Lutherans, 86 percent of Presbyterians, 85 percent of Congregationalists, 81 percent of Baptists, 79 percent of members of the Christian Church, and 67 percent of Methodists could describe their church's stances on no such issues. Moreover, the larger proportion of Methodists than other Protestants so informed was primarily due to awareness of the long-standing opposition by the Methodist Church to consumption of alcohol.

doubtedly resulted in more weight and authority being accorded by its laymen to the views expressed in its pronouncements than to church views among Protestants. This observation, if valid, would help to explain the more prevalent congruence of international opinions of regular Catholic churchgoers with the public stance of their leadership, contrasted with the apparent irrelevance of church attendance in this regard among Protestants.

Though the "winds of change" in the Vatican have not resulted in such dramatic change among diocesan priests as many progressives hoped, significant parallel trends have taken place among clergy in direct contact with parishioners. A number of archbishops, bishops, and older pastors remain quite conservative on foreign policy as well as on domestic public and social issues, but in very few instances have they taken active public positions against the international points of view emanating in the sixties from Rome and advanced by more liberal colleagues of similar station within the Church. Furthermore, the younger parish clergy, usually closer to most parishioners than bishops or even their own pastor-monsignor, are on the whole more interested in the foreign-policy implications of the gospel and more liberal in their international thinking than the older clergy.[4]

Catholic diocesan priests as a group were probably no more liberal on such issues as helping the less-developed world than ministers in N.C.C.-affiliated denominations in the 1960's. They may even have been somewhat more conservative on U.S. relations with the communist world. However, priests seem somewhat more willing than their Protestant counterparts to express views contrary to those prevailing in the pews. Although the vast majority of the liberal comments by priests in their parishes have dealt with race relations or other issues nearer to home, an increasing minority have also argued now and then for improved international cooperation, deescalation of the war in Vietnam, and the like.

Perhaps because of stronger controls by the congregation, insecurity about their careers, responsibilities for the livelihoods of wives and children, and other considerations more pertinent to Protestant than Catholic clergy, liberal Protestant ministers have seemed more cautious or circumspect about expressing views opposed to those apparent in politically conservative congregations. Probably owing to their anxieties about

4. E.g., Joseph H. Fichter, *Priests and People* (New York: Sheed and Ward, 1965), p. 101.

generating divisive controversies in their parishes,[5] many such Protestant ministers elect to do most of their social (including international) witnessing outside their churches where they are less vulnerable, in secular bodies or unofficial religiously oriented groups such as Clergy and Laymen Concerned About Vietnam.

Catholics who have been little informed about the international substance of encyclicals and other church pronouncements are at least vaguely aware of a new atmosphere of change and debate about change—of questioning older traditions, habits, and assumptions—in their church. This more dynamic milieu tends to loosen former inhibitions and attitudes and to facilitate reconsideration and modification of long-held views—especially on domestic social and personal issues but also on foreign affairs. The widely publicized growth of interest among their religious leaders in the implications of the faith for international issues—dramatized by such actions as papal visits to India, the Middle East, the UN, Latin America, and Africa—has at least suggested to many Catholics who know little of the issues involved that they are both important and relevant in some way to their religion.

Election of President Kennedy

The advent of a cosmopolitan internationalist Irish Catholic in the White House, popular among his coreligionists, and the related appointment of Catholics—like his brother-in-law, Sargent Shriver—to prominent foreign-policy roles, undoubtedly accounted for a part of the modification of Catholic opinion toward congruence with the policies of his administration. Conversely, President Kennedy's religion and ethnic background may have alienated not only some Protestant voters who might have preferred a Protestant Democrat over Republican candidate Nixon, but also some Protestant support for his international programs.

However, the impact of John F. Kennedy on Catholic international attitudes relative to that of other factors should not be overestimated.

5. Other motivations for emphasis on activities outside their parishes are involved as well. Ministers may feel more effective cooperating or working with interested, capable groups in their locales rather than with less interested (or even opposed), less able members of their own congregations. Some ministers focus their efforts in the secular community because on principle they feel the role of the church there in such fields is as crucial or more crucial than its role vis-à-vis its parishioners. They also argue that it is preferable to strengthen promising cooperative endeavors in the community rather than to attempt to organize weaker, less effective ones in their churches.

The shift of foreign-policy opinions of rank-and-file Catholics in a liberal direction relative to those of Protestants began at least a year or two before his election to the presidency. Catholic legislators in both houses of Congress were voting more favorably than Protestants for broad foreign-aid programs even earlier—by the mid-fifties. John F. Kennedy was more popular among Jewish than Catholic voters. Moreover, though Irish Catholics have been somewhat more liberal on foreign affairs than Italian Catholics, the latter (as well as some other Catholic ethnic groups) voted for Kennedy in 1960 in larger proportions than did his Irish Catholic compatriots.[6] Nor did Catholics accord all of his foreign policies more support than did Protestants—only in those fields where Catholic opinion had already begun to shift in a liberal direction relative to Protestant opinion during the second Eisenhower administration. Moreover, in these areas—developmental and other nonmilitary aid, technical assistance, negotiation and compromise with the communist powers, entry of Mainland China into the UN, intercultural exchange, immigration, and the like—Catholic-Protestant differences continued to be at least as large under the Johnson administration as under its predecessor. But on tariffs and trade, national defense, military aid, and collective security Catholics did not differ consistently from Protestants during either the Kennedy years, the preceding administration, or the following one.

Shifts Within the Catholic Population

Demographic and sociological changes within the Catholic citizenry—changes unrelated to their religion or developments within their churches per se—have also had a bearing on the relative shifts in Catholic and Protestant international attitudes. The passing of the immigrant Catholic population, the improved education, emergence from ghettoes, assimilation of their descendants into the middle class, and the decline in relative importance of international issues with unique emotional implications for particular Catholic ethnic groups—such as aid to Britain against Germany and Italy—have been significant factors.

Until relatively recently, a disproportionately large number of the few Catholic specialists in international affairs were émigré intellectuals from central and eastern Europe whose countries had come under com-

6. Andrew M. Greeley, "Ethnicity as an Influence on Behavior" (unpublished paper presented at the National Consultation on Ethnic Behavior sponsored by the American Jewish Committee at Fordham University, 20 June 1968).

munist control following the retreat of the Nazi armies. Although a small Catholic Left in international affairs existed as far back as the 1930's, the Catholic cosmopolitan elite seemed for the most part to the right of center. Native-born Catholic Americans—most of whose parents were immigrants or the children of immigrants, members of the working class, and unexposed to college—were too busy climbing the educational, economic, and social ladders to become specialists or even thoughtful amateurs in world affairs. Most of the small cosmopolitan minority in the country generally, however, were not only college-educated themselves; they were also the sons and daughters of college-educated parents. The cosmopolitan elite of relatively liberal orientations was thus primarily a Protestant and Jewish group.

The ghettoized, defensive character of most Catholics extended to international affairs as well as to other spheres. Neither priests nor laymen received much encouragement from local diocesan headquarters to take part in secular discussions of foreign affairs outside their church structure. Thus in 1946 only 8 percent of Catholic whites, contrasted with 13 percent of Protestant whites, belonged to any organization in which world affairs were discussed.[7] The more sophisticated the level of discussion, the smaller the proportion of Catholics in it was; the Council on Foreign Relations, for example, included extremely few Catholic members, and the proportions among its affiliated Committees on Foreign Relations and among groups associated with the Foreign Policy Association were not much greater.

Since World War II an ever increasing number of Catholics have not only been exposed to Catholic higher education but have also been influenced by experience in major public and secular private educational institutions where systematic attention was more often paid to foreign affairs and where the general foreign-policy orientation was more liberal than in most traditional Catholic colleges. Gradually a generation of U.S.-born and U.S.-trained Catholics seriously interested in international affairs emerged from the graduate schools as a new, articulate, and on the whole liberal intellectual elite. Related to this development was the increase in the number of college-educated Catholics who exposed themselves to thoughtful discussions of foreign affairs in the better secular or ecumenical, religiously oriented periodicals, the corresponding growth during the two decades following the Second World War in circulation of such Catholic-associated publications as *The Commonweal, The*

7. SRC survey of June–Aug. 1946.

National Catholic Reporter, America, Jubilee,[8] *Cross Currents, Ave Maria, Catholic World,* and *Ramparts* and the inclusion of more sophisticated international content in diocesan newspapers and other popular Catholic periodicals.

Thus by the mid-sixties the minority of Catholics seriously interested and well informed in foreign affairs, though still proportionally smaller than that among Protestants (and much smaller than that among Jews), had increased considerably. Although still underrepresented among readerships of such periodicals as *Harper's,* the *Atlantic,* and the *New York Times,* and in groups outside the church where foreign policy was responsibly discussed, Catholics of the mid-sixties constituted larger fractions of these then ever before.

Some Interreligious Differences Smaller Than Others

The liberalization of thought, public statements, and actions at the top of the Catholic Church since the late fifties seems to have been accompanied more in some fields than in others by parallel changes in rank-and-file American Catholic opinion. The most marked differences between Catholic and white Protestant thinking in world affairs which developed during the decade following the mid-fifties seemed related to various aspects of foreign nonmilitary aid.

Catholics were more enthusiastic than their Protestant compatriots at least as far back as the late 1930's for domestic counterparts of foreign aid, such as the Roosevelt New Deal, social welfare, aid to dependent children, social security, unemployment compensation, and the Truman Fair Deal. Although the lower average economic status of Catholics than white Protestants and the somewhat larger fraction of Catholics likely to benefit directly from such transfers of wealth at home during this earlier period partly explain their more favorable attitudes, relatively prosperous Catholics were likewise more favorably disposed than equally privileged white Protestants. Ethnic identifications, low education, economic underprivilege, the desire to become Americanized prevalent among religious groups of recent foreign origins, and perhaps other factors among Catholics apparently impeded their application of their approval of help for the less fortunate at home to their counterparts abroad until recently—after these inhibiting demographic factors had been much attenuated.

The broader international composition and social heterogeneity

8. Merged in 1968 with the *U.S. Catholic.*

within the United States of the Catholic Church in contrast with the largely American membership and experience of most Protestant denominations and the limited variety of socioeconomic and ethnic groups within each of them has also perhaps had some bearing on Catholic-Protestant opinion differences with respect to international assistance. The more diverse character of the Catholic Church has probably also had some connection with Catholic-Protestant differences on immigration, international exchanges, and perhaps relations with cultures different from one's own in general.

Divergence in theological traditions and in the social values related to them may also underlie Catholic-Protestant differences on both domestic and foreign aid, as well as on some other international issues. Protestant theology, especially that of Calvinism (and to a lesser degree Lutheranism), has accented social and economic individualism: the individual alone is responsible for himself and progress results primarily from individual competence and hard work. Evangelical Protestantism has tended either to ignore social and public questions or to argue that such problems will be resolved through individual conversion to Christ. Catholic theology, on the other hand, views the well-being of the whole community of man as the concern of everyone and the salvation of each person as dependent on the community of the faithful. Catholic ethics accord more emphasis to social in contrast to individual responsibility, expect less of individuals and their achievements, and are more lenient and forgiving toward individual shortcomings than austere, puritanical Calvinism.[9]

It is true that both Catholics and Protestants have long financed charitable and relief programs abroad under church auspices. The efforts of progressive churchmen and others to extend the sensitivities of churchgoers beyond missionary objectives and charity to encompass justice, understanding of the social, economic, and institutional factors responsible for the plight of the unfortunate both at home and abroad, and support for governmental and intergovernmental as well as church and other private action in these fields have been frustrating and marginally successful among both religious groups.

9. The finding by Stark and Glock among white Christians that religious orthodoxy was negatively correlated with social ethicalism among Protestants, but slightly positively related among Catholics, likewise suggests that these differences in theological emphases have been transmitted to at least some degree to American churchgoers. Rodney Stark and Charles Y. Glock, *American Piety: The Nature of Religious Commitment*, pp. 75–76.

However, the individualistic, free-enterprise ethic of Protestantism has probably been a more inhibiting factor to achievement of these objectives than the Catholic emphasis on social interdependence. Thus there seems little connection among many Protestants between approval of church programs and other privately operated charitable programs in the less-developed world and support for more ambitious, systematic U.S. governmental and international organizational action to assist in basic economic and political development.[10] In fact, the relationship may be slightly negative in some instances, especially where church-related endeavors are perceived as encouragement of self-sufficiency, "food for work," or the like. Among Catholics, on the other hand—most of whom are less hesitant than white Protestants about governmental social and economic action generally—there seems more carry-over from endorsement of church-run programs in Asia, Africa, and Latin America to approval of governmental and intergovernmental action.

Perhaps the support, slightly more widespread among Catholic whites than Protestant whites in the 1960's for liberalization of relations with the U.S.S.R., its allies, and the People's Republic of China[11] is also connected with the more cosmopolitan composition and less austere, eye-for-an-eye-and-tooth-for-a-tooth ethic of the Catholic Church.

WHY SO LITTLE IMPACT ON PARISHIONERS?

Despite these recent developments in the Catholic Church, its overall influence on the international thinking of its followers is only marginally greater than that of the non-fundamentalist Protestant establishments. Regardless of even more liberal and articulate pronouncements from the top, of growing agreement with the views advanced by these statements among parish clergy (wider than among their parish-

10. For example, the Missouri Synod Lutherans and the Southern Baptists have on the whole been more active in missionary activities and in charitable and relief enterprises both at home and abroad than have the theologically less conservative Episcopalians. In 1965, for instance, only a minority among Episcopal churchwomen in northern California considered the dispatching of missionaries abroad among the important roles of their church. Ralph Luther Moellering, "The Missouri Synod and Social Relations: A Theological and Sociological Analysis" (Ph.D. dissertation, Harvard University, 1964), and Earl R. Babbie, "A Religious Profile of Episcopal Churchwomen," *Pacific Churchman* 97, no. 1 (Jan. 1967). Nevertheless, both laymen and clergymen of the former two denominations have been less supportive of foreign economic aid than have their Episcopal counterparts (see above, pp. 172–74).

11. Protestant attitudes toward the People's Republic of China have probably also been influenced by the historic Protestant missionary involvement there and Protestant affinities for Methodist Chiang Kai-shek and his Nationalist government.

ioners), and the growth in the number of interested, informed, and cosmopolitan Catholic laymen, both Catholic and Protestant institutions have largely failed to communicate their leaders' perceptions of the general ethical implications of Christian faith for world affairs to more than a handful of their members. Neither Catholic nor Protestant churches have yet become major determinants of their members' thinking on even the international issues with obvious ethical connotations.

These are not, of course, observations applicable to churches alone. Most secular institutions—national trade unions, the American Bar Association, the U.S. Chamber of Commerce, etc.—are also frustrated in their attempts to influence foreign-policy making and to communicate the views of national leaders to members. They too encounter special difficulties when the basic purposes of their organization and the motivations which attracted their members are quite distant from foreign affairs. Thus when the leaders of the AFL-CIO and major national unions express views on wages, hours, working conditions, and other issues which politicians believe to be a proper concern of the unions and of active interest among their members, both the Executive and Congress take notice, and union members pay some attention. But when the same union leaders speak out on foreign aid, trade with eastern Europe, U.S. policy toward Mainland China, or the like, federal officials doubt whether they represent the views of many union members. Most members, in fact, pay little attention to what their leaders are saying on such issues.[12]

Christian churches encounter many of the same problems as other voluntary organizations in their efforts to transmit the views of leaders to the rank and file and to gain serious consideration of their views by the federal government.[13] Religious institutions constitute only one of many stimuli affecting their parishioners. Churchgoers, like members of secular organizations, are involved in a number of other institutions and interpersonal relationships, which sometimes reinforce, but often countervail, church utterances on world affairs. However, churches also face other problems, peculiar to them. It is to these that we now turn our attention.

12. See Alfred O. Hero, Jr., and Emil Starr, *The Reuther-Meany Foreign Policy Dispute: Union Leaders and Members View World Affairs* (Dobbs Ferry, N.Y.: Oceana Publications, 1970).

13. For further discussion of those barriers to effective communication and influence, see Alfred O. Hero, Jr., *Voluntary Organizations in World Affairs Communication* (Boston: World Peace Foundation, 1960), esp. pp. 108–13.

Dearth of Coordinated Action

Few church members have ever been exposed to serious discussion of the implications of the traditions of their faith for world affairs. Little successful communication relevant to such content from national church headquarters and the elites who are interested in this area downward into church structures to local parishioners has so far taken place. Some spasmodic attempts have been made since the Second World War by one or another denomination or by the F.C.C. or N.C.C. But they did not include the combination of components essential to long-run effectiveness—interesting substantive content presented through educational techniques appropriate to religious group structures and to the target audiences; adequate material resources and trained personnel; forceful, imaginative national, regional, and local leaderships; systematic orchestration of the diverse means of communication potentially available to the major churches working together; and continuation over an extended period of time. Only recently have churches begun to consider seriously what groups they should try to reach first with their limited resources; to think through the international substance they should attempt to communicate to them; to examine systematically institutional and other complex practical problems of involving them; and to inventory critically pertinent experience of secular agencies and the few successful programs sponsored by churches, in search of useful ideas.[14]

Organizational, structural, and related phenomena at the national level have been, in part, responsible for this dearth of effective action, or even of a sense or feel for action, to implement the many policy utterances on the local or even regional, state, diocesan, synod, or comparable intermediate levels. The N.C.C., the organization best equipped to design and execute effective programs, has been a confederation of denominations whose utterances are only nonbinding recommendations and whose constitution and traditions prohibit it from dealing

14. The Peace Priority Program, initiated by the N.C.C. in 1966, provided for examination, evaluation, experimentation, and innovation in international-affairs education. The Departments of International Affairs and of Educational Development of the N.C.C. established a Joint Project Committee on International Affairs Education in 1967, involving international affairs and education specialists from both the N.C.C. and its member denominations, as well as outside consultants, to consider such matters and to provide recommendations for improved programs. A year later, discussion and planning began between the Department of International Affairs of the N.C.C. and the Division of World Justice and Peace of the U.S. Catholic Conference to establish a joint educational endeavor devoted to the less-developed world. However, even should such enterprises prove relatively fruitful, the development, pilot testing, and implementation of effective educational programs are still some years away.

directly with subordinate levels within its affiliated denominations. In order to implement its policies downward it must either stir the national denominational leaders and their staffs to take action or energize state councils of churches to bestir their local denominational affiliates.

Moreover, at least as of 1960, many socially aware Protestant clergymen who have been familiar with the N.C.C. pronouncements and programs have regarded them as timid, bland, and generally unexciting, reflecting least common denominators of agreement among representatives of heterogeneous affiliated denominations.[15] Those in the few denominations relatively active in this field, such as the United Church of Christ and the Methodist Church, tend to feel that the efforts of the latter are less cautious and more lively than those of the ecumenical body. Others have complained that many N.C.C. utterances are couched in vague generalities and have not dealt at appropriate times and in suitable language with the relevant policy aspects of such general issues as arms control; U.S. relations with eastern Europe, the U.S.S.R., and the People's Republic of China; or the less-developed world. Furthermore, clergy in the member denominations tend to judge N.C.C. programs in "international affairs and peace" more frequently as failures than they so regard the N.C.C.'s other "social action" activities.[16]

Most of the denominations, in turn, on the one hand tend to be jealous of their own prerogatives vis-à-vis the N.C.C. in respect of communications relevant to world affairs among their own clergy and members, while on the other hand they show but marginal interest in that field themselves. Few denominations allocate much time, energy, or talent to that domain. Thus only a minority of these affiliated with the N.C.C. see fit to employ on their staff even one full-time member professionally trained in either international affairs per se or in education and communication in that field. In most denominations the individual responsible for foreign affairs and, especially, for educational activities relevant to that domain has also been charged with other substantive spheres of Christian social relations. Some denominations, e.g., most of those composed primarily of Negroes, show even less real concern, through any assignment of personnel and material resources, for international affairs. Participation of their representatives in N.C.C. committees and other N.C.C. enterprises constitutes the principal activity

15. "The Clergy Views the National Council of Churches" (unpublished research report, Bureau of Applied Social Research, Columbia University, 1960), pp. VI–6 and VII–23.

16. Ibid., pp. VI–7 and 8.

in international relations for many religious bodies;[17] moreover, the influence of such participants upon their denominations thereafter has been at most marginal. Even in denominations which have assigned individuals full-time to this content area, these have typically operated on subordinate levels of church bureaucracies, from which roles they have been able to exert little influence on top-level denominational decision making, determination of priorities, and allocation of resources relevant to their field.

Most utterances of both the N.C.C. and the denominations in international affairs are largely the products of a few staff members in cooperation with committees composed of members interested more in their substance than in creating materials to raise issues and generate discussion and action in religious bodies below. Rather than being designed for educational purposes within church structures, with the aid of specialists in education and communication in the same headquarters, they have been phrased for, and directed primarily toward, others already seriously interested in and sophisticated about world affairs, federal officials and members of Congress involved in that field, and interested editors of the religious press and of a handful of more internationally concerned newspapers and magazines.

Only a few of these statements have been accorded much coverage in the secular or popular religious press. Denominational presses could deal more adequately than they have with utterances and activities of the N.C.C. and of the denominations in world affairs, but they have predominantly been house organs devoted to the issues emphasized by their respective denominational officialdoms. Moreover, only minuscule minorities of church people read much material when it appears in either secular or religious periodicals.[18] Such utterances may provide

17. Some observers surmise that the sending of representatives to meetings and other activities outside the denomination has served as a substitute for action, or even as an excuse for doing little in international-affairs education within some denominations. Moreover, the predominantly Negro denominations have for the most part not even participated actively in the international deliberations and programs of the N.C.C. or other ecumenical agencies. Even when they have been prevailed upon to name representatives or participants for such endeavors, the individuals named have frequently, in practice, failed to take an active role.

18. Thus among adult United Presbyterians of the mid-sixties, 60 percent "knew nothing about" the *Atlantic*, 68 percent *Harper's Magazine*, 68 percent the *Saturday Review*, 77 percent the *National Review*, 91 percent the *Reporter*, 66 percent the *Christian Herald*, 86 percent *Christianity Today*, and 87 percent the *Christian Century*. "United Presbyterian National Educational Survey" (Philadelphia: Board of Christian Education of the United Presbyterian Church, 1966), vol. IIA, tables III, VI, and XVII. Only one in eight members of the United Church of Christ read its denominational periodical

sermon materials or emotional support from on high for some atypically interested and outspokenly liberal parish clergy, but seldom are their style and language particularly suitable for educational use in typical parishes.

Staffs charged with the substance of international affairs seldom have either the training, the responsibility, or the resources and authority to design and execute regional or local educational programs. They work primarily with their own small, atypically interested constituencies rather than with Christian education staffs capable of translating their ideas into educational materials and programs or otherwise communicating their basic content into church structures below. Seldom have educational specialists been brought intimately into the planning, designing, wording, and execution of international communications, as they have in missionary and some other fields of social action. Conversely, relatively few Christian educators are sufficiently interested or sophisticated in world affairs or in education in that field to consider the area central to their tasks or to write effective materials and to organize high-content programs on their own. In general, rapport between them and international-affairs people in the churches is poor to nonexistent. Christian educators often confuse two objectives, foreign missionaries and international affairs, and emphasize the former in their materials and programs, while international-affairs personnel often regard their colleagues in Christian education as intellectually unexciting technicians.[19]

"regularly" in 1966, only one out of a thousand *Social Action*, 1 percent the *Christian Century*, 3 percent the *Christian Herald*, and less than 3 percent any of the liberal news analysis magazines, such as the *Reporter*, the *New Republic*, or the *Nation*. Yoshio Fukuyama, *The Parishioners* (New York: United Church Board of Homeland Ministries, 1966), p. 15. Certainly no more than minorities of these minorities who exposed themselves more or less frequently to such publications paid much attention to the very limited coverage of the position of the churches on world affairs within them.

19. In an unpublished survey performed in 1969 on the status of international-affairs education in selected denominations the N.C.C. found that (1) most available materials had a general orientation rather than a specific focus on particular issues; (2) most denominations accorded much less educational emphasis to international affairs than to either foreign missions or domestic political or social issues; (3) whereas missionary education was directed primarily at church school audiences, international affairs education was focused mostly on special groups relatively interested in that field outside church schools and individual parishes; (4) only four of the thirteen persons responsible for international affairs were members of educational curriculum committees in their respective denominations; (5) most educational personnel studied were unable to differentiate adequately between missionary and international affairs education; and (6) the war in Vietnam and, to a lesser extent, general issues of war and peace constituted the substance of most denominational educational programs relevant to world affairs, while economic development and most other issues received but minor (or virtually no) attention.

The foreign-mission leadership has enjoyed much greater financial and personnel resources, prestige, and influence, both within national church bureaucracies and at regional and parish levels, than have the handful of individuals seriously concerned with international affairs. Missionary groups also have the intimate involvements and practical experiences abroad, especially in the less-developed world, and the deep roots in local churches that let them make a greater impact on the international thinking of rank-and-file churchgoers than is made by international-affairs groups in the same religious bodies.

In fact, little has been done to translate the opportunities of missionary leaders into action to cosmopolitanize and broaden international conceptions in American pews. Although church mission boards and staffs have gradually become more sophisticated themselves about international affairs and have shifted their own emphases abroad from "converting the heathen" and paternalism to service in health, education, agriculture, and the like,[20] discussions and prevailing perceptions relevant to foreign missions in local churches in the U.S. have changed much less. Mission personnel have much more influence on the international content of church materials than do church specialists in international affairs, and the quality of that content has certainly improved substantially since the 1930's. However, the thrust of such materials from the frame of reference of broad education in world affairs still leaves much to be desired. Parish activities relative to missions have typically devoted little attention to underlying economic, social, and political phenomena in societies where missions have been active, and even less to the interrelatedness of missionary endeavors with those of secular agencies, particularly of the indigenous and U.S. governments, with respect to these complex matters. Improved cooperation between mission and international-affairs personnel in religious institutions, and coordination of the considerable resources, talents, and appeals of missionary efforts with the overall purposes of internationalizing the thinking of American churchgoers, remain priority objectives for the future.

State and metropolitan councils of churches and regional, state, diocesan, synod, and other levels of denominational jurisdiction between the national and parish levels seldom fill these gaps. Here and there

20. For a critique of the performance of foreign missions relative to development of the third world, see Richard Dickinson, *Line and Plummet* (Geneva, Switzerland: World Council of Churches, 1968).

some stronger, better-staffed state or local council of churches or denominational agency has conducted ad hoc conferences or other discussions for clergy and/or laymen on ethics and world affairs. But for the most part such agencies have neither the strong motivation and energy, the trained staff, the active lay support, nor other prerequisites to design and carry out, on any continuing basis, effective programs in this field. Such intermediate-level bodies at best consider themselves brokers for materials, programs, and other projects designed at the national level or offered them by secular agencies. Without more leadership and assistance from above, it seems doubtful whether much more is to be anticipated from these levels of ecclesiastical organization.[21]

Noncommunication in the Parishes

Lacking substantial encouragement and help from above, few parishes have made much of an effort to awaken and sensitize their members to the ethical implications of international phenomena.[22] Local clergymen—the crucial element in energizing and leading any such programs—are more interested, better informed, and more liberal than most of their parishioners in respect of international affairs, more aware of and more in agreement with the expressions of their denominations and the N.C.C. in that domain, and more apt to feel it to be a proper sphere of concern of Christian churches.[23] However, only a small minority of them have the systematic training, the knowledge, or the intellectual interest to lead their congregation in that field. In few instances has their formal education in colleges and seminaries or their other experiences prepared them for such a role.

Moreover, many other more immediately and locally pressing substantive problems demand the limited time and energy of the parish minister, and only a small minority of ministers view foreign relations as worthy of priority consideration in their congregation. Particularly in one-minister churches the clergyman is swamped with the administrative and pastoral duties of keeping the machinery going, chores which absorb his energies. But even in larger parishes with several clergymen

21. For an empirical study of the reasons for underimplementation of projects of the national Presbyterian Church (U.S.A.) and of its recommendations relevant to such fields as foreign affairs by synod and presbytery agencies in Illinois in the early and mid-1950's, see Gordon L. Shull, "The Presbyterian Church in American Politics" (Ph.D. dissertation, University of Illinois, 1955), pp. 129–33.

22. For a discussion of the lack of attention to such fields of public policy as international affairs in local Presbyterian churches in Illinois, see Shull, pp. 134–89.

23. See above, pp. 165–72, and Stark and Glock, *American Piety*, p. 69.

there has usually been little encouragement to develop special knowledge in such fields as foreign affairs; on the contrary, one's clerical associates and influential laymen in one's parish may resent such demanding intellectual interests, which take time from calls and other more traditional parish activities.

Even where thoughtful, well-read clergymen are willing to brave these perils, the vehicle with which they can reach most parishioners most often, the sermon, provides but limited possibilities. In some churches, particularly the Roman Catholic and the Anglican, the sermon has a quite restricted role in the service and is kept short. Even if a sermon deals with some important aspect of world affairs, the time available is often too limited for effective development of the subject. Many parishioners pay little attention or miss the major points. Selective somnolence, selective attention, selective perception, and selective remembrance operate in churches on Sunday mornings as they do elsewhere. Many of the large number who are uninterested in world affairs, or who feel they should not be on churches' agenda either pay little attention or reject much of the message. Most of the many who disagree with the interpretations or views advanced from the pulpit resist or exclude the offending message.

In fact, comparatively few sermons deal with controversial international issues in a forceful way. Although sermons, prayers, and church services generally call for peace and other widely accepted objectives of mankind, few clergymen are competent to deal responsibly with international affairs, and most hesitate to express themselves from their pulpits on controversial issues in that field, particularly when they feel that many in the audience will disagree with them and some may be better informed than they. Many other issues closer to home demand attention, and priests and ministers prefer to deal with a single field of human activity only now and then—especially areas, like world affairs, which they feel to be of low parishioner interest. If the pastor deals with Vietnam one Sunday, he normally hesitates to focus on foreign aid or some other international problem for some weeks or months. In more orthodox denominations clergymen usually feel obligated to consider international affairs in the context of Biblical exposition; in theologically conservative churches homilies ordinarily stay so close to the Scriptures that world affairs are seldom included. Moreover, clergy are reluctant to express clear-cut views on problems on which not only their congregations but also experts do not agree and with respect to which their own impressions may later prove to be in error—especially in monologic sermons where their congregations are unable to advance alternative interpretations.

But the principal reason why more of the small minority of parish ministers who are interested in foreign affairs have not spoken out more frequently seems to be their hesitation about irritating many of their parishioners by discussing issues fraught with controversy. In particular, they are often reluctant to take public positions on such issues more liberal than or contrary to the opinions of most in their congregation. Regardless of their formal structures, even Episcopal and Methodist parishes are congregation-oriented and controlled, in fact if not so much in theory. The vulnerability of local (and higher-echelon) Protestant clergy to the reactions of laity aroused by emotional issues has often been demonstrated forcefully to ministers.[24]

But even when local clergymen feel that most of their communicants would accord them the right to express ideas on such questions (if not that most would more or less agree with their views), many are timid in their comments for fear of alienating influential minorities, "splitting the congregation," undermining participation in parish activities, and rendering fund raising, pastoral counseling, and other traditional functions of the church more difficult. Ministers are especially hesitant to risk such dissension over matters like world affairs which they suspect most of their members do not consider a proper area (or at least not an important one) for church discussion and which clergymen themselves do not view as being vital enough to their central objectives to warrant the negative effects that might be thus entailed for other, "less distant," concerns. Given such hazards, most clergy choose the safer and generally more acceptable emphasis on personal needs of their flocks.

Nor are many adult parishioners exposed to much Christian ethics

24. A study of a national sample of 1,530 Episcopal parishioners and 259 of their local ministers in 1951–52 discovered that on those public issues where parishioner sentiment was relatively homogeneously more conservative than the stance of the Episcopal Church, the ability of the Church and of its local clergy who agreed with it to deviate from those views and to influence rank-and-file opinion was severely limited. Such was the case with respect to support of the right of conscientious objection, liberalized immigration, and outlawry of use of nuclear weapons against noncombatants, as well as most domestic economic and welfare questions. An exception was the UN, toward which the vast majority of parishioners as well as of clergymen held basically favorable views. See Charles Y. Glock and Benjamin D. Ringer, "Church Policy and the Attitudes of Ministers and Parishioners on Social Issues," *American Sociological Review* 21, no. 2 (April 1956). For the hesitations of parish ministers to deal candidly with controversial issues which may result in discord in their congregations, see Jeffrey K. Hadden, *The Gathering Storm in the Churches*, pp. 216–22.

relative to international affairs in their formative years as children and adolescents in churches. Only minorities of school-age offspring of nominal members of most Protestant churches attend church schools regularly. Particularly in theologically less conservative churches (where attention to this field is less unlikely) many participate only now and then; a majority in recent years seems to take part less than once every two weeks or so. Moreover, many parents regard church school in a rather perfunctory way, from primarily a baby-sitting arrangement on Sunday mornings to a means of spasmodic exposure of their children to some religious values. It is difficult to teach youngsters in a systematic fashion under such limitations even if teachers are competent, motivated to teach, and provided with proper literature and other teaching materials.

Very little that was relevant to the Christian conscience pertinent to foreign peoples and cultures and international aspects more generally was presented as late as the end of the 1940's to those who did attend church schools more or less frequently.[25] Since then, most of the major denominations have revised their church-school literature to include responsible attention to this field. Some recent popular publications of the N.C.C.'s Friendship Press and other publishers containing such substance are available for local parish educational programs. However, a systematic content analysis of materials actually used in church schools would probably discover little attention to this important area even in the late 1960's.[26] Moreover, much of what content there is seems derived from the purposes and experiences of foreign missions,[27] little of which has dealt with ethical problems of development and of policies of the U.S. government in these matters. Indeed, some of this content would probably still be regarded by sensitive people from underdeveloped societies as offensive.

Parish church schools—probably even more than churches themselves—tend to gloss over, bypass, or suppress conflict and controversy

25. In a survey of religious education in greater Pittsburgh in 1948, for example, only 19 percent of 504 Protestant parishes dealt with any aspect of international relations in their Sunday or other church schools. Cited in Albert T. Rasmussen, *Christian Social Ethics* (Englewood Cliffs, N.J.: Prentice-Hall, 1956), p. 100.

26. Such a content analysis of the quantity and also the quality and tone of widely used church-school and other religious education materials would seem a priority research task, perhaps as a Ph.D. dissertation under the supervision of a mature specialist in religious education.

27. Overseas mission boards seem to have greatly influenced much of the treatment of foreign affairs in church-school texts.

such as that inherent in forthright discussions of Christian perspectives on U.S. foreign policy, rather than to deal candidly with them. Furthermore, few church-school teachers (or their supervisors)—the vast majority of them volunteers with little training in pedagogy and virtually none in international affairs—are sufficiently interested or qualified to bring Christian perspectives to bear responsibly on international phenomena to which increasing numbers of their students are exposed by their secular schools and the communications media.[28] Even where instructional materials provide a basis for adequate discussion, the quality of presentation usually leaves much to be desired because of inadequacies of volunteer teachers.

The Personalized, Pietistic Religion of Most Churchgoers

The anxieties of many perceptive local clergymen relative to presenting forthrightly controversial international issues to their parishioners are for the most part well founded. The meagerness of effort by the clergy and their ecclesiastical superiors to communicate to parishioners on ethical aspects of foreign policy is crucial, but it is matched by another factor that is in considerable measure responsible for inaction—the pietistic, otherworldly, and individual-salvationist mentalities and traditions that still prevail in most denominations other than the small, nontrinitarian ones. The gradual development of wider concern for the social and public-policy implications of the Christian faith since the rise of the social-gospel movement in the latter part of the nineteenth century has been rather a clerical than a lay phenomenon among Americans active in local churches.[29]

Even among denominations composed largely of the educationally

28. Thus, 83 percent of parish church schools of the United Presbyterian Church in the mid-sixties had no professionally trained director or minister in charge; they were run by volunteer amateurs. Church-school teachers in United Presbyterian parishes were, in fact, somewhat less apt to read analytical periodicals and the like than adult parishioners as a whole. Ninety-two percent said they did not know of the *Reporter*, 84 percent of the *Christian Century*, and 80 percent the *National Review*. Although 62 percent felt the church should take an active part in solving "such issues as liquor and gambling," only 31 percent felt it should do so for "disarmament" and only 38 percent for any aspect of world affairs—such as foreign aid, the UN, or relations with communist countries. Moreover, most church-school teachers reported that "the Church had helped her (him) very little to understand people of different cultures . . . [and to] work for justice in her community and the world." Oscar J. Hussel and Gerald L. Klever, *Church School Teachers of the United Presbyterian Church* (Philadelphia: Board of Christian Education of the United Presbyterian Church in the United States of America, 1967), pp. 16, 142, and 169.

29. See Glock and Stark, *American Piety*, pp. 69 ff., and Hadden, pp. 6 ff.

privileged, such as the Episcopalians, the United Presbyterians, and members of the United Church of Christ, majorities have perceived their churches and their religion mostly in terms of such personal needs as peace of mind, respite from secular insecurities, social support, or individual salvation—needs only vaguely related to the controversial public issues of the era. If ethical concerns are considered, attention traditionally focuses (especially in the more "Protestant" groups) on drinking, gambling, smoking, and sexual morality. Such individual virtues as honesty, piety, decency, and character are viewed as causes and cures of both domestic and international problems. The pre-social-gospel view that such problems will take care of themselves if men can be taught to be Christians remains the predominant orientation in the pews of even the denominations and parishes composed of more educated members.

Only minorities, in many parishes quite small minorities, perceive much connection between their supposed Christian convictions and international matters, feel that their clergy and religious institutions should speak out on them, or view such questions as properly part of the agenda for their churches. To their local clergy most Christians continue to ascribe primarily the traditional roles of priest, preacher, leader of worship, comforter of the sick and bereaved, and worker with children and youth—not those of social prophet, intellectual stimulator and leader, or challenger of their parishioners' social consciences.[30]

30. In an AIPO survey of March 1968, 52 percent of Protestants (55 percent of white Protestants) and 57 percent of Catholics in America felt the churches should "keep out of political and social matters," only 42 percent (40 percent of white Protestants) and 35 percent, respectively, thought they should "express their views" on such issues. Among United Presbyterians in the mid-sixties, only 26 percent felt the church should try to take an active part in solving problems of disarmament or arms control, 33 percent those of foreign aid, communism, or world affairs in general. *United Presbyterian National Educational Survey* (vol. II A, 1966), pp. 53–54. At about the same time only 25 percent of urban members of the United Church of Christ felt "work for social justice" was a necessary attribute of being a Christian, and only 37 percent thought the denominations, including their own, should have the right to issue policy statements on social or political issues. Yoshio Fukuyama, *The Parishioners* (Philadelphia: Research Dept. of the United Church Board for Homeland Ministries, 1966), pp. 9–14 and 38–42. Even among active Episcopal churchmen in the Diocese of (Northern) California in the mid-sixties, only 35 percent considered Christian education of its members on current social issues a "very important" role for their church, contrasted with 93 percent who so viewed providing the sacraments, 92 percent who so characterized education of children in the traditional beliefs of the Christian church, and 62 percent who likewise considered pastoral counseling for individual church members. Whereas majorities said they would turn to their church for help in solving personal problems, only minorities would do so for even domestic, including community, problems of public import. Fifty-four percent agreed "frequently the Church becomes so involved

Most Protestant parishes show a limited range of social backgrounds, largely drawn from the middle and upper classes, agreeing in general on most political issues, and unenthusiastic about their religious institutions' criticizing the status quo.

Seldom has an interest in the value of religion for social, political, or international concerns been a significant motive for joining or continuing with a church. Involvement is determined for the most part by factors unassociated with such concerns or even counter to them. Traditional, family, and personal considerations, along with unreflective piety, account for the presence of most parishioners in churches. They seek personal satisfactions, social contacts, religious exposure for their children, personal emotional comforting, or religious values for themselves.

Only quite recently have large minorities of white churchgoers, particularly Protestants, perceived such ethically relevant issues as domestic poverty and racial discrimination as bearing much connection to their religious commitments. It is therefore not surprising that only minuscule minorities in the 1960's linked their faith with experientially and psychologically more remote fields such as U.S. military and security policy and U.S. relations with the third world. Even the few who were interested in critical analysis and interpretation of world affairs normally sought such insights and stimulation elsewhere rather than in their churches.

However, most such thoughtful individuals are no longer active in churches. The greater one's commitment to and involvement in the organization life of the church, the less inclined has one been to want

---

in problems of society that it loses sight of the needs of its own members"; only 33 percent disagreed. Survey conducted by the Survey Research Center of the University of California at Berkeley, reported in Earl R. Babbie, "A Religious Profile of Episcopal Women," *Pacific Churchmen* 97, no. 1 (Jan. 1967). For similar findings in the early 1950's on a national sample of Episcopalians, see Benjamin B. Ringer and Charles Y. Glock, "The Political Role of the Church as Defined by Parishioners," *Public Opinion Quarterly* 18, no. 4 (Winter 1954), pp. 337–48, and Charles Y. Glock, Benjamin B. Ringer, and Earl R. Babbie, *To Comfort and to Challenge* (Berkeley: Univ. of California Press, 1967), pp. 202 ff. The percentages who have thought churches should express views on social and public questions have been higher among Negro than white churchgoers. Thus a survey of the mid-fifties reported in Leonard Broom and Norval D. Glenn, "Negro-White Differences in Reported Attitudes and Behavior," *Sociology and Social Research* 50, no. 2 (Jan. 1966), p. 192, found that 61 percent of Negroes versus 47 percent of whites expressed this opinion. Racial differences were larger when education was held constant. However, this racial difference has undoubtedly been primary related to the view among Negroes that churches should be outspoken and generally active in race relations. Negroes on the whole have seemed considerably less interested than whites in churches speaking out on international affairs.

one's church to get into controversial public questions, including foreign policy. People more interested in such fields and in their ethical implications to which local churches should be (but seldom are) devoting some attention have been much less likely than their more pietistic and theologically individualistic compatriots to attend church on Sunday, participate in church organizations, spend time in religious activities, listen to religious programs on the radio, watch them on television, read religious literature, or otherwise ascribe importance to organized religion.[31] When those most apt to be interested in the implications of the gospel for public affairs have participated in recent years, their involvement has often been limited to occasional attendance on Sunday mornings and, perhaps, participation in committees and other church-connected bodies above the parish level. Activists in world affairs among Protestants have been for the most part inactive church members or unaffiliated with churches.

These would normally be the individuals most apt to inject vitality and international content into local social action, Christian education, and similar groups which most N.C.C.-affiliated denominations encourage their congregations to organize. The failure of most local parishes to establish and continue such groups seriously interested in social and public issues, the quiescence of many of those which exist on paper, and the dearth of serious attention devoted to international issues by even the more active ones[32] are undoubtedly related, probably in a

31. Ringer and Glock, "The Political Role of the Church as Defined by Parishioners," discovered during the Korean War that the Episcopal parishioners most committed to and actively involved in their church and those to whom the church was most important in their personal life were the least permissive toward participation of their church in public issues, including international affairs. Rodney Stark and Charles Y. Glock, "Will Ethics Be the Death of Christianity?" *Transaction* 5, no. 6 (June 1968), pp. 7–14, discovered a relatively high correlation between more traditional evangelical, individualistic religious beliefs and church involvement generally among both Protestants and Catholics, but particularly the former. Stark and Glock, *American Piety*, pp. 84–213, found that the more conservative his theology, the more apt the Protestant church-member was to go to church, spend time during the week in church activities, give money to the church, and otherwise take part in church-related enterprises. Denominations of more liberal theological bent—those in which such matters as international affairs have been more apt to be discussed—were less able to attract their members to activities connected with the church than such denominations as the Southern Baptists and the fundamentalist sects. Similar findings were reported by Hadden, pp. 23 ff.

32. Rasmussen, p. 100, cited a survey of 504 churches in Greater Pittsburgh in 1948 which found that only 19 percent had either social action or education committees. Shull, pp. 146–56, discovered that only 45 of 199 Presbyterian (U.S.A.) churches in Illinois in the early and mid-1950's had social action or education committees, notwithstanding some fifteen years of resolutions and other efforts by national, synod, and presbytery assemblies and staffs exhorting churches to activate such groups.

circular way, to the absence of lively, internationally sophisticated participants and the pervasive tendency of such talent to focus its energies elsewhere, outside the churches.

Most of the individuals who populate men's clubs, singles' clubs, couples' groups, women's weekly meetings, and other ongoing activities between Sunday mornings in local churches in recent years tend to be people who are not particularly intellectually alert, socially effective, or in wide demand in secular endeavors devoted to social and public issues. They seem to be seeking social acceptance, emotional support, and refuge in their churches—havens from complex, frustrating, and divisive problems in the secular world—rather than ethical challenges unsettling to their traditional habits and attitudes rooted in the social milieux in which they live. They shy away from conflict and controversy rather than face up to it; many have little understanding of discussion as an approach to examining controversial issues or the philosophy of agreement to disagree; most would undoubtedly oppose the transformation of their churches into forums for discussion of the relevance of the gospel to divisive international (or other) questions; and a majority would probably feel hurt, alienated, or irritated if such a transformation came about.[33] Indeed, many would probably cease participation in the parish church or in activities of their church which dealt straightforwardly with controversy if it became the locus of such debate of issues on which many were sharply divided. The financial health of the parish might thus suffer, unless the more lively intellectual atmosphere attracted as many (and as prosperous and generous) new, issue-oriented members as it repelled. Those who remained though opposed to the new climate or the particular views advanced within it, and the many who seek escape and comforting rather than intellectual stimulation and challenge, might cease to come to the local clergy for counsel in their personal problems. It may well be difficult for one and the same clergy and parish both to serve pastoral needs effectively and to deal candidly and prophetically with divisive issues.

Thus it is not surprising that most of the little discussion of inter-

---

Women's groups excepted, there had been no organized study of any of the rather numerous Presbyterian study literature on social and public issues in three out of four churches; only one out of seven had studied more than one piece (or subject) of such discussion material; and extremely few had devoted attention to any international topic other than the proposed diplomatic recognition of the Vatican and universal military training.

33. For some documentation of these impressions, see Ringer and Glock, "The Political Role of the Church as Defined by Parishioners," and Hadden, p. 222.

national affairs in parishes has been confined to crisis-type issues, such as the war in Vietnam, and that the vast majority of parishioners have seldom heard such matters as U.S. relations with the less-developed world, U.S. nuclear retaliation policy, arms control, or other ethically relevant issues discussed in these terms within their religous institutions. Nor is it difficult to understand why there has been so little connection between the thinking of most church members and that of the clergy in their own parishes on such questions. Indeed, most members probably never hear their ministers or priests express themselves on such issues.

This state of affairs is unlikely to change significantly until local churches learn to deal with real issues in a forthright way, which must include willingness to deemphasize consensus and tranquillity and to face debate and inevitable disagreement. Major change in this direction at the popular level with respect to international affairs will probably not come except as part of a long-term overhaul in traditional theological preconceptions about roles for religion, churches, and clergy still rooted in the minds of American churchgoers. Although this process among younger clergy, religious intellectuals, national church staffs and boards, and the better seminaries was well along by the end of the sixties, the gap between them and the grass roots remains formidable. The hoped-for transformation in the pews will not be achieved either quickly or easily.

The Catholic Situation: Only Somewhat Different

These comments derive primarily from discussions and impressions, buttressed by some research, within Protestant churches. However, the observations seem to apply with but limited amendments to Roman Catholic institutions as well. Although the Catholic Church has advantages over a number of Protestant denominations in some respects, it is also more affected by other limitations on communications to its members pertinent to world affairs.

Perhaps Catholic bishops and priests continue to enjoy more authority and influence over such opinions among their members than do their Protestant counterparts. There has been little anticlericalism among American Catholic laymen comparable to that prevalent in many other countries. In contrast with the decentralization and paucity of structures to achieve effective local action in most Protestant denominations, the Catholic Church has both the potential organizational instruments and institutional resources to get its views and objectives into its parishes once it decides to get them there.

Moreover, Catholics continue to attend church oftener than Protestants and are thus more exposed to their clergy. Although Catholics interested in international affairs (and other fields relevant to social ethics) grow more and more critical and restless within tradition-minded parishes, they have so far remained more inclined than their intellectually alert Protestant counterparts to participate in the church rather than to drift away.[34] They perhaps provide more of a nucleus of support for socially and internationally aware clergy than has been available in much smaller Protestant congregations. The generally more populous Catholic than Protestant parishes have likewise provided greater material and manpower resources, including more clergymen per parish. Whereas it is next to impossible for one-minister-parish Protestant clergy to become knowledgeable in many fields, multi-priest Catholic parishes should permit development of more specialized interests and intellectual sophistication among their clergy.

Religious prophets, like other critics of the status quo, need a sense of personal security to challenge prevailing attitudes and policies. Bachelor priests are free of the concern for the economic security of wives and children. Moreover, the Catholic Church provides them with more institutional support than most Protestant ministers enjoy. Although conservative Catholic bishops have at times shifted outspoken liberal priests from more desirable to less desirable jobs, sometimes responding to pressures from local parishioners, parish clergy cannot be fired by influential members of the parish in the way that many Protestant ministers can be. Nor do Catholic priests feel as often pressed as Protestant ministers by competition to keep their parishioners from moving to another church nearby with a more popular or less controversial clergyman, or to attract members from other churches (even churches of the same denomination). Catholic parishes also tend to be less apt to emphasize social cohesiveness and smooth interpersonal relations among parishioners, who are both more numerous and more socially heterogeneous than in a typical Protestant parish. At least theoretically, pressure to conform for both priests and laity, against divisive or controversial ideas, should be less compelling.

But Catholic bishops, with a few notable exceptions, seem no more interested in achieving effective action in their churches in this area than their Protestant equivalents. Only Rome can require a bishop to act; the U.S. Catholic Conference has no more authority over him than

34. See also Stark and Glock, *American Piety*, pp. 182 and 219.

does the N.C.C. vis-à-vis the Protestant denominations. Competent Catholic staffs working in this field have hardly existed until quite recently, and their influence in their church has certainly been no greater than that of their more numerous Protestant equivalents. Even fewer material resources have been available for activities in this area than among Protestants. Catholic philanthropists more than their Protestant counterparts seem to limit their giving to traditional charities like hospitals, schools, and asylums, mostly in their own dioceses. There is little tradition of support among the Catholic wealthy for such intellectual concerns as international relations, and the Church itself has not elected to fill this gap. Moreover, archdiocesan and diocesan authorities seldom bestir their staffs or local parishes in this field.

At the parish level few priests, especially few older priests, have the education or intellectual interests that would lead them to discuss complicated issues responsibly. (Indeed, some cosmopolitan laymen have been anxious about what priests might say on world affairs if many more of them did speak out.) Even younger priests are minimally exposed to such matters in their formal training in diocesan seminaries, and few of them have been encouraged to develop the knowledge afterwards. Very few local or regional pastoral institutes aimed at in-service training or other educational programs for diocesan priests address themselves to international questions. Furthermore, Catholic sermons are short, many more immediate issues demand attention, and it is difficult for even interested priests to prepare sermons on such a complex field that will be both interesting and understandable across the broad range of sophistication and education represented in the congregation of the typical Catholic church.

Nor have Catholic laymen been any more favorably disposed than Protestants to the entry of their churches and clergy into controversial public issues.[35] As among many Protestants, non-controversial (in the local parish, not abroad!) missionary activities in the less-developed world have provided convenient alternatives to potentially more divisive thought and action on U.S. foreign policy and international relations. Catholics interested in the ethical significance of their religion for U.S. policy are, like Protestants, a limited minority. Parish priests, like ministers, prefer to deal with problems which interest large numbers in their pews. They too want to run solvent, socially and economically viable parishes, rather than to work among irritated, tense congregations, split

35. AIPO survey of April 1968.

over such emotional issues as the war in Vietnam, foreign aid, and Communist China.

It is not surprising that insofar as parish priests have spoken out on public matters, they usually focus on domestic issues, especially race relations and community problems. Except for according some publicity to papal encyclicals and other pronouncements from above and isolated sermons on the war in Vietnam, few speak from the pulpit on Christian ethics in relation to world issues. Nor have sodalities, Holy Name Societies, Catholic Action groups, or other diocesan organizations done so. The greater independence from congregational pressures enjoyed by Catholic than Protestant clergymen is perhaps reflected in regard to more immediate issues, but seems to have little practical outcome, as of the late 1960's, with respect to international affairs.

Thus, although the Catholic Church has apparently had slightly more influence in recent years on international views of its active adherents than have most Protestant denominations, neither the vigor of effort nor the effects of the Church approach those apparent in more traditional areas of Church interest such as marriage and divorce, birth control, and abortion. Even in international fields like economic assistance where rank-and-file Catholics have in recent years been consistently more liberal than Protestants, differences seem to spring as much from the traditional Catholic emphasis on charity, contrasted with Protestant emphasis on laissez-faire individualism, as from any communication of information or ideas pertinent to the ethical aspects of foreign policy per se.

The shift at the top of the Catholic Church from anticommunism to negotiation and reconciliation seems to make less impact at the grassroots level than do the Vatican's stances on foreign aid. Most rank-and-file Catholics are likewise unaware of or have not agreed with the communications from the Catholic elite on this range of issues. Regardless of rethinking and major amendment of the theory of the just war among a number of Catholic intellectuals, the residues of that tradition seem relatively strong among most American Catholics—to judge from their expressed views on the use of military force in U.S. foreign policy. The views expressed from Rome in favor of freer trade, especially with underdeveloped societies, are apparently accompanied by little change in thinking on this issue among typical parishioners.

CHAPTER 11. TOWARD CHURCHES MORE EFFECTIVE IN WORLD AFFAIRS

The obstacles facing those who would develop more widespread interest and understanding in the ethical aspects of international affairs through religious institutions in America are clearly frustrating, multiple, and often mutually reinforcing. No one program or even several programs, however carefully designed and ably executed, are likely to result in significant, lasting effects unless they are part of a congeries of vigorous efforts focused on diverse elements and issues within the churches and carried out over several decades. Marked improvement in the current situation is apt to be apparent only after international dimensions have become integrated and institutionalized into the major means of communication and ongoing life of the churches from their national and international offices through their local congregations.

Moreover, meaningful inroads against the prevailing lethargy, indifference, and resistance to forthright treatment of controversial ethical considerations in foreign affairs, particularly among laity at the parish level, seem unlikely unless similar advances are achieved with respect to social, political, and other living issues in general, including such domestic questions as race relations and poverty. A basic shift of popular theology in the pews from individual pietism to social and political relevancy, supported by major reinvigoration, focusing, and perhaps restructuring of the churches will probably be necessary before notable changes will be apparent in respect of international affairs among large numbers of more typical churchgoers.

Many thoughtful educators and others interested in helping improve public understanding of critical issues facing their country abroad argue that these difficulties are so formidable and effective long-range action so improbable within existing church structures that the limited talent and resources available should be focused elsewhere—for example, on schools, mass media, or certain secular voluntary institutions. A number of internationally aware clergymen and laymen tend to agree or feel that they are more likely to make some impact on policy, public opinion, and thinking in the churches themselves through working with other interested minorities in and out of churches in such groups as Clergy and Laymen Concerned About Vietnam and Negotiation Now which are independent of the restraints and indifference endemic to most ecclesiastical bodies. They reason that such activist groups, if ably led, can dramatize issues for a wider public in and out of the churches, attract the energies of able churchmen which might remain dormant or otherwise be lost in more traditional church atmospheres, provide emotional support, encouragement, and leadership for similarly inclined minorities in pulpits and pews to speak out themselves, develop climates in which cautious leaders and staffs of formal religious bodies can and will do more than they would normally, and take more vigorous action with respect to policy making itself than cumbersome denominational or ecumenical agencies. Moreover, they feel that such lively extra-church bodies can attract a wider range of able talent than can the churches or even ecumenical groups alone.

Certainly any systematic analysis of opportunities for education, communication, and political action in world affairs relevant to church-men should devote careful attention to possibilities for more fruitful collaboration with secular agencies at all levels from the local church to the national and international denominational or ecumenical head-quarters (see below, pp. 240–45). Such an analytical examination should include what might be done outside formal church establishments, including work through relatively "radical" groups, to develop ideas and modes of action, to reinforce the efforts of internationally alert minorities within the churches, and generally to encourage religious institutions to assign higher priority to and deal more effectively with international phenomena. As will be the case for efforts within the churches themselves, potentially efficacious techniques for achieving such ends will vary from one group to the next and must be developed em-pirically, for particular topics, groups, and circumstances. Certainly the potential long-term impacts of the congeries of heterogeneous outside groups—some of them composed largely of ethically conscious church-men, others primarily secular in composition and concern—on individual clergymen and laymen and ultimately on the quality of thought and dis-cussion of international phenomena within the churches themselves are substantial.

However, the problems of encouraging more thoughtful attention to such issues outside formal religious bodies—insofar as the objective is one of communicating beyond the small minority already relatively interested and informed in international affairs—though in some respects different, are likewise typically mutually supporting and difficult to resolve short of major, coordinated, long-continuing efforts. Trade

unions, business and professional organizations, and other mass membership organizations are unlikely to be any more effective in this respect
than churches (see above, p. 214). Sophisticated groups devoted to
international affairs, or to public policy more generally, whether or not
they are concerned with ethical dimensions, typically involve no more
than a relative handful of intellectually alert churchmen, considerably
fewer than are potentially reachable with information and ideas about
ethical aspects of foreign policy through ongoing religious bodies. Furthermore, only a few such groups have broad, analytically oriented
concerns in foreign relations. A number of those in which churchmen
are actively involved focus on only one or a limited range of issues,
advance only particular interpretations and policy recommendations,
attract primarily individuals who agree with their views rather
than stimulating critical thought and discussion, and lose their vitality
once the issue which brought them into existence becomes less important or changes its character.

Although American religious bodies can constitute only one of a
number of influences on public thought, opinion, and policy in regard
to world affairs, their potential long-run contributions seem sufficiently
unique and generally important to warrant more serious thought and
systematic application of talent, energy, and material resources than
has so far obtained. With the exception of school systems and perhaps
mass media, churches would appear to have more potential in this field
than other vehicles.

No other institutions are as well situated to organize expertise to
deal responsibly and effectively with ethical considerations in international relations. If the churches do not bring rigorous thought in that
area vigorously to bear on policy makers, elites who influence their
decisions, and at least potentially interested segments of the public,
no other agencies are apt to do so on any continuing basis, and such
considerations are unlikely to be taken into serious account. Churches
have the contacts, or could establish them, with competent specialists
on international relations, social ethicists, and individuals intimately
familiar with foreign-policy making inside government to develop substantively excellent and provocative comment on a continuing basis.
Churches could likewise enlist the assistance of experts in communication
and education pertinent to world affairs, both in and outside their own
membership rolls, to develop effective techniques to generate more discussion of these phenomena among many more of their members (and

perhaps nonmembers) than has so far prevailed. Able individuals in all these categories are still to be found on church roles; indeed, they may well drift away from organized religion if the churches do not make more intelligent use of their talents.

No other institutions have as many adherents or can communicate as often face to face with so many of the citizenry, including those in public office. Different from their situation in most of Europe and much of the rest of the "Christian" world, churches in America still have considerable strength, prestige, audiences, and ability to take effective action. The central concerns of religious bodies should have more direct connections in the public interest with most broad and many specific international phenomena than do those of trade unions, business and professional organizations, or other populous nongovernmental groups. Moreover, although few clergymen either in local churches or in intermediate or national-level ecclesiastical bodies have adequate training and experience to organize attractive, high-content programs in world affairs on their own, most of them ascribe greater importance to this field within church life and hold views closer to those of foreign-affairs specialists and national religious agencies than do general church memberships. Most ministers and priests would approve of more active and generally effective programs in this field if they were developed and organized by competent church agencies.[1] Furthermore, churches enjoy considerably more latitude—both by law and by practical politics— than do foundations, educational institutions, and other nonprofit organizations to take forthright positions and marshal public opinion and political influence on controversial issues before the Executive and

---

1. In 1960, 69 percent of parish clergymen in N.C.C.-affiliated denominations said they agreed with N.C.C. goals in "international affairs and peace," 63 percent agreed in general with the basic direction of most N.C.C. pronouncements in public affairs, 61 percent disagreed that the "N.C.C. is too concerned with national and international social problems," only 22 percent felt the N.C.C. tended to act too independently of its member denominations, 56 percent would have liked "very much to see church-sponsored examinations of major ethical issues in American life," and 48 percent felt the "N.C.C. has not adequately involved local clergymen in its programs." Majorities of clergymen in most N.C.C.-affiliated denominations seemed likewise to agree in general with the utterances of their own denominations in foreign affairs. See "The Clergy Views the National Council of Churches" (New York: Bureau of Applied Social Research, Columbia University, 1960), pp. III–4, IV–2, IV–5, IV–9a, V–5, VII–16, IX–5, and IX–10. A decade later, in February–March, 1971, 78 percent of Protestant, 90 percent of Catholic, and 91 percent of Jewish clergymen in America agreed that "churches . . . should . . . express their views on . . . social and political questions"; only 21, 6, and 5 percent, respectively, preferred that they "keep out" of these spheres. *Gallup Opinion Index*, April 1971, p. 19. For attitudes of clergymen toward international issues, see above, pp. 165–72.

Congress. Hardly a congressional district in the country would be immune to the effects of well-organized, substantively sophisticated endeavors in international affairs under religious auspices.

The pages following will offer some general suggestions relative to how American churches might over the coming generation improve communication, education, and understanding of ethical dimensions of international affairs, primarily among their own adherents. Although impacts of religious institutions on foreign-policy making will be intimately connected with public understanding of the issues among their members, only tangential attention will be devoted to that complex range of matters. Some of the following recommendations may be applicable to Jewish religious bodies as well, but they are designed to apply primarily to Christian groups.

No exhaustive, detailed, or even semidefinitive discussion of how the churches might proceed can be attempted here. Given the limited practical experience, the paucity of systematic research pertinent to the complex processes involved,[2] and so far only the beginnings of organized thought and discussion within and outside churches of such matters,[3] no more than a few impressionistic suggestions will be offered. The gradual evolution of the diversity of effective programs on the range of substantive issues for the heterogeneous elements reachable by American religious organizations which seems called for will ultimately depend on the imagination and expertise of a number of different individuals, including local clergymen and laymen; the refinement of pilot endeavors through testing on small groups, application to wider audiences, and built-in systems of systematic evaluation; the building of a body of critical thought and empirical research on the relevant educational and communications processes; and a general expansion of talent, energy, material resources, and importance ascribed to this domain within American religious life.

2. For a systematic inventory, abstracts, and a critical evaluation of pertinent research through 1968, see Alfred O. Hero, Jr., "Communication of World Affairs Within and By American Churches: Bibliography and Abstracts" (Boston: World Peace Foundation, 1969), 234 pp.

3. The suggestions following benefited greatly from the author's participation as a consultant in 1968–69 in the deliberations of the Joint Project Committee on International Affairs Education of the Department of International Affairs and the Department of Educational Development of the N.C.C. Readers who participated in those discussions will doubtless recognize herein variations of ideas advanced in the Committee. However, the report of the Committee has not been made public and the judgments and emphases herein are those of the author alone.

PINPOINT EFFECTIVE ELITES AND WORK WITH THEM

Religious institutions should examine more systematically than they have the actual and potential patterns of communication, influence, and action pertinent to ethical perspectives in world affairs within their own structures, decide on priority audiences for their attention and on what they want to achieve with each of them, and then secure whatever outside help they may need in addition to the expertise already available to them to design techniques to gain the desired results with the particular groups in question. Church programs of the past, often designed supposedly for church people (or just people) in general or for whoever might volunteer to participate, have for the most part been of but limited appeal to such influential or potentially influential minorities among the reachable audiences of religious bodies.

Two general types of influentials or potential influentials seem worthy of focused effort: (1) those at every level, including local congregations, who either have entree or could gain entree to one aspect or another of the foreign-policy-making process itself and (2) the considerably larger number at each level who may be of assistance in the long-term, multifaceted effort required to generate concern and understanding in this field among more typical churchmen. Although there is undoubtedly some overlap between these two groups, many who could be involved in thoughtful efforts directed at the federal Executive or Congress might not be effective, or interested, in taking much of a part in the educational processes within the churches. Moreover, the composition of each of these elites probably varies considerably from one issue to the next within the general field of international affairs. Objectives, techniques, and contents of efforts designed to enlist their talents and energies appropriately should also differ among the diverse elements composing these two rather heterogeneous categories. The task of fathoming these complex patterns of communication and influence, locating the pertinent individuals, and designing techniques to deal appropriately with them should be worth considerable discussion with perceptive observers in and out of churches, close observation of the processes themselves, systematic research, and practical action over the next several decades.

Several groups would seem particularly worthy of more focused and continuous attention than they have so far received: (1) specialist in international affairs in universities, research institutions, national governments, international organizations, and, in some cases, theological schools, a number of them already on church rolls; (2) professionals in communication and education in public affairs, especially foreign affairs; (3) persons responsible for preparing or editing religious education materials, periodicals, and printed, electronic, and face-to-face programs, including those pertaining to foreign missions; (4) clergy at all levels, from local ministers and priests through officials at national denominational and ecumenical headquarters, and the seminary and other educators charged with their continuing education and with the formation of coming generations of religious professionals; (5) active laymen at all levels, including the local congregation, who, while not experts in foreign affairs, show well above average interest in that field; and (6) churchmen active in areas of social concern other than international, such as domestic race relations and urban problems. Some specific suggestions relative to each of these groups will be advanced in the sections following.

ECUMENICAL AND SECULAR COOPERATION AND SPECIALIZATION

Interchurch Collaboration Essential

No one Protestant denomination, nor even a combination of Protestant groups such as the N.C.C., nor the Catholic Church in America, will alone be likely to generate the talent, enthusiasm, funds, and popular support to achieve the desired objectives. Coordinated orchestration of efforts is much more apt to exert some long-term impact.

General agreement on important substantive issues should not be an unrealistic objective; basic ethical orientations of the leaderships of the Catholic Church and the major Protestant denominations now differ relatively little on most international issues other than population problems. More divergence of opinion is apparent within each communion than between their respective encyclicals, policy statements, and other officially proclaimed positions on world issues. Although each denomination has developed its own approaches and relationships within its structure, sectarian differences in strategies and techniques of communication and education should not be insurmountable obstacles. Catholic authorities have become increasingly interested in cooperative ventures. Nor should there be much opposition from Protestant religious professionals, even in local parishes.[4]

Closer cooperation between Catholic and Protestant communions would have multiple advantages over the current, unorganized situation. Although there are some differences of practical import at the parish level between Catholic and Protestant churches and among the Protestant denominations, most of their problems of generating interest and thought among communicants seem similar. Projects or techniques which have experienced some success within the United Church of Christ, for instance, might be of some value in other Protestant denominations and in the Catholic Church, and vice versa. Duplication could be minimized and sparse intellectual and financial resources spent more effectively through joint development and implementation of new programs. Ecumenical endeavors should be more attractive to busy specialists in international affairs, adult education, and other fields, as well as to the desired participants. The range of views advanced is likely to be broader, less biased by narrow preoccupations or assumptions, and generally more interesting. Such programs on state council of churches or diocesan levels would generate better understanding of the diversity and international character of Christian churches, as well as develop acquaintances and rapport for subsequent joint educational programs and political action. Moreover, interdenominational and Catholic-Protestant enterprises, particularly if substantively competent and linked with effective involvement of respective communicants, should command broader interests on the part of mass media and wider attention among the public, as well as more marked impacts on Congress and the Executive.

Specialization and Rapport with Nonreligious Groups

Expanded ecumenical cooperation should also include more active collaboration with secular agencies. Many non-church citizens will neither participate in churches' programs, nor pay much attention to

4. In a national survey of a numerous sample of clergy in N.C.C.-affiliated denominations in 1960, majorities in all denominations said they would like to see "close ties between Protestant and Roman Catholic clergy" and expanded cooperation among Protestant denominations. A majority of all N.C.C.-affiliated denominational clergy also said they would "very much like to see increased emphasis on interdenominational world-wide service." "The Clergy Views the National Council of Churches," pp. VII-and 5a and VIII-15. Although most approved of the tones of both N.C.C. stances and those of their own denominations on social and public questions, they reported that most of their program materials and suggestions in these fields in fact came from their own denominations. Ibid., pp. VII-16, Table 7-12, and VIII-10.

their communications—unless they are conducted cooperatively or otherwise linked with secular agencies which have better rapport with these Americans. Moreover, churches will in any event be only one of a number of forces (some of them contradictory) acting on their own faithful, currently less effective on their behavior in this field than mass media, formal education, and even some other voluntary organizations. The impacts of the churches acting in collaboration with other groups interested in improving public understanding and action in world affairs are apt to be considerably greater than those of religious bodies acting more or less in isolation. Furthermore, the churches will need to make use of the experience and expertise available to such groups in developing their own educational programs. In conjunction with such non-church bodies religious institutions may hope to make a substantial as well as a unique contribution.

Such programs as may be developed should also make more of an attempt than has typically been the case to inject provocative questions, interpretations, perceptions, and insights from outside the United States into their content. To some extent this objective may be achieved by involving individual foreigners in the preparation and execution of projects under the more or less complete control of their American sponsors. However, such enterprises are apt to have a more dynamically international flavor if they are designed jointly by American and non-American institutions, preferably for use abroad as well as in this country. More effort might also be applied to searching out with international and foreign institutions opportunities for participation of clergy, seminary students, and other churchmen in roles abroad wherein they will be exposed directly to practical aspects of international affairs.

Considerable specialization or differing emphases as to subject matter, audiences, and techniques by religious agencies as contrasted with secular bodies in the United States seem advisable. Each institution should concentrate its limited resources on those aspects of the world scene in which it has or can readily develop particular expertise, on those groups within the body politic with whom it already has some rapport, or has reasonable hope of establishing some, and on those means of communication which are appropriate for its institutional structure and the groups at which the pertinent ideas are to be directed. Rather than duplicating programs or strategies which may be executed better by others, each agency should carefully consider and, where appropriate, make use of the experiences and programs of such others, cooperate in joint ventures where feasible, provide programs which complement or stimulate efforts by others, and emphasize aspects which are least likely to be dealt with as ably by any other source.

These principles, together with those advanced above relative to designing programs to achieve specific objectives with particular elements reachable by religious groups, suggest a major shift from the couching of program goals in vague moral terms and the general lack of precision and clarity of purposes and audiences which have marked a number of church endeavors of the past. Within the general field of international relations religious bodies should concentrate on ethical and moral factors and direct their efforts mainly at church member and those other Americans who, though not affiliated with churches, ar likely to be realistically reachable by them.

Ethics cannot, of course, be considered in the abstract, in isolation from the international and domestic political realities to which they ar supposedly applicable. Churches will need more active assistance of specialists in international relations in universities and research institutions and of individuals intimately familiar with the relevant policy making processes than has so far eventuated to determine what the ethically relevant questions are and to think and program constructively about them. However, there seems no point in the churches' devoting much of their very limited energies for this field to becoming one mor source of descriptive or analytical programs about international relation per se, the content and purposes of which differ little from those of secular bodies.

Similarly with respect to target audiences, the churches seem hardl likely to marshal the resources to make a major impact on their ow adherents. If they cannot succeed with their own people, it seems ver unlikely that they will do better with many of the unchurched, most of whom are apt to be more indifferent, if not hostile, to ideas emanatin from religious sources. If religious institutions can develop understandin of relevancies of their faith for world affairs among even an influentia minority of their own parishioners over the next twenty years, they wi have achieved a great deal more than many thoughtful observers believ them capable of doing.

The types of cooperation and mutual assistance likely to be benefici to the common objectives of churches and secular agencies are un doubtedly numerous, depending on the opportunities, the personaliti involved, and other factors. Influential authorities in at least sever agencies involved in serious education in foreign affairs have been more interested in working with churches than the latter appear to have been in cooperating with them. Several types of cooperative activities seem particularly promising.

Rather than attempting to design comparable programs of their own, religious institutions should make more use of *bona fide* educational programs already developed and successfully tested out on groups comparable to those in churches. Some of these, such as the Great Decisions discussion program of the Foreign Policy Association, some materials of the United Nations Association, and some programs of the Center for War/Peace Studies and affiliated groups, have been used successfully in some—too few—local parishes. Many, perhaps most, parishes include at least a dozen or so members sufficiently interested and informed to benefit from participating in such discussions if they could be attracted to them in the parish hall, or motivated by their church to take part in them elsewhere, sponsored perhaps ecumenically or by secular groups. More active efforts by churches to motivate their ethically alert people to take part in secular public policy study, discussion, and action groups could not only expand the understanding of pertinent issues among these participants but also bring their ethical frames of reference to the attention of influential groups which might otherwise accord little attention thereto. Some existing programs, designed for leadership groups, could be sponsored in somewhat amended forms by diocesan or ecumenical agencies, to the benefit of clergymen and laymen interested in more intensive, in-depth discussions of more complex international phenomena. In some cases cooperating organizations may even have field staffs able to advise and work with local church groups in organizing such programs, securing resource experts to lead or assist discussions, and helping attract the desired participants.

Churches could also show more active interest in working with other organizations, including those with specialized talents in international relations, in designing and executing joint programs of both education and political action. Able ethicists who are sophisticated about foreign affairs might thus succeed in achieving wider attention to ethical aspects in programs implemented under secular auspices, provided that the ethics involved were not parochial to a particular religious group, or even to Christians alone. The experience of secular educational groups could likewise be valuable to religious institutions in designing programs of their own, specially tailored for their audiences and their substantive interests. For example, individuals intimately familiar with the design and execution of the Great Decisions programs of the Foreign Policy Association and the World Politics programs of the former American Foundation for Continuing Education could cooperate with specialists in international affairs and ethicists in producing ethically provocative reading and discussion materials. Religious institutions might also enlist their assistance in writing brief supplementary materials which pose searching ethical questions, to be used under church auspices in conjunction with descriptive and analytical materials already produced by secular agencies. Likewise with the help of experienced educators from other walks of life, churches could make wider use than heretofore of some of the more effective techniques developed elsewhere in recent years, such as analytical case studies designed to sharpen practical ethical issues, simulation and games, video tape, and closed-circuit television combined with telephone circuits.

Churches could furthermore cooperate more effectively with secular groups at all levels in action-oriented programs and, especially, in enterprises which tied together in interdependent fashion objectives of political action and education. Insofar as their general policy preferences might be similar, religious bodies might, for example, collaborate with such groups as the League of Women Voters and even more internationally thoughtful trade unions, such as the United Auto Workers, from the national to the community levels in efforts to make some impact on the federal Executive, congressmen, or influential opinion in their political constituencies during periods when pertinent policies were under active discussion in Washington. These organizations could at the same time launch coordinated educational efforts among their respective audiences relative to the same issue areas, be they relations with the less-developed world, arms control, or other questions.

In broader terms, churches should relate more effectively to the education and communication endeavors and potentialities in foreign affairs of other institutions and take more into consideration in their own programs the other sources of information and interpretation to which their likely participants have been or may be exposed. Thus, for example, they ought to take advantage of growing sophistication in attention to world affairs in local junior high and high schools in their own church school discussions of similar questions from ethical frames of reference (see below, p. 267). Churches might likewise develop techniques to encourage serious discussions of ethical aspects of international issues raised by presidential and congressional candidates during electoral campaigns.

SHARPEN ETHICAL ISSUES AND UTILIZE SPECIALIZED TALENT

Focus Systematically on a Limited Number of Issues

In terms of tactics and perhaps even medium-term educational strategy, the churches would perhaps be wise to focus their energies not only on influential minorities but also on a few broad issues of continuing significance wherein ethical considerations are especially important and, preferably, relatively easily demonstrated. It would also be helpful if the issues chosen could be approached to some extent from the personal experiences of churchmen and if some potentially effective action with respect to them by church people were feasible. Selecting fewer issues and dealing with them in depth in coordinated programs should have more profound, lasting effects then trying to cover the whole range of ethically relevant international phenomena more or less simultaneously and, necessarily, in relatively cursory and superficial fashion.

Participation of affluent societies in the economic, political, and social development of Asia, Africa, and Latin America has rightly been selected by the Department of International Affairs of the N.C.C. and the Division of World Justice and Peace of the National Catholic Conference for systematic attention. The long-term objectives of the churches should include a gradual transformation of basic attitudes of churchmen from traditional short-run relief and charity, paternalism, and conceptions of relations with these countries mainly in terms of strategic security, national defense, and stopping "communism" toward long-term, fundamental change in the direction of social, economic, and political justice. Foreign aid should constitute only one of the policy areas examined. The human consequences of the world market structure and the importance of liberalized international trade policies on the part of industrialized societies—seldom visible issues in religious bodies—should receive careful attention. Interrelationships between economic and social change and resurgent nationalism, political instability, and violence should be considered, as well as implications of racialism, military aid, and armed intervention from the West. Controversial roles of church-connected activities, especially missions, with respect to more general long-range objectives of less developed countries, should receive particularly critical consideration.[5] Religiously and ethically motivated public support could become a major political force which, along with others, could bring about a reversal in the decline of U.S. aid in recent years, more progressive U.S. trade policies, and a deemphasis of military means.

The role of U.S. power in world affairs in general over the coming generation might be another focus of organized church effort. If that complex topic proved to be too broad, ethical dimensions of U.S. military, defense, and collective security policies might be a more manageable one. The latter might encompass the applicability of the traditional theory of the just war to modern problems of nuclear and guerrilla warfare, U.S. second strike or nuclear retaliation doctrines, the use of military power against left-wing nationalist unrest in the underdeveloped world, and the alleged overreliance of the U.S. on military rather than on diplomatic, economic, political, and other less violent means.

The classic Judeo-Christian commitment to the universal value of every individual human being as equal to that of every other human being—be his government friend, neutral, or foe of ours, or be he a poor illiterate in an underdeveloped country or a more sophisticated person in an industrialized society—could be a frame of reference for examining and humanizing a wide variety of issues of U.S. policy and action abroad, including major aspects of those mentioned so far. This fundamental religious value could motivate churchmen to empathize more with peoples, modes of thought, and ways of life in cultures different from our own, to view issues from their perspectives as well as from ours, to challenge narrow national loyalties, and to view social and political institutions here and elsewhere in more compassionate and relative terms and to consider them as dynamic rather than static secular structures, in need of continuing revision in the light of real human needs.

Interrelate with Domestic Issues

From multiple points of view, the churches should do a great deal more than they have so far to interrelate ethically provocative inter-

5. See, for example, Richard Dickinson, *Line and Plummet* (Geneva, Switzerland: World Council of Churches, 1968), and *World Development: The Challenge to the Churches* (Geneva, Switzerland: Official Report to the World Council of Churches and the Pontifical Commission on Justice and Peace by the Exploratory Committee on Society, Development and Peace, 1968).

national questions with critical domestic issues to which they have recently devoted increasing attention. Such internal problems are typically more easily relatable to the personal experiences and current interests of church people. The churches have developed more coherent ethical thought and more effective strategies and practical techniques for educating and engaging churchmen in domestic race relations and, to a lesser degree, such other domestic issues as urban affairs, exploitation of migratory and other unorganized labor, and environmental problems. Insofar as religious bodies and their members have been interested in social ethics, that concern has been focused primarily on such internal questions. Indeed, the upsurge of church concern with such matters may so monopolize the attention of ethically conscious minorities, including local, regional, and national elites, in the churches as to reduce even further the current minimal resources accorded to international phenomena.

Given the concomitant shift of emphasis from the international to the domestic scene among socially and intellectually aware groups in American society generally, it seems unrealistic to assume that the churches can be induced in the foreseeable future to devote more than tangential efforts to the international sector unless such attention is related in a meaningful (rather than token or artificial) way to domestic areas of central social concern. Moreover, although the limited advances made by the churches since the mid-fifties and their further anticipated progress in such fields as domestic race relations will not automatically result in wider understanding of the gospel's relevance to foreign affairs, they should help to develop ethical sensitivities, acceptance of social relevancy for religious institutions, potentially useful techniques, and a number of practical educational opportunities for educational endeavors involving international content. Conversely, even if church efforts in foreign affairs are only partially successful, they should in the long run reinforce the effects of comparable enterprises focused on domestic issues and generally assist in livening up and invigorating church life.

The dichotomous viewing of domestic versus international phenomena prevalent in most churches seems furthermore inherently erroneous and counterproductive in terms of the substance of the issues, fundamental educational objectives, and long-run political effectiveness. Most of the domestic issues to which churches have been devoting attention are neither unique to the United States nor causally independent of developments abroad nor understandable or resolvable in the artificial confines of limited American experience, insights, and values alone. Discussions of domestic issues should be infused with international experience, programs devoted primarily to international problems should profit from interest and experience of participants in internal phenomena, and future educational endeavors and political action should treat foreign and domestic issues as dynamic wholes.

Relate Newsworthy Events to More General Phenomena

More systematic, intensive attention by the churches to a limited range of continuing, underlying international issues of long-term ethical significance and to their interconnections with equally important domestic questions should not, of course, be so inflexible as to exclude vigorous reaction to dramatic, immediate crisis developments to which ethical perspectives can make significant contributions. Events prominent on the front pages of the popular press and on national television newscasts will often command more widespread attention than will the basic historical, economic, and social phenomena from which those happenings emerge. All too few churchmen heard any ethical comment in their churches on such events as the shootings at Sharpeville in 1960, the murder of hundreds of thousands of so-called "communists" in Indonesia in 1965, or the killing of North Vietnamese noncombatants prior to deescalation of U.S. bombing there in the spring of 1968.

However, if the churches develop ethically, empirically, and otherwise intellectually sophisticated thought and educational and political action with respect to several long-term phenomena of really broad significance, most particular events should be readily relatable to such fields of continuing central concern. Such interest-generating developments should be utilized as concrete examples and as opportunities and points of departure for discussion of more basic issues rather than simply as ad hoc, isolated events worthy of particular comment during or immediately after their occurrence. For example, developments in the Vietnam war could readily provide points of entry into discussions of ethical aspects of U.S. relations with the underdeveloped or third world generally and of U.S. military intervention in such areas. One or more interrelated developments could provide material for discussable case studies involving provocative discussion materials which relate them to more general processes and issues and raise controversial ethical issues of wider significance.

Dealing with Ethical Complexity

Some specialists in social ethics and others in international affairs, plus a few others, have together already produced a not inconsiderable literature, part of it of excellent quality, on ethical dimensions of one or another international problem. Nevertheless, a general sharpening and refining of the intellectual and empirical qualities of ethical analysis, criticism, and questions raised relative to international phenomena and their connections with U.S. domestic issues, and enlistment and development of a considerably expanded stable of articulate, able specialists in the relevant fields will constitute a major precondition for more adequate attention to ethical aspects among policymakers, international affairs experts, the minority attentive to world affairs among the American public, influential elements at all levels within the churches, and, indirectly, church members and the populace generally as well.

The churches need particularly over coming decades to dispel the widely held impression—oversimplified though it may be—in the government and among the international affairs community generally that much of what religious bodies have to say is "beating the air" by utopian idealists who are unwilling or unable to take the time to "do their homework" on the pragmatic realities, or even the moral complexities, of the issues to which they address themselves. Many professionals in international affairs continue to feel the analyses and ideas contributed from ethical perspectives do not meet the intellectual and scholarly standards of secular specialists whose thinking they respect. Long-run effectiveness with respect to these crucial elites will depend on the success of the churches in developing equally dynamic and perceptive thought and equally sophisticated people in a range of substantive fields who stay with critical world problems for years, acquiring competence and respect as peers of these elites and establishing themselves as forces to be reckoned with in the government, the community of world-affairs specialists, and internationally alert elements in and out of the churches. Collectively this empirically oriented, yet morally sensitive interdisciplinary elite should become expert and articulate in the diversity of important and potentially important international phenomena to which ethical perspectives may be relevant.

Since most foreign-policy decisions and actions involve choices between conflicting value alternatives, ideally the range of issues and talents pertinent to ethical reflections should be virtually as broad and varied as the secular fields of international affairs. In some international phenomena significant ethical aspects are relatively clear-cut and simple to understand without much knowledge beyond that available in the popular media. Such may be the reported torture, killing, or other maltreatment of noncombatants, political prisoners, and prisoners of war in South Vietnam; the low level of U.S. nonmilitary aid; the tendency of officials to clothe in self-righteous, moralistic pretensions amoral or even immoral actions taken in the supposedly short-run national interest; the related inclinations of many Americans to perceive the foreign adversaries of the U.S. as evil devils and ourselves as crusaders for the good; and the misleading of the American (and foreign) public by federal officials about the salient facts of our international actions and the real reasons for carrying them out.

But most important international issues involve multiple, often conflicting moral elements. No clear demarcations between right and wrong are readily apparent. No single policy alternative is likely to be agreed upon among morally sensitive experts as more ethical than one or more others. Considerable expertise is necessary to isolate and accord priority to the complex moral considerations involved. Moreover, the most ethical approach to many issues may vary over time, as detailed changes take place in the relevant situations. In many complicated situations even the experts may be unaware of facts necessary to arrive at a solution which incorporates both idealism and realism. Some problems are so highly technical that specialized knowledge is essential to sort out ethical issues and deal with them in terms not only helpful to the technicians but also convincing to the policymakers and other generalists who are obliged to make interpretations and decisions without fully understanding the technical details. Unanticipated international crises may call for rapid decisions wherein only those highly informed about the details may be able to come to reasonably moral judgments. Furthermore both the moral and practical consequences of each alternative line of U.S. action may be very difficult to anticipate, since U.S. policies may have but a marginal influence on the course of events in foreign societies where other powers are also likely to take independent and unanticipated actions.

The wiser course may frequently be to try to identify the conflicting ethical issues inherent in the pertinent international phenomenon and the policy alternatives facing Americans with respect to it and to pose provocative, preferably readily discussable ethical questions, rather than to attempt particular ethical "answers." Pinpointing complex ethical dilemmas and posing penetrating questions designed to provoke constructive controversy and discussion is likely to be less polemical, presumptuous, and, in the long run, erroneous than offering "solutions." Moreover, whereas forceful advocacy of particular policies as more ethical than others may polarize, narrow artificially, or even close down discussion, provocative ethical questions and analysis of the ethical implications of alternative lines of action should be more intellectually stimulating of critical and imaginative thought, more educationally effective, and less vulnerable to attack by those who disagree with the particular ethical judgment and resulting policy alternative proposed.[6]

Furthermore, if the churches are to have significant impacts on more typical churchmen, beyond the small minorities who are analytically inclined and/or already relatively attentive to world affairs, social ethics, or both, they will have to devise affective and personalized, as well as intellectual, techniques and to integrate educational processes into types of individual and group action which are popularly attractive. Different personality types in the churches must be attracted initially to international affairs through varied sorts of experiences, only part of which are likely to be primarily rational. Once so emotionally involved, a number of them may be reached with more theoretical or analytical material. Moreover, even the more internationally and intellectually oriented minority can be influenced by affective experiences and motivated toward more intensive interest and more serious thought through involvement in practical action.

Some aspects of ethical reflection in foreign affairs are, of course, more readily translatable into personal involvement and affective appeals than others. For example, empathy and compassionate sensitivity with respect to other cultures can be advanced through face-to-face intercultural experiences under high-rapport circumstances with foreigners available to the churches. However, many aspects of ethics in world affairs could be translated into relatively simple messages or ideas and integrated into such ongoing vehicles of the churches as hymns, prayers, and church-school materials so as to be understandable to most churchmen.

6. A majority of parish clergy in N.C.C.-affiliated denominations likewise preferred in 1960 that the N.C.C. and their own denominations define issues, line out ethical ramifications, pose searching questions, and encourage people to make their own decisions rather than offer particular recommendations for solutions.

Improve Utilization of Talent

Continuing definitions of ethical dimensions and drawing up of searching questions with respect to even a limited number of complex issues and their articulation and packaging for optimal effectiveness among heterogeneous target audiences will require orchestration of diverse energies and talents which religious institutions have so far done little to develop or organize. Crucial will be the attraction, training, and intellectual development of more theologically trained professionals in social ethics, religious education, overseas missions, and other fields who have a serious interest in relating ongoing processes and events in foreign affairs to Christian theology, faith, traditions, and practices. In addition to helping to improve the quality of analysis, reflection, and education and communication techniques with respect to ethics vis-à-vis foreign affairs, they would assist in preparing a new generation of clergymen sensitive to this area and reeducating current clergy and laymen through graduate and continuing education. A number of this elite should likewise become sufficiently respected for their insights that they will gain access to policymakers in both the Executive and Congress who deal with problems in which they are expert.

The training and effective utilization of such talent in seminaries; religion departments of universities; social action, overseas missions and education departments of denominational and ecumenical organizations on the national, middle judicatory, state, diocesan, and even local levels; and diverse special agencies and ministries will at best require a generation or more of concerted action by religious institutions. The quality of international content and experience available to theological students will have to be substantially upgraded, opportunities for continuing and graduate education in this field broadened, and interesting and varied careers throughout church life expanded to attract, develop, keep, and actively use such a body of able talent.

Moreover, it is unrealistic to expect that such a group of church-connected people will be able to achieve the multiple long-range objectives of religious institutions without considerably expanded, continuing intellectual interchange and practical collaboration with the wide range of internationally sophisticated talent in universities, research institutions, government, international governmental and nongovernmental organizations, and such diverse other secular walks of life as international business, agriculture, and public health. The churches at all levels should exert themseves much more than heretofore to pinpoint, energize, and appropriately involve such outside competence potentially available to them.

Although rapport between social ethicists and other professionals in the churches and the relevant diverse specialized communities in secular life has improved somewhat in recent decades, for the most part the former continue to think and work in relative intellectual and social isolation from the latter. Most nontheologically trained people seriously concerned with world affairs, on the other hand, tend to regard much of the literature and discussion of ethics in relation to that field produced by theologically oriented specialists as difficult to follow, overly abstract, and of little intellectual and practical interest and thus to pay little heed to it.

Even though a number of Americans with specialized knowledge relevant to church objectives in international affairs have been at least nominally affiliated with churches, typically neither their own parish clergy, seminary professors and administrators, nor church officials at higher ecclesiastical echelons have shown much interest in their special talents. For the most part they are pressed to spend the very limited time they devote to churches on canvassing for funds and members, calling, ushering, and other traditional church functions which they regard as tedious or trivial, rather than on activities in which they might make unique contributions. Small wonder that many of these individuals tend to drift away from organized religion, to become nominal members, or, if they continue to participate, to see little connection between their central secular interests and their churches. Visitors from other nations and cultures with special expertise on their own or other countries, some of them affiliated with churches, others not, have likewise hardly been tapped for the many purposes of American religious bodies wherein their observations and insights would be helpful.

The intellectual problems of juxtaposing international realities and their domestic concomitants with ethical perspectives should be sufficiently interesting and important that the churches should have reasonable success in gaining the cooperation of secular specialists if they applied themselves intelligently to that task. Many of these professionals, including a number who are already rather concerned about ethical considerations relevant to their field—would be pleasantly surprised to learn that the churches were really interested in meaningful activities related to their career interests and in making use of their expertise. Some who are but nominal church members, or who have largely left the churches, might thus be attracted back to some extent into organized religion.

The purposes and means of involving them will necessarily vary with the task at hand and the individual. Some already have access to policymakers in Washington in their own fields of knowledge. Once convinced of the validity of the arguments of the churches, particularly if they had themselves helped to develop those arguments, a number would undoubtedly be willing to help communicate them to policymakers and opinion leaders both in and out of the churches. Others who have specialized understanding of foreign-policy-making processes could help religious institutions in thinking through how most effectively to get their ideas seriously considered in those processes. A number could be invited to help perfect churches' thinking and positions on complex international problems and in developing educational materials and other communications directed at clergy, laymen, and the public. More could be enticed into serving as speakers, resource experts, discussion leaders, and the like in regional, state, diocesan, synod, and even parish programs.

Once involved in such endeavors, a number of these specialists would undoubtedly learn a good deal about the ethical problems of their own secular fields through such participation. A considerable fraction of them would probably read more widely and otherwise attempt to broaden their own expertise in that field. Some might become sufficiently motivated to devote enough of their intellectual energies over a long enough period to the problems of special interest to the churches to be of continuing practical assistance to them and even to make original contributions to thought in this neglected field.

International Communication Within the Churches

Improvement of the substantive quality of ethically relevant international content, the development of a larger body of sophisticated talent in this field, and closer cooperation with substantive specialists outside religious institutions should facilitate communication to a wider audience, but even the most valid, important, and provocative ideas will not move very far beyond the small, interested minority without systematic efforts to move them. Moreover, whereas substantial thoughtful attention has already been focused on the substance of ethics and foreign affairs, virtually no research and only the beginnings of serious thought have been devoted to the educational problems pertinent to communicating that substance.[7]

Ideas generated by specialists will ultimately have to be translated into language and programs understandable and attractive to every level in the churches, from readers of *Foreign Affairs* to working-class housewives who did not finish high school and youngsters in typical church schools, and then integrated into their usual activities, habits, and ways of life. Since no one type of program is likely to be appropriate for much more than a relatively homogeneous minority of church people, and significant impacts on even a single individual will typically require exposure to a number of different stimuli, the identification of the forms of activity which will involve and indicate these heterogeneous elements and the designing, testing, implementation, evaluation, and continuous refinement of techniques to broaden their understanding promise to require more originality, time, energy, application of talent, material resources, and organization than the development of the substantive ideas.

The creation and improvement of such programs will not be achieved alone from the top—the national headquarters—of the churches or of any combination of them. A few dioceses, synods, state and municipal councils, and other intermediate level ecclesiastical agencies have experimented with clergy and/or laymen seminars, conferences, study groups, and other vehicles—usually populated by more internationally interested and sophisticated minorities. They and others could be encouraged to experiment further, and the resulting programs and experiences could be evaluated with a view toward wider use of refined versions of the successes and avoidance of repetition of the failures. Regional and local-level church organizations should likewise be brought into planning and pilot testing programs initiated from above; they typically have a more realistic feel for the local situation, they know the local people, and their active participation and cooperation will be essential in carrying out most programs that may be developed. Their early involvement may thus result not only in generally more attractive programs but also in more effective local cooperation when the programs are implemented on a large scale in the field.

7. See Alfred O. Hero, Jr., "Communication of World Affairs Within and By American Churches: Bibliography and Abstracts," mimeographed (Boston: World Peace Foundation, 1969).

National and intermediate-level agencies should likewise carefully search for interesting ideas for programs in local parishes which might provide prototypes or suggestions for trial elsewhere. Some more interested and able parish clergymen and laymen should similarly be brought into planning and pilot testing new programs at an early stage.

Nevertheless, much of the basic impetus, coordination, and even detailed development of programs must necessarily come from the national level, preferably ecumenically organized and pressed. Only a few rather atypical state councils of churches, dioceses, synods, or the like have the trained staff, experience, funds, contacts, or, especially, motivations to move ahead without outside assistance. Only a minuscule fraction of local congregations are likely to do much more than they are doing—very little—without example, help, and judicious pressure from above. Individual, parish, and even intermediate-level action will be most likely when there is a flow of accurate and timely information and ideas and encouragement for expression at appropriate times and places. Centralized groups, with the assistance of staffs and consultants which only they are likely to be able to muster on a sufficient scale, must continuously inventory and evaluate ongoing efforts in the field, must design, test, and distribute programs of their own, organize cooperative ventures with other communions and secular groups at the national level for implementation in local areas, and provide thoughtful guidance required for extended nationwide efforts to educate churchmen. National agencies primarily must likewise arrange for the required training of clerical and lay cadres and elites required for effective local leadership in whatever programs may eventuate.

Upper-echelon church authorities should be under no naive illusions about the magnitude of the task of achieving effective use of such ideas and materials below their national offices. The very concept of doing something in this field, as well as the desirability and feasibility of specific actions, will have to be sold to hundreds of local bishops, seminary deans, and other influential clerical and lay church leaders throughout the United States who currently are at most only marginally interested. With the help of the more interested and activist of these and any other local allies who can be secured inside and outside the churches, particularly within individual parishes, comparable sales jobs will have to be performed on thousands of currently little interested pastors and lay leaders on vestries and comparable parish boards. But even where such time-consuming, often frustrating efforts seem relatively successful, little useful action is likely to transpire without concerted, well-organized, face-to-face hand-holding and rather detailed assistance by individuals intimately familiar with and seriously interested in the pertinent programs.[8] Otherwise, even the most promising ideas and materials are very likely to remain largely intellectual exercises for the few who develop them.

Institutionalize International Affairs in Church Education and Communication Media

Little long-term effect on churchmen's thinking beyond the small already quite interested and generally cosmopolitan minority will be forthcoming unless and until responsible information and ideas and effective educational techniques are integrated regularly and normally into the published materials read and used by clergy, seminarians, laymen, church school teachers and students, and other churchmen in their ongoing habits and activities.

More active interchange and practical collaboration should be vigorously furthered between church and outside specialists in international affairs on the one hand and boards of education and staffs charged with drawing up curricula and providing teaching materials on the other. Together they should be able to produce lively, internationally sophisticated materials which make use of new educational designs such as games, simulation, case studies, drama, and closed-circuit television and, at the same time, appear in formats, as parts of series, and otherwise in forms conventional enough to assure their widespread utilization. Over time a corps of educationally competent and organizationally influential people should be developed who can not only produce good educational materials but also press the cause of international-affairs education through denominational, regional, and lower-echelon judicatory structures.

Active collaboration between international-affairs expertise in and out of the churches and overseas mission boards and staffs responsible for materials and programs aimed at American audiences should be accorded as high, if not even higher, priority. The task of utilizing mis-

8. The effort of the Foreign Policy Association to assist the National Council of Catholic Women in the early 1960's to design and execute a discussion program for members of its affiliated local chapters is instructive in this regard. Good discussion materials and program instructions were produced, but little actually transpired outside of a handful of dioceses with atypically interested leaderships. The F.P.A. finally committed its own staff to organizational work at the local level, still with only limited results.

sionary experience and interest as a vehicle for thoughtful discussions of optimal roles of churches and U.S. society generally vis-à-vis the less-developed world would be greatly facilitated by the revamping of missionary work itself to relate it more closely to the overall problems and objectives of development and to the efforts of secular agencies in the same countries. Nevertheless, a good deal could be done under more or less current conditions to enhance the quality of international content of materials and programs relevant to foreign missions used in American churches.

The Crucial Role of Seminaries

Theological schools, along with religion departments of universities and colleges, should undoubtedly provide the principal home bases for the required expanded community of theologically and ethically oriented analysts of the international and attendant domestic scenes. Seminaries will also be largely responsible for the sensitivity, substantive competence, and educational effectiveness of the next generation of clergy, by far the most important elite with respect to communication and education in international affairs in religious institutions. They are likewise at least a potentially significant vehicle in broadening competence in both substance and educational approaches of the current generation of religious professionals and interested laymen.

The little pertinent research and critical observation in existence[9] suggest that only a few seminaries—for the most part larger ones, with more numerous and specialized faculties, good research libraries, and active associations with major universities—offer even a single one-semester course which deals more or less sytematically with world

9. Ernest W. Lefever conducted a survey by mail of teaching at a sample of sixty-four Protestant seminaries in 1954, when he was associate executive director of the Department of International Justice and Goodwill (predecessor of the Department of International Affairs) of the N.C.C. Another was mailed to seminary presidents and deans by Calvin J. Sutherlin in 1961. Some relevant observations were also generated by the study reported in H. Richard Niebuhr, Daniel D. Williams, and James M. Gustafson, *The Advancement of Theological Education* (New York: Harper, 1957), esp. pp. 15, 51–52, and 100–102. See also the articles in the special issue of the *Christian Century* of 23 April 1969 (vol. 86, no. 17), "World Politics in the Seminary," and mimeograhed papers prepared by Connolly C. Gamble, Jr., and Emma Lou Benignus, respectively, for the meeting of the Joint Committee on International Affairs Education of the Departments of International Affairs and Christian Education of the N.C.C. devoted to seminary education in foreign affairs, 18–20 Dec. 1968. The comments following profited significantly from the author's participation in the subcommittee of the Joint Committee devoted to seminaries and from discussion with members of the task force of the American Society of Christian Ethics charged with thinking through the role of international affairs in theological education.

affairs. Normally such courses have been taught by an atypically internationally concerned professor of social ethics. Perhaps as many as half of recent seminary graduates have been exposed to some ethical reflection in this field, along with a number of others, in general survey courses in social ethics. Much of this very limited treatment has been rather abstract, theoretical, and lacking in political realism; rarely have such general courses probed systematically concrete world issues.[10]

Most of whatever other little attention seminary curricula have devoted to foreign affairs seems to have been given in teaching relevant to world missions, but its quality in terms of critical analysis of basic economic, social, cultural, and political phenomena in the societies in which missions have operated usually has left much to be desired. Courses in other fields have been primarily domestic in tone, except insofar as a visiting teacher from abroad or an atypically cosmopolitan faculty member may have introduced transnational dimensions. Nor have courses on such subjects as practical and pastoral theology, Christian education, or homiletics done much to prepare future clergymen to deal constructively in sermons, church schools, or other parish milieux with conflict and change inherent in critical discussion of controversial ethical issues such as those of foreign policy. Seminaries and their faculties have been small, specialized international expertise among them infrequent, and the priorities accorded to international aspects low in contrast with other subjects more traditionally associated with theological education competing for attention in already tight curricula.[11]

As more and more seminaries have become associated with universities since the Second World War, systematic, empirically oriented courses in international and related domains in these institutions have

10. Moreover, most of this limited attention to international affairs has been centered on (if not largely restricted to) North American and European phenomena. Whole fields of major ethical salience, such as trade and other economic relations between industrialized and underdeveloped societies, have received hardly any attention (though domestic economic issues were a central concern of the social gospel movement in the United States).

11. These observations seem to apply with some moderate amendment to the seminary education of Roman Catholic diocesan priests as well. Curricula have typically been drawn under a more structured body of theory about theological education than in most Protestant seminaries. Although some attention has recently been accorded to encyclicals and other papal literature dealing with international issues, little systematic, cause-versus-effect analysis of the international phenomena at which these statements have been directed seems to have taken place. Seldom have church utterances been put into meaningful contexts. It seems unlikely that major change in these directions will transpire unless basic theories of Catholic theological education are modified or a few examples or ideas drawn from world affairs can be squeezed into the current system.

become available for academic credit to seminarians. However, in fact neither faculty advisors nor other influences in most seminary environments have actively encouraged many students to take such courses, and only a rather atypical handful, largely advanced students, have done so. Moreover, most of these few have gone into specialized ministries or other careers rather than into parish work or the general life of the churches. Given the relatively few seminarians who were exposed to systematic study of world affairs as undergraduates, the result has been clergy most of whom, though more idealistically liberal in their international opinions and more willing to see their churches involved in the world than most of their flocks, have neither the knowledge, the analytical qualities, nor the communication talents to deal with this field responsibly and effectively.

Continuing education for clergy—accorded but very low priority in terms of talent, material resources, and prestige in most seminaries (and elsewhere)—has offered very little in international affairs and the number of those who have actually availed themselves of the few opportunities offered has been minuscule indeed. Subjects of more apparent immediate utility in typical parishes have dominated continuing education and attracted most of its participants. Continuing education provided for laymen has so far been little more than token gestures, virtually none of which have included much attention to international issues.

The prognosis for internationalization of theological education in its diverse formal and informal aspects in more intellectually isolated, more traditional seminaries—largely trade schools rather than lively centers of thought, discussion, and inquiry—seems unpromising. The quality of their offerings and their general atmosphere pertinent to world affairs seem unlikely to improve substantially short of closing a number of them, the merger or close cooperation of others with larger or more intellectually alert ones of either the same or other denominations, and the physical displacement of those in isolated locales to dynamic university communities.

On the other hand, the rather highly visible, prestigious interseminary ecumenical centers in Greater Boston, San Francisco–Berkeley, Chicago, Atlanta, and several other metropolitan areas, along with the score or so of other theological schools which offer advanced degrees and research and teaching programs and are connected with major universities, could develop over the coming decade a number of interesting pilot programs.

If broadly publicized the more effective of these could serve as examples or prototypes for many other theological schools, which tend in the long run to follow their lead. Moreover, lively programs at these elite institutions would have significant impacts on their own students from whom most future faculty members at other seminaries will be drawn. Programs of systematic research at the doctoral, master, and even bachelor levels, focused on ethics and international affairs per se and on related communication in religious bodies, could provide useful factual data and insights, develop an increasingly important community of theologically trained specialists, and generally lift the quality of thought and teaching in this field in American churches.

Perhaps improvement of the international content of social ethics and world mission courses should receive top priority. Most of these elite theological educational institutions could develop either on their own, or in cooperation with other local seminaries, at least one, and preferably several, high-content, basically analytical courses devoted specifically to international subjects. Cooperative endeavors with local universities and other internationally oriented institutions, such as that focused on defense and arms control between Wesley Seminary and the American University in Washington, D.C., might be attempted elsewhere. Joint courses taught together by theologically trained seminary professors and university-based specialists in foreign affairs might be so conducted as to attract both seminarians and university graduate students. Exchanges of faculty members with other institutions, especially abroad, could be expanded, and more visiting experts on international problems could be brought into programs frequented by theological students. General courses in social ethics and overseas missions to which most students preparing for the B.D. are exposed could make more use of empirical examples and case studies drawn from world affairs to highlight basic moral issues.

However, cosmopolitanization of seminary education should not be limited to formal courses in one or two fields, but extended across most of seminary life from course work in the sociology of religion, pastoral and systematic theology, Christian education, church history, comparative religion, ecumenics, and field work through informal student activities and internships in international governmental and non-governmental bodies and in pertinent offices of the United States Executive and Congress. Matured foreign students, both at seminaries and in nearby institutions, could be more creatively employed to broaden horizons on theological campuses. Multidisciplinary courses related to education and communication, particularly in the local parish, could be attempted, perhaps with the participation of faculty members of affiliated universities and other "outside" experts. Finally, seminary curricula demands could be liberalized and students—including those preparing for the B.D.—more actively encouraged to take part in courses at related universities insofar as their thrusts might differ from those available at the seminary.

A number of the approaches and techniques that might prove effective in the larger, stronger centers of theological education may, of course, not be feasible in seminaries less well endowed with talent, university connections, and financial resources. Other programs would have to be modified substantially to be applicable in more typical seminaries. No one model, or even several, will apply in most places. However, some pertinent programs are undoubtedly feasible in most seminaries where a nucleus of even one faculty member and a few students interested in world affairs is on campus.

Significant upgrading of the quality of analysis and teaching relevant to international affairs and its communication in religious bodies in the seminaries would undoubtedly exert some indirect effects on the current staffs and laymen in the churches. However, more direct efforts to involve them through continuing education seem essential if there is to be much impact in local congregations in the reasonably near future. Opportunities for full-time study in more internationally oriented seminary complexes and universities while on leave from regular tasks for a semester or more, along with systematic courses offered part-time, need to be extended and diversified. However, only relatively few individuals are apt to become involved in such intensive, extended courses. Attractive weekend, one-day, and other briefer experiences should be developed, where feasible in cooperation with ecumenical group and secularly based expertise.

Some Thoughts on Local Parishes

A central target audience for such continuing education by seminaries, state, local, and ecumenical ecclesiastical bodies and other agencies should be the limited minority of clergy and laymen in local congregations who, while not professionals in either international affairs or social ethics, have considerable interest in either or both. Some may follow international developments in semipopular periodicals like *Har-*

per's Monthly, the *Atlantic,* the *New Republic,* the *New York Times,* or in ethically oriented publications like the *Commonweal, Christianity and Crisis,* or the *Christian Century.* A smaller number may be active in World Affairs Councils, Committees on Foreign Relations, Leagues of Women Voters, or other organizations concerned about international relations. Most of them have made little connection between their religious convictions and their thinking on world problems. Others, though concerned about the implications of their faith for domestic social, economic, or political issues, such as race relations and poverty at home, have devoted little attention to its significance for foreign policy. Some may be concerned about one or two timely controversial issues of foreign affairs in an ethical frame of reference, such as the war in Vietnam, but not much about others.

Collectively such partially aware individuals may number only two or three in some small, isolated parishes to a considerably larger minority of the members of others. Some of them hold positions of influence on staffs or advisory or other committees of intermediate-level church agencies or on church-connected newspapers or other publications. A number have some influence on the views of others both inside and outside churches. They originate and carry out whatever activities in world affairs now go on in churches, and they will be the prime movers, executors, influencers, and allies of most future endeavors that can be energized in this field. They will also constitute the nuclei of efforts by churches to exert constructive direct impacts on congressmen in their constituencies. Perhaps a quarter of clergymen and one out of a dozen or so laymen—more in some denominations than others—approach one or a combination of these descriptions.

Fortunately many of these people also constitute a generally more accessible and manageable target audience than most other churchmen. They could compose an influential audience for the analyses, discussions, and insights on ethics and foreign affairs of the specialists, provided that these ideas were presented to them in suitable form. These individuals are more familiar with analytical approaches to problems and with dispassionate examinations of controversial issues than most Americans. Furthermore, they can be attracted to intensive discussions of public questions with less difficulty than more typical churchmen. And those who could be induced to participate in particular seminary, state, metropolitan community, or even ecumenical programs are likely to be both few enough and homogeneous enough in their relevant aptitudes to permit relatively sophisticated discussions with articulate specialists in this field. Over the next generation the churches might succeed to a considerable degree both in broadening and deepening their ethical perceptions with respect to the major continuing international issues of the remainder of the twentieth century and in developing their skills in respect of disseminating and stimulating thought and insights in the field among others, both in and out of the churches. A by-product of endeavors involving both clergy and laity might be a gradual narrowing of the gaps between them and the forging of more effective rapport for local action.

Some parishes include enough such individuals and enough talents and resources to perform part of this educational role at that level. More parishes could secure competent speakers or discussants now and then for Lenten programs, discussion groups, men's clubs, senior citizens' and youth groups, and other regular or ad hoc activities within the parish. Some could even organize all-day sessions on Saturdays or a series of evening discussions in depth once a week or less often, led by competent persons. A few churches have the required resource people on their rolls; if not, they could be brought in from nearby seminaries or universities, from among foreign visitors, or from other sources. Some churches might see fit to develop parish policy statements as means of generating discussion and interest.

But most programs aimed at this important audience will have to be organized jointly either by clusters of nearby churches, by diocesan, synod, state, regional and other intermediate-level ecclesiastical agencies, by seminaries and continuing-education bodies, or, particularly, under ecumenical auspices—perhaps including Jews and secular bodies such as World Affairs Councils and Leagues of Women Voters. The experience of the Workshops of the Church Center for the United Nations, the Council on Religion and International Affairs, the Foreign Policy Association, and other sophisticated groups could be applied more widely at regional and local levels. Two-day and longer retreats and conferences already conducted by some state councils of churches and regional denominational bodies could be attempted elsewhere.

The long-term task of drawing the attention of more typical parishioners to ethical dimensions in international affairs could be considerably facilitated through more effective organization and education of local clergy and their more interested lay minority. However, there is no "mass" public audience in the churches, insofar as that expression implies a large minority with similar levels of knowledge, interests, and attitudes in world affairs or social ethics, reachable through any particular type of communication or technique. Most congregations include a broad continuum in such attributes, in basic personality and modes of thought and participation, and in their potential influence on secular political processes relevant to foreign policy. They must be reached and involved through a multiplicity of heterogeneous approaches from primarily analytical ones such as those envisaged above to basically affective, emotive, and other nonintellectual experiences.

Thus, some parishioners with but slightly above-average interest in world affairs who would not go to the parish hall of another church or elsewhere outside their own parish to participate in a program might do so if it took place in familiar surroundings, especially if they were pressed to do so by their pastor or an associate in the same church or if the program were part of some more general activity in which they were already active. Or they might be attracted if a well-known or prestigious speaker were involved. Others more apolitical or, at least, uninterested in analyses of international political or economic issues, even in ethical terms, might be willing to take part in face-to-face informal encounters with clergymen, students, or other visitors from abroad. Some of them might also be educable through their interests in foreign missions, or in domestic issues with international implications or counterparts.

Nevertheless, it is doubtless unrealistic to hope to involve more than a minority, albeit larger in some parishes than others, in systematic discussions of ethical dimensions in world affairs. Most churchgoers are not sufficiently interested to participate. They tend to opt out of such activities unless they are under considerable social obligation or pressure to stay. Moreover, they have neither the familiarity with international phenomena nor the analytical approach which are essential to their learning much even if they did volunteer to expose themselves to such programs.

Considerable ingenuity on all levels of religious institutions will be required to extract from the sophisticated discussions of the specialists the more important, relatively simple, and yet basically valid ideas about which rank-and-file parishioners should be aware; word them clearly in language they are likely to listen to and understand; and integrate them into activities in which they are apt to take part. Even if typical churchmen grasped only a relatively few uncomplicated, affective rather than intellectual messages about their religion's bearing on foreign affairs, substantial changes in their basic attitudes might ensue.

Such fundamental concepts must be communicated particularly at such times and under such conditions that less interested or more conservative communicants are present, that is, when voluntary aspects are minimal. For most adult church members, this means at general Sunday services, primarily through sermons, or through discussions directly connected with Sunday church attendance. For most children and adolescents the primary instrument must be church schools, religious instruction during released times from secular schools, or, for those who attend them, Catholic private or parochial schools. Means must be devised to circumvent or minimize the problems of utilizing sermons and church schools more effectively and deliberately for this important purpose (see above, pp. 220–24).

If parishioners cannot be reached by sermons, it is unlikely they can be reached by discussion groups, lectures, or other means available to their parish. They might pay more attention to sermons if they were livened up through introduction of more controversial material. Clergymen who hesitate to take personal positions might achieve desirable results through posing searching moral questions that Christians should consider in making up their own minds on particular issues rather than trying to answer them themselves. Guest preachers, including priests and ministers from underdeveloped and communist countries, can express controversial views from the pulpit which the local pastor wishes aired but is cautious about expressing himself. Once such ideas have been advanced by visitors, then the parish clergy may find it easier to deal frankly themselves with the issue in question. Clergymen who do not feel well enough informed themselves or who are otherwise hesitant about advancing their own interpretations and policy preferences could make better use of the pronouncements of their denominations, specifically citing them where desirable, to put these ideas before their communicants. More churches might experiment with open, or "talk back," discussions following sermons, where the preacher can entertain questions and expressions of alternative views on the sermon topic. Such discussions could be varied from time to time by having one or more members of the parish familiar with the topic expand on, ramify, or disagree with parts of the sermon.

If one or more general international issues were accorded prominence by higher echelons in the denomination, by the N.C.C., or ecumenically by both Catholic and Protestant authorities, local clergymen would undoubtedly feel freer to devote more sermons to these issues and to deal with them in a more controversial (and interesting) manner. Even two or three thoughtful sermons a year devoted to Christian ethics in foreign affairs would be a great deal more than currently transpires. But international content should not be limited to two or three sermons *per annum* or to special occasions when some dramatic event on the world scene calls for focused attention from the pulpit. General Christian theological and ethical points or arguments can be illustrated with one or two international phenomena, along with national or local issues, in only several sentences in a larger number of sermons, even on successive Sundays.

It seems unlikely that church schools will provide more lively educational experiences in international affairs (or other fields) unless the parishes of which they are integral parts become more intellectually vibrant places themselves. Moreover, the task will be difficult indeed unless more is done to involve the parents in discussing the same field and in supporting the efforts of their Sunday schools in this regard. Furthermore, even if the quality of church-school materials pertinent to ethics and world affairs were improved, most current volunteer teachers in Sunday schools would not be competent to use them effectively.

A number of well-informed observers therefore feel that only a radical transformation of the current Sunday school system will result in much improvement in the quality of religious education in social ethics, including foreign affairs. They argue for expansion of analytical teaching of religion in secular public and private schools, as has been the practice in Britain, and suggest that parish church schools be replaced by ecumenically organized and supervised, relatively centralized, courses conducted during release time from secular schools, in the afternoon after school, and/or on Sunday mornings. Financial resources, talent, and physical facilities of a number of nearby churches could thus be combined and utilized more effectively. Such agencies would need use only the more able volunteer teachers, and they could be trained more intensively both in teaching and in substantive fields of Christian ethics. Sufficient resources would be available to hire professional educators in more difficult fields insofar as able volunteers were not forthcoming. Content in such areas as foreign affairs could be systematically coordinated with that presented to the same youngsters in social studies in secular schools. Religious courses might emphasize interconnections of Christian doctrine therewith. Such more professional, centralized, ecumenical instruction could likewise have more effect on parents through their children and more directly through involving parents on governing boards, committees, and specially designed programs for them.

Undoubtedly such agencies would offer more attractive opportunities than the current system for better religious education in international affairs. Depending on the details, such a development should be actively supported. But if such ecumenical institutions should eventuate on any extensive scale, they are at least a number of years, perhaps decades, in the future. Action to improve youngsters' understanding of this field should not await this eventuality. More could be done under more or less the current system, inadequate though it may be.

In fact, unless church-school instruction comes to grips more competently than it now does with the important issues of our era, the drift of intelligent parents and their more socially aware offspring away from this pastime will probably accelerate. Bright youngsters above roughly age twelve already balk in large numbers at routine participation in boring Sunday morning sessions which seem so much duller than their experiences in the better public and private secular schools.[12] Many parents who are more interested in the content than the forms of religious experience are coming to agree sufficiently with their offspring to let them drop out of church schools.

Invigoration of church-school literature with more provocative material which dealt forthrightly with major world issues and linked ethical considerations to content learned in secular schools would be a major step in the right direction. More use might be made by teachers at junior high and high church-school levels of articles in such publications as *World View*, the *Commonweal*, and *Christianity and Crisis* as background materials. More promising teachers at the upper levels might be strongly urged to participate in some of the serious discussions about international affairs at higher church echelons mentioned earlier, or in specially designed programs in social ethics for church school teachers at seminaries or elsewhere. Team teaching might be tried, whereby persons especially familiar with specific fields of ethical concern

12. F. H. Hilliard, "The Influence of Religious Education Upon the Development of Children's Moral Ideas" *British Journal of Educational Psychology* 29, pt. 1 (Feb. 1959), pp. 50–59, reported on a number of studies that suggested that many adolescents tended to reject mystical or traditional religious beliefs and practices in favor of pragmatically and ethically oriented religion.

meet periodically with each class, or with the combined classes of the older age groups. Able, busy individuals—including foreign students at seminaries and universities and more matured foreigners—not now active as church school teachers might thus be enticed to take part in their areas of expertise. Informal sessions with foreign high-school students in this country under programs such as the American Field Service might also be helpful. More use might be made of interesting films and other visual or auditory aids, followed by discussion. More ad hoc joint church-school meetings with other churches with particularly interesting personalities might be attempted.

Parents might be assembled with pertinent teachers to help think through the sort of world their children will probably face in adulthood and the goals of Christian education suggested thereby. They should also discuss their own roles vis-à-vis those of the church school in developing their offspring's sensitivities to such phenomena. Some programs for parents and their adolescent youngsters together might be attempted, perhaps with a foreign speaker or American who is both expert on the pertinent subject and articulate with adolescents.

DEVELOPMENT OF RELEVANT RESEARCH

Systematic research on the relevant processes of education, communication, and influence within American religious institutions and between them and the actual making of foreign policy should go hand in hand with the development, pilot testing, and implementation of practical programs.[13] Insofar as feasible, educational programs themselves should have built in from their inception means of empirical evaluation, a form of applied research which, if well grounded in theory and methodology, will itself provide insights of wider import than the particular program in question.

However, the gradual filling of the void of basic empirical knowledge about these important processes would undoubtedly provide many useful guides and hunches for the design of effective practical programs. Moreover, both researchers and imaginative practitioners are likely to benefit from cooperative arrangements in selecting priority topics, generating perceptive hypotheses, providing entrees for interviews, interpreting

13. For further suggestions for future research, see Alfred O. Hero, Jr., "Christian Ethics and World Affairs in American Churches: A Bibliographic Review of Non-Communication," *Religious Education* 65, no. 5 (Sept.–Oct. 1970), pp. 436–46.

findings, and implementing results. Opportunities for interesting and useful studies in these unexplored areas are almost infinite. Only a few suggestions about studies of rather obvious potential value can be mentioned here.

The actual and potential roles of the churches in the making of foreign policy in such ethically relevant fields as arms control, defense policy, the use of military means in various international contexts, and trade, aid, and investment with respect to less-developed countries seem priority research topics which should be interesting to able social scientists and apt to produce results valuable to practitioners. Such studies could begin with careful examinations of whatever literature is relevant to interactions of religious bodies with the federal Executive and Congress and the body of serious research and thought on foreign policy making itself, particularly in the field of foreign relations in question and in policy areas related thereto. A number of perceptive hypotheses could probably be drawn from a combination of such sources and some preliminary discussions with a few interested congressmen, their assistants, and participant observers within the Executive.

However, priority should be accorded to systematic interviews and direct observations on Capitol Hill, in the Department of State, in the Department of Defense, in the Arms Control and Disarmament Agency, in the Executive Office of the President, and in other agencies involved in the area of policy in question. The relevant political processes, and hence the potential points of entry and interaction of the churches, probably vary from one international issue to the next, though there may be some general principles which apply to a number of policy areas.

Such research should consider a number of practical questions, as well as more theoretical ones. What, for example, is likely to be the effectiveness of approaching congressmen at home, in their districts, as compared with approaching them in Washington? What sorts of approaches, by what types of individuals representing religious bodies (specialists on the particular issue at hand, leading churchmen, active churchmen of considerable influence in their districts, etc.) are apt to be most effective? At what points in the development of policy are churches most likely to have an impact? Where in both the executive and legislative processes should the churches expend their energies and what sorts of church-sponsored activities at those points are appropriate? Should the churches generally focus on one timely issue at a time in their encounters with congressmen, or on several simultaneously? How aware of church pronouncements in the foreign-policy areas in question are congressmen and executive officials, especially those affiliated with the churches uttering such statements, and what do these policymakers think of them? Should religious groups coalesce with secular non-governmental groups in their efforts, or is such cooperation apt to dilute or distort unduly the churches' objectives and messages? To what extent do such considerations vary from issue to issue in world affairs?

The pinpointing and examining of those minorities within religious bodies who have or might have significant influences on either these foreign-policy-making processes or on thought, sensitivity, attitudes, and actions toward foreign affairs within the churches themselves deserve systematic study. Research focused on these individuals and the processes in which they have or may have significant roles should not only consider who they are, what their international thinking is like, what their views are of the proper roles for churches in this field, and what they do within religious structures relevant to world affairs, but also what they might be motivated to do and how they might be encouraged to do it.

The identity of these influential or potentially influential groups and the relevant processes through which they may have some impact on either policy making or opinion in the churches will undoubtedly vary from issue to issue. However, the clergy and the educational system that forms their thinking would seem priority research topics in any event.

For instance, little is known about how clergy (or laymen) have developed whatever expertise and views they have in international affairs. From what sources have they learned their information and interpretations? What roles have religious publications or institutions played in these processes, in contradistinction to secular sources, and how might the understanding of world affairs among clergy be improved? What has been, and what might be, the roles of seminary education, continuing education, seminars, leaves of absence for study, and so forth in this regard?

Even less is known about what theologically trained religious professionals, particularly in local churches, do or might be encouraged to do with their interest, information, and ideas in this field. Perhaps analysis of this area should form part of wider studies of local parishes as social and communications systems, in which clergy typically form an important element. Analysis of the actual and potential roles of clergy in the total parish system would require not only careful interviewing of clergymen but also of laymen in their parishes who work with them, are affected by them, and affect them. Interviews could be supplemented with systematic observations of the parish system in operation. Potentially practical results of such studies could include the pinpointing of activities which have been effective in one or more churches as possible prototypes for use elsewhere, as well as providing ideas for programs and materials sponsored by higher-level religious bodies for local clergy and potentially interested laymen. Ideas might also be generated on improving the impacts by local clergy and their churches on the surrounding secular community and on local congressmen.

Little is known about the relative effectiveness of different techniques of communication and education; the relative impacts of diverse types of educational, intercultural, or emotional experiences; or how church-men of heterogeneous backgrounds, interests, and aptitudes become concerned enough to think about ethical aspects of foreign affairs and gradually to develop their understanding in that field. The secular literature in education, communications, learning theory, social psychology, sociology, political socialization, and other related fields could be systematically searched and synthesized for hypotheses to be put to the test in local parishes and in other milieux within church bodies. Such research could consider, inter alia, the potential roles in these basic processes of international awakening and learning of the diverse in-strumentalities available in parish life—sermons, church schools, couples' clubs, women's groups, discussions following Sunday services, Lenten meetings, activities related to overseas missions, ecumenical cooperation with other parishes nearby, collaboration with seminaries and secular agencies in the area, and so on.

Systematic quantitative and qualitative content analyses might be used to determine, inter alia, the degree to which ideas prevalent among national religious leaders and intellectuals interested in foreign affairs and propounded by official statements have found their way into printed materials used in missionary education, church schools, or other activities of local churches, or read by large numbers or important groups of clergy and laymen. The international assumptions, images, and attitudes in widely used teaching materials and popular religious period-icals would seem priority subjects for such research. Content analyses could be especially rewarding if they were coordinated with audience studies of even small samples to determine reactions to the content, the uses to which it is put, and its functions for its readers.

Empirical examination of at least a small, carefully chosen sample of both Protestant and Catholic seminaries in international affairs likewise seems well overdue. A study might begin with questionnaires administered by mail to a much larger sample from which a dozen or so heterogeneous seminaries could be chosen for more intensive study. Interviews and on-the-spot observations should include not only teaching of social ethics and overseas missions but also the diverse aspects of seminaries through which cosmopolitan influences might be brought to bear—field work; pastoral theology; sociology of religion; homiletics; international exchanges of professors and students; cooperative arrangements with international affairs, political science, and other relevant research and teaching at nearby universities; informal student activities; etc. (see above, pp. 258–62). Areas in which teaching is relatively strong versus areas in which it is particularly weak could be scrutinized. Opportunities for internationalization of both future clergymen and, through continuing education, of clergy already ordained and active laymen could be searched out, perhaps in conjunction with studies of practical career opportunities and demands in local churches, higher-level ecclesiastical bodies, special ministries, and elsewhere.

Some of the needed research would probably require funds and other resources well beyond those likely to be available to individual scholars and, especially, graduate students. However, in most cases useful pilot studies or research on particular aspects of more general phenomena could be effectively pursued as thesis topics by properly trained and ably guided Ph.D., Th.D., and even masters candidates. Some of this research could be pursued in such seminary-related fields as the sociology of religion, world missions, Christian education, and social ethics; other studies could be performed by theologically trained and other graduate students pursuing advanced degrees in one or another social science department of affiliated universities.

Certainly a number of these phenomena should be more generally interesting and potentially more significant thesis topics for both graduate students and faculty servicing them than many subjects chosen in the past. Field studies of nearby parishes and local, state, and regional ecclesiastical bodies, of congressional districts, and of other entities within commuting distances of seminaries and secular universities should be manageable as well as financially and otherwise feasible for potentially interested graduate students. Modest fellowships could undoubtedly be secured for studies requiring interviews over extended periods in Washington or elsewhere.

The possibilities of successfully encouraging the performance of such research are intimately related to the general problem of raising the priority accorded to this field among pertinent faculty members of major theological schools and of relevant graduate departments of associated universities. Perhaps some carefully organized discussions in which practitioners and research and academic talent outlined major research areas worthy of attention over the next decade and considered procedures for funding, cooperation, and other administrative matters would be useful. Such sessions might also work out more ambitious interdisciplinary research proposals to be executed on larger scales which might be worthy of financial support by foundations or other sources.

CONCLUSION

Thus the churches could over the coming generation become more effectively relevant to ethical reflection in respect to American foreign policy and international phenomena generally and exert significant impacts on the thinking of their own members, on the body politic generally, and on the policy-making process generally. However, they would be obliged to shift considerably their current priorities. As of the early 1970's the prognosis for their doing so unfortunately does not seem optimistic.

APPENDIX: TESTS OF STATISTICAL SIGNIFICANCE OF DIFFERENCES

Differences in percentages between replies of any two groups may be due merely to sampling error. Assuming random or representative samples of the groups in question, the larger the number of respondents, the less the probability is that a given difference may be due to such error alone, and the more likely it is that this difference reflects a true difference between the total populations from which the samples were drawn.

If one hypothesizes in advance that a group will be more (or less) favorable or opposed to a particular alternative than some other group, then differences in excess of 1.29 standard deviations of the difference (σ_{diff}) may be expected to occur less than once out of ten times due to chance factors alone. Standard deviations may be calculated through the formula

$$\sigma_{diff} = \sqrt{\frac{P_1(100-P_1)}{N_1} + \frac{P_2(100-P_2)}{N_2}}$$

where P_1 is the percentage of the sample of one group expressing the relevant view, P_2 that of the sample of the other group, and N_1 and N_2 the number of interviewees in the respective samples. Table A–1, deduced from applying this formula, provides handy estimates of minimum percentage differences at the 10 percent level of confidence for typical sample sizes for percentages near 35 or 65 percent, 20 or 80 percent, and 10 or 90 percent, respectively.

However, if it is not anticipated that there is a true difference in the behavior between two groups, then percentage differences must be larger, 1.65 σ_{diff}, to occur less than once in ten times due to sampling errors, that is, greater than those indicated in Table A–2.

Table A-1. Sampling errors of differences: one-tail □ $P = .10$

Sample size	500	300	200	100	75	50	25
		For percentages around 35 and 65 percent					
3000	3	4	4				
2000	3	4	5	6			
1000	3	4	5	6	7		
500	4	4	5	7	8	10	
300		5	6	7	8	10	14
200			7	8	9	10	14
100				9	10	11	14
75					10	12	15
50						13	16
25							18

		For percentages around 20 and 80 percent					
3000	2	3	4				
2000	3	3	4	5			
1000	3	3	4	5	6		
500	3	4	4	6	6	8	
300		4	5	6	7	8	
200			5	6	7	8	
100				7	8	9	
75					9	10	
50						10	

		For percentages around 10 and 90 percent					
3000	2	2	3				
2000	2	2	3	4			
1000	2	3	3	4	5		
500	2	3	3	4	5		
300		3	4	4	5		
200			4	5	5		
100				6			

Table A-2. Sampling errors of differences: two-tail □ $P_6 = .10$

Sample size	500	300	200	100	75	50	25
		For percentages around 35 and 65 percent					
3000	4	5	6				
2000	4	5	6	8			
1000	4	5	6	8	9		
500	5	6	7	9	10	12	
300		7	8	9	11	13	17
200			8	10	11	13	17
100				12	13	14	18
75					13	15	19
50						17.	20
25							23

	For percentages	around	20 and 80	percent		
3000	3	4	5			
2000	3	4	5	7		
1000	4	4	5	7	8	
500	4	5	6	7	8	10
300		5	6	8	8	10
200			7	8	9	11
100				9	11	12
75					12	12
50						13

	For percentages	around	10 and 90	percent	
3000	2	3	4		
2000	2	3	4	5	
1000	3	3	4	5	6
500	3	4	4	5	6
300		4	5	6	7
200			5	6	7
100				7	

Table 1-1.   U.S. participation in World War I

	Catholics	Protestants	Jews	Non-church-members
AIPO 147, 2-2-39				
(N)	(571)	(1588)	(93)	(859)
U.S. entry into World War I a mistake	52%	42%	37%	44%
Not a mistake	33	44	48	42
No opinion	15	14	15	14
AIPO 229, 1-22-41				
(N)	(566)	(1589)	(91)	(849)
Entry a mistake	46%	38%	33%	42%
Not a mistake	38	47	52	41
No opinion	16	15	15	17

Table 1-2.   The League and world trade

	Catholics	Protestants	Jews	Non-church-members
AIPO 133, 9-23-38				
(N)	(528)	(1690)	(56)	(867)
U.S. failure to join League partly responsible for European troubles	15%	19%	27%	15%
Not at all responsible	64	62	61	63
No opinion	21	19	12	22
AIPO 181, 1-10-40				
(N)	(537)	(1638)	(41)	(901)
Could describe correctly "reciprocal trade treaties"	7%	10%	18%	9%
Approve reciprocal policy[a]	67	71	76	69
Disapprove[a]	33	29	23	31

[a] Question was posed only to the 41 percent of the public who said they had heard of "Secretary Hull's reciprocal trade treaties." Percentages are of those who expressed opinions.

Table 1-3.   Fascism, Communism, and Franco

	Catholics	Protestants	Jews	Non-church--members
AIPO 141, 12-16-38				
(N)	(488)	(1578)	(73)	(789)
In Spanish Civil War, sympathize with				
Loyalists	19%	31%	38%	34%
With Franco	25	7	5	6
With neither	22	26	25	24
No opinion	34	36	32	36
Remove Neutrality Act prohibition on sales of munitions to either side in Spain	15	18	34	18
Do not	64	61	46	57
No opinion	21	21	20	25
AIPO 145, 1-20-39				
(N)	(591)	(1628)	(72)	(839)
If had to choose, would choose Fascism over				
Communism	34%	24%	19%	27%
Prefer Communism	17	25	45	23
No opinion	49	51	36	50
AIPO 147, 2-2-39				
(N)	(547)	(1613)	(107)	(802)
Sympathize with				
Loyalists[a]	36%	54%	71%	50%
With Franco[a]	37	15	5	17
With Neither[a]	18	19	11	20
No Opinion[a]	9	12	13	13

[a]   This question was posed to only the 61 percent of the public who
    said they had followed events in the Spanish Civil War. Percentages
    are of those queried.

Table 1-4.   Compromises with Hitler and Mussolini

	Catholics	Protestants	Jews	Non-church-members
AIPO 133, 9-23-38				
(N)	(528)	(1690)	(56)	(867)
England and France mis-taken to accept Germany's demands on Czechoslavakia	51%	52%	73%	52%
Not a mistake	28	30	27	30
No opinion	21	19	0	18
Would like F.D.R. to openly criticize Hitler and Mussolini	28	30	33	31
Would not	65	63	60	60
No opinion	7	7	7	9
AIPO 145, 1-20-39				
(N)	(591)	(1628)	(72)	(839)
Return colonies to Hitler	20%	14%	4%	14%
Do not	66	73	90	72
No opinion	14	13	6	14

Table 1-5.   Implications of an Axis triumph

	Catholics	Protestants	Jews	Non-church-members
AIOP 229, 1-22-41				
(N)	(566)	(1589)	(91)	(849)
Would personally be affected if Germany defeats Britain	64%	71%	86%	71%
Would not	28	17	11	17
No opinion	8	12	3	12
Germany would attack U.S. if Royal Navy defeated	48	59	68	58
Would not	42	31	28	30
No opinion	10	10	4	12

Table 1-6.   Neutrality policy before the fall of France

	Catholics	Protestants	Jews	Non-church-members
AIPO 149, 2-22-39				
(N)	(595)	(2079)	(61)	(997)
Allow Britain and France to buy warplanes here	49%	52%	60%	49%
Do not	37	35	33	36
No opinion	14	13	7	15
Allow Germany and Italy to buy them	16	13	8	14
Do not	73	77	87	74
No opinion	11	10	5	12
AIPO 172A, 10-3-39				
(N)	(293)	(833)	(48)	(411)
Congress should change Neutrality Law so Britain and France or any other nations can buy war supplies here	21%	26%	31%	24%
Qualified approve[a]	8	9	10	9
Disapprove	68	63	56	62
No opinion	3	2	3	5
AIPO 180A, 12-22-39				
(N)	(324)	(801)	(39)	(373)
Approve U.S. lending Britain and France money to buy war supplies here	13%	17%	21%	16%
Disapprove	79	74	71	75
No opinion	8	9	8	9
AIPO 180B, 12-22-39				
(N)	(320)	(796)	(38)	(374)
Approve such loans if they start paying something on World War debts	19%	24%	30%	24%
Still disapprove	74	68	60	67
No opinion	7	8	10	9

[a] The most frequent reservation was that purchasers pay cash.

Table 1-7.   Helping Britain win

	Catholics	Protestants	Jews	Non-church-members
AIPO 209, 9-3-40				
(N)	(567)	(1629)	(57)	(871)
More important to try to				
(1) keep out of war ourselves	53%	43%	32%	45%
(2) help England win, even at risk of getting into war ourselves	45	53	66	50
No opinion	2	4	2	5
AIPO 213, 9-30-40				
(N)	(599)	(1602)	(71)	(827)
More important to try to				
(1) keep out of war	43%	34%	15%	35%
(2) help England win	52	61	76	59
No opinion	5	5	9	6
If the question were put to a national vote, would vote to enter the war	16	19	34	18
Would vote to stay out	75	71	66	71
No opinion	9	10	0	11
AIPO 214T, 10-5-40				
(N)	(294)	(797)	(29)	(428)
If Britain unable to pay cash for aircraft				
(1) Sell on credit supplied by our government	48%	61%	89%	51%
(2) Do not	40	32	8	38
No opinion	12	7	3	11
AIPO 214 K, 10-5-40				
(N)	(239)	(762)	(28)	(441)
Change Johnson Act so Britain can borrow money from U.S. government	42%	51%	58%	46%
Do not	48	36	30	43
No opinion	10	13	12	11

	Catholics	Protestants	Jews	Non-church
AIPO 215, 10-9-40				
(N)	(564)	(1625)	(53)	(871)
Change Neutrality Law to let England borrow money from U.S. government to buy more food and war materials here	39%	45%	51%	44%
Do not	49	43	39	43
No opinion	12	12	10	13
AIPO 215, 10-9-40				
(N)	(564)	(1625)	(53)	(871)
Revise Neutrality Law so American ships can carry war materials to Britain	31%	37%	41%	35%
Do not	56	50	46	49
No opinion	13	13	13	16
If appears Britain will be defeated unless U.S. supplies more food and war materials, favor giving Britain more help	83	87	91	80
Opposed	11	8	7	12
No opinion	6	5	2	8
Composite of AIPO 217 and 220, 10-22-40 and 11-5-40				
(N)	(2089)	(6157)	(206)	(3274)
More important to try to				
(1) keep out of war	56%	45%	25%	43%
(2) help England win	39	50	71	50
No opinion	5	5	4	7
AIPO 229, 1-22-41				
(N)	(566)	(1589)	(91)	(849)
More important to try to				
(1) keep out of war	49%	32%	19%	35%
(2) help England win	47	63	73	59
No opinion	4	5	8	6
Congress should pass Lend Lease bill	45	56	63	54
Qualified	12	15	17	14
Congress should not pass	34	22	16	22
No opinion	9	7	4	11

	Catholics	Protestants	Jews	Non-church
AIPO 240, 6-24-41				
(N)	(287)	(912)	(79)	(342)
Pres. Roosevelt has gone too far in helping Britain	21%	13%	8%	17%
Hasn't gone far enough	25	34	42	31
Has helped about right amount	48	46	46	46
No opinion	6	7	4	6
U.S. Navy should convoy ships carrying war materials to Britain	52%	57%	61%	55%
Should not	41	35	27	34
No opinion	7	8	12	11
AIPO 248, 9-17-41				
(N)	(533)	(1592)	(93)	(791)
Agree with Lindbergh	20%	13%	2%	15%
Disagree	57	65	93	64
No opinion	23	22	5	21
More important to try to				
(1) keep out of war	40	25	18	29
(2) help England win	55	68	77	66
No opinion	5	7	5	5
Change Neutrality Act so American ships with American crews can carry war materials to Britain	38	48	58	49
Do not	47	36	27	37
No opinion	15	16	15	14
U.S. Navy should shoot at German submarines and warships on sight	55	64	68	62
Should not	35	28	20	25
No opinion	10	8	12	13

Table 1-8.   Finland and the USSR

	Catholics	Protestants	Jews	Non-church-members
AIPO 181, 1-10-40				
(N)	(537)	(1638)	(41)	(901)
Approve of $60 million loan for Finland	52%	58%	61%	51%
Disapprove	42	36	33	43
No opinion	6	6	6	6
AIPO 240, 6-24-41				
(N)	(541)	(1701)	(72)	(741)
Want USSR to win	65%	75%	79%	75%
Want Germany to win	6	4	2	4
No difference which wins	21	17	15	16
No opinion	8	4	4	5
U.S. gov't should supply USSR with war materials on same basis as Britain	33	36	41	36
Should not	56	54	49	52
No opinion	11	10	10	12

Table 1-9.   The Far East

	Catholics	Protestants	Jews	Non-church-members
AIPO 149T, 2-22-39				
(N)	(265)	(765)	(23)[a]	(509)
In case of a Russian-Japanese war				
(1) think Russia would win	55%	55%	52%	56%
(2) think Japan would win	20	21	26	20
No opinion	25	24	22	24
AIPO 149K, 2-22-39				
(N)	(293)	(1027)	(29)[a]	(448)
Rather Russia win	46%	50%	72%	54%
Rather Japan win	13	9	0	5
Makes no difference	30	29	24	26
No opinion	11	12	4	15
AIPO 213K, 9-30-40				
(N)	(277)	(838)	(35)[a]	(457)
U.S. government should forbid sale of arms, gasoline, etc., to Japan	79%	84%	84%	83%
Should not	13	9	5	7
No opinion	8	7	11	10
Let Japan get control of China	31	29	37	27
Other isolationist answers	15	13	11	16
Risk war to stop Japan	28	32	34	28
No opinion	26	26	17	29

[a] Note the small size of the Jewish sample.

Table 2-1.   Knowledge of world affairs

	Catholics	Protestants	Jews
AIPO 408, Nov.'47			
(N)	(623)	(1975)	(142)
Heard or read about recent G.A.T.T. signed at Geneva to lower tariffs reciprocally	30%	38%	47%
NORC 155, 2-25-48			
(N)	(276)	(887)	(64)
Heard of Palestine partition	72%	71%	97%
NORC 156, 4-26-48			
(N)	(294)	(885)	(60)
U.N. favors partition (correct)	26%	25%	56%
U.N. opposes	15	12	22
Don't know	59	63	22
U.S. favors partition	23	20	13
U.S. opposes (correct)	27	30	77
Don't know	50	50	10
USSR favors partition (correct)	19	20	63
USSR opposes	19	20	12
Don't know	62	60	25
Correct on all three	17	17	48
NORC 157, 4-22-48			
(N)	(252)	(917)	(72)
Heard something of recent defense agreement between England, France, and other countries of western Europe	38%	39%	63%
NORC 159, 6-29-48			
(N)	(260)	(923)	(67)
Knew fighting stopped in Palestine (correct)	52%	47%	62%
Thought large-scale fighting still going on	31	28	38
Thought agreed on final peace	3	1	0
Don't know	14	24	0
NORC 161, 10-13-48			
(N)	(258)	(845)	(76)
Heard something of Bernadotte Plan recommended to U.N.	21%	23%	76%
Had not	79	77	24
Spontaneously named Bernadotte as famous person assassinated in Palestine	43	34	92
Selected name from 5 alternatives	27	27	7
No knowledge	30	39	1

	Catholics	Protestants	Jews
NORC 280, 4-17-50			
(N)	(301)	(866)	(44)
Heard of Point Four	19%	24%	34%
AIPO 526, Jan. '54			
(N)	(312)	(1085)	(47)
Heard or read anything about tariffs and trade issue	39%	44%	68%
AIPO 540, Nov. '54			
(N)	(321)	(1006)	(87)
Heard or read anything about tariffs and trade issue	45%	50%	62%
AIPO 546, 4-12-55			
(N)	(380)	(1058)	(51)
Heard or read of trouble in Formosa area	83%	81%	96%
Knew Quemoy and Matsu controlled by Nationalist China	38	45	67
NORC 404, 4-26-57			
(N)	(307)	(865)	(55)
Number of African countries or territories correctly mentioned:			
None	58%	60%	23%
One	17	19	20
Two	13	9	16
Three	4	6	11
Four	4	3	4
Five or more	4	3	26
AIPO 614, 5-27-59			
(N)	(360)	(1071)	(51)
Heard or read anything about tariffs and trade issue	39%	35%	55%
AIPO 653, 12-5-61			
(N)	(372)	(1123)	(53)
Heard or read anything about tariffs and trade issue	55%	50%	60%
AIPO 656, 3-6-62			
(N)	(354)	(1134)	(53)
Heard or read about Kennedy administration's proposed Trade Expansion Act to increase U.S. trade with other countries	46%	45%	66%

SRC 473, Sept-Oct. '64	Catholics	Protestants	Jews
(N)	(326)	(996)	(38)
Knew Mainland China both communist-controlled and not a member of the U.N.	75%	68%	87%

Table 2-2.   Importance ascribed to world affairs

Roper 916, Sept. '56	Catholics	Protestants	Jews
(N)	(750)	(1951)	(117)
Foreign affairs or some aspect of foreign policy the most important issue in the forthcoming presidential election (volunteered)	9%	9%	20%
NORC 393, 9-13-56			
(N)	(301)	(805)	(47)
Get good deal of world affairs information from			
Radio	19%	26%	28%
TV	41	37	34
Newspapers	46	45	62
Magazines	16	17	30
Talking to people	15	14	23
Roper 925, Oct. '56			
(N)	(757)	(1954)	(97)
Foreign affairs more important than domestic affairs	28%	26%	29%
AIPO 577, 1-15-57			
(N)	(380)	(1017)	(53)
If you had time to spare, which one of these would interest you the most?			
Schools, education	36%	36%	42%
Natural resources, preserve wild life	10	13	8
Church, religious work	33	38	6
Voting, political affairs, politics	2	2	3
World affairs, the U.N.	12	8	34
Others or don't know	7	3	5

Table 2-3.   Support for active international role

	Catholics	Protestants	Jews
NORC 144, 9-20-46			
(N)	(265)	(905)	(55)
U.S. fought World War II only because attacked at Pearl Harbor	35%	27%	31%
Fought for some other reasons too	56	62	62
No opinion	9	11	7
SRC survey of June-Aug.'46			
(N)	(245)	(855)	(50)
U.S. should keep to self, have nothing to do with rest of world	10%	8%	0%
Qualified agree	7	5	2
Disagree	69	69	92
Qualified disagree	6	7	2
No opinion	8	11	4
Roper 737, Aug.'53			
(N)	(846)	(2298)	(167)
U.S. should have taken larger part since last war in world affairs	5%	18%	25%
Has taken on whole about right part	67	48	64
Should have taken definitely smaller part	23	20	9
No opinion	5	14	2
AIPO 525, 1-7-54			
(N)	(325)	(1003)	(69)
Heard or read anything of Bricker amendment	25%	26%	51%
Approve of it	4	5	0
Disapprove	6	7	32
No opinion	15	14	19
SRC 417, Sept.-Oct.'56			
(N)	(372)	(1287)	(56)
Strongly agree U.S. would be better off if stayed home, did not concern self with problems in other parts of world	15%	13%	12%
Agree, but not strongly	8	11	7
Depends	5	6	2
Disagree, but not strongly	14	14	14
Strongly disagree	42	46	54
No opinion	16	10	11

	Catholics	Protestants	Jews
AIPO survey of Feb.'69[a]			
Better if U.S. kept independent in world affairs	24%	21%	12%
Better if worked closely with others	70	73	84
No opinion	6	6	4

a *Gallup Opinion Index,* March 1969.

Table 2-4.   Approval of conduct of foreign policy

	Catholics	Protestants	Jews
NORC 157, 4-22-48			
(N)	(220)	(785)	(70)
Approve of the way our relations with other countries being handled by Secretary of State Marshall	56%	60%	50%
Disapprove	11	11	32
No opinion	33	29	18
NORC 280, 4-17-50			
(N)	(301)	(866)	(44)
Secretary of State Acheson doing a good job	25%	20%	18%
Fair job	30	30	34
Poor job	13	12	16
No opinion	32	38	32
NORC 339, 4-1-53			
(N)	(302)	(872)	(40)
Approve of Secretary of State Dulles	61%	61%	53%
Disapprove	4	3	12
No opinion	35	36	35
Approve of way our federal officials are handling foreign affairs	73	73	62
Disapprove	10	13	18
No opinion	17	14	20
NORC 348, 9-24-53			
(N)	(163)	(325)	(32)
Approve of way Dulles handling job as secretary of state	56%	58%	54%
Disapprove	7	10	16
No opinion	37	32	30
Approve of way officials in Washington are handling our foreign affairs	66	63	55
Disapprove	19	21	22
No opinion	15	16	23

Table 2-5.   The United Nations

	Catholics	Protestants	Jews
NORC 144, Sept.-Oct.'46			
(N)	(266)	(905)	(55)
Which likely to provide best chance of keeping world peace?			
(1) Making U.N. strong	64%	67%	80%
(2) Trying to keep ahead of other powers ourselves	34	26	20
NORC 157, 4-22-48			
(N)	(252)	(915)	(72)
U.N. is important to world peace	69%	65%	79%
Outlook for peace would be just about as good without U.N.	20	22	15
No opinion	11	13	6
Present weaknesses of U.N. due chiefly to			
(1) Way U.N. is set up	16	16	31
(2) Way the countries have acted	62	61	62
(3) No opinion	27	23	7
U.S. has done all should to make U.N. successful	71	63	25
U.S. should have done more	14	22	71
No opinion	15	15	4
Good idea to transform U.N. into world government	35	38	60
Bad idea	44	43	32
No opinion	21	19	8
NORC 280, 4-17-50			
(N)	(301)	(866)	(44)
Approve of channeling at least some technical assistance to less-developed countries through U.N.	37%	33%	52%
Handle all technical assistance bilaterally	34	33	20
Oppose all technical assistance	21	22	21
No opinion	8	12	7
AIPO 507, 10-15-52			
(N)	(794)	(2137)	(97)
Very important that the U.S. try to make U.N. a success	76%	77%	89%
Fairly important	10	9	5
Not so important	6	7	1
No opinion	8	7	5

	Catholics	Protestants	Jews
Roper 737, Aug.'53			
(N)	(846)	(2298)	(105)
How best to achieve peace:			
(1) Don't get tied up in any more alliances or joint commitments and pull out of as many as can as soon as can	9%	10%	5%
(2) Continue to work with U.N. as have, gradually trying to make it better	20	26	20
(3) Immediately get behind strengthening U.N.; give it enough authority to keep even major power from starting war	37	32	44
(4) In addition to staying in U.N., form world government with friendly democratic countries	6	4	6
(5) Transform U.N. into world government	11	10	14
(6) None of these will work, so don't rely on any of them	7	6	5
(7) No opinion	10	12	6
AIPO 575, 11-20-56			
(N)	(385)	(1016)	(58)
Very important that U.S. try to make U.N. a success	85%	85%	86%
Fairly important	7	8	8
Not so important	4	4	2
No opinion	4	3	4
U.N. doing good job in trying to solve problems it has had to face	51	52	31
Fair job	25	27	40
Poor job	13	9	25
No opinion	11	12	4
AIPO 577, 1-30-57			
(N)	(374)	(987)	(53)
Chances of U.N. keeping peace good	48%	39%	42%
Fair	30	31	30
Poor	14	23	23
No opinion	8	7	5
AIPO 631, 7-14-60			
(N)[a]	(668)	(1888)	(80)
UNEF a good idea	71%	73%	85%
Poor one	14	10	3
No opinion	15	17	12

	Catholics	Protestants	Jews
AIPO 654, 1-9-62			
(N)[a]	(826)	(2377)	(88)
U.N. doing good job	54%	48%	50%
Fair	24	30	40
Poor	13	12	9
No opinion	9	10	1
Give up U.N. membership	9	7	9
Stay in	86	86	91
No opinion	5	7	0
Very important to make U.N. successful	81	83	92
Fairly important	12	9	0
Not so important	3	4	7
No opinion	4	4	1
AIPO 659, 5-29-62			
(N)[a]	(750)	(2254)	(77)
U.N. doing good job	54%	47%	65%
Fair	28	29	22
Poor	11	15	8
No opinion	7	9	5
AIPO 666, 12-11-62			
(N)[a]	(756)	(2206)	(99)
Approve of Stevenson's performance at U.N.	71%	52%	81%
Disapprove	4	20	1
No opinion	25	28	18
AIPO 679, 11-8-63			
(N)[a]	(925)	(3073)	(110)
Give up U.N. membership	9%	8%	0%
Stay in	80	77	100
No opinion	11	15	0
AIPO 680, 11-20-63			
(N)[a]	(913)	(2274)	(74)
U.N. doing good job	57%	50%	64%
Fair	25	29	25
Poor	5	8	3
No opinion	13	13	8
Very important to make U.N. successful	80	79	91
Fairly important	8	9	2
Not so important	3	4	2
No opinion	9	8	5

	Catholics	Protestants	Jews
AIPO 689, 4-22-64			
(N)[a]	(745)	(2503)	(122)
UNEF a good idea	69%	60%	71%
Poor one	18	20	5
No opinion	13	20	24
AIPO 695, 7-21-64			
(N)[a]	(725)	(2532)	(107)
UNEF a good idea	77%	63%	70%
Poor one	14	17	15
No opinion	9	20	15
U.N. Army should deal with problems			
of S.E. Asia and Vietnam	67	55	67
Should not	18	20	18
No opinion	15	25	15
AIPO 712, 6-2-65			
(N)[a]	(742)	(2383)	(104)
Would likely have been World War III			
but for U.N.	62%	58%	72%
U.N. made no difference	26	25	23
No opinion	12	17	5
AIPO 715, 8-3-65			
(N)[a]	(942)	(2309)	(99)
Approve of asking U.N. to try to			
work out own formula for			
peace in Vietnam	79%	71%	94%
Disapprove	12	13	0
No opinion	9	16	6
AIPO 723, 12-29-65			
(N)[a]	(707)	(2135)	(118)
Good idea for U.S. to submit			
Vietnam case to U.N. or			
I.C.J. and agree to accept			
decision	55%	45%	61%
Bad idea	32	39	22
No opinion	13	16	17
AIPO 724, 2-8-66			
(N)[a]	(938)	(2205)	(104)
Favor U.N. trying to work out			
Vietnam solution	60%	57%	79%
Oppose	5	5	2
No opinion	35	38	19
U.N. would be able to achieve			
peaceful settlement of			
differences in Vietnam	25	19	27

	Catholics	Protestants	Jews
AIPO survey of Aug.'66[b]			
Good idea for U.S. to submit			
Vietnam case to U.N. or I.C.J.	56%	51%	62%
Bad idea	30	32	25
No opinion	14	17	13
AIPO survey of July '67			
Very important to make U.N.			
successful	82%	79%	–
Fairly important	8	10	
Not so important	5	6	
No opinion	5	5	
Give up U.N. membership	8	10	
Stay in	88	84	
No opinion	4	6	
AIPO survey of Aug.'67[c]			
U.N. doing good job	49%	50%	–
Poor	36	34	
No opinion	15	16	
AIPO survey of Oct.'67[d]			
Favor turning Vietnam problem			
over to U.N. Both sides			
agree in advance to accept			
U.N. decision. U.N. police			
border.	63%	58%	–
Opposed	30	33	
No opinion	7	9	

a AIPO samples starting in 1960 were weighted to compensate for
underrepresentation of lower educational and socio-economic
groups in the sample. These figures are weighted ones. Actual
N's were typically approximately one-half the weighted N's indicated for Catholics and Protestants and two-thirds those
provided for Jews.
b *Gallup Political Index,* Sept. 1966.
c *Gallup Opinion Index,* Sept. 1967.
d *Gallup Opinion Index,* Nov. 1967.

Table 3-1.   Anticipated relations with the USSR, 1943-1950

	Catholics	Protestants	Jews	Non-church-members
AIPO 287, 1-7-43				
(N)	(489)	(1535)	(68)	(684)
Think Russia can be trusted to cooperate with us after the war	39%	47%	82%	47%
Russian cooperation cannot be trusted	32	27	9	29
No opinion	29	26	9	24
SRC survey of June '46				
(N)	(120)	(428)	(23)	
Can count on Russian gov't being friendly to us	28%	37%	41%	-
Cannot	58	42	41	
No opinion	14	21	18	
SRC survey of Aug.'46				
(N)	(125)	(427)	(26)	
Can count on Russian govt being friendly to us	23%	25%	36%	-
Cannot	63	57	55	
No opinion	14	18	9	
NORC 144, 9-20-46 to 10-6-46				
(N)	(265)	(895)	(55)	
Newspapers generally make Russia look better than she really is	23%	16%	9%	-
Worse than she is	43	41	51	
About as she is	21	21	24	
No opinion	13	22	16	
One country entirely to blame for U.S.-USSR differences	28	14	22	-
Both partly to blame	64	78	69	
No opinion	8	8	9	
Present disagreements serious enough to consider going to war about	24	15	13	-
Not serious enough	64	68	82	
Not yet, could be soon	6	6	5	
No opinion	6	11	0	
Expect U.S. to fight war within 25 years	67	63	45	-
Do not	22	24	44	
No opinion	11	13	11	

	Catholics	Protestants	Jews	Non-church
NORC 280, 4-17-50				
(N)	(301)	(866)	(44)	
Expect U.S. to fight war within 10 years	63%	68%	48%	-
Do not	29	22	34	
No opinion	8	10	18	

Table 3-2.   Preferred U.S. posture toward communist world, 1948-1956

	Catholics	Protestants	Jews
NORC 157, 4-22-48			
(N)	(252)	(917)	(72)
U.S. should be more willing to compromise with USSR	6%	8%	33%
Present policy about right	17	20	11
Should be even firmer than we are	65	63	43
No opinion	12	9	13
SRC survey of June-Aug.'48			
(N)	(245)	(855)	(49)
Use army and navy to make other countries do what we think they should	18%	14%	9%
Disapprove of this suggestion	68	70	83
No opinion	14	16	8
AIPO 454, 3-24-50			
(N)	(341)	(991)	(78)
U.S. government spending on national defense should be increased	72%	61%	56%
Kept at present level	18	26	31
Decreased	5	7	9
No opinion	5	6	4
NORC 280, 4-17-50			
(N)	(301)	(866)	(44)
Very important to stop spread of communism	93%	80%	62%
Only fairly important	3	8	18
Not important at all	1	4	9
No opinion	3	8	11
NORC 339, 4-1-53			
(N)	(302)	(872)	(40)
Important to liberate eastern Europe	78%	70%	78%
No concern of ours	15	22	20
No opinion	7	8	2
U.S. government should do something now to free them from communist rule[a]	48	39	43
Should not	26	26	33
No opinion	4	5	2

	Catholics	Protestants	Jews
AIPO 514, 4-17-53			
(N)	(338)	(1102)	(48)
Would favor international control and inspection of atomic energy and arms	56%	57%	85%
Would oppose	33	30	13
No opinion	11	13	2
Roper 737, Aug.'53			
(N)	(846)	(2298)	(137)
Preferred orientation toward USSR[a]			
(1) Go to war with Russia as soon as our military leaders think we can win and get it over with	8%	6%	1%
(2) Rely completely on building up our military strength and keep it strong enough to handle the Russians as long as we need to	31	24	18
(3) While keeping up our military strength, make every reasonable attempt to find a way to live peacefully with Russia	57	66	78
(4) Stop relying on military strength and start right now working out some agreement with the Russians, even if we have to give in to them on some important things	4	4	7
SRC 417, Sept.-Nov.'56			
(N)	(372)	(1287)	(56)
Strongly agree best way to deal with USSR and Com. China is to act as tough as they do	57%	51%	55%
Agree, but not strongly	10	12	11
Depends	4	6	7
Disagree, but not strongly	4	7	4
Strongly disagree	6	9	7
No opinion	19	15	16

a Percentages of those with opinions; "no opinions" eliminated.

Table 3-3.   Diplomatic relations with USSR, 1948-1957

	Catholics	Protestants	Jews
NORC 157, 4-22-48			
(N)	(252)	(917)	(72)
Approve of Truman meeting with Stalin in Europe to try to settle U.S.-USSR differences	45%	53%	53%
Disapprove	40	40	40
No opinion	15	7	7
Why disapprove?			
(1) USSR cannot be trusted to live up to any agreements	19	15	14
(2) Would show American weakness	19	11	10
World peace more likely if Russia out of U.N.	37	30	23
Peace less likely if Russia out of U.N.	28	32	46
No difference	20	19	24
No opinion	15	19	7
NORC 404, 4-26-57			
(N)	(307)	(865)	(55)
Break all diplomatic relations with USSR	23%	18%	9%
Continue to exchange ambassadors	75	76	89
No opinion	2	6	2

Table 3-4.   Summit negotiations and exchanges of persons with communist countries, 1948-1957

	Catholics	Protestants	Jews
NORC 157, 4-22-48			
(N)	(252)	(917)	(72)
Let communist reporters into U.S. to report facts as they see them	49%	50%	79%
Do not	44	44	18
No opinion	7	6	3
Allow U.S. reporters to report from communist countries	74	69	90
Do not	18	25	10
No opinion	8	6	0
AIPO 454, 3-24-50			
(N)	(344)	(991)	(78)
Good idea for Pres. Truman to take lead in arranging summit meeting with Soviet and other leaders	47%	42%	60%
Fair idea	8	8	8
Poor idea	40	41	24
Qualified answers	1	2	1
No opinion	4	7	7
NORC 401, 12-28-56			
(N)	(279)	(870)	(42)
Good idea for Pres. Eisenhower to invite top Soviet leaders to visit U.S.	54%	57%	76%
Bad idea	40	36	21
No opinion	6	7	7
NORC 404, 4-26-57			
(N)	(307)	(865)	(55)
Good idea to exchange visits of musicians and athletes with USSR	75%	69%	84%
Bad idea	20	27	15
No opinion	5	4	1

Table 3-5.   Collective security and defense against communist expansionism, 1948-1957

	Catholics	Protestants	Jews
NORC 157, 4-22-48			
(N)	(252)	(917)	(72)
U.S. should promise to go to war to defend W. Europe if it is attacked	43%	40%	24%
Should not	46	48	51
No opinion	11	12	25
AIPO 432, 11-24-48			
(N)	(661)	(1942)	(141)
U.S. should join W. Europe in a permanent military alliance	69%	70%	49%
Should not	19	17	40
No opinion	12	13	11
AIPO 506, 10-7-52			
(N)	(822)	(2051)	(111)
Continue to give money and send troops to help Europe build up defense against Russia	51%	47%	69%
Qualified approval	5	5	3
Withdraw and let Europe take care of herself	31	33	15
No opinion	13	15	13
Composite of Roper surveys of Aug. and Oct.'52			
(N)	(1807)	(5047)	(311)
What do now in Korea?			
(1) Continue to try to negotiate end of fighting	30%	28%	54%
(2) Stop fooling around, knock communists out even at risk of World War III	40	39	25
(3) Pull out entirely	18	18	14
(4) No opinion	12	15	7
NORC 339, 4-1-53			
(N)	(302)	(872)	(40)
Korea worth fighting	38%	36%	45%
Not worth it	55	55	43
No opinion	7	9	2

	Catholics	Protestants	Jews
AIPO 577, 1-15-57			
(N)	(385)	(1029)	(53)
Approve if U.S. promised to send armed forces if Soviet troops attack Middle East	48%	50%	51%
Disapprove	37	34	34
Neither or depends	3	3	4
No opinion	12	13	11
Roper 939, April '57			
(N)	(339)	(1042)	(43)
Essential to get NATO fixed up after Suez Crisis	63%	67%	74%
Desirable, but not essential	19	17	12
Doesn't really matter whether fix up our relations with Britain and France	10	8	2
No opinion	8	8	12
Eisenhower Doctrine to resist communist aggression in Middle East with U.S. armed forces a good one	23	25	19
Could be improved	34	31	30
Not adequate	7	9	21
Stay out of Middle East	22	19	12
No opinion	14	16	18

Table 3-6.   Relations with the People's Republic of China, 1955-1957

	Catholics	Protestants	Jews
AIPO 546, 4-12-55			
(N)	(380)	(1058)	(51)
Invite Russia, Communist China, other interested governments to work out peaceful solution	75%	73%	82%
Disapprove	14	18	10
No opinion	11	9	8
NORC 401, 12-28-56			
(N)	(279)	(870)	(42)
Approve of Americans carrying on trade with Communist China, if did not include war materials	41%	47%	57%
Disapprove	53	46	31
No opinion	6	7	12
AIPO 577, 1-15-57			
(N)	(385)	(1029)	(53)
Drop out of U.N. if Communist China admitted	24%	21%	17%
Do not	57	64	77
No opinion	19	15	6

Table 3-7.   Relations with Yugoslavia, 1951-1956

	Catholics	Protestants	Jews
AIPO 470-TPS, 1-2-51			
(N)	(327)	(917)	(29)
If communist troops from Hungary and Rumania attack Yugoslavia, U.S. should			
(1) Send planes, tanks, guns, other war equipment	43%	44%	57%
(2) Also send American soldiers	13	13	15
(3) Send neither to help Yugoslavia	30	27	18
(4) No opinion	14	16	10
NORC 401, 12-28-56			
(N)	(279)	(870)	(42)
Good idea to invite Tito to visit U.S.	59%	61%	76%
Bad idea	32	26	21
No opinion	9	13	3
Can count on Yugoslavia to cooperate with U.S.	38	29	36
Cannot	31	36	45
No opinion	31	35	19

Table 3-8.   Communist influence in the U.S., 1948-1954

	Catholics	Protestants	Jews
NORC 157, 4-22-48			
(N)	(252)	(917)	(72)
Allow communists to speak over			
radio	30%	33%	78%
Do not	62	60	21
No opinion	8	7	1
Allow newspapers to criticize			
form of government	68	68	94
Do not	26	29	6
No opinion	6	3	0
AIPO 454, 3-24-50			
(N)	(341)	(991)	(78)
Senator McCarthy's claims about			
communists in State Depart-			
ment are true	49%	52%	37%
Agree, with reservations	18	17	10
McCarthy's claims "just a case			
of politics"	28	28	49
No opinion	5	3	4
NORC 280, 4-17-50			
(N)	(301)	(866)	(44)
All people in State Department			
are probably loyal	24%	21%	32%
At least some not loyal	62	66	57
No opinion	14	13	11
Communists in State Department			
doing great deal of harm to			
U.S. interests	28	29	14
Some harm	32	32	27
No significant harm or			
no opinion	40	39	59
Favorable impression of officials			
in State Department	60	55	52
Unfavorable	27	28	21
Neither or no opinion	13	17	27
Composite of Roper surveys of			
Aug. and Oct.'52			
(N)	(1807)	(5047)	(311)
Keeping communists out of			
government jobs should be			
one of 2 or 3 most important			
things for next administration			
to do	52%	52%	37%

	Catholics	Protestants	Jews
AIPO 513, 3-26-53			
(N)	(335)	(1095)	(51)
Former communists should be allowed to teach in colleges	27%	20%	38%
Need a congressional investigation of communism in our churches	28	40	12
NORC 341-2, 6-30-53			
(N)	(302)	(831)	(50)
State Department doing all it should to keep disloyal people out of Department	80%	79%	88%
Not doing all it should	11	11	6
No opinion	9	10	6
NORC 365, 11-26-54			
(N)	(278)	(757)	(48)
American communists a great danger	37%	37%	25%
Only some danger	42	45	40
Practically no danger	15	13	31
No opinion	6	5	4

Table 3-9.   Senator Joseph McCarthy's popularity

	Catholics	Protestants	Jews
AIPO release 1-15-54			
Impressions of Sen. Joseph R. McCarthy:			
(1) Favorable	58%	49%	15%
(2) Unfavorable	23	28	71
(3) Neither or no opinion	19	23	14
AIPO release 3-14-54			
Impressions of Sen. Joseph R. McCarthy:			
(1) Favorable	56%	45%	12%
(2) Unfavorable	29	36	83
(3) Neither or no opinion	15	19	5
AIPO release 4-4-54			
Impressions of Sen. Joseph R. McCarthy:			
(1) Favorable	46%	37%	10%
(2) Unfavorable	41	46	85
(3) Neither or no opinion	13	17	5
AIPO release 6-23-54			
Approve of Senator McCarthy			
"Intensely"	21%	12%	5%
Disapprove "intensely"	24	31	65
NORC 365, 11-26-54			
Impressions of Sen. Joseph R. McCarthy:			
(1) Favorable	58%	43%	15%
(2) Unfavorable	23	36	79
(3) Neither or no opinion	19	21	6

Table 3-10.   National defense

	Catholics	Protestants	Jews
AIPO 625, 2-29-60			
(N)[a]	(849)	(1810)	(114)
U.S. is spending too little			
for national defense	21%	20%	50%
Spending about right amount	49	44	23
Spending too much	18	18	19
No opinion	12	18	8
AIPO 639, 12-6-60			
(N)[a]	(718)	(1953)	(74)
New President and Congress			
should spend more money to			
strengthen national defense	32%	27%	32%
AIPO 691, 5-20-64			
(N)[a]	(721)	(2533)	(85)
If U.S. reduced military spend-			
ing drastically, serious			
depression would result	31%	29%	32%
Savings thus entailed would be			
spent on other things, without			
serious depression	51	48	42
No opinion	18	23	26
POS 655, 2-15-65			
(N)	(359)	(1152)	(46)
Extremely well satisfied with			
U.S. military strength	33%	28%	39%
Considerably well satisfied	42	48	37
Somewhat satisfied	18	16	19
Not satisfied at all	4	6	3
No opinion	3	2	2
AIPO 712, 6-2-65			
(N)[a]	(742)	(2383)	(104)
Every able-bodied male 18 years			
old should be required to serve			
one year in armed forces	68%	64%	65%
Should not	27	31	33
No opinion	5	5	2
AIPO survey of July '69[b]			
U.S. spending too much for defense			
and military purposes	56%	48%	–
About right amount	29	34	
Too little	6	9	
No opinion	9	9	

	Catholics	Protestants	Jews
AIPO survey of July '70[c]			
Rate Pentagon highly favorable	24%	34%	-
Highly unfavorable	6	3	

[a] AIPO samples since 1960 have been weighted. Actual samples of Catholics and Protestants were approximately one-half of the N's indicated herein, while the actual N's of Jews approximated two-thirds of the figures listed.

[b] *Gallup Opinion Index,* Aug. 1969.

[c] *Gallup Opinion Index,* Aug. 1970.

Table 3-11.   Defense of Berlin

	Catholics	Protestants	Jews
AIPO 648, 7-25-61			
(N)[a]	(770)	(2140)	(72)
Should keep U.S. forces, along with British and French, in Berlin even at risk of war	88%	84%	81%
Should not	6	4	9
No opinion	6	12	10
AIPO 651, 10-17-61			
(N)[a]	(770)	(2371)	(105)
If had to make decision, would prefer all-out nuclear war to communist rule	85%	81%	64%
Would rather live under communist rule	3	6	11
No choice	12	13	25
U.S. and allies should fight way into Berlin if access obstructed by communists	67	61	40
Should not	19	20	31
No opinion	14	19	29

[a] Weighted N's were approximately twice the size of actual N's interviewed by the AIPO among Christians and 1.5 times actual Jewish N's.

Table 3-12.   Intervention in Latin America

	Catholics	Protestants	Jews
AIPO 640, 1-10-61			
(N)[a]	(643)	(1875)	(58)
U.S. should fight to prevent Castro take-over of Guantanamo by force	76%	77%	95%
Should not	11	10	5
No opinion	13	13	0
AIPO 663, 9-18-62			
(N)[a]	(885)	(2495)	(105)
Agree that U.S. should send armed forces into Cuba to overthrow Castro	22%	26%	25%
Disagree	66	62	57
No opinion	12	12	18
AIPO 668, 2-5-63			
(N)[a]	(841)	(2602)	(76)
Agree that U.S. should send armed forces into Cuba to overthrow Castro	20%	19%	22%
Disagree	62	63	78
No opinion	18	18	0
Cuban situation is serious threat to peace	63	63	82
Not serious threat	14	12	5
No opinion	23	25	13
POS 655, 2-15-65			
(N)	(359)	(1152)	(46)
Preferred policy toward Cuba:			
March in and get rid of Castro	11%	13%	12%
Continue as we have	48	43	49
Set up exile government	32	30	25
No opinion	9	14	14
AIPO 720, 11-16-65			
(N)[a]	(920)	(2366)	(70)
U.S. did right thing in sending troops into Santo Domingo	57%	51%	44%
Did wrong thing	17	22	27
No opinion	26	27	29

[a]   These weighted N's were approximately twice actual N's among Christians, 1.5 times actual N's among Jews.

Table 3-13.   Likelihood of war with communist countries, 1957-1968

	Catholics	Protestants	Jews
NORC 404, 4-26-57			
(N)[a]	(307)	(865)	(55)
Expect major war in two years	13%	19%	7%
Have to fight eventually	39	41	11
Can avoid war entirely	40	34	78
No opinion	8	6	8
AIPO 617, 8-18-58			
(N)	(385)	(959)	(58)
Western countries can continue to live peacefully with the Russians	47%	40%	57%
Bound to be major war sooner or later	38	45	26
Likely to get into world war in next five years	16	22	10
No opinion	15	15	17
AIPO 628, 6-24-60			
(N)[a]	(751)	(2489)	(113)
Western countries can continue to live peacefully with the Russians	44%	33%	60%
Bound to be a major war sooner or later	43	59	28
Likely to be major war in next five years	18	26	12
No opinion	13	8	12
AIPO 631, 7-14-60			
(N)[a]	(760)	(2307)	(107)
U.S. likely to get into another world war within five years	42%	50%	15%
Not likely	46	35	58
No opinion	12	15	27
AIPO 642, 3-8-61			
(N)[a]	(752)	(2518)	(115)
World war likely within five years	25%	35%	11%
Not likely	61	46	70
No opinion	14	19	19
AIPO 651, 10-17-61			
(N)[a]	(770)	(2371)	(105)
If Berlin problem is solved peacefully:			
There will be a long period of peace	16%	11%	31%
The Russians will stir up strife again in near future	74	78	60
No opinion	10	11	9

	Catholics	Protestants	Jews
AIPO 654, 1-9-62			
(N)[a]	(862)	(2377)	(88)
Is possible to reach peaceful settlement of differences with USSR	54%	51%	74%
Impossible	24	36	20
No opinion	22	13	6
AIPO 659, 5-29-62			
(N)[a]	(750)	(2254)	(77)
There is much danger of world war	28%	40%	20%
Not much danger	64	48	66
No opinion	8	12	14
AIPO 674, 6-19-63			
(N)[a]	(771)	(2411)	(138)
It is possible to reach peaceful settlement of differences with USSR	54%	46%	51%
Impossible	30	40	25
No opinion	16	14	24
AIPO 676, 8-13-63			
(N)[a]	(861)	(2466)	(134)
It is possible to reach peaceful settlement of differences with USSR	46%	42%	58%
Impossible	37	40	31
No opinion	17	18	11
AIPO 701, 11-4-64			
(N)[a]	(742)	(2342)	(162)
It is possible to reach peaceful settlement of differences with USSR	61%	54%	67%
Impossible	22	27	16
No opinion	17	19	17
POS 655, 2-15-65			
(N)	(359)	(1152)	(46)
War with USSR and/or China over Cuba likely	17%	20%	13%
War not likely with either over Cuba	68	65	72
No opinion	15	15	15
Western countries can live peacefully with USSR	42	37	62
There is bound to be a major war sooner or later	42	48	23
No opinion	16	15	15

	Catholics	Protestants	Jews
Western countries can live peacefully with Communist China	21	19	32
Bound to be a major war sooner or later with China	58	61	44
No opinion	21	20	24

AIPO 713, 6-22-65

	Catholics	Protestants	Jews
(N)[a]	(914)	(2325)	(133)
U.S. likely to get into another world war within five years	32%	36%	24%
Not likely	57	51	54
No opinion	11	13	22

AIPO 725, 3-1-66

	Catholics	Protestants	Jews
(N)[a]	(875)	(2328)	(172)
U.S. likely to get into World War III in next year	16%	24%	10%
Not likely	71	63	80
No opinion	13	13	10

AIPO survey of Dec. '66[b]

	Catholics	Protestants	Jews
Vietnam war will probably be settled before end of 1967	21%	13%	-
Will probably not be settled	72	75	
No opinion	7	12	

AIPO survey of March '67[c]

	Catholics	Protestants	Jews
Major war between U.S. and Communist China very likely	22%	27%	-
Fairly likely	19	15	
Not very likely	49	46	
No opinion	10	12	

AIPO survey of Feb. '68[d]

	Catholics	Protestants	Jews
Present N. Korean situation likely to lead to war	44%	50%	-
Not likely	43	36	
No opinion	13	14	

a These weighted N's were approximately twice the N's actually interviewed by the AIPO among Christians and 1.5 times those interviewed among Jews.

b *Gallup Opinion Index*, Jan. 1967. Replies of Jews were not provided.

c *Gallup Opinion Index*, April 1967.

d *Gallup Opinion Index*, March 1968.

Table 3-14.   Summit contacts, 1956-1959

	Catholics	Protestants	Jews
NORC 401, 12-28-56			
(N)	(279)	(870)	(42)
Good idea for President Eisenhower to invite top Soviet leaders to visit U.S.	54%	57%	76%
Bad Idea	40	36	21
No opinion	6	7	3
Roper 939, April '57			
(N)	(339)	(1042)	(43)
Should invite Tito to U.S.	49%	59%	61%
Should not	35	28	28
No opinion	16	13	11
AIPO 617, 8-18-59			
(N)	(385)	(960)	(58)
Approve of Khrushchev's forthcoming visit to U.S.	62%	66%	76%
Disapprove	27	19	9
No opinion	11	15	15
Approve of Eisenhower's planned visit to USSR	69	70	84
Disapprove	19	15	5
No opinion	12	15	11

Table 3-15.   Arms limitations

	Catholics	Protestants	Jews
NORC 404, 4-26-57			
(N)	(307)	(865)	(55)
Approve of further negotiations for arms control with international safeguards	48%	45%	49%
Disapprove	48	50	42
No opinion	4	5	9
AIPO 620, 11-10-59			
(N)	(385)	(1144)	(60)
Extend H-bomb testing agreement another year	75%	75%	88%
Do not	13	13	10
No opinion	12	12	2
AIPO 635, 9-7-60			
(N)[a]	(709)	(1973)	(84)
If USSR agrees to disarm under careful U.N. inspection:			
U.S. should agree to disarm to same extent	46%	45%	63%
U.S. should not agree	43	42	31
No opinion	11	13	6
AIPO 656, 3-6-62			
(N)[a]	(780)	(2481)	(87)
U.S. should resume atmospheric nuclear tests	73%	65%	71%
Should not	21	26	24
No opinion	6	9	5

[a] Weighted roughly 2:1 for Christians, 3:2 for Jews.

Table 3-16.   Nonmilitary relations with communist states, 1954-1964

	Catholics	Protestants	Jews
AIPO 526, Jan.'54			
(N)	(312)	(1075)	(47)
U.S. and USSR should work out business arrangement to buy and sell goods to each other	39%	40%	62%
Oppose this idea	46	46	32
No opinion	15	14	6
AIPO 639, 12-6-60			
(N)[a]	(718)	(1953)	(74)
New President and Congress should find a new way to deal with the USSR	46%	37%	49%
AIPO 676, 8-13-63			
(N)[a]	(861)	(2466)	(134)
Heard of test-ban agreement with USSR	80%	74%	98%
Senate should ratify[b]	67	57	81
Should not	18	20	11
No opinion	15	23	8
Make further arms control agreements with USSR	51	44	47
Do not	36	41	40
No opinion	12	15	13
SRC 473, pre-election, Sept.-Oct.'64			
(N)	(329)	(1005)	(45)
Mind made up, definitely favor negotiations with communist leaders to settle differences	71%	65%	80%
Favor but with doubts, hesitancy	3	7	4
Depends	4	4	4
Mind made up, definitely against negotiations	9	8	0
Against, but with doubts, hesitancy	1	1	0
No opinion	3	3	5
No interest in this issue	9	12	7

	Catholics	Protestants	Jews
SRC 473, post-election, Nov.'64			
(N)	(326)	(996)	(38)
U.S. farmers and businessmen should be allowed to trade with communist countries in nonmilitary goods	31%	25%	45%
Depends	6	5	3
U.S. government should prohibit trade	43	47	32
No opinion	1	3	2
No interest in this issue	19	20	18

a Actual N's were approximately one-half these weighted N's among Christians, two-thirds of weighted N's among Jews.

b Percentages are of those who said they had heard of the test-ban agreement.

Table 3-17. Relations with the People's Republic of China, 1961- 1970

	Catholics	Protestants	Jews
AIPO 689, 4-22-64			
(N)[a]	(745)	(2503)	(122)
By 1970 China will be greater threat to peace	65%	52%	66%
USSR will still be greater threat	21	30	13
No opinion	14	18	21

AIPO survey	642, 3-8-61			650, 9-19-61		
Religion	Cath.	Prot.	Jews	Cath.	Prot.	Jews
(N)[a]	(752)	(2518)	(115)	(777)	(2380)	(110)
Admit Communist China to U.N.	18%	17%	41%	20%	16%	19%
Do not	70	65	46	66	65	61
No opinion	12	18	13	14	19	20

AIPO survey	684, 1-28-64			706, 2-17-65		
Religion	Cath.	Prot.	Jews	Cath.	Prot.	Jews
(N)[a]	(607)	(2304)	(49)	(756)	(2547)	(45)
Admit Communist China to U.N.	17%	13%	20%	26%	20%	42%
Do not	70	71	61	59	66	53
No opinion	13	16	19	15	14	5
Go along with U.N. majority to admit	46	37	49	57	45	58
Do not	38	46	37	29	39	27
No opinion	16	17	14	14	16	15

AIPO survey	726, 3-22-66			Sept. '66[b]		
Religion	Cath.	Prot.	Jews	Cath.	Prot.	Jews
Admit Communist China to U.N.	25%	23%	55%	27%	22%	38%
Do not	59	56	21	54	58	51
No opinion	16	21	24	19	20	11
Go along with U.N. majority	48	48	67	55	51	69
Do not	34	31	16	29	36	19
No opinion	18	21	17	16	13	12
Favor Communist Chinese membership if would improve U.S.-Communist China relations				60	53	79
Still oppose				27	32	12
No opinion				13	15	9

	Catholics	Protestants	Jews	Catholics	Protestants	Jews
AIPO survey Feb.'69[c]						
Admit Communist						
China to U.N.	39%	28%	–			
Do not	50	58				
No opinion	11	14				
Go along with						
U.N. majority	60	53				
Do not	30	36				
No opinion	10	11				
AIPO survey Oct.'70[d]						
Admit Communist						
China to U.N.	38%	32%	–			
Do not	48	52				
No opinion	14	16				
SRC 473, Sept.-Oct.'64						
(N)				(326)	(996)	(38)
Admit Communist China to U.N.				18%	13%	29%
Opposed, but U.S. stay in U.N. if admitted				33	33	39
Opposed, don't know if U.S. should stay in				4	5	8
U.S. withdraw from U.N. if admitted				6	7	3
No opinion				14	10	8
Did not know mainland under communist government and not in U.N.				25	32	13
AIPO survey of March 1967[e]						
USSR likely to be greater threat to world peace than China a few years from now				16%	20%	–
China likely to be greater threat				74	68	
No opinion				10	12	

a Weighted N's were roughly twice actual N's among Christians and 1.5
   times actual N's among Jews.

b *Gallup Opinion Index,* Oct. 1966.

c *Gallup Opinion Index,* March 1969.

d *Gallup Opinion Index,* Nov. 1970.

e *Gallup Opinion Index,* April 1967.

Table 3-18.   U.S. involvement in Vietnam, 1964-1970

	Catholics	Protestants	Jews
AIPO 697, 8-25-64			
(N)[a]	(950)	(2712)	(156)
U.S. should continue present policy and keep troops in Vietnam	14%	12%	15%
Get tougher, apply more military pressure	15	23	2
More military action to stop further aggression	5	5	0
Go all the way or pull out	7	15	1
Strengthen U.N. role, send U.N. troops	2	2	6
More economic aid	4	3	9
More advisors, help straighten out their government	2	1	5
AIPO 704, 1-5-65			
(N)[a]	(735)	(2503)	(133)
If had to choose either escalation or withdrawal:			
(1) Take our men out of Vietnam	32%	32%	41%
(2) Send more in	46	45	50
(3) No opinion	22	23	9
Should have become involved with our armed forces in Southeast Asia	56	49	48
Should not have	25	28	25
No opinion	19	23	27
AIPO 706, 2-17-65			
(N)[a]	(756)	(2547)	(45)
U.S. should continue its efforts in Vietnam	63%	57%	51%
Should pull armed forces out	17	17	16
No opinion	20	26	33
Should continue efforts, even at risk of nuclear war	49	38	36
Should not risk nuclear war	32	34	51
No opinion	19	28	13
Agree with suggestion that President Johnson try to arrange a conference with leaders of S.E. Asia and China to see if peace can be worked out	68	64	73
Disagree	13	13	16
No opinion	9	7	2
Hadn't heard of developments in Vietnam	10	16	9

	Catholics	Protestants	Jews
AIPO survey of Aug.'66[b]			
In view of developments, was mistake to send troops to fight in Vietnam	27%	37%	43%
Not a mistake	54	46	46
No opinion	19	17	11
AIPO survey of Sept.'66[c]			
Approve of way President Johnson is handling situation in Vietnam	54%	39%	41%
Disapprove	31	43	41
No opinion	15	18	18
AIPO survey of Oct.'66[d]			
In view of developments, U.S. made mistake in sending troops to fight in Vietnam	27%	31%	29%
Not a mistake	58	49	39
No opinion	15	20	12
Favor raising income taxes to pay for Vietnam war	24	17	17
Oppose	67	76	80
No opinion	9	7	3
AIPO 710, 4-21-65			
(N)[a]	(797)	(2481)	(105)
Should have become involved with our armed forces in Southeast Asia	59%	49%	59%
Should not have	23	27	21
No opinion	18	24	20
Should continue to bomb North Vietnam	65	57	66
Should stop	19	22	16
No opinion	16	21	18
AIPO 713, 6-22-65			
(N)[a]	(914)	(2325)	(133)
If S. Vietnamese government ends war and stops fighting:			
U.S. should withdraw from war	67%	63%	69%
U.S. should continue war alone	18	20	15
No opinion	15	17	16

	Catholics	Protestants	Jews
AIPO 719, 10-27-65			
(N) [a]	(973)	(2236)	(123)
Less inclined to vote for congressional candidate if advocated trying harder to reach compromise peace in Vietnam	18%	21%	17%
More inclined to vote for him	66	65	75
No opinion	16	14	8
Should have become involved with our armed forces in Southeast Asia	70	61	72
Should not have	16	23	15
No opinion	14	16	13
If congressional candidate advocated sending a great many more men to Vietnam, would be more inclined to vote for him	49	46	37
Less inclined	28	33	29
Neither and no opinion	23	21	34
AIPO 724, 2-8-66			
(N) [a]	(784)	(2395)	(128)
Extend bombing to include N. Vietnamese cities	28%	28%	30%
Do not	58	60	50
No opinion	14	12	20
AIPO 725, 3-1-66			
(N) [a]	(875)	(2328)	(172)
In view of developments, U.S. made mistake sending troops to fight in Vietnam	22%	26%	34%
Not a mistake	64	57	56
No opinion	14	17	10
AIPO 726, 3-22-66			
(N) [a]	(878)	(2454)	(85)
Agree with hawks who would step up fighting in Vietnam	45%	48%	22%
Agree with doves who want to slow fighting down	26	24	39
No opinion	29	28	39
AIPO survey of June '66 [e]			
Approve of U.S. bombing oil dumps in Haiphong and Hanoi in N. Vietnam	71%	70%	65%

	Catholics	Protestants	Jews
AIPO survey of Feb.'67 [f]			
Approve way Pres. Johnson is			
handling situation in Vietnam	51%	35%	-
Disapprove	32	48	
No opinion	17	17	
U.S. did right thing in sending			
troops to Vietnam	63	52	
Should not have become so			
involved	24	38	
No opinion	13	10	
U.S. should continue bombing			
N. Vietnam	68	67	
Should stop	23	23	
No opinion	9	10	
AIPO survey of March '67 [g]			
If Robert Kennedy were President,			
he would deal better with			
Vietnam than Pres. Johnson	27%	25%	-
Worse	13	14	
Not much difference	50	51	
No opinion	10	10	
Knew difference between Kennedy			
and Johnson positions on Vietnam	49	45	
Like Kennedy's better [h]	28	30	
Johnson's better	63	58	
No opinion	9	12	
AIPO survey of April '67 [i]			
Approve of way Pres. Johnson is			
handling situation in Vietnam	48%	39%	-
Disapprove	38	48	
No opinion	14	13	
AIPO survey of May '67 [j]			
Approve of way Pres. Johnson is			
handling situation in Vietnam	54%	38%	-
Disapprove	36	46	
No opinion	10	16	
In view of developments U.S.			
made mistake in sending troops			
to fight in N. Vietnam	30	39	
Not a mistake	60	47	
No opinion	10	14	
Our participation in Vietnam			
war is morally justified	67	56	
Is not	20	38	
No opinion	13	16	

	Catholics	Protestants	Jews
Should go all-out to win military victory, using atomic weapons	25	26	
Disagree	69	62	
No opinion	6	12	
AIPO survey of June '67[k]			
Approve of way Pres. Johnson is handling Vietnam situation	50%	38%	–
Disapprove	34	48	
No opinion	16	14	
AIPO survey of July '67[l]			
In view of developments, U.S. made mistake in sending troops to fight in Vietnam	36%	42%	–
Not a mistake	55	46	
No opinion	9	12	
Favor sending 100,000 more troops in addition to 460,000 there now	36	42	
Opposed	52	47	
No opinion	12	11	
Think U.S. and allies losing ground in Vietnam	10	10	
Standing still	42	47	
Making progress	38	34	
No opinion	10	9	
AIPO survey of Aug.'67[m]			
Approve way Pres. Johnson handling Vietnam situation	39%	30%	–
Disapprove	49	57	
No opinion	12	13	
AIPO survey of Oct.'67[n]			
In view of developments, U.S. made mistake in sending troops to fight in Vietnam	41%	47%	–
Not a mistake	52	42	
No opinion	7	11	
Halt in bombing N. Vietnam would improve chances of meaningful peace talks	26	25	
Better to continue bombing	65	65	
No opinion	9	10	
Personal policy preference:			
Should begin U.S. troop withdrawal	29	30	
Should continue present level of fighting	11	10	
Should increase strength of attacks against N. Vietnam	34	55	
No opinion	6	5	

	Catholics	Protestants	Jews
Reactions to alternative proposed policies:			
Press S. Vietnam to draft more men, train them better to do more of fighting, gradually replace U.S. troops with S. Vietnamese. U.S. continue supplying war materials and economic aid			
Favor	73%	71%	-
Oppose	18	21	
No opinion	9	8	
Continue bombing selected N. Vietnam targets and other military pressures until N. Vietnam agrees to reduce military efforts and to negotiate			
Favor	58	56	
Oppose	32	35	
No opinion	10	9	
Let military leaders win war as see fit, give them men and supplies they say need to run war. Increase bombing N. Vietnam and pressures on enemy ground forces. Escalate bombing to include Haiphong, use nuclear weapons if military so decides			
Favor	40	44	
Oppose	50	46	
No opinion	10	10	
Withdraw our troops now. Vietnam war not worth fighting			
Favor	32	36	
Oppose	60	55	
No opinion	9	9	
Stop bombing for long period (even if N. Vietnam does not promise reciprocal action) to bring on negotiations. Offer long-range economic aid			
Favor	23	23	
Oppose	68	66	
No opinion	9	11	
Vietnam war may start World War III	47	39	
More likely to prevent it	35	41	
No opinion	18	20	
If situation like Vietnam developed elsewhere U.S. should send troops	33	28	
Should not	54	58	
No opinion	13	14	

	Catholics	Protestants	Jews
AIPO survey of Nov.'67[o]			
Extend ground war into N. Vietnam	39%	38%	-
Do not	46	43	
No opinion	15	19	
AIPO survey of Jan.'68[p]			
Consider self "hawk", should step up U.S. military effort in Vietnam	53%	53%	-
"Dove", should reduce military effort	35	34	
No opinion	12	13	
AIPO survey of Feb.'68[q]			
Consider self "hawk", should step up U.S. military effort in Vietnam	57%	61%	-
"Dove", should reduce military effort	26	24	
No opinion	17	15	
In view of developments, U.S. made mistake in sending troops to fight in Vietnam	43	47	
Not a mistake	46	41	
No opinion	11	12	
Halt in bombing N. Vietnam would improve chances for meaningful peace talks	18	15	
Better to continue bombing	68	71	
No opinion	14	14	
AIPO survey of March '68[r]			
Think most S. Vietnamese want U.S. to get out of S. Vietnam	40%	40%	-
Most do not	48	44	
No opinion	12	16	
U.S. should go all out to win military victory using atomic weapons	26	29	
Disagree	66	63	
No opinion	8	8	
U.S. should stop bombing of N. Vietnam	45	37	
Should not	47	53	
No opinion	8	10	
If U.S. government decided that best to stop bombing and fighting and gradually withdraw, would approve such decision	56	55	
Disapprove	34	35	
No opinion	10	10	

	Catholics	Protestants	Jews
Consider self "hawk", should step up U.S. military effort in Vietnam	40	43	
"Dove", should reduce military effort	43	40	
No opinion	17	17	
In view of developments, U.S. made mistake in sending troops to fight in Vietnam	44	49	
Not a mistake	47	41	
No opinion	9	10	

AIPO survey of April '68^s

	Catholics	Protestants	Jews
In view of developments, U.S. made mistake in sending troops to fight in Vietnam	48%	47%	-
Not a mistake	43	40	
No opinion	9	13	
Consider self "hawk", should step up U.S. military effort in Vietnam	42	41	
"Dove", should reduce military effort	40	41	
No opinion	18	18	
Approve Pres. Johnson's decision to cease bombing N. Vietnam	69	61	
Disapprove	22	26	
No opinion	9	13	

AIPO survey of Aug.'68^t

	Catholics	Protestants	Jews
In view of developments, U.S. made mistake in sending troops to fight in Vietnam	50%	53%	-
Not a mistake	38	35	
No opinion	12	12	

AIPO survey of Oct.'68^u

	Catholics	Protestants	Jews
In view of developments, U.S. made mistake in sending troops to fight in Vietnam	50%	54%	-
Not a mistake	41	37	
No opinion	9	9	
Consider self "hawk", should step up U.S. military effort in Vietnam	40	47	
"Dove", should reduce military effort	43	39	
No opinion	17	14	

	Catholics	Protestants	Jews
AIPO survey of Jan.'69^V			
Should reduce forces month by			
month in Vietnam	64%	53%	-
Should not	23	31	
No opinion	13	16	
AIPO survey of Feb.'69^W			
In view of developments, U.S.			
made mistake in sending troops			
to fight in Vietnam	51%	52%	-
Not a mistake	43	39	
No opinion	6	9	
AIPO survey of Feb.'69^X			
U.S. should continue Paris peace			
talks	73%	66%	-
Should not	18	20	
No opinion	9	14	
AIPO survey of June '69^Y			
U.S. should call for cease fire			
with both sides staying where			
they are	59%	51%	-
Disapprove	30	35	
No opinion	11	14	
Favor withdrawing all U.S. troops			
immediately	31	27	
Oppose	61	63	
No opinion	8	10	
U.S. should withdraw troops			
faster than 25,000 over next			
three months as ordered by Nixon	47	38	
Slower	15	18	
Same rate	28	30	
No opinion	10	14	
AIPO survey of Oct.'69^Z			
U.S. should withdraw troops at			
faster rate	50%	40%	-
Slower rate	10	12	
Present rate	28	34	
No opinion	12	14	
Congress should pass proposal			
requiring withdrawal of all			
U.S. troops by end of 1970	62	53	
Should defeat	24	33	
No opinion	14	14	
In view of developments, U.S.			
made mistake in sending troops			
to fight in Vietnam	53	59	
Not a mistake	35	32	
No opinion	12	9	

	Catholics	Protestants	Jews
AIPO survey of Nov.'69[aa]			
Consider self "hawk", should step up U.S. military effort in Vietnam	27%	32%	-
"Dove", should reduce military effort	60	53	
No opinion	13	15	
AIPO survey of Jan.'70[bb]			
In view of developments, U.S. made mistake in sending troops to fight in Vietnam	58%	56%	-
Not a mistake	35	32	
No opinion	7	12	
AIPO survey of Feb.'70[cc]			
Favor withdrawing all U.S. troops immediately	36%	33%	-
Oppose	56	57	
No opinion	8	10	
AIPO survey of March '70[dd]			
U.S. should withdraw all troops immediately	24%	18%	-
Withdraw all troops within 18 months	24	25	
Withdraw all troops, but take as long as needed to turn war over to S. Vietnamese	33	41	
Send more troops and step up fighting	9	7	
No opinion	10	9	
AIPO survey of May '70[ee]			
Approve of way Pres. Nixon is handling situation in Vietnam	51%	57%	-
Disapprove	41	32	
No opinion	8	11	
Approve of way Pres. Nixon is handling Cambodian situation	44	54	
Disapprove	47	29	
No opinion	9	17	
Should send U.S. troops to help Cambodia	19	28	
Shoud not	70	54	
Qualified	5	8	
No opinion	6	11	
U.S. will be able to avoid major military involvement in Cambodia	28	31	
Will not	59	52	
No opinion	13	17	

	Catholics	Protestants	Jews
U.S. should send arms and material to help Cambodia	47	50	
Should not	39	32	
Qualified	6	6	
No opinion	8	12	

a Weighted N, roughly 2 times real N among Christians and 3/2 times actual N among Jews.

b *Gallup Political Index,* Sept. 1966.

c AIPO release of 9-21-66.

d *Gallup Political Index,* Nov.-Dec. 1966.

e *Gallup Political Index,* July 1966.

f *Gallup Opinion Index,* March 1967.

g *Gallup Opinion Index,* April 1967.

h Question asked only among those who knew the difference between the two positions.

i *Gallup Opinion Index,* May 1967.

j *Gallup Opinion Index,* June 1967.

k *Gallup Opinion Index,* July 1967.

l *Gallup Opinion Index,* Aug. 1967.

m *Gallup Opinion Index,* Sept. 1967.

n *Gallup Opinion Index,* Nov. 1967.

o *Gallup Opinion Index,* Dec. 1967.

p *Gallup Opinion Index,* Feb. 1968.

q *Gallup Opinion Index,* March 1968.

r *Gallup Opinion Index,* April 1968.

s *Gallup Opinion Index,* May 1968.

t *Gallup Opinion Index,* Sept. 1968.

u *Gallup Opinion Index,* Nov. 1968.

v *Gallup Opinion Index,* Feb. 1969.

w *Gallup Opinion Index,* March 1969.

x *Gallup Opinion Index,* April 1969.

y *Gallup Opinion Index,* July 1969.

z *Gallup Opinion Index,* Nov. 1969.

aa *Gallup Opinion Index,* Dec. 1969.

bb *Gallup Opinion Index,* Feb. 1970.

cc *Gallup Opinion Index,* March 1970.

dd *Gallup Opinion Index,* April 1970.

ee *Gallup Opinion Index,* June 1970.

Table 4-1.   The Marshall Plan

	Catholics	Protestants	Jews
AIPO 411, 1-21-48			
(N)	(594)	(2254)	(143)
Had heard or read of Marshall Plan	78%	83%	90%
Among those who had heard or read only:			
Approve Marshall Plan	54	53	55
Approve with qualifications ("if they repay," "if properly administered," "if they work themselves," "if we can afford it," etc.)	10	9	11
Disapprove	18	21	21
No opinion	18	17	14
AIPO 411 (T only), 1-21-48			
(N)	(308)	(1134)	(81)
Congress should vote full $6.8 billions for first 15 months of ERP requested by President	47%	43%	75%
Congress should appropriate smaller amount	7	10	2
Approval with provisos, reservations ("if necessary," "if properly handled," "if spent right," "if it doesn't go on too long," etc.)	3	4	3
Congress should vote no money for ERP	33	33	16
No opinion	10	10	4
AIPO 411 (K only), 1-21-48			
(N)	(286)	(972)	(62)
Favor sending $17 billion in goods over 4 years to W. Europe to improve conditions and keep it from going communistic	52%	47%	63%
Favor lesser amount	6	5	3
Favor with qualifications	6	9	7
Oppose	29	33	23
No opinion	7	6	4
NORC 155, 2-25-48			
(N)	(276)	(887)	(64)
Congress should appropriate $5 billion requested by Secretary Marshall for next year for ERP	19%	24%	30%
Congress should reduce it	33	28	25
Disapprove of ERP in general	42	43	38
No opinion	6	5	7

	Catholics	Protestants	Jews
AIPO 454, 3-24-50	(341)	(991)	(78)
U.S. spending on Marshall Plan			
should be increased	10%	11%	17%
Should be decreased	47	48	29
Kept the same	33	32	44
No opinion	10	9	10
NORC 280, 4-17-50			
(N)	(301)	(866)	(44)
Continue Marshall Plan aid to			
W. Europe	58%	55%	66%
Discontinue	32	34	27
No opinion	10	11	7
U.S. spending too much on			
Marshall Plan	50	53	52
Right amount	33	29	22
Not enough	5	4	17
No opinion	12	14	9
Pres. Truman proposed $3 billion			
for next year, contrasted with			
$4 billion appropriated for			
fiscal year 1950:			
(1) Still too much	31	34	38
(2) About right amount	45	39	29
(3) Not enough	14	10	20
(4) No opinion	10	17	13
Composite of Roper surveys of			
Aug. and Oct.'52			
(N)	(1807)	(5047)	(311)
Continuation of aid to W. Europe			
1 of 2 or 3 most important of			
10 things for new administration			
to do	8%	8%	18%

Table 4-2.   Military aid

	Catholics	Protestants	Jews
NORC 155, 2-25-48			
(N)	(276)	(884)	(64)
Send arms to South America	49%	46%	42%
Bad idea	33	37	45
No opinion	18	17	13
Send military supplies to Chiang			
regime	35	32	33
Do not	58	60	58
No opinion	7	8	9
NORC 157, 4-22-48			
(N)	(252)	(917)	(72)
Send military supplies to W. Europe now to strengthen them against future attack	58%	51%	49%
Opposed	33	40	43
No opinion	9	9	8
Send military supplies to help Chinese government against the communists	62	55	48
Do not	26	31	49
No opinion	12	14	3
AIPO 423, 11-1-48			
(N)	(661)	(1952)	(141)
Favor spending $2 billion next year to help W. Europe rearm	35%	32%	25%
Oppose this proposal	50	55	69
No opinion	15	13	6
AIPO 445, 7-21-49			
(N)	(605)	(1948)	(123)
Had heard or read of NATO Pact	57%	64%	80%
Send arms and war materials to NATO members[a]	58	57	31
Do not	29	30	58
No opinion	13	13	11
Roper survey of Aug.'52			
(N)	(908)	(2414)	(136)
Keep on building armed strength of W. Europe	31%	26%	41%
Continue some aid, but cut amount	43	44	42
Get out of Europe's affairs	16	16	12
No opinion	10	14	5

	Catholics	Protestants	Jews
Roper survey of Oct.'52			
(N)	(899)	(2633)	(175)
Keep building armed strength of			
W. Europe	31%	27%	41%
Continue some aid, but cut amount	44	45	40
Get out of Europe's affairs	15	16	12
No opinion	10	12	7
AIPO 506, 10-7-52			
(N)	(822)	(2051)	(111)
U.S. should train and equip			
S. Korean army of 2 million men	72%	69%	69%
Should not	15	19	18
No opinion	13	12	13

a Asked only of those who had heard of the North Atlantic Pact.

Table 4-3.   Aid to less-developed countries--general, 1950-1957

	Catholics	Protestants	Jews
NORC 280, 4-17-50			
(N)	(301)	(866)	(44)
Had heard or read of Point Four Program	19%	24%	34%
Could describe in general terms the main purpose of Point Four as technical assistance to underdeveloped countries	3	4	23
Good policy for U.S. to try to help backward countries raise their standards of living	75	72	77
No concern of our government	21	22	21
No opinion	4	6	2
Aid to such countries really helps U.S. interests	75	68	70
Does not help U.S. at all	17	23	21
No opinion	8	9	9
AIPO 514, 4-17-53			
(N)	(388)	(1099)	(48)
Favor sending less economic and military aid to W. Europe and more to allies in Asia	48%	44%	42%
Qualified approval	3	4	4
Disapprove	30	25	42
No opinion	19	27	12
AIPO 546, 4-12-55			
(N)	(380)	(1058)	(51)
Good idea to send economic aid similar to ERP to noncommunist Asian countries	56%	55%	71%
Bad idea	29	26	12
No opinion	15	19	17
SRC 417, Sept.-Oct.'56			
(N)	(372)	(1287)	(56)
Strongly agree U.S. should give economic help to poorer countries even if can't pay for it	21%	21%	30%
Agree, but not strongly	21	21	21
Depends	14	16	20
Disagree, but not strongly	10	10	4
Strongly disagree	16	16	9
No opinion	18	16	16

	Catholics	Protestants	Jews
NORC 401, 12-38-56			
(N)	(279)	(870)	(42)
Aid we're sending abroad helps U.S.	73%	61%	71%
Does not	23	31	19
No opinion	4	8	10
AIPO 577, 1-15-57			
(N)	(385)	(1029)	(53)
Approve sending economic--i.e., financial--help to friendly Middle Eastern countries	69%	69%	76%
Disapprove	18	19	9
No opinion	13	12	15
Approve sending arms and war materials to help build up their armies	50	53	57
Disapprove	38	32	30
No opinion	12	15	13
Roper 939, March '57			
(N)	(339)	(1042)	(43)
Increase amount of foreign economic aid	2%	4%	21%
Keep the same	24	24	26
Cut a little	35	30	21
Cut drastically	26	28	16
Stop altogether	3	3	2
No opinion	10	11	14
Increase amount of foreign military aid	4	6	12
Keep the same	50	46	58
Cut a little	21	20	14
Cut drastically	10	15	5
Stop altogether	3	2	2
No opinion	12	12	9
NORC 404, 4-26-57			
(N)	(307)	(865)	(55)
$4 billion for military plus economic aid next year is:			
(1) Too much	38%	36%	31%
(2) Not enough	3	2	5
(3) About right	47	50	35
(4) No opinion	12	12	29

Table 4-4.   National defense and military vs. economic aid

	Catholics	Protestants	Jews
AIPO 514, 4-17-53			
(N)	(388)	(1099)	(48)
If defense spending can safely be cut, would favor U.S., along with other countries, using part of money thus saved to help needy countries	57%	70%	77%
Opposed	25	23	21
No opinion	18	7	2
Roper 939, March '57			
(N)	(339)	(1042)	(43)
Increase or keep military aid about the same, but cut or stop economic aid	31%	26%	23%
Increase or keep economic aid about the same, but cut or stop military aid	4	4	7
NORC 404, 4-26-57			
(N)	(307)	(865)	(55)
Continue economic aid to countries that have agreed to stand with us against communist aggression	82%	79%	91%
Do not continue	16	16	7
No opinion	2	5	2
More important to send allies economic aid	64	71	73
More important to send them military aid	20	15	11
No opinion	16	14	16

Table 4-5.   Communism, neutralism, and aid

	Catholics	Protestants	Jews
SRC 417, Sept.-Oct.'56			
(N)	(372)	(1287)	(56)
Strongly agree U.S. should help countries not as much against communism as we are	11%	12%	20%
Agree, but not strongly	16	17	14
Depends, not sure	12	12	13
Disagree, but not strongly	11	10	9
Strongly disagree	24	20	20
No opinion	26	29	25
AIPO 576, 12-12-56			
(N)	(418)	(1053)	(43)
Congress should appropriate $4 billion for next year for other countries to help prevent their going communistic	61%	56%	77%
Congress should not appropriate so much	25	29	14
No opinion	14	15	9
NORC 401, 12-28-56			
(N)	(279)	(870)	(42)
U.S. should continue economic aid to countries like India, which have not joined us as allies against the communists	59%	47%	76%
Should stop aid to such countries	36	46	24
No opinion	5	7	0
Composite of NORC 401, 12-28-56, and NORC 404, 4-26-57			
(N)	(586)	(1635)	(97)
U.S. can in general count on India to cooperate in world affairs	37%	41%	43%
Cannot	34	31	33
No opinion	29	28	24
Roper 939, March '57			
(N)	(339)	(1042)	(43)
Neutralist, nonaligned policy of Nehru has had generally good effect on world peace and understanding	29%	31%	30%
More bad than good	35	30	30
No opinion	36	39	40

	Catholics	Protestants	Jews
NORC 404, 4-26-57			
(N)	(307)	(865)	(55)
U.S. should continue economic aid to countries like India, which have not joined as allies	43%	38%	69%
Should stop aid to such countries	52	56	27
No opinion	5	6	4
Send economic aid to communist countries like Poland	55	42	57
Do not	42	51	40
No opinion	3	7	9

Table 4-6. Foreign aid, 1958-1968

	Catholics	Protestants	Jews
AIPO 596, 3-4-58			
(N)	(362)	(1148)	(46)
Estimated annual aid level within $1 billion of correct figure of approximately $4 billion	6%	6%	13%
Knew of both economic and military objectives of aid	10	11	36
In general for foreign aid	58	48	65
Against it	30	35	24
No opinion	12	17	11
SRC 431, Sept.-Oct.'58			
(N)	(381)	(1329)	(61)
Agree U.S. should give economic help to poorer countries even if they can't pay for it	53%	49%	61%
Disagree (U.S. should not)	17	21	12
Depends	14	13	15
No interest and no opinion	16	17	12
AIPO 596, 3-4-58			
(N)	(362)	(1148)	(46)
Congress should appropriate more money than President asked for foreign aid for next year	4%	3%	7%
Should appropriate what he asked for	37	36	33
Should appropriate less or nothing	36	34	28
No opinion	23	27	32
AIPO 617, 8-18-59			
(N)	(385)	(960)	(58)
Favor Congress setting aside money to fit out hospital, food, training, etc., ships for needy abroad	74%	72%	78%
Opposed	18	17	12
No opinion	8	11	10
SRC 440, Sept.-Oct.'60			
(N)	(413)	(1427)	(68)
Agree U.S. should give economic help	56%	50%	63%
Disagree	16	21	10
Depends	17	15	21
No opinion	11	14	6

	Catholics	Protestants	Jews
AIPO 640, 1-10-61			
(N)[a]	(660)	(1856)	(58)
Favor sending qualified young men at gov't expense on technical assistance to underdeveloped countries	73%	70%	67%
Opposed	13	20	12
No opinion	14	10	21
Would want son to participate	70	63	71
Would not	20	27	9
No opinion	10	10	20
AIPO 646, 5-26-61			
(N)[a]	(817)	(2466)	(110)
Willing to make sacrifices for foreign aid, even if means increasing our taxes	15%	8%	12%
AIPO 647, 6-21-61			
(N)[a]	(722)	(1927)	(72)
Communism would be in greater position of world power if Congress had not appropriated $3-4 billion annually for foreign aid	68%	58%	51%
Would not or no difference	21	24	22
No opinion	11	18	27
AIPO 649, 8-22-61			
(N)[a]	(687)	(2304)	(64)
Favor U.S. taking lead in establishing university in Africa open to all qualified Africans	67%	57%	63%
Opposed	24	27	34
No opinion	9	16	3
Favor U.S. doing likewise in Southeast Asia	59	49	53
Opposed	28	32	34
No opinion	13	19	13
AIPO 652, 11-15-61			
(N)[a]	(703)	(1873)	(57)
U.S. and West not doing enough in financial and technical aid for less-developed countries	16%	13%	42%
Are doing enough (or too much)	67	69	42
No opinion	17	18	16
Interests of U.S. have been helped by foreign aid in last five years	55	49	44
Have not	25	27	56
No opinion	20	24	0

	Catholics	Protestants	Jews
AIPO 657, 4-4-62			
(N)[a]	(896)	(2238)	(75)
Favor aid to Yugoslavia	27%	24%	39%
Opposed	39	40	36
No opinion	34	36	25
AIPO 659, 5-29-62			
(N)[a]	(750)	(2254)	(77)
Send food to Communist China if China requests it	50%	46%	69%
Do not	43	45	26
No opinion	7	9	5
Like to see U.N. try to solve feeding and resettling of Chinese refugees	68	64	84
Would not	23	33	12
No opinion	9	3	4
AIPO 664, 10-17-62			
(N)[a]	(953)	(3009)	(103)
Had heard or read of Peace Corps	81%	68%	81%
Approve in general of job being done by Peace Corps	64	49	73
Disapprove	5	6	3
No opinion	12	13	5
AIPO 665, 11-14-62			
(N)[a]	(1073)	(3095)	(106)
U.S. should do something to help India[b]	61%	52%	69%
Should not	14	11	16
No opinion	10	21	13
Never heard of any fighting between India and China	15	16	2
AIPO 667, 1-9-63			
(N)[a]	(1074)	(3008)	(137)
In general for foreign aid	61%	57%	70%
Against it	29	31	16
No opinion	10	12	14
AIPO 678, 10-9-63			
(N)[a]	(813)	(2301)	(85)
Spontaneously mentioned foreign aid as a program on which U.S. gov't spends too much	37%	42%	42%

	Catholics	Protestants	Jews
AIPO 682, 12-10-63			
(N)[a] (All self-declared			
Democrats excluded)	(324)	(1276)	(20)
U.S. foreign aid should be kept			
at present level at least	38%	30%	62%
Should be reduced	49	51	38
Should be cut out entirely	6	8	0
No opinion	7	11	0
SRC 473, Sept.-Oct.'64			
(N)	(350)	(1078)	(45)
Definitely favor giving aid, mind			
made up	51%	43%	56%
Favor, but some doubts	6	7	11
Depends	19	18	16
Each country should make own way,			
but some doubts	2	4	0
Each country should make own way,			
mind made up	13	17	9
No interest and no opinion	9	11	8
POS 655, 2-15-65			
(N)	(359)	(1152)	(46)
U.S. has obligation to help			
poorer nations	56%	45%	60%
Does not	23	25	18
Depends, conditional	19	26	22
No opinion	2	4	0
$1 in aid for $200 of GNP is			
too little	12	9	17
About right or depends	38	35	37
Too much	34	35	22
No opinion	16	21	24
Extremely well satisfied with			
U.S. aid to poor nations	24	19	29
Considerably well satisfied	27	24	31
Only somewhat satisfied	25	32	22
Not at all satisfied	22	24	18
No opinion	2	1	0
Should spend most aid			
in Latin America	50	39	35
in Asia	12	8	14
in Africa	7	15	10
Neither or equally	8	8	21
No opinion	23	30	20

	Catholics	Protestants	Jews
AIPO 706, 2-17-65			
(N)[a]	(756)	(2547)	(45)
In general for foreign aid	60%	56%	67%
Approve without conditions or qualifications:			
Percent of total	35	29	43
Percent of those in general for aid	59	52	63
Against it	29	35	29
No opinion	11	9	4
AIPO 706, 2-17-65			
(N)[a]	(786)	(2547)	(45)
$3.4 billion, or about 3% of federal budget, requested by President of Congress for foreign aid next year should be increased	5%	6%	8%
Should be authorized as requested	41	31	36
Should be decreased	43	51	29
No opinion	11	12	18
Reasons given for disapproving of foreign aid (among those against it only):			
Charity begins at home, should be devoted to poor here, etc.	49	41	15
Our overall expenditures or national debt too large	10	16	0
How this money could be better used (among only those who would cut or stop aid):			
Help poverty in U.S., aid U.S. underprivileged	38	32	31
Improve unemployment, job opportunities, etc., here	11	7	0
Don't spend it at all, cut taxes, national debt, or balance of payments	21	28	38
Most important purpose of foreign aid is:			
Raising living standard, economic growth	29	22	39
AIPO 707, 3-1-65			
(N)[a]	(878)	(2393)	(119)
Had heard or read about great population increase predicted in world in next few decades	74%	72%	90%
Worried about this anticipated increase	20	23	26

	Catholics	Protestants	Jews
AIPO 718, 10-6-65			
(N) [a]	(837)	(2467)	(71)
Our gov't should help other countries with birth-control programs if they ask us	39%	54%	73%
Should not	54	38	21
No opinion	7	8	6
AIPO 724, 2-8-66			
(N) [a]	(784)	(2395)	(128)
Approve of inclusion of following in foreign aid program:			
Provide birth control information	31%	48%	63%
Train teachers, provide books, build schools	62	66	67
Build highways, railroads, other communications	24	21	21
Build hospitals, train nurses and physicians, provide medicines	58	63	57
Send surplus food	42	41	57
Help improve farming methods	58	63	59
Build up military strength	22	17	9
Construct factories and industries	35	33	34
AIPO 724, 2-8-66			
(N) [a]	(784)	(2395)	(128)
In general for foreign aid	53%	52%	62%
Against it	33	37	27
No opinion	14	11	11
Continue aid to a country that fails to support U.S. in major foreign-policy decision, e.g., Vietnam	17	14	17
Reduce aid to that country	29	31	36
Cut aid off completely	45	47	30
No opinion	9	8	17

	Cath.	Prot.	White Prot.	Nonwhite Prot.	Jews
AIPO 724, 2-8-66					
(N) [a]	(784)	(2395)	(2022)	(371)	(128)
Lack of indigenous effort primarily accounts for poverty and economic underdevelopment	36%	39%	42%	24%	30%
Circumstances beyond their control does	32	28	30	22	43
Both equally responsible	24	26	22	35	24
No opinion	8	8	6	19	3

	Catholics	Protestants	Jews
AIPO 726, 3-22-66			
(N) [a]	(878)	(2454)	(85)
Fast rate of world population			
growth is a serious problem	57%	72%	73%
Is not	35	20	15
No opinion	8	8	12
AIPO survey of May '67 [c]			
Have followed some of discussions			
about U.S. foreign aid program	38%	41%	-
Have not followed any	62	59	
Would like to see amount requested			
by Pres. Johnson, $3.1 billion			
or 2% of U.S. budget, increased	8	6	
Decreased	46	52	
Kept same	36	29	
No opinion	10	13	
AIPO survey of Aug.'68 [d]			
Favor U.S. gov't helping other			
nations who request aid in			
birth control	65%	70%	-
Opposed	25	22	
No opinion	10	8	

a   Weighted N's indicated were approximately twice the numbers of
    Christians interviewed and one-and-a-half times the number of Jews.

b   This question was asked only of persons who said they had heard or
    read of the fighting between India and China. Percentages are,
    however, based on all interviewees.

c   *Gallup Opinion Index,* June 1967.

d   *Gallup Opinion Index,* Sept. 1968.

Table 4-7.   World trade

	Catholics	Protestants	Jews
AIPO 408, Nov.'47			
(N)	(623)	(1975)	(142)
Favor GATT to lower tariffs			
reciprocally	65%	66%	81%
Oppose	12	12	9
No opinion	23	22	10
AIPO 526, Jan.'54			
(N)	(312)	(1085)	(47)
Favor higher tariffs	14%	10%	13%
Lower tariffs	29	29	47
About current level	21	22	21
No opinion	36	39	19
AIPO 540, Nov.'54			
(N)	(321)	(1006)	(87)
Favor higher tariffs	19%	18%	18%
Lower tariffs	36	30	50
About current level	18	23	9
No opinion	27	29	23
Roper 939, March '57			
(N)	(339)	(1042)	(43)
All tariffs should be fairly high to protect jobs and industry from foreign competition	33%	34%	32%
Should be low to keep prices down and encourage world trade	39	33	33
Should be medium	11	9	18
Depends	3	7	5
No opinion	14	17	12
AIPO 614, 5-27-59			
(N)	(360)	(1071)	(51)
Favor higher tariffs[a]	18%	9%	14%
Lower tariffs[a]	9	15	33
About current level[a]	8	7	6
No opinion[a]	4	4	2
Never heard or read anything of trade and tariffs discussion	61	65	45
AIPO 653, 12-5-61			
(N)	(372)	(1123)	(53)
Favor higher tariffs[a]	18%	16%	16%
Favor lower tariffs[a]	22	19	33
Keep tariffs at current levels[a]	8	7	8
No opinion	7	8	3
Haven't heard or read anything about tariffs or trade	45	50	40

	Catholics	Protestants	Jews
AIPO 655, Feb.'62			
(N)	(396)	(1133)	(39)
Like to see more foreign goods imported into U.S.	10%	11%	19%
Put on more import restrictions	56	48	52
Keep trade barriers and imports at current level	19	18	13
Depends	8	6	11
No opinion	7	17	5
Put more restrictions on textile imports	39	32	35
Keep as are	37	38	40
Import more textiles	10	11	13
No opinion	14	19	12
Put more restrictions on oil imports	30	26	20
Keep as are	36	31	55
Import more oil	18	18	15
No opinion	16	25	10
Put more restrictions on automobile imports	56	49	52
Keep as are	32	28	30
Import more cars	5	9	12
No opinion	7	14	6
Put more restrictions on steel imports	49	37	43
Keep as are	28	27	33
Import more steel	11	13	10
No opinion	12	23	14
AIPO 656, 3-6-62			
(N)	(354)	(1134)	(53)
Important to increase goods we buy from and sell to other countries	66%	66%	79%
Not important	19	17	13
No opinion	15	17	8
Favor higher tariffs	17	14	9
Favor lower tariffs	35	27	44
Keep at current levels	15	18	21
No opinion and never heard of tariffs	33	41	26

a Question was posed only to those who said that they had heard or read something of tariffs and/or trade.

Table 5-1.   Relations with the Vatican

	Catholics	Protestants	Jews
AIPO 482, 11-9-51			
(N)	(470)	(1362)	(120)
U.S. Senate should approve appointment of ambassador to Vatican	43%	12%	22%
Should not	12	35	33
No opinion	10	11	14
Never read or heard anything about naming of such an ambassador	35	42	31
AIPO 645, May '61			
(N)	(351)	(1040)	(56)
Like U.S. gov't to send representative to Vatican	68%	26%	39%
Opposed	17	43	35
No opinion	15	31	26

Table 5-2.   Franco Spain

	Catholics	Protestants	Jews
NORC T-46, DU-1, 5-21-46			
(N)	(103)	(311)	(18)
Favorable impressions of Franco gov't	14%	6%	2%
Unfavorable impressions	46	60	78
No opinion	40	34	20
Franco gov't a threat to international peace[a]	31	38	47
U.N. should do nothing, but leave the problem to the Spanish themselves[a]	27	31	31
U.N. should break diplomatic relations with Franco, but go no further to get rid of his gov't[a]	7	6	8
U.N. should take further action, but not at risk of another Spanish civil war[a]	2	2	2
U.N. take whatever action necessary to eliminate that regime, even at risk of civil war[a]	8	17	22
No opinion	2	4	15
NORC 161, 10-13-48			
(N)	(268)	(845)	(76)
Add Spain to countries receiving ERP aid	32%	24%	22%
Disapprove of such aid to Spain	41	50	69
No opinion	27	26	9
Of those who approved:			
Feel strongly	32%	33%	27%
Do not feel strongly	68	67	73
Of those who disapproved:			
Feel strongly	62	61	92
Do not feel strongly	38	39	8
AIPO release 5-11-49			
Franco Spain should be invited to join U.N.[b]	47%	30%	23%
Should not[b]	33	50	68
No opinion[b]	20	20	9
AIPO 489, 3-25-52			
(N)	(436)	(1445)	(117)
U.S. should join Spain in mutual defense pact	47%	37%	29%
Should not	27	35	68
No opinion	26	28	3

	Catholics	Protestants	Jews
NORC 339, 4-1-53			
(N)	(302)	(872)	(40)
Approve of U.S. sending military			
supplies to Franco gov't	57%	53%	50%
Disapprove	28	32	38
No opinion	15	15	12
NORC 349, 11-25-53			
(N)	(233)	(909)	(47)
Approve of recent agreement to			
give economic and military			
aid to Spain in return for			
bases	81%	77%	75%
Disapprove	10	13	15
No opinion	9	10	10

_a_ These questions were posed only to those who expressed unfavorable
impressions of Franco.

_b_ Asked only of those who could identify General Franco. Percentages
are based only on those confronted with this query.

Table 5-3.   Perception of foreigners and their governments

	Catholics	Protestants	Jews
AIPO 445, 7-21-49			
(N)	(593)	(1909)	(116)
Germany has been punished enough			
for World War II	56%	53%	32%
Has not	27	28	58
No opinion	17	19	10
NORC 280, 4-17-50			
(N)	(297)	(866)	(40)
Can trust the Germans now	31%	21%	7%
Cannot	60	67	88
No opinion	9	12	5
NORC 401, 12-28-56			
(N)	(279)	(870)	(42)
Can count on Japan to cooperate			
with us	70%	65%	64%
Cannot	5	19	26
No opinion	15	16	10
NORC 404, 4-26-57			
(N)	(307)	(865)	(55)
Can count on England to cooperate			
with us	77%	74%	82%
Cannot	17	16	14
No opinion	6	10	4
AIPO 630, 6-28-60			
(N)[a]	(820)	(2187)	(119)
Send teachers to study abroad at			
U.S. expense	70%	58%	74%
Poor idea	24	34	23
No opinion	6	8	3
AIPO 650, 9-19-61			
Which two can be depended on as			
most friendly to U.S.?			
(1) India	12%	12%	6%
(2) Indonesia	3	2	2
(3) Japan	20	18	13
(4) Pakistan	3	4	2
(5) South Korea	12	13	14
(6) Thailand	4	2	2
(7) Philippines	38	36	43
No opinion	8	13	18

	Catholics	Protestants	Jews
AIPO 668, 2-5-63			
(N)[a]	(841)	(2602)	(76)
Britain is a dependable ally			
of U.S.	63%	63%	82%
Is not	14	12	5
No opinion	23	25	13
West Germany is a dependable ally	63	57	46
Is not	11	13	34
No opinion	26	30	20
France is a dependable ally	38	31	21
Is not	33	35	66
No opinion	29	34	13
AIPO 723, 12-29-65			
(N)[a]	(959)	(2284)	(148)
Japan is a dependable ally	44%	39%	48%
Is not	38	35	24
No opinion	18	26	28
AIPO survey of June '66[b]			
France is a dependable ally	18%	15%	16%
Is not	56	56	56
No opinion	26	29	28

a These weighted N's were approximately twice the N's of Protestants
   and Catholics actually interviewed, and 1.5 times the actual N's
   of Jews.

b *Gallup Political index,* July 1966.

Table 5-4.   Immigration

	Catholics	Protestants	Jews
NORC 231, Dec.'44			
(N)	(523)	(1729)	(107)
Jews should have same chance as others to settle in all countries after the war	81%	73%	99%
Jews should not	15	20	0
No opinion	4	7	1
Jews should have same chance as non-Jews to settle in America after war	66	57	99
Jews should not	13	12	0
No opinion	21	31	1
NORC 243, 8-21-46			
(N)	(527)	(1810)	(108)
Let some of 800,000 homeless Europeans come here now	22%	20%	82%
Do not	72	74	14
No opinion	6	6	4
Let some of them come here if other countries take some too	56	47	92
Do not	40	48	3
No opinion	4	5	5
NORC 157, 4-22-48			
(N)	(252)	(917)	(72)
Let 200,000 D.P.'s from eastern Europe come to live in next two years	44%	36%	85%
Do not	47	57	14
No opinion	9	7	1
NORC 401, 12-28-56			
(N)	(279)	(870)	(42)
U.S. is letting in too many Hungarian refugees	30%	37%	5%
About right number	51	46	67
Not enough	13	9	26
No opinion	6	8	2
Louis Harris Survey of 1965			
Favor letting more immigrants come to U.S., as proposed by Pres. Johnson	33%	18%	44%
Oppose	44	65	41
No opinion	23	17	15

	Catholics	Protestants	Jews
AIPO 713, 6-22-65			
(N)[a]	(914)	(2325)	(133)
Increase rate of immigration	9%	5%	33%
Keep at present level	46	37	32
Decrease or stop	26	37	14
No opinion	19	21	21
Change quota system based on national origins to system based on occupational skills	51	48	75
Prefer present quota system to that proposed by the President	32	35	12
No opinion	17	17	13

a Weighted N's.

Table 5-5.   Israel and the Arab states

	Catholics	Protestants	Jews
NORC 231, Dec.'44			
(N)	(522)	(1724)	(107)
Agree with Zionists, Britain should set up Jewish state in Palestine	36%	34%	69%
Agree with Arabs against establishing Jewish state	27	22	7
Neither	10	9	16
No opinion	27	35	8
U.S. should officially demand that Palestine be made into Jewish state	20	18	59
NORC 155, 2-25-48			
(N)	(276)	(887)	(64)
Approve proposed partition of Palestine between Arabs and Jews	38%	35%	88%
Disapprove	22	19	6
No opinion	12	17	3
Never heard of proposed partition	28	29	3
Sympathize with the Jews in this conflict	32	32	92
Sympathize with the Arabs	19	16	0
Neither and no opinion	49	52	8
Continue embargo of arms to the area	83	85	33
Cease embargo	9	7	58
No opinion	8	8	9
Sell arms to both sides	5	4	14
Sell only to Jews	2	2	44
No opinion	2	1	0
Approve sending U.S. troops as part of U.N. force in Palestine, if requested	36	42	91
Disapprove	60	51	8
No opinion	4	7	1
Approve sending U.S. troops independently if no U.N. force is sent	11	7	28
Disapprove	84	85	61
No opinion	5	8	11

	Catholics	Protestants	Jews
NORC 156, 3-25-48			
(N)	(294)	(885)	(60)
Favor partition into two countries, one for Jews, other for Arabs	48%	47%	82%
Against	27	28	13
No opinion	25	25	5
Approve change of U.S. policy from support of to opposition to partition	36	40	10
U.S. should have continued support of partition	35	31	85
No opinion	29	29	5
If Jews independently set up Jewish state anyhow, U.S. should encourage them	44	50	85
Should oppose them	14	10	0
Neither, stay out of this issue	23	21	10
No opinion	19	19	5
NORC 159, 6-29-48			
(N)	(229)	(887)	(51)
Sympathize with Jews in Palestine conflict	31%	34%	93%
Sympathize with Arabs	22	12	0
Sympathize with neither and no opinion	47	54	7
NORC 349, 11-25-53			
(N)	(233)	(909)	(47)
Arabs more to blame for dispute with Israel	9%	9%	67%
Israel more to blame	9	9	0
Both equally to blame	11	11	12
Neither to blame	2	2	5
No opinion	22	23	16
Never heard of Arab-Israeli dispute	47	46	9
Very important to cooperate closely with Israel	30	33	79
Only fairly important	32	28	19
Not so important	14	10	0
No opinion	24	29	2
Very important to cooperate closely with Arab states	29	31	51
Only fairly important	32	28	32
Not so important	12	11	15
No opinion	27	30	2

	Catholics	Protestants	Jews
Supply arms to Israel	17	16	85
Do not	69	63	10
No opinion	14	21	5

NORC 404, 4-27-57			
(N)	(306)	(752)	(55)
Egypt more to blame for conflict with Israel	38%	41%	83%
Israel more to blame	15	11	2
Both equally	20	13	11
Neither	2	3	2
No opinion	25	32	2
Very friendly to Israel	11	14	87
Somewhat friendly	33	31	11
Neither	42	41	2
Somewhat unfriendly	7	7	0
Very unfriendly	3	1	0
No opinion	4	6	0
More friendly now	17	16	40
Less friendly now	17	18	5
Same, no change	59	57	53
Don't know	7	9	2

Roper 939, April '57			
(N)	(339)	(1042)	(43)
Have high opinion of Israel	7%	10%	63%
Although Israel has done some things disapprove of, in general think well of her	42	45	23
Although understand Israel's position, in general don't think well of her	19	13	5
Have low opinion of Israel	5	5	0
No opinion	27	27	9

AIPO survey of June '67[a]			
Approve of way Johnson is handling Middle East situation	51%	47%	-
Disapprove	13	13	
No opinion	36	40	

AIPO survey of July '68[b]			
If full-scale Arab-Israeli war developed, U.S. should supply arms and materials to Israel	21%	23%	-
Should not	66	58	
No opinion	13	19	
In case of such war, should send troops to help Israel	5	8	
Should not	84	76	
No opinion	11	16	

	Catholics	Protestants	Jews
In case of such a war, should			
supply arms and material to Arabs	3	3	
Should not	83	76	
No opinion	14	21	
In case of such a war, should send			
troops to help Arabs	1	2	
Should not	87	80	
No opinion	12	18	
AIPO survey of Jan.'69[c]			
Heard or read of troubles between			
Israel and Arab nations	89%	83%	–
Sympathize more with Israel	44	50	
Sympathize more with Arabs	7	4	
Neither and no opinion	49	46	
AIPO survey of March '70[d]			
Heard or read of troubles between			
Israel and Arab nations	87%	86%	–
Sympathize more with Israel	34	45	
Sympathize more with Arabs	6	2	
Neither	39	31	
No opinion	21	22	

a *Gallup Opinion Index*, July 1967.

b *Gallup Opinion Index*, Aug. 1968.

c *Gallup Opinion Index*, Feb. 1970.

d *Gallup Opinion Index*, April 1970.

Table 5-6.　Optimism about the future

	Catholics	Protestants	Jews
POS 655, 2-15-65			
(N)	(359)	(1152)	(46)
U.S. world influence will increase			
over next 20 years	59%	49%	52%
Will decrease	26	32	32
Will stay same	4	8	6
No opinion	11	11	10
AIPO survey of Dec.'66[a]			
1967 will likely be a year of:			
(1) Economic prosperity	49%	42%	—
(2) Economic difficulty	41	45	
(3) No opinion	10	13	
(1) Full employment	65	61	
(2) Rising unemployment	24	30	
(3) No opinion	11	9	
(1) Strikes and industrial disputes	56	60	
(2) Industrial peace	29	25	
(3) No opinion	15	15	
(1) Rising taxes	89	93	
(2) Falling taxes	6	3	
(3) No opinion	5	4	
(1) Increasing American power in			
the world	70	65	
(2) Declining American power	15	21	
(3) No opinion	15	14	
(1) increasing Red Chinese power	58	58	
(2) Declining Chinese power	26	20	
(3) No opinion	16	22	
(1) Increasing Soviet power	45	50	
(2) Declining Soviet power	29	25	
(3) No opinion	26	25	
AIPO survey of Dec.'69			
Think following will happen by 1990:			
U.S. standard of living will			
have doubled	47%	41%	—
U.S. life expectancy will have			
risen to 100 years	32	23	
A cure for cancer will be found	75	72	
Man will live on moon	22	16	
No Russian communism	11	6	
Russia and West will be living			
peacefully together	24	20	
Atomic weapon production will			
have ceased	16	14	
Passports unnecessary for			
world travel	18	16	

a Gallup Opinion Index, Jan. 1967.　Jewish replies were not provided.
b Gallup Opinion Index, Dec. 1969.

Table 6-1. Race and knowledge of world affairs

	Negroes				All	Whites	
	All	Protestant	North	South		Protestant	Catholic
AIPO 401, 7-23-47							
(N)	(177)		(134)	(43)	(2883)		
Heard or read of Marshall Plan	48%		49%	44%	62%		
Could correctly describe it	2		5	1	7		
AIPO 406, 10-22-47							
(N)	(190)		(160)	(30)	(2733)		
Heard or read of Marshall Plan	54%		55%	47%	69%		
Roper survey of Nov.'47							
(N)	(306)				(3241)		
Regarded helping Europe to recover as among two most important of nine alternative endeavors for U.S. gov't	4%				14%		
So regarded strengthening the U.N.	6				22		
AIPO 408, Nov.'47							
(N)	(102)	(91)	(63)	(39)	(2797)	(1883)	(611)
Heard or read of recent GATT signed in Geneva by 22 states, to lower tariffs	18%	18%	22%	13%	37%	38%	30%
AIPO 411, 1-28-48							
(N)	(190)				(2971)	(2064)	(580)
Heard or read of Marshall Plan	67%				83%	84%	78%
AIPO 412, 2-4-48							
(N)	(211)				(2974)		

	Negroes				All	Whites	
	All	Protestant	North	South		Protestant	Catholic
Heard or read of Marshall Plan	75%				85%		
Could correctly describe it	4				10		
AIPO 439, 3-17-49							
(N)	(189)		(164)	(25)	(2004)		
Heard or read of Marshall Plan	56%		79%	36%	82%		
Could correctly describe it	2		4	0	5		
Heard or read of North Atlantic Security Pact	33		50	16	59		
Could correctly describe it	15		18	0	26		
AIPO 446, 8-12-49							
(N)	(227)				(2824)		
Makes much difference to U.S. whether Britain continues to be strong	55%				66%		
Little or no difference	31				26		
No opinion	14				8		
Heard or read of Britain's money difficulties	50				64		
AIPO 455, 4-28-50							
(N)	(132)				(1374)		
Heard or read of Point Four	20%				27%		
Could provide generally correct description of Point Four	1				5		
Composite of Roper surveys of Aug. and Oct.'52							
(N)	(840)	(698)	(365)	(475)	(7152)	(4349)	(1781)
One of 2 or 3 most important issues in election campaign is to continue aid to W. Europe	3%	3%	4%	1%	9%	9%	8%

	Negroes				All	Whites	
	All	Protestant	North	South		Protestant	Catholic
Roper survey of Aug.'52							
(N)	(387)				(2021)		
Economic aid to W. Europe one of most important of 10 policies for next administration to continue	3%				9%		
AIPO 517, 7-2-53							
(N)	(128)		(74)	(54)	(1417)	(885)	(311)
Read regularly any columnist on national or international affairs	21%		23%	18%	32%	52%	45%
AIPO 540, Nov.'54							
(N)	(141)	(129)			(1329)		
Heard or read anything of trade or tariffs	38%	37%			51%		
AIPO 546, 4-12-55							
(N)	(195)	(189)	(100)	(95)	(1340)	(863)	(368)
Heard or read of any trouble in Formosa area	66%	65%	82%	50%	84%	85%	83%
Knew Quemoy and Matsu in noncommunist hands	34	33	44	24	46	47	39
Could not locate 1 of 7 European countries on a map	30	36	23	49	22	23	21
AIPO 558, 1-4-56							
(N)	(166)		(92)	(74)	(1217)		
Heard or read of recent French elections	16%		21%	10%	49%		

| | Negroes | | | | | Whites | |
	All	Protestant	North	South	All	Protestant	Catholic
NORC 404, 4-26-57							
(N)	(117)				(1162)	(766)	(299)
Could name no countries or territories in Africa	70%				55%	56%	54%
Could name as many as five	1				6	6	5
AIPO 653, 12-5-61							
(N)	(165)	(150)			(1439)	(973)	(362)
Heard or read recently of any discussion of tariffs or trade	23%	23%			55%	54%	56%

Table 6-2. Race and foreign policy before Pearl Harbor

	Negroes				All	Whites	
	All	Protestant	North	South		Protestant	Catholic
AIPO 149A, 2-22-39							
(N)	(20)	(19)			(1508)	(747)	(258)
Prefer Japan win if Soviet-Japanese war	20%	21%			9%	9%	14%
Prefer USSR win	40	37			51	50	45
Neither, no choice	30	31			29	30	30
No opinion	10	11			11	11	11
AIPO 181, 1-10-40							
(N)	(100)	(90)	(100)	(0)	(3031)	(1584)	(537)
Change U.S. Constitution to require national vote before Congress could draft Americans for war overseas	64%	64%	64%		60%	58%	63%
Disapprove	29	28	29		35	37	31
No opinion	7	8	7		5	5	6
Approve lending Finland $60 million to help fight USSR	50	50	50		55	58	52
Disapprove	37	38	37		39	36	42
No opinion	13	12	13		6	6	6
Roper 22, March '40							
(N)	(403)		(110)	(293)	(4813)		
U.S. should							
Lend Finland money to buy whatever she needs to fight USSR	28%		36%	26%	38%		
Lend Finland money only to buy food and medicine, but not munitions	27		25	28	31		
Lend her no money under any circumstances	22		28	19	22		
No opinion	23		11	27	19		

		Negroes				Whites	
	All	Protestant	North	South	All	Protestant	Catholic
Next administration should							
Lower tariffs	42		40	43	19		
Not lower tariffs	19		24	16	39		
No opinion	39		36	41	42		
Continue making reciprocal trade agreements	59		57	59	56		
Stop making them	13		15	11	13		
No opinion	28		28	30	31		
AIPO 213, 9-30-40							
(N)	(57)	(44)			(1559)	(794)	(275)
Let Japan control China rather than risk war	33%	34%			30%	28%	31%
Other isolationist replies	14	15			15	14	15
Risk war to stop her	25	24			29	32	28
No opinion	28	27			26	26	26
Embargo munitions to Japan	72	71			83	84	80
Do not	14	13			9	9	13
No opinion	14	16			8	7	7
AIPO 214T, 10-5-40							
(N)	(42)				(1595)	(777)	(292)
Sell Britain military aircraft on credit if can't pay cash	48%				57%	62%	48%
Do not	43				34	31	40
No opinion	9				9	7	12

	Negroes				Whites		
	All	Protestant	North	South	All	Protestant	Catholic
	(56)	(72)			(1428)	(736)	(238)
AIPO 214K, 10-5-40							
Liberalize Johnson Act to permit Britain to borrow from U.S. govt	39%				48%	51%	42%
Do not	50				40	36	48
No opinion	11				12	13	10
	(108)				(2936)		
AIPO 232, 3-7-41							
Approve of leasing 40 more destroyers to Britain	47%				51%		
Qualified approval	6				14		
Disapprove	35				26		
No opinion	12				9		
Approve of Lend-Lease bill	46				61		
Disapprove	20				23		
Never heard of it and no opinion	34				16		
	(81)	(72)			(2985)	(1631)	(539)
AIPO 240, 6-24-41							
F.D.R. has gone too far in helping Britain	11%	10%			17%	16%	19%
About right	62	61			51	51	51
Not far enough	18	19			25	26	23
No opinion	9	10			7	7	7
U.S. should supply USSR on same basis as Britain	37	36			35	34	36
Should not	42	42			54	56	54
No opinion	21	22			11	10	10

	Negroes				Whites		
	All	Protestant	North	South	All	Protestant	Catholic
AIPO 244, Aug.'41							
(N)	(99)		(92)	(7)	(2875)		
U.S. should include USSR in Lend-Lease	32%		33%	29%	38%		
Should exclude USSR	15		16	0	28		
Undecided	17		16	29	13		
Never heard of Lend-Lease and no opinion	36		35	42	21		

Table 6-3.   Race and aid to Europe

	Negroes				Whites		
	All	Protestant	North	South	All	Protestant	Catholic
NORC 233, March '45							
(N)	(215)		(57)	(15)	(2585)		
Best chance of prosperity here if we help other countries get back on feet after war	65%				81%		
Help even if it doesn't help U.S. prosperity (volunteered)	2				2		
Makes no difference	6				2		
Best chance if we don't help	14				9		
Don't help regardless	3				2		
No opinion	10				4		
AIPO 405K, 10-1-47							
(N)	(73)				(1345)		

| | Negroes | | North | South | All | Whites | |
	All	Protestant				Protestant	Catholic
Willing to go back to food rationing if necessary to feed hungry in Europe	44%		46%	25%	50%		
Not willing	47		48	38	43		
No opinion	9		6	37	7		
AIPO 392, 3-12-47 (N)	(114)	(100)			(2720)	(1519)	(481)
Approve of U.S. lending Greece $250 million	22%	21%			48%	49%	49%
Disapprove	32	33			27	27	25
No opinion	46	46			25	24	26
AIPO 394, 4-9-47 (N)	(102)				(2447)		
Like own Congressman to vote for $250 million to aid Greece	33%				52%		
Like him to vote against it	44				37		
No opinion	23				11		
Like own Congressman to vote for $150 million to aid Turkey	29				39		
Like him to vote against it	42				45		
No opinion	29				16		
Turn matter of aid to Greece and Turkey over to U.N. and have U.S. supply the money	29				33		
Opposed	36				53		
No opinion	35				14		

| | Negroes | | | | All | Whites | |
	All	Protestant	North	South		Protestant	Catholic
AIPO 401, 7-23-47							
(N)	(177)		(134)	(73)	(2883)		
Give Europe credits of about $5 billion annually for 3 to 4 years as Marshall suggests	42%		42%	42%	50%		
Opposed	36		41	21	33		
No opinion	22		17	37	17		
Willing to pay more taxes for ERP	30		30	30	35		
Not willing	51		52	51	53		
No opinion	19		18	19	12		
AIPO 405, 10-1-47							
(N)	(157)		(142)	(15)	(2666)		
Favor lending W. Europe about $20 billion over 4 years to buy goods in U.S.	41%		42%	33%	48%		
Qualified approval	5		6	0	6		
Disapprove	33		32	40	34		
No opinion	21		20	27	12		
AIPO 406, 10-22-47							
(N)	(190)				(2733)		
Approve of Marshall Plan	29%				38%		
Qualified approval	1				2		
Disapprove	5				8		
No opinion	17				21		
Never heard of Marshall Plan	48				31		
Approve of lending $20 billion over 4 years to Europe	47				50		
Qualified approval	4				6		
Disapprove	33				33		
No opinion	16				11		

| | Negroes | | | | All | Whites | |
	All	Protestant	North	South		Protestant	Catholic
AIPO 411, 1-21-48							
(N)	(190)	(175)			(2971)	(2064)	(580)
Approve of Marshall Plan	34%	34%			44%	47%	43%
Qualified approval	7	7			9	8	8
Disapprove	11	12			17	19	14
No opinion	17	16			13	10	13
Never heard of Marshall Plan	33	33			17	16	22
AIPO 411T, 1-21-48							
(N)	(97)	(92)			(1504)	(1036)	(301)
Congress should vote $6.8 billion for first 15 months of ERP	32%	32%			46%	44%	47%
Should vote less (or other qualifications)	8	10			12	14	9
Should not vote $6.8 billion	49	48			32	32	34
No opinion	11	10			10	10	10
AIPO 412, 2-4-48							
(N)	(211)		(169)	(42)	(2974)		
Approve of Marshall Plan	38%		37%	43%	46%		
Qualified approval	6		6	5	8		
Disapprove	10		11	2	13		
No opinion	21		22	21	18		
Never heard of it	25		24	29	15		
ERP could be cut without hurting it	43		45	33	44		
Cut would do significant damage	23		24	21	28		
No opinion	34		31	46	26		
AIPO 439, 3-13-49							
(N)	(189)		(164)	(25)	(2004)		

	Negroes				Whites		
	All	Protestant	North	South	All	Protestant	Catholic
Congress should vote money needed to continue ERP							
next year	39%		42%	20%	51%		
Congress should not	22		24	8	17		
No opinion	13		13	8	14		
Never heard of ERP (Marshall Plan)	26		21	64	18		
U.S. should supply war materials to W. Europe if it provides us with the help it is able to							
give in return	65		64	76	73		
U.S. should not	20		22	4	16		
No opinion	15		14	20	11		
AIPO 446, 8-12-49 (N)	(227)		(195)	(32)	(2824)	(902)	
Britain will need more money from U.S. than Congress is providing under ERP to get out of her difficulties	26%		26%	22%	33%		
Will not	15		15	9	21		
No opinion	10		11	6	10		
Never heard of her financial difficulties	49		48	63	36		
Favor new loan of $1-2 billion to Britain	10		11	3	14		
Oppose	35		36	28	44		
No opinion	6		5	6	6		
Never heard of her financial difficulties	49		48	63	36		
AIPO 454, 3-24-50 (N)	(89)	(86)	(73)	(16)	(1369)		(337)

	Negroes					Whites	
	All	Protestant	North	South	All	Protestant	Catholic
U.S. should increase amount of ERP	9%	9%	7%	19%	12%	12%	10%
Keep it at current level	31	30	33	25	33	33	33
Decrease it	44	44	47	31	46	48	47
No opinion	16	17	13	25	9	7	10
AIPO 455, 4-28-50 (N)	(132)		(100)	(32)	(1374)		
$3 billion for Marshall Plan next year too little	1%		1%	0%	5%		
About right	26		29	16	33		
Too much	15		20	0	25		
No opinion	10		13	3	9		
Never heard of Marshall Plan	48		37	81	28		
NORC 292, 11-22-50 (N)	(114)		(31)	(83)	(1153)		
U.S. should continue Marshall Plan in fiscal year 1952 if Europe needs it	37%		39%	36%	45%		
Stop it whether Europe needs it or not	40		35	42	42		
No opinion	23		26	22	13		
NORC 314, 11-22-51 (N)	(95)				(1182)		
Continue economic aid to W. Europe	60%				63%		
Stop it	31				31		
No opinion	10				6		
AIPO 490, 4-11-52 (N)	(136)		(109)	(27)	(1929)		

	All	Negroes			All	Whites	
		Protestant	North	South		Protestant	Catholic
U.S. gov't should continue to give money and military equipment to W. Europe to help build up defenses	47%		46%	52%	56%		
Should not	40		40	37	36		
No opinion	13		14	11	8		
$8 billion for military aid to W. Europe next year too much	65%		67%	56%	61%		
About right	12		10	18	17		
Too little, not enough	0		0	0	1		
No opinion	23		23	26	21		
Composite of Roper surveys of Aug. and Oct. '52 (N)	(840)	(689)	(365)	(475)	(7152)	(4349)	(1781)
Keep on building up armed strength of W. Europe	17%	18%	18%	16%	29%	28%	32%
Give some aid, but reduce amount	35	33	39	27	44	45	44
Get out of European affairs, let them build own defenses	26	26	29	24	15	14	15
No opinion	22	23	14	33	12	13	9

Table 6-4. Race and aid to colored and less-developed countries, 1949-1957

	Negroes					Whites	
	All	Protestant	North	South	All	Protestant	Catholic
AIPO 439, 3-17-49							
(N)	(189)		(164)	(25)	(2004)	(797)	(289)
U.S. should do more to help Japan get back on feet	30%		31%	24%	32%		
Should not	51		53	40	56		
No opinion	19		16	36	12		
AIPO 473, 3-24-51							
(N)	(78)				(1997)		
U.S. should give grain to India	60%				54%		
Qualified should	5				7		
Should not	18				30		
No opinion	17				9		
NORC 280, 4-17-50							
(N)	(114)				(1153)	(797)	(289)
Good policy for the U.S. to help backward countries raise standards of living	47%				64%	65%	65%
No concern to our gov't	34				30	31	30
No opinion	19				6	4	5
AIPO 455, 4-28-50							
(N)	(132)		(100)	(32)	(1374)		
Approve of Point Four technical assistance to backward countries	0%		0%	0%	4%		
Approve with qualifications	1		1	0	2		
Disapprove	3		3	3	6		
Disapprove with qualifications	0		0	0	0.5		
No opinion	16		17	13	15		
Never heard of Point Four	80		79	84	73		

| | Negroes | | | | Whites | | Catholic |
	All	Protestant	North	South	All	Protestant	
AIPO 477, 7-6-51							
(N)	(85)		(69)	(16)	(1901)		
Favor U.S. helping rebuild war damage in S. Korea	48%		52%	31%	55%		
Opposed	39		36	50	37		
No opinion	13		12	19	8		
NORC 329, 8-28-52							
(N)	(116)				(1176)		
More important to send our allies economic aid	33%				47%		
More important to send them military aid	52				35		
No opinion	15				18		
AIPO 506, 10-7-52							
(N)	(247)	(219)	(116)	(131)	(2879)	(1832)	(801)
U.S. should train and equip S. Korean army of 2 million	68%	69%	69%	68%	70%	69%	72%
Should not	14	15	16	11	18	20	15
No opinion	18	16	15	21	12	11	13
AIPO 514, 4-17-53							
(N)	(144)	(130)	(72)	(72)	(1376)	(969)	(331)
U.S. should give less economic and military aid to W. Europe, more to allies in Asia	44%	44%	49%	39%	45%	44%	48%
Qualified answer	4	3	8	0	3	4	3
Disapprove	14	15	18	10	28	26	30
No opinion	38	38	25	51	24	26	19

		Negroes				Whites	
	All	Protestant	North	South	All	Protestant	Catholic
AIPO 514, 4-17-53							
(N)	(144)	(140)	(72)	(72)	(1376)	(955)	(336)
If defense spending can safely be cut, U.S. along with other nations should spend part of savings on aid to needy countries	54%	53%	56%	51%	65%	68%	57%
Opposed	22	22	33	11	26	23	34
No opinion	24	25	11	38	9	9	9
AIPO 517, 7-2-53							
(N)	(128)		(74)	(54)	(1417)		
Favor authority for President to lend or give surplus grain to underfed abroad	53%		50%	57%	71%		
Opposed	23		28	15	22		
No opinion	24		22	28	7		
NORC 365, 11-26-54							
(N)	(86)				(1115)		
U.S. should help South and Central America improve their education and health conditions	72%				83%		
U.S. shouldn't concern self with that	19				12		
No opinion	9				5		
U.S. should put up some money for this purpose (asked only of those who said U.S. should help)	20				37		
U.S. should just help in other ways and let them provide all the money	47				43		
No opinion	5				3		

	Negroes				All	Whites	
	All	Protestant	North	South		Protestant	Catholic
U.S. should help these countries build industries	59				66		
U.S. shouldn't concern self with that	31				24		
No opinion	9				10		
U.S. gov't should lend them money to industrialize (asked only of those who said U.S. should help)	20				19		
U.S. should merely encourage U.S. businessmen to take care of this	34				43		
No opinion	5				4		
AIPO 541, 12-29-54							
(N)	(166)		(110)	(56)	(1280)		
Withdraw aid to nations which refuse to cooperate with us	70%		74%	59%	74%		
Continue aid to them	13		13	14	19		
No opinion	17		13	27	7		
AIPO 546, 4-12-55							
(N)	(195)	(189)	(100)	(95)	(1340)	(866)	(376)
Good idea to send aid similar to Marshall Plan to noncommunist Asia	52%	52%	47%	57%	57%	56%	56%
Bad idea	25	25	32	18	27	26	29
No opinion	23	23	21	25	14	18	15
AIPO 558, 1-4-56							
(N)	(166)		(92)	(74)	(1217)		

	Negroes				All	Whites	Catholic
	All	Protestant	North	South		Protestant	
Congress should appropriate same amount, $4 billion, this year as in recent years to help prevent foreign countries							
going communistic	56%		52%	61%	57%		
Congress should not	16		23	8	26		
No opinion	28		25	31	17		
NORC 382, 1-26-56							
(N)	(120)				(1118)		
Our gov't should try harder to win friendship of countries like India, Egypt, and Burma							
Doing all we should now	47%				39%		
	46				53		
No opinion	7				8		
What should it do? (asked only of those who replied it should do more)							
Less strings attached to aid, etc.	14%				10%		
More food, clothing, relief	5				11		
More equipment, capital assistance	10				9		
More technical assistance, education	6				6		
More food	1				4		
All who mentioned some form of foreign aid	22				29		
More or better propaganda	2				4		
More intercultural exchanges, students, etc.	5				3		
Teach them Christianity	2				3		
Improve diplomatic relations	0				2		
More friendly attitude, understanding	7				1		

	Negroes					Whites	
	All	Protestant	North	South	All	Protestant	Catholic
Less emphasis on military, more on peace	0				1		
No suggestions	22				15		
Give Eisenhower authority to put part of economic aid on long-term basis	15				26		
Do not	76				64		
No opinion	9				10		
NORC 386, 4-20-56 (N)	(109)				(1115)		
Good for our gov't to spend money on technical assistance to help backward countries solve farming and health problems	73%				86%		
Bad idea	19				10		
No opinion	7				4		
Continue economic aid to countries that have agreed to stand with us against communist aggression	80				87		
Stop it	15				9		
No opinion	5				4		
Continue economic aid to countries like India which have not joined as allies against communists	31				44		
Stop it	63				48		
No opinion	6				8		

	Negroes				Whites		
	All	Protestant	North	South	All	Protestant	Catholic
Good idea to put some economic aid on long-term basis	49				50		
Depends	4				7		
Bad idea	39				33		
No opinion	8				10		
Good idea to send military supplies to help build up armies of friendly countries	62				67		
Bad idea	32				28		
No opinion	6				5		
NORC 390, 6-26-56 (N)	(120)				(1155)		
Such nonaligned countries as India and Burma have duty to join our side to stop spread of communism	50%				52%		
Are justified in refusal to take sides	39				36		
No opinion	11				12		
Continue economic aid to such nonaligned countries	43				48		
Stop it	54				47		
No opinion	3				5		
More important to send allies economic aid	56				72		
More important to send them military aid	30				16		
No opinion	14				12		

	Negroes				Whites		
	All	Protestant	North	South	All	Protestant	Catholic
NORC 399, 11-15-56							
(N)	(127)				(1158)		
Continue economic aid to countries that have agreed to stand with us against communist aggression	79%				91%		
Stop it	15				6		
No opinion	6				3		
Approve economic aid to countries like Poland	37				55		
Disapprove	48				38		
No opinion	15				7		
NORC 401, 12-28-56							
(N)	(113)	(97)			(1119)	(757)	(268)
Continue economic aid to such nonaligned countries	46%	45%			53%	48%	60%
Stop it	46	46			42	46	36
No opinion	8	9			5	6	4
AIPO 576, 1-8-57							
(N)	(126)	(117)	(40)	(86)	(1414)	(936)	(410)
Congress should appropriate $4 billion this year as in recent years to help prevent foreign countries going communistic	49%	50%	47%	51%	59%	57%	61%
Congress should not	29	29	35	26	27	30	25
No opinion	22	21	18	23	14	13	14

	Negroes					Whites	
	All	Protestant	North	South	All	Protestant	Catholic
AIPO 577, 1-15-57							
(N)	(160)	(149)	(112)	(48)	(1334)	(881)	
Send military supplies to friendly Middle Eastern countries	54%	54%	59%	42%	52%	53%	50%
Opposed	25	25	28	18	35	32	38
Neither	3	2	4	0		3	2
No opinion	18	19	9	40	10	12	10
Send economic aid to these countries	64	64	68	54	70	70	69
Opposed	17	18	20	10	18	19	18
Neither	2	1	3	0	2	2	3
No opinion	17	16	9	36	10	9	10
NORC 404, 4-26-57							
(N)	(117)	(101)	(33)	(84)	(1162)	(766)	(299)
Continue economic aid to countries that have agreed to stand with us against communist aggression	73%	72%	64%	77%	81%	81%	82%
Stop it	18	18	30	13	16	16	16
No opinion	9	10	6	10	3	3	2
Continue economic aid to such nonaligned countries	32	33	39	29	41	41	42
Stop it	61	59	58	62	53	54	52
No opinion	7	8	3	9	6	5	6
More important to send allies economic aid	62	61	67	59	70	73	64
More important to send them military aid	20	20	15	21	16	14	20
No opinion	18	19	18	20	14	13	16

		Negroes				Whites	
	All	Protestant	North	South	All	Protestant	Catholic
Good idea to put some economic aid on long-term basis							
Bad idea	34	35	40	32	40	41	38
No opinion	51	51	46	54	51	50	52
	15	14	14	14	9	9	10
Approve economic aid to countries like Poland							
Disapprove	32	31	18	37	47	46	55
No opinion	60	60	76	54	48	48	42
	8	9	6	9	5	6	3
$4 billion for foreign aid next year too much							
Not enough	39	40	46	37	37	35	38
About right	1	0	0	1	3	4	3
No opinion	44	44	42	46	48	50	48
	16	16	12	18	12	11	11

Table 6-5. Race and aid since 1956

	Negroes					Whites	
	All	Protestant	North	South	All	Protestant	Catholic
SRC 417, Sept.-Oct.-56							
(N)	(147)	(101)	(64)	(83)	(1609)	(1151)	(364)
Strongly agree U.S. should help poorer countries	29%		27%	36%	21%	20%	21%
Agree, but not so strongly	15		16	15	22	22	21
Depends, not sure	7		6	9	16	17	16
Strongly disagree	12		15	12	16	17	16
Disagree, but not so strongly	8		11	6	10	10	10
No opinion	29		25	32	15	14	16
Strongly agree should help even if not as much against communism as we	15		13	17	12	12	12
Agree, but not so strongly	12		22	4	17	18	16
Depends, not sure	3		2	4	13	13	12
Strongly disagree	11		14	10	22	21	24
Disagree, but not so strongly	6		6	6	11	11	11
No opinion	53		43	59	25	25	25
NORC 404, 4-26-57							
(N)	(117)	(101)	(33)	(84)	(1162)	(766)	(299)
Very important to help Africa improve living standards	56%	55%	82%	46%	39%	40%	36%
Only fairly important	9	8	12	7	35	36	33
Not important at all	3	4	3	4	15	14	20
No opinion	32	33	3	43	11	10	11
Roper 939, April '57							
(N)	(145)	(135)	(49)	(96)	(1361)	(904)	(328)

	Negroes				Whites		
	All	Protestant	North	South	All	Protestant	Catholic
Economic aid to Asia and Africa should be increased	10%	10%	21%	5%	3%	3%	2%
Should be kept at current levels	27	27	33	24	24	24	24
Should be cut a little	28	28	20	31	31	31	35
Should be cut drastically	17	17	20	15	29	30	26
Should be stopped completely	4	4	0	6	3	4	3
No opinion	14	14	6	19	10	8	10
Increase military aid	10	11	12	9	5	5	5
Keep at current levels	46	46	49	44	47	45	50
Cut a little	21	19	25	19	20	20	21
Cut drastically	10	9	6	11	14	16	10
Stop completely	1	1	0	2	2	2	2
No opinion	12	14	8	15	12	12	12
AIPO 593, 12-31-57							
(N)	(190)		(120)	(70)	(1332)		
Willing to have income taxes raised to meet Soviet economic competition and promises of economic aid to Africa and Asia	38%		33%	46%	32%		
Not willing	41		51	23	56		
No opinion	21		16	31	12		
Roper 963, Jan.'58							
(N)	(149)		(53)	(96)	(1344)		
Expand economic aid to under-developed Asia and Africa	27%		43%	19%	17%		
Keep at current levels	36		45	30	43		
Cut it back or terminate it	19		8	25	22		
No opinion	18		4	26	18		

	Negroes					Whites	
	All	Protestant	North	South	All	Protestant	Catholic
AIPO 596, 3-4-58							
(N)	(162)	(147)	(68)	(94)	(1447)	(1007)	(350)
In general for foreign aid	47%	46%	68%	32%	51%	48%	58%
Against it	27	27	17	34	33	36	30
No opinion	26	27	15	34	15	16	12
Congress should appropriate more money than the President requested for foreign aid	1	1	0	2	4	4	4
Should appropriate about same amount	32	33	38	28	36	37	36
Should appropriate less	32	33	38	28	35	34	36
No opinion	35	33	24	42	25	25	24
AIPO 617, 8-18-59							
(N)	(154)		(95)	(59)	(1322)		
Good idea to equip hospital, training, food, etc., ships at U.S. expense	64%		65%	61%	74%		
Bad idea	17		17	19	17		
No opinion	19		18	20	9		
Congress should appropriate money for this[a]	50		46	54	57		
Should not	8		13	0	9		
No opinion	6		6	7	8		
AIPO 639, 12-6-60[b]							
(N)	(371)	(359)	(208)	(163)	(2475)	(1635)	(695)
New President and Congress should increase foreign aid	7%	6%	6%	8%	7%	6%	6%
Should reduce or stop it	45	44	45	46	40	40	45

	All	Negroes Protestant	North	South	All	Whites Protestant	Catholic
AIPO 640, 1-10-61 (N)[b]	(244)	(228)	(102)	(142)	(2405)	(1840)	(650)
Favor Peace Corps for technical assistance to less-developed world	79%	78%	85%	75%	71%	69%	73%
Opposed	6	6	7	6	19	22	13
No opinion	15	16	8	19	10	9	14
AIPO 641, 2-8-61 (N)[b]	(256)		(152)	(104)	(2617)		
U.S. should offer surplus foods to famine-racked Communist China	62%		66%	56%	52%		
Should not	25		25	26	38		
No opinion	13		9	18	10		
AIPO 646, 5-26-61 (N)[b]	(281)	(254)	(144)	(137)	(3241)	(2216)	(802)
Willing to make personal sacrifices, including higher taxes, for foreign economic aid	14%	14%	27%	1%	22%	19%	27%
Willing to make similar sacrifices for military aid	9	9	16	2	9	8	15
AIPO 652, 11-15-61 (N)[b]	(410)	(371)	(245)	(165)	(2355)	(1502)	(682)
U.S. and West doing enough for less-developed countries	52%	51%	67%	31%	70%	71%	68%
Not doing enough	18	18	15	22	14	13	16
No opinion	30	31	18	47	16	16	16
Foreign aid of last five years has helped U.S. interests	43	43	51	32	52	51	55
Has not	22	21	22	23	28	29	25
No opinion	35	36	27	45	20	20	20

		Negroes				Whites	
	All	Protestant	North	South	All	Protestant	Catholic
AIPO 657,[b] 4-4-62							
(N)[b]	(467)	(430)	(271)	(196)	(2936)	(1839)	(875)
Favor economic and military aid to Yugoslavia	32%	33%	38%	23%	24%	22%	27%
Oppose	24	24	28	18	42	44	39
No opinion	44	43	34	59	34	34	34
AIPO 659,[b] 5-29-62							
(N)[b]	(436)	(400)	(265)	(171)	(2800)	(2071)	(730)
Send food to Communist China if she asks for it	44%	44%	47%	39%	49%	46%	50%
Do not	39	39	40	36	44	44	43
No opinion	17	17	13	25	7	10	7
AIPO 664,[b] 10-17-62							
(N)[b]	(384)	(357)	(277)	(107)	(3864)	(2652)	(980)
Approve of job being done by Peace Corps	47%	48%	56%	24%	54%	50%	64%
Disapprove	2	1	0	6	7	7	6
No opinion	9	9	4	22	12	13	12
Never heard of Peace Corps	42	42	40	48	27	30	18
AIPO 665,[b] 11-14-62							
(N)[b]	(429)	(399)	(313)	(116)	(3997)	(2635)	(1040)
U.S. should do something to aid India in fighting with China	43%	44%	49%	26%	56%	54%	61%
Should not	7	7	7	4	13	12	14
No opinion	23	22	22	29	18	21	10
Never heard or read anything of Sino-Indian fighting	27	27	22	41	13	13	15

		Negroes				Whites	
	All	Protestant	North	South	All	Protestant	Catholic
AIPO 667, 1-9-63							
In general for foreign aid	53%				59%		
Against it	26				31		
No opinion	21				11		
AIPO 678, 10-9-63							
(N)[b]	(432)	(402)	(273)	(159)	(2905)	(1895)	(798)
Volunteered foreign aid as something on which gov't spends too much money	27%	27%	29%	23%	43%	45%	37%
Have very great deal of trust in way Pres. Kennedy and his administration are handling foreign aid	33	33	32	35	16	13	27
Considerable trust	28	28	29	26	32	31	35
Not much trust	10	10	10	11	27	28	23
None at all	7	7	4	12	14	17	6
No opinion	22	22	25	16	11	11	9
AIPO 682, 12-10-63							
(N)[b] (no self-identified Democrats included)	(101)	(92)			(1609)	(1184)	(318)
Kept U.S. gov't aid abroad at current level at least	58%	58%			31%	28%	38%
Reduce aid	19	19			51	54	49
End it	4	4			7	8	5
No opinion	19	19			11	10	8
SRC 473, Sept.-Oct.'64							
(N)	(159)	(148)	(81)	(78)	(1399)	(857)	(313)
Definitely agree, mind made up, should give aid to other countries if need help	43%	42%	46%	40%	46%	43%	52%

	Negroes				Whites		
	All	Protestant	North	South	All	Protestant	Catholic
Agree, but with some doubts, mind not made up	7	7	6	8	7	7	6
Depends	7	7	11	2	19	19	20
Definitely feel each country should make own way as best can, mind made up	16	16	18	13	16	17	12
Each should make own way, but mind not made up	3	3	3	4	3	4	2
No opinion	5	5	0	10	2	2	2
No interest in aid issue	19	20	16	23	7	8	6
POS 655, 2-15-65							
(N)	(182)	(165)	(137)	(45)	(1438)	(987)	(352)
U.S. spends too much on foreign aid	18%	18%	19%	16%	36%	38%	34%
Too little	18	17	17	20	9	8	12
About right amount, or depends	27	28	28	24	37	26	29
No opinion	37	37	36	40	18	18	15
Should spend most foreign aid in							
(1) Latin America	14	14			45	43	50
(2) Asia	8	8			9	9	12
(3) Africa	33	33			10	11	7
(4) Neither or equally	7	6			9	10	8
No opinion	38	39			27	27	23
Have obligation to help under-developed countries	46	47			49	44	55
Do not	27	26			24	26	23
Depends, conditional	18	17			25	27	21
No opinion	9	10			2	3	1
Extremely well satisfied with U.S. help to poorer countries	25	25			20	17	23
Considerably well satisfied	36	36			25	22	26

	Negroes				Whites		
	All	Protestant	North	South	All	Protestant	Catholic
Somewhat satisfied	27	27			29	32	29
Not satisfied at all	9	10			25	28	21
No opinion	3	2			1	1	1
AIPO 706, 2-17-65 (N)	(386)	(359)	(268)	(118)	(3120)	(2237)	(697)
In general for foreign aid	58%	58%	57%	60%	57%	56%	61%
Against it	26	24	27	24	34	35	29
No opinion	16	18	16	16	9	9	10
Would like Pres. Johnson's request for $3.4 billion for aid of Congress increased	13	13	14	13	5	5	5
Would like it cut	35	35	34	36	50	46	45
Keep it the same	29	30	25	38	34	40	41
No opinion	23	22	27	13	11	9	9
AIPO 724, 2-8-66 (N)	(400)	(371)			(3117)	(2022)	(771)
In general for foreign aid	57%	57%			53%	52%	52%
Against it	19	20			37	39	34
No opinion	24	23			10	9	14
Lack of effort by nation's gov't accounts for economic under-development	21	24			40	42	36
Circumstances beyond its control	23	22			31	30	33
Both	36	35			23	22	24
No opinion	20	19			6	6	7
Continue aid to countries which fail to support U.S. in major foreign policy decision, such as Vietnam	21	21			15	14	17

	Negroes				All	Whites	
	All	Protestant	North	South		Protestant	Catholic
Reduce aid to such countries	28	28			30	31	29
Cut it off completely	33	33			47	49	45
No opinion	18	18			8	6	9
Include the following within U.S. aid:							
Promote birth control information	32	33			45	49	31
Train teachers, provide books, build schools	49	48			67	69	62
Build highways, railroads, transportation	26	25			21	19	24
Build hospitals, train M.D.'s and nurses, give medicine	50	49			62	64	59
Send surplus food	40	40			41	41	42
Build factories and industries	28	27			34	32	35
Help improve farming methods	43	42			64	66	58
Build up military strength	26	27			17	16	22
No opinion	19	20			7	6	10

a Posed only to those who considered the action "a good idea" in the preceding question. Percentages are of total samples, including those who felt this "a bad idea" or who offered no opinion.

b Weighted N's here were approximately twice actual N's among whites and 2.3 times those among Negroes.

Table 6-6. Race vs. trade

	Negroes		All	Whites	Catholic
	All	Protestant		Protestant	
AIPO 408, Nov.'47					
(N)	(102)	(91)	(2797)	(1883)	(611)
Favor GATT to lower tariffs	64%	63%	67%	67%	65%
Oppose	6	6	12	12	12
No opinion	30	31	21	21	23
AIPO 526, Jan.'54					
(N)	(72)	(65)	(1421)	(1025)	(307)
Favor higher tariffs	13%	11%	11%	10%	14%
Lower tariffs	40	41	29	28	29
Current level	17	15	22	22	21
No opinion	30	33	38	40	36
AIPO 540, Nov.'54					
(N)	(141)	(129)	(1329)	(885)	(311)
Favor higher tariffs	13%	11%	19%	19%	19%
Lower tariffs	33	34	33	30	36
Tariffs as they are	18	18	21	23	18
No opinion	36	37	27	28	27
AIPO 541, 12-29-54					
(N)	(166)		(1280)		
Favor reducing general level of tariffs	27%		25%		
Opposed	25		43		
No opinion and never heard anything of tariffs	48		32		

| | Negroes | | | Whites | |
	All	Protestant	All	Protestant	Catholic
AIPO 614, 5-27-59					
(N)	(144)	(130)	(1392)	(944)	(351)
Favor higher tariffs[a]	1%	1%	12%	11%	18%
Lower tariffs[a]	7	9	15	16	9
Tariffs as they are[a]	5	4	7	7	8
No opinion[a]	3	3	5	5	4
Had neither heard nor read of any discussion of tariffs or trade	84	83	61	61	61
AIPO 653, 12-5-61					
(N)	(165)	(143)	(1439)	(973)	(362)
Favor higher tariffs[a]	3%	4%	18%	17%	19%
Lower tariffs[a]	11	12	21	21	22
Tariffs as they are[a]	4	2	7	7	8
No opinion[a]	5	6	8	9	7
Had neither heard nor read of any discussion of tariffs or trade	77	76	46	46	44
AIPO 655, Feb.'62					
(N)	(172)	(153)	(1468)	(978)	(386)
Like to see more goods imported	18%	19%	11%	9%	10%
Put on more trade restrictions	25	25	52	53	56
Keep restrictions about as they are	18	16	18	18	19
Depends	10	11	6	5	8
No opinion	29	29	13	15	7
Put more restrictions on textile imports	17	18	35	35	39
Keep as are	35	33	38	38	37
Encourage more imports	17	15	11	10	10
No opinion	31	34	16	17	14

	Negroes All	Negroes Protestant	All	White Protestant	Catholic
Put more restrictions on oil imports	17	17	28	28	30
Keep as are	34	35	33	30	36
Encourage more imports	15	14	19	19	18
No opinion	34	34	20	23	16
Put more restrictions on automobile imports	36	34	52	51	56
Keep as are	30	31	29	28	32
Encourage more imports	10	12	9	9	5
No opinion	24	23	10	12	7
Put more restrictions on steel imports	25	23	42	40	49
Keep as are	25	27	28	27	28
Encourage more imports	20	19	12	12	11
No opinion	30	31	18	21	12
AIPO 656, 3-6-62					
(N)	(127)	(111)	(1473)	(1024)	(345)
Important to increase goods we buy and sell to foreign countries	41%	40%	68%	69%	66%
Not important	32	31	16	15	19
No opinion	27	29	16	16	15
Favor higher tariff[a]	5	3	15	15	17
Favor lower tariffs[a]	17	17	30	29	35
Keep tariffs at current level[a]	19	18	18	18	15
No opinion and never heard of tariffs	59	62	37	38	33

[a] Posed only to those who said they had heard or read something of tariffs and world trade.

Table 6-7.   Race vs. international exchange and immigration

| | Negroes | | Whites | | |
	All	Protestant	All	Protestant	Catholic
AIPO 630, 6-28-60					
(N)[a]	(298)	(274)	(2951)	(1912)	(793)
To increase good will and understanding, good idea to send U.S. teachers who so desire abroad at federal expense in summer	75%	75%	60%	56%	70%
Poor idea	8	9	33	38	24
No opinion	17	16	7	6	6
Good idea to invite foreign teachers to U.S. at federal expense	59	59	54	49	63
Poor idea	24	24	39	43	30
No opinion	17	17	7	8	7
AIPO 713, 6-22-65					
(N)[a]	(425)	(395)	(3111)	(1930)	(890)
Increase the number of foreigners permitted to immigrate to U.S.	9%	8%	7%	5%	9%
Keep at current level	35	35	39	37	46
Reduce immigration	23	23	35	39	26
No opinion	33	34	18	19	19
Favor changing from country of origin quota system to one based on skills	55	56	50	48	51
Oppose	20	20	34	36	32
No opinion	25	24	16	16	17

a Weighted N's.

Table 6-8.   Race and the United Nations

	Negroes			Whites	
	All	Protestant	All	Protestant	Catholic
NORC 280, 4-17-50					
(N)	(114)		(1153)	(797)	(289)
At least some U.S. aid to backward countries should be spent through the U.N.	18%		35%	35%	34%
All U.S. aid should be handled bilaterally by U.S. gov't	24		34	33	38
No opinion	5		5	5	4
Against aid generally	34		20	21	20
No opinion on aiding backward countries	19		6	6	4
AIPO 541, 12-29-54					
(N)	(166)		(1280)		
U.S. should give strong support to U.N.	67%		73%		
Should give only a little or no support	17		16		
No opinion	16		11		
AIPO 631, 7-14-60					
(N)[a]	(365)	(281)	(2418)	(1587)	(631)
Good idea to build up standing U.N. emergency force to deal with small wars	64%	64%	73%	74%	71%
Poor idea	13	12	12	10	14
No opinion	23	24	15	16	15
AIPO 654, 1-9-62					
(N)[a]	(421)	(372)	(2991)	(2004)	(801)
U.S. should withdraw from U.N.	7%	7%	9%	10%	7%
Should not	75	74	87	87	87
No opinion	18	19	4	3	6

	Negroes			Whites	
	All	Protestant	All	Protestant	Catholic
AIPO 679, 11-8-63					
(N)[a]	(651)	(605)	(3630)	(2468)	(894)
U.S. should withdraw from U.N.	7%	7%	8%	9%	9%
Should not	69	67	80	79	80
No opinion	24	26	12	12	11
AIPO 680, 11-20-63					
(N)	(442)	(407)	(2942)	(1867)	(885)
U.N. doing a good job	54%	53%	51%	49%	56%
Fair job (volunteered)	32	33	27	28	26
Poor job	2	2	8	9	5
No opinion	12	12	14	14	13
Very important to try to make U.N. a success	79	78	79	79	80
Fairly important	15	16	8	8	9
Not so important	1	1	4	5	3
No opinion	5	5	9	8	8
AIPO 695, 7-21-64					
(N)[a]	(447)	(411)	(3068)	(2121)	(701)
Good idea to build up standing U.N. emergency force to deal with small wars	69%	68%	66%	62%	78%
Poor idea	5	5	18	19	13
No opinion	26	27	16	19	9
Approve of U.N. army dealing with problems of Southeast Asia and Vietnam	60	59	57	54	68
Disapprove	8	7	21	21	18
No opinion	32	34	22	25	14

	Negroes		Whites		
	All	Protestant	All	Protestant	Catholic
AIPO 712, 6-2-65 (N)[a]	(475)	(432)	(2875)	(1951)	(721)
If U.N. had not existed, would likely have been another world war	57%	57%	59%	58%	61%
No difference	22	21	26	25	26
No opinion	21	22	15	17	13
AIPO 715, 8-3-65 (N)[a]	(361)	(335)	(3166)	(1974)	(901)
Approve of asking U.N. to try to work out formula for peace in Vietnam	60%	59%	76%	73%	79%
Disapprove	14	13	12	13	12
No opinion	26	28	12	14	9
AIPO 723, 12-29-65 (N)[a]	(303)	(271)	(3225)	(2013)	(938)
Good idea to submit Vietnam case to U.N. or International Court of Justice and accept the decision	38%	37%	50%	46%	55%
Poor idea	33	33	36	39	33
No opinion	29	30	14	15	12
AIPO survey of Aug.'66[b]					
Good idea to submit Vietnam to U.N. and accept decision	51%		50%		
Poor idea	28		34		
No opinion	21		16		

a Weighted N's were approximately twice actual N's among whites, 2.3 times among Negroes.

b Gallup Political Index, Sept. 1966.

Table 6-9. Race vs. war and defense

	Negroes		Whites		
	All	Protestant	All	Protestant	Catholic
AIPO 541, 12-29-54					
(N)	(166)		(1280)		
U.S. will find itself in another world war within one year	14%		11%		
Not so soon, but within 5 years	40		37		
No world war within 5 years	23		31		
No opinion	23		21		
AIPO 558, 1-4-56					
(N)	(166)		(1217)		
U.S. likely to be in World War III in five years	32%		22%		
Not so soon, but in respondents' lifetimes	31		39		
World War III not likely in respondents' lifetimes	15		24		
No opinion	22		15		
AIPO 631, 7-14-60					
(N)[a]	(382)	(349)	(2993)	(1958)	(741)
Anticipate another world war in five years	50%	51%	49%	50%	42%
World war unlikely in five years	28	29	37	36	46
No opinion	22	20	14	14	12
AIPO 639, 12-6-60					
(N)[a]	(371)	(359)	(2475)	(1635)	(695)
The new President and Congress should spend more money to strengthen national defense than spent recently	30%	29%	28%	27%	32%

	Negroes		All	Whites	
	All	Protestant		Protestant	Catholic
POS 655, 2-15-65					
(N)	(182)	(165)	(1438)	(987)	(352)
Extremely well satisfied with U.S. military strength	31%	31%	30%	28%	33%
Considerably well satisfied	50	49	45	48	44
Somewhat satisfied	13	14	17	16	17
Not at all satisfied	0	0	6	6	3
No opinion	6	6	2	2	3
AIPO 712, 6-2-65					
(N)[a]	(475)	(442)	(2383)	(1940)	(727)
Every able-bodied male aged 18 years should be required to serve in armed forces for one year	62%	63%	66%	64%	68%
Should not	31	32	30	31	27
No opinion	7	5	4	5	5
AIPO 713, 6-22-65					
(N)[a]	(425)	(395)	(3111)	(1927)	(899)
U.S. likely to get into another world war in 5 years	45%	45%	33%	35%	31%
Not likely	36	35	55	54	58
No opinion	19	20	12	11	11
AIPO 725, 3-1-66					
(N)[a]	(249)	(231)	(3309)	(2091)	(863)
U.S. likely to get into another world war in next year	31%	31%	20%	25%	16%
Not likely within a year	52	51	67	64	72
No opinion	17	18	13	11	12

	Negroes All	Whites All
AIPO survey of Sept.'66 [b]		
Every able-bodied male aged 18 years should be required to serve in armed forces for one year		
Should not	69%	69%
No opinion	22	24
	9	7

[a] Weighted N's.

[b] *Gallup Political Index*, Oct. 1966.

Table 6-10. Race and arms control

	Negroes		Whites		
	All	Protestant	All	Protestant	Catholic
AIPO 635, 9-7-60					
(N)[a]	(349)	(325)	(2558)	(1648)	(691)
If USSR agrees to disarm under careful U.N. inspection, U.S. should agree					
to disarm to same extent	41%	40%	47%	46%	47%
U.S. should not	34	34	42	43	42
No opinion	25	26	11	11	11
AIPO 676, 8-13-63					
(N)[a]	(464)	(432)	(3096)	(2033)	(843)
Senate should ratify nuclear test ban treaty[b]	31%	30%	49%	45%	54%
Should not[b]	10	10	15	16	14
No opinion[b]	11	12	16	19	12
Never heard of test ban agreement	48	48	20	20	20
AIPO 691, 5-20-64					
(N)[a]	(536)	(498)	(2987)	(2033)	(691)
Would be serious depression if U.S. reduced drastically armed forces and armaments	37%	37%	29%	27%	31%
No serious depression likely	31	32	51	51	51
No opinion	32	31	20	22	18

a Weighted N's.

b Posed only to those who had heard of agreement.

Table 6-11. Perception of the communist problem

| | All | Negroes | | | All | Whites | |
		Protestant	North	South		Protestant	Catholic
AIPO 454, 3-24-50							
(N)	(89)	(79)	(73)	(16)	(1369)	(889)	(337)
Senator McCarthy's claims are true	43%	41%	44%	38%	51%	52%	50%
Largely politics, exaggerated, or untrue	29	29	30	25	29	29	23
No opinion	28	30	26	37	20	19	27
AIPO 455, 4-28-50							
(N)	(132)		(100)	(32)	(1374)		
Senator McCarthy doing more harm than good	18%		20%	13%	31%		
Doing more good than harm	38		44	19	39		
No opinion	44		36	68	30		
AIPO 517, 7-2-53							
(N)	(128)				(1417)		
Russia is trying to become the ruling world power	53%				79%		
Just building protection against attack in another war	14				5		
No opinion	33				16		
NORC 365, 11-26-54							
(N)	(86)	(78)			(1115)	(679)	(273)
Favorable impression of McCarthy	31%	30%			45%	44%	58%
Unfavorable	35	37			35	36	23
No opinion	34	33			20	20	19
American communists a great danger	38	38			37	37	37
Some danger	29	27			44	46	42
Practically none	20	21			14	13	15
No opinion	13	14			5	4	6

	Negroes		Whites		
	All	Protestant	All	Protestant	Catholic
AIPO 541, 12-29-54					
(N)	(166)		(1280)		
There are some communists in federal gov't	60%		72%		
How many?					
A great number	11		14		
Relatively few	45		55		
Don't know	4		3		
There are no communists in the federal gov't	17		11		
No opinion	23		17		
Approve of Senate's censure of McCarthy	44		47		
Disapprove	23		35		
No opinion	33		18		
AIPO 674, 6-19-63					
(N)a	(455)	(431)	(3036)	(2030)	(733)
Possible to reach peaceful settlement of differences with USSR	43%	43%	48%	47%	55%
Impossible	27	26	39	41	30
No opinion	30	31	13	12	15
POS 655, 2-15-65					
(N)	(182)	(165)	(1438)	(987)	(352)
Will be able to live peacefully with Communist China	17%	17%	22%	21%	19%
Will not	57	56	59	61	58
No opinion	26	27	19	18	23

	Negroes		Whites		
	All	Protestant	All	Protestant	Catholic
Left wing groups, such as the Communist Party, in U.S. are					
(1) A very great danger	22	22	34	37	31
(2) A considerable danger	25	25	33	34	34
(3) Not very much danger, or none at all	37	36	28	25	29
No opinion	16	17	5	4	6

a Weighted N's.

Table 6-12.   Race and policies toward communist powers

	Negroes				All	Whites	
	All	Protestant	North	South		Protestant	Catholic
AIPO 439, 3-17-49							
(N)	(189)		(164)	(25)	(2004)		
U.S. should join defense pact with W. Europe							
Should not	75%		74%	80%	78%		
Should not	11		12	8	13		
No opinion	14		14	12	8		
Roper 694, Aug.'52							
(N)	(398)	(357)	(129)	(269)	(3556)	(2057)	(888)
Support further negotiations over Korea	36%	36%	35%	36%	29%	27%	33%
Want Korean war carried further	20	22	23	20	38	41	38
Withdraw from Korea	27	24	26	27	16	15	18
No opinion	17	18	16	17	17	17	11
AIPO 517, 7-2-53							
(N)	(128)				(1417)		
Favor meeting of leaders of West with those of USSR	42%				56%		
Oppose	20				30		
No opinion	38				14		
AIPO 526, Jan.'54							
(N)	(72)				(1421)	(1025)	(307)
U.S. and USSR should work out business arrangement to buy and sell goods to each other	46%				41%	41%	39%
Should not	29				45	45	46
No opinion	25				14	14	15

	Negroes All	Negroes Protestant	Whites All	Whites Protestant	Catholic
AIPO 541, 12-29-54					
(N)	(166)		(1280)		
Should blockade coast of Communist China					
Should	27%		35%		
Should not	31		39		
No opinion	42		26		
SRC 417, Sept.-Oct.'56					
(N)	(147)		(1609)	(1149)	(359)
Strongly agree the best way to deal with USSR and Com. China is to act as tough as they do	41%		52%	51%	57%
Agree, but not strongly	10		12	12	10
Depends, not sure	7		5	6	4
Disagree, but not strongly	4		6	7	4
Strongly disagree	7		8	9	6
No opinion	31		17	15	19
AIPO 648, 7-25-61					
(N)[a]	(1331)	(308)	(2828)	(1832)	(736)
Should keep U.S. forces in Berlin with British and French forces, even at risk of war	75%	74%	85%	86%	88%
Should not do so at risk of war	10	10	5	3	5
No opinion	15	16	10	11	7
AIPO 650, 9-19-61					
(N)[a]	(347)	(323)	(2685)	(2057)	(684)
Try to fight way into Berlin with allies if roads and airways get blockaded by communists	68%	68%	70%	72%	68%
Do not	12	13	19	17	20
No opinion	20	19	11	11	12

| | Negroes | | Whites | | |
	All	Protestant	All	Protestant	Catholic
AIPO 668, 2-5-63[a]					
(N)	(418)	(389)	(3234)	(2212)	(816)
U.S. should send armed forces into Cuba to overthrow Castro	15%	16%	20%	20%	21%
Should not	46	44	65	66	63
No opinion	39	40	15	14	16
SRC 473, Sept.-Oct.'64					
(N)	(172)	(148)	(1398)	(857)	(313)
Favor negotiations with leaders of communist gov'ts to try to settle our differences	69%	69%	72%	72%	74%
Depends	0	0	4	4	4
Refuse to have anything to do with them	6	5	10	10	10
No opinion	5	5	3	3	3
No interest in this issue	20	21	11	11	9
Farmers and businessmen should be allowed to do business in nonmilitary goods with communist countries	30	29	28	24	31
Depends	4	4	5	5	6
Such trade should be forbidden	32	29	44	47	43
No opinion	1	1	3	3	1
No interest in this issue	33	37	20	21	19
POS 655, 2-15-65					
(N)	(182)	(165)	(1438)	(987)	(352)
Invade Cuba and overthrow Castro	13%	14%	13%	13%	11%
Continue current policies	39	39	44	43	49
Set up a Cuban gov't in exile	19	19	32	21	33
No opinion	29	28	11	13	7

		Negroes		Whites	
AIPO 720, 11-16-65	All	Protestant	All	Protestant	Catholic
(N)[a]	(371)	(345)	(2903)	(2021)	(889)
U.S. right in sending troops into Santo Domingo	50%	50%	53%	51%	58%
Wrong to intervene militarily	17	16	22	23	17
No opinion	33	34	25	26	25

[a] Weighted N's were roughly 2 times and 2.3 times actual white and Negro N's respectively.

Table 6-13.   Vietnam

	Negroes				Whites		
	All	Protestant	North	South	All	Protestant	Catholic
AIPO 710, 4-21-65 (N)[a]	(388)	(357)			(3111)	(2123)	(780)
In light of developments, should have become involved with U.S. military forces in Southeast Asia							
Should	45%	44%			53%	49%	59%
Should not	20	20			27	29	23
No opinion	35	36			20	22	18
AIPO 713, 6-22-65 (N)[a]	(425)	(395)			(3111)	(1930)	(890)
Continue war alone if S. Vietnam gov't decides to end war and stop fighting	16%	16%			19%	20%	19%
Stop fighting ourselves too	63	62			65	64	67
No opinion	21	22			16	16	14
AIPO 719, 10-27-65 (N)[a]	(329)	(306)			(3056)	(1930)	(961)
More inclined to vote for congressional candidate if advocated sending great many more men to Vietnam	36%	35%			47%	47%	49%
Less inclined	40	39			30	31	28
No opinion	24	26			23	22	23
More inclined to vote for congressional candidate if advocated trying harder to reach a compromise settlement in Vietnam	77	76			65	64	65
Less inclined	9	9			20	24	18
No opinion	14	15			15	12	17

	Negroes		Whites		
	All	Protestant	All	Protestant	Catholic
AIPO 724, [a] 2-8-66					
(N) [a]	(400)	(371)	(3117)	(2022)	(771)
Favor bombing big cities in N. Vietnam	25%	25%	29%	29%	28%
Oppose	55	53	60	61	58
No opinion	20	22	11	10	14
AIPO 725, [a] 3-1-66					
(N) [a]	(249)	(231)	(3309)	(2091)	(851)
In view of developments, U.S. made mistake sending troops to fight in Vietnam	18%	18%	26%	28%	22%
Not a mistake	50	49	59	58	64
No opinion	32	33	15	14	14
AIPO survey of Sept. '66 [b]					
Approve way Pres. Johnson is handling Vietnam	48%		42%	37%	54%
Disapprove	32		41	45	31
No opinion	20		17	18	15
Begin to withdraw from Vietnam	20		17		
Carry on	18		18		
Expand our military effort there	50		56		
No opinion	12		9		

a Weighted N's were roughly twice and 2.3 times as large as actual white and Negro N's respectively.

b Gallup release of 9-21-66.

Table 6-14. Admission of the People's Republic of China to the United Nations

	Negroes			Whites	
	All	Protestant	All	Protestant	Catholic
SRC 473, Sept.-Oct.-64					
(N)	(172)	(148)	(1398)	(857)	(313)
Communist China should be admitted to U.N.	11%	10%	16%	13%	18%
Should not, but U.S. to stay in if admitted	15	16	36	36	34
U.S. should pull out if admitted	3	2	7	8	5
Don't know if should be admitted or what U.S. should do if admitted	10	9	15	15	19
Did not know Mainland China has communist regime, but not in U.N.	61	63	26	28	24
AIPO 684, 1-28-64					
(N)	(369)	(354)	(2740)	(2950)	(587)
Admit China	18%	18%	14%	12%	17%
Do not	50	48	72	74	70
No opinion	32	34	14	14	13
AIPO 706, 2-17-65					
(N)	(386)	(359)	(3120)	(2237)	(397)
Admit China to U.N.	28%	29%	21%	18%	26%
Do not	41	39	66	70	60
No opinion	31	32	13	12	14
AIPO 726, 3-22-66					
(N)	(385)	(347)	(3139)	(2093)	(857)
Admit China to U.N.	30%	29%	24%	22%	25%
Do not	35	32	58	59	58
No opinion	35	39	18	19	17

Table 6-15.   Relations with the Vatican

| | Negroes | | All | Whites | | |
| | | | | Protestant | | |
	All	Protestant		North	South	Catholic
AIPO 181, 1-10-40						
(N)	(100)	(92)	(3034)	(1374)	(264)	(537)
U.S. should send ambassador to Vatican						
Should	32%	30%	38%	29%	31%	64%
Should not	30	31	42	51	41	22
No opinion	38	39	20	20	28	14
AIPO-TPS 457, 6-27-50						
(N)	(117)		(1246)			
Was good idea for Pres. Roosevelt and Truman to have a personal representative at the Vatican	53%		46%			
Only a fair idea	1		5			
Poor idea	3		14			
No opinion	43		35			
Like to see federal gov't send an American representative to Vatican in future	54		46			
Opposed	4		15			
Indifferent	0		8			
No opinion	42		31			
AIPO 482, 11-9-51						
(N)	(87)	(82)	(1935)	(1063)	(227)	(464)
U.S. Senate should approve appointment of ambassador to Vatican	17%	17%	22%	14%	11%	46%
Should not	10	13	33	42	31	15
No opinion	12	10	11	11	13	10
Never heard or read anything about this	61	60	34	33	45	29

AIPO 645, April '61	Negroes		Whites			
				Protestant		
	All	Protestant	All	North	South	Catholic
(N)	(180)	(163)	(1366)	(602)	(278)	(362)
Like present administration to send representative to Vatican	38%	35%	35%	23%	25%	68%
Opposed	19	20	40	52	41	17
No opinion	43	45	25	25	34	15

Table 7-1. Place of birth of one or both parents (whites only) [a]

	Italy	Germany	Ireland	Britain	White Commonwealth[b]	Poland	Russia	Other Axis-invaded Europe	Other foreign origins	All other whites
AIPO 147A, 2-2-39										
(N)	(45)	(89)	(71)							(1463)
If Germany and Italy go to war against Britain and France, U.S. should do everything possible to help them except										
go to war itself	29%	40%	48%							69%
Should not	56	53	44							26
No opinion	15	7	8							5
AIPO 147 B, 2-2-39										
(N)	(32)	(67)	(52)							(1241)
If Germany and Italy attack France and Britain, agree with F.D.R. that U.S. should help short of going into war	34%	43%	50%							63%
Should not	60	55	43							31
No opinion	6	2	7							6
AIPO 147 A+B, 2-2-39										
(N)	(77)	(156)	(123)							(2704)
If Germany and Italy defeat Britain and France, would start war against U.S.	14%	34%	41%							54%
Would not	71	49	44							31
No opinion	15	17	15							15

AIPO 148, 2-16-39	Italy	Germany	Ireland	All other whites
(N)	(80)	(144)	(107)	(2778)
Sell war materials to Britain and France for cash	37%	43%	46%	55%
Do not	54	54	39	38
No opinion	9	3	5	7
Sell them food	53	65	65	72
Do not	38	31	29	23
No opinion	9	4	6	5
Send U.S. Army and Navy abroad to fight enemies of England and France	12	7	13	18
Do not	79	89	82	76
No opinion	9	4	5	6

	Italy	Germany	Ireland	Britain	White Common-wealth[b]	Scandi-navia	Poland	Russia	Other Axis-invaded Europe	Other foreign origins	Both parents U.S. born
Composite of AIPO 169, 170, 171, and 172, Sept.'39											
(N)	(237)	(444)	(348)	(283)	(192)		(118)	(195)	(180)	(673)	(6161)
Change Neutrality Act so Britain and France and others can buy munitions											
here	45%	37%	52%	59%	55%		60%	60%	57%	50%	53%
Do not	41	50	39	28	39		28	33	32	39	37
No opinion	14	13	9	13	6		12	7	11	11	10
Should declare war and send Army and Navy to fight											
Germany	4	3	4	8	7		10	3	8	7	5
Should not	93	93	92	86	87		86	94	87	89	91
No opinion	3	4	4	6	6		4	3	5	4	4
AIPO 171, 9-22-39											
(N)	(70)	(135)	(105)	(90)	(57)		(45)	(51)			(2403)
U.S. should fight to keep out European invasion of any country within 1500 miles of Panama Canal	51%	58%	67%								69%
Should not	34	31	24								20
No opinion	15	11	9								11

	Italy	Germany	Ireland	Britain	White Commonwealth		Poland	Russia			Both parents U.S. born
European war just another struggle for power and wealth	49	50	47	35	39		45	59			43
Is a struggle of democracy against spread of dictatorship	34	35	44	55	47		40	35			44
No opinion	17	15	9	10	14		15	6			13
Composite of AIPO 211, 212, and 213, Sept.'40											
(N)	(198)	(422)	(277)	(381)	(174)	(260)	(329)	(453)			(5402)
Would vote to enter war against Germany and Italy	11%	12%	21%	23%	19%	19%	22%	20%			18%
Would vote to stay out of war	82	82	72	70	72	69	69	72			73
No opinion	7	6	8	7	9	12	9	8			9
AIPO 215, 10-9-40											
(N)	(74)	(159)	(128)	(141)	(80)	(149)	(61)	(59)	(136)	(140)	(2005)
Increase food and war supply aid to Britain if appears she will be defeated	58%	71%	81%	92%	86%	88%	82%	90%	77%	84%	86%
Do not	18	19	11	4	9	9	10	10	17	10	9
No opinion	24	10	8	4	5	3	8	0	6	6	5
Composite of AIPO 209, 210, 213, and 221, Jan-Nov.'40											
(N)	(352)	(693)	(508)	(352)	(301)	(357)	(585)	(392)			(8652)
Think Germany and Italy will win war	26%	18%	12%	9%	10%	9%	9%	11%			11%
Think Britain will win	32	44	66	66	67	64	56	58			61
Neither will win	4	5	4	4	4	4	5	4			4
No opinion	38	33	18	21	19	23	30	27			24

	Italy	Germany	Ireland	Britain	White Commonwealth	Scandinavia	Poland	Russia	Other Axis-invaded Europe	Other foreign origins	Both parents U.S. born
Composite of AIPO 216, 217, and 220, Sept.-Oct.'40											
(N)	(286)	(689)	(489)	(542)	(408)	(507)	(149)	(201)	(469)	(208)	(9430)
More important for U.S. to try to keep out of war	72%	68%	51%	36%	38%	46%	36%	37%	47%	45%	44%
More important to help Britain at risk of war	22	27	43	60	58	47	58	57	47	47	51
No opinion	6	5	6	4	4	7	6	6	6	8	5
AIPO 219, 10-24-40											
(N)	(119)	(239)	(43)	(49)	(34)	(69)			(203)	(31)	(3568)
Think U.S. will enter the war in Europe	26%	26%	26%	31%	27%	36%			31%	45%	35%
Will stay out	47	34	53	43	44	30			40	29	29
Go in if a long war	6	12	7	4	12	9			3	16	8
Go in if Germany and Italy win	2	7	12	8	3	12			7	7	9
Other	3	11	2	10	6	6			5	0	7
No opinion	16	10	0	4	8	7			14	3	14
AIPO 229, 1-22-41											
(N)	(147)	(183)	(132)	(101)	(40)	(137)			(285)	(130)	(1839)
Congress should pass Lend-Lease bill (with or without qualifications)	49%	44%	56%	76%	70%	70%			70%	68%	71%
Should not	41	48	35	17	23	25			22	28	21
No opinion	10	8	9	7	7	5			8	9	8
Composite of AIPO 229, 806, 809, 241, 242, and 248, Jan.-Oct.'41											
(N)	(396)	(756)	(582)	(673)	(381)	(499)	(163)	(226)	(340)	(475)	(10,430)
More important to try to keep out of war	63%	56%	43%	24%	33%	36%	33%	21%	32%	39%	31%
More important to help Britain	33	41	52	71	62	60	66	75	64	56	64
No opinion	4	3	5	5	5	4	1	4	4	5	5

AIPO 240, 6-24-41	Italy	Germany	Ireland	Britain	White Common- wealth	Scandi- navia	Russia	Other foreign origins	Both parents (U.S. born)
(N)	(77)	(153)	(124)	(123)	(80)	(100)	(49)	(305)	(821)
U.S. Navy should convoy supplies to Britain	22%	39%	45%	73%	62%	52%	69%	53%	60%
Should not	71	58	45	24	31	44	29	36	31
No opinion	7	3	10	3	7	4	2	11	9
U.S. gov't should supply war and other materials to USSR on same basis as to Britain	16	33	38	40	28	37	59	38	37
Should not	74	60	56	52	60	52	39	55	52
No opinion	10	7	6	8	12	11	2	7	11

a In the few cases where parents were natives of two different countries, the individual appears in two national
  groups in this table.

b Mostly Canada.

Table 7-2.   Ethnic origins (non-Jewish whites only)[a]

	Britain	Ireland	Germany	Scand-inavia	Italy	Other W. Europe	Poland	Other E. Europe	All others
AIPO 307, 11-23-43[b]									
(N)	(235)	(77)	(104)		(30)				(2225)
Willing to continue to put up with shortages of butter, sugar, meat, other rationed food after war to give food to Europe	66%	64%	65%		63%				64
Not willing	25	30	28		27				29
No opinion	9	6	7		10				7
Republicans and Democrats should both take stand for future active part in world affairs									
Should	69	65	67		63				65
Should not	12	16	13		13				15
No opinion	19	19	20		24				20
Combined Roper surveys of Aug. and Oct. '52[c]									
(N)	(530)	(432)	(828)	(283)	(306)	(213)	(221)	(508)	(228)
Most important 2 or 3 things for next administration to do:									
Continue aid to W. Europe	10%	10%	7%	9%	10%	11%	9%	13%	7%
End war in Korea quickly	56	60	56	62	63	53	61	61	48
Keep communists out of gov't jobs	58	50	54	53	51	56	43	40	54
What best to do in Korea?									
Continue negotiations	26	32	27	29	30	31	37	41	33
Expand war	43	40	40	38	35	42	35	29	38
Pull out	16	16	17	19	22	12	16	18	15
No opinion	15	12	16	14	13	15	12	12	14

	Britain	Ireland	Germany	Scandinavia	Italy	Other W. European	Poland	Other E. European	All others
What best to do in Europe?									
Keep building its armed strength	30	28	25	26	35	28	27	38	36
Cut aid	46	47	47	51	34	48	47	40	40
Get out of Europe	16	17	16	13	17	15	16	14	13
No opinion	8	8	12	10	14	9	10	8	11
Roper 737, Aug.'53[c]									
(N)	(166)	(169)	(289)	(113)	(112)	(86)	(107)	(111)	(127)
U.S. should have taken larger part in world affairs since 1945	19%	21%	19%	13%	10%	21%	18%	14%	14%
Just about right	47	39	42	45	44	38	36	47	49
Definitely smaller part	18	31	25	33	27	28	26	24	17
No opinion	16	9	14	9	19	13	20	15	20
Way of handling Russia with which most agree:									
Go to war as soon as U.S. military leaders think we can win and get whole thing over with	2	8	8	2	6	5	6	2	10
Rely completely on building own military strength	24	33	26	18	30	17	28	25	26
While keeping up military strength, make every reasonable attempt to find way to live peacefully with Russia	68	53	56	71	53	71	57	64	49
Stop relying on military strength; work out agreement even if we have to give in to Russia on important things	3	4	4	6	3	6	2	8	6
No opinion	3	2	6	3	8	1	7	1	9

	Britain	Ireland	Germany	Scandi-navia	Italy	Other W. European	Poland	Other E. European	All others
Way to achieve peace with which most agree:									
No more alliances or joint commitments; get out of as many as soon as we can	1	5	5	4	4	4	5	6	6
Continue to work with U.N. as we have, gradually trying to improve it	28	25	20	28	25	24	22	17	23
Immediately get behind strengthening U.N.; give it enough power to keep even a strong nation from starting war	19	22	18	15	23	22	21	27	21
In addition to continuing with U.N., unite with friendly democratic gov'ts into one gov't	13	8	10	15	9	13	5	16	12
Work toward transforming U.N. into world gov't	12	13	11	4	6	14	12	12	9
None of these	6	11	16	16	16	13	19	10	8
No opinion	21	16	20	18	17	10	16	12	21
SRC 417, Sept.-Oct.'56[d]									
(N)	(140)	(93)	(162)	(58)	(58)	(60)	(39)	(97)	(901)
Should give economic help to poorer countries	41%	43%	40%	43%	50%	47%	56%	39%	44%
Depends or not sure	19	14	18	21	14	13	15	16	14
Should not	25	25	29	26	14	27	21	29	26
No opinion	15	18	13	10	22	13	8	16	16
Give help even if recipients not as much against communism as we	29	23	38	29	14	42	39	25	30
Depends or not sure	14	17	12	21	16	15	10	9	12
Do not help	32	40	32	31	34	27	33	35	29
No opinion	25	20	18	19	36	16	18	31	29

	Britain	Ireland	Germany	Scandinavia	Italy	Other W. European	Poland	Other E. European	All others
SRC 440, Sept.-Oct.'60[e]									
(N)	(331)	(177)	(242)	(44)	(58)	(104)	(22)	(30)	(1213)
U.S. better off if stayed home, did not concern self with world problems	13%	15%	18%	23%	14%	10%	14%	20%	17%
Depends on or not sure	7	7	8	5	3	8	0	0	6
Disagree with this view	75	71	71	59	66	75	77	74	67
No opinion	5	7	3	13	17	7	9	6	10
Should give economic help to poorer countries	57	68	49	43	60	57	55	34	53
Depends or not sure	16	10	16	14	23	16	23	13	14
Should not	19	17	22	36	7	18	18	37	21
No opinion	8	5	13	7	10	9	4	16	12
SRC 473, Sept.-Dec.'64[f]									
(N)	(241)	(138)	(161)	(27)	(21)	(78)	(23)	(19)	(417)
Give aid to countries if they need help	51%	54%	52%	52%	48%	53%	62%	68%	50%
Depends or not sure	25	18	28	33	24	21	0	11	15
Each country should make own way as best it can	17	23	13	7	14	18	31	16	23
No opinion	7	5	7	8	14	8	7	5	12
Our gov't should meet with communist leaders to try to settle our differences	68	80	80	67	67	74	92	84	68
Depends or not sure	7	6	3	11	0	6	0	0	3
Should refuse to have anything to do with them	15	3	9	11	0	12	0	11	11
No opinion	10	11	8	11	33	8	8	5	18

	Britain	Ireland	Germany	Scandi-navia	Italy	Other W. European	Poland	Other E. European	All others
U.S. farmers and businessmen should be able to trade with communist countries in nonmilitary goods	26	25	26	26	14	28	15	32	26
Depends or not sure	5	7	7	0	10	10	23	5	3
Such trade should be forbidden	50	42	45	63	52	44	31	42	43
No opinion	19	26	22	11	24	18	31	21	28
Did not know Mainland China is communist and not in U.N.	16	23	24	19	24	19	39	26	36
Should be admitted to U.N.	16	14	19	19	14	21	8	11	12
Should not be admitted	58	53	47	55	38	48	46	48	42
But U.S. should stay in if admitted	41	41	38	48	33	33	31	37	29
Don't know if U.S. should stay in	10	3	4	7	0	5	15	11	4
U.S. should get out	7	9	5	0	5	10	0	0	9
No opinion	10	10	10	7	24	12	7	15	10
Harris survey of 1965 Favor liberalized immigration as proposed by Pres. Johnson	10%	26%	12%	38%	38%	23%	40%	38%	20%
Oppose	70	53	76	30	30	57	44	46	61
No opinion	20	21	12	7	32	20	16	16	19

a Except where otherwise indicated, individuals whose parents or grandparents were natives of more than one foreign country appear in more than one ethnic category.

b Based on place of birth of father or mother.

c Based on place of birth of grandparents.

d Based on place of birth of respondent, either parent, or father's parent.

e Based on place of birth of foreign-born parent(s) and country family came from originally on father's side for those both of whose parents were born in the U.S. Interviewees whose parents were natives of two different foreign countries were eliminated.

f Based on place of birth of parents and/or grandparents. Where more than one foreign country was mentioned, ethnic origin was determined by replies to "Aside from American, what nationality do you think of your family as being, mainly?"

Table 7-3.   Regional religious differences (whites only)

	South				Non-South			
	Prot.	Cath.	Unaf.	Tot.[a]	Prot.	Cath.	Unaf.	Tot.[a]
AIPO 133, 9-23-38								
(N)	(284)	(15)	(83)	(388)	(1359)	(512)	(784)	(2748)
Britain and France mistaken in accepting Germany's demands on Czechoslovakia	46%	80%	59%	51%	51%	50%	51%	52%
Not mistaken	33	13	23	29	32	29	31	31
No opinion	21	7	18	20	17	21	18	17
U.S. failure to join League partly responsible for European troubles	20	20	10	17	17	18	15	17
Not responsible	61	67	58	61	63	62	63	63
No opinion	19	13	32	22	20	20	21	20
Like to see F.D.R. openly criticize Hitler and Mussolini	31	47	31	31	29	28	31	30
Would not	60	53	58	60	64	65	60	62
No opinion	9	0	11	9	7	7	9	8
AIPO 145, 1-20-39								
(N)	(280)	(34)	(81)	(399)	(1321)	(556)	(758)	(2719)
Prefer fascism over communism	18%	21%	17%	18%	26%	35%	18%	25%
Communism over fascism	26	26	20	25	25	17	30	25
No opinion, or neither	56	53	63	37	50	48	52	50
Return colonies to Germany	7	14	17	10	15	20	13	15
Do not	77	77	65	74	72	66	73	72
No opinion	16	9	18	16	13	14	14	13
AIPO 149A, 2-22-39								
(N)	(130)	(12)	(52)	(187)	(617)	(255)	(396)	(1321)
Rather USSR win if a war with Japan	57%	67%	60%	58%	48%	45%	53%	50%
Rather Japan win	8	0	2	6	10	14	＼6	9
No choice	25	25	25	25	31	10	26	29
No opinion	10	8	13	11	11	31	15	12
AIPO 181, 1-10-40								
(N)	(264)	(31)	(86)	(381)	(1320)	(506)	(771)	(2683)
Congress should vote $60 million for Finland	68%	74%	58%	66%	57%	51%	50%	53%
Should not	28	23	36	30	38	44	44	41
No opinion	4	3	6	4	5	5	6	6
U.S. should send ambassador to Pope	31	48			29	65		
Should not	41	32			51	21		
No opinion	12	20			20	9		

Northeast				Midwest				West				All Whites		
Prot.	Cath.	Unaf.	Tot.[a]	Prot.	Cath.	Unaf.	Tot.[a]	Prot.	Cath.	Unaf.	Tot.[a]	Prot.	Cath.	Unaf.
(496)	(294)	(260)	(1106)	(665)	(169)	(337)	(1197)	(198)	(49)	(187)	(445)	(1643)	(527)	(867)
49%	52%	48%	51%	54%	48%	55%	53%	49%	49%	50%	49%	52%	51%	52%
31	27	31	30	32	30	29	31	33	33	32	33	32	28	30
20	21	21	19	14	22	16	16	18	18	18	18	16	21	18
20	19	20	20	16	16	12	14	17	16	15	16	18	14	15
60	64	60	61	66	59	65	65	58	61	65	62	62	65	63
20	17	20	19	18	25	23	21	25	23	20	22	20	21	22
30	29	30	31	26	23	30	27	33	35	34	34	29	32	31
61	65	61	61	68	69	59	65	59	55	58	58	64	58	60
9	6	9	8	6	8	11	8	8	10	8	8	7	10	9
(459)	(323)	(257)	(1093)	(668)	(177)	(319)	(1184)	(199)	(56)	(182)	(442)	(1601)	(590)	(839)
28%	36%	19%	28%	26%	39%	19%	26%	17%	18%	18%	17%	24%	34%	18%
23	15	32	24	24	17	26	24	30	23	34	31	25	17	29
49	49	49	48	50	44	55	50	53	59	49	52	51	49	53
15	18	9	14	17	23	18	18	12	27	11	13	14	20	14
72	67	78	73	71	64	67	69	76	64	75	75	73	66	72
13	15	13	13	12	13	15	13	12	9	14	12	13	14	14
(224)	(155)	(147)	(556)	(302)	(75)	(179)	(569)	(91)	(25)	(70)	(196)	(747)	(258)	(448)
45%	43%	52%	48%	46%	48%	54%	49%	62%	48%	51%	56%	50%	45%	54%
9	15	5	9	13	12	8	11	3	16	3	4	9	14	5
33	30	29	31	32	32	21	28	23	32	32	28	30	30	26
13	12	14	12	9	8	17	12	12	4	14	12	11	11	15
												(1584)	(537)	(857)
												58%	52%	51%
												36	42	43
												6	6	6
												30	64	
												50	22	
												20	14	

	South				Non-South			
	Prot.	Cath.	Unaf.	Total	Prot.	Cath.	Unafil.	Total
AIPO 213, 9-30-40								
(N)	(134)	(17)	(51)	(204)	(660)	(258)	(392)	(1355)
Forbid sale of strategic								
goods to Japan	86%	82%	71%	82%	84%	79%	85%	83%
Do not	7	0	10	7	10	14	6	10
No opinion	7	18	19	11	6	7	9	7
Risk war to prevent Japan								
from getting control of								
China	29	27	29	32	29	27	27	28
Do not	21	12	18	19	33	33	30	32
Other isolationist replies	17	12	8	14	13	15	17	15
No opinion	33	29	45	35	25	25	26	25
AIPO 214T, 10-5-40								
(N)	(114)	(10)	(42)	(170)	(663)	(282)	(355)	(1367)
Sell Britain aircraft on								
credit supplied by our								
gov't if can't pay								
cash	73%	80%	64%	71%	60%	47%	50%	55%
Do not	22	10	21	21	33	41	40	36
No opinion	5	10	15	8	7	11	10	9
AIPO 214K, 10-5-40								
(N)	(120)	(19)	(38)	(177)	(616)	(231)	(382)	(1316)
Change Johnson Act so								
Britain can borrow								
money from U.S. gov't	55%	66%	69%	67%	48%	42%	44%	45%
Do not	29	22	21	21	39	49	45	43
No opinion	16	12	10	12	13	9	11	12
AIPO 240, 6-24-41								
(N)	(285)	(25)	(86)	(401)	(1346)	(514)	(650)	(2604)
F.D.R. has gone too far								
in helping Britain	5%	4%	6%	5%	19%	20%	21%	20%
About right	51	56	45	50	51	51	50	51
Not far enough	36	36	37	37	22	22	23	23
No opinion	8	4	12	8	8	7	6	6
Supply USSR on same basis								
as Britain	39	76	36	**41**	31	34	37	33
Do not	48	20	48	46	58	55	52	56
No opinion	13	4	16	13	11	11	11	11
AIPO 248, 9-17-41								
(N)	(246)	(21)	(74)	(345)	(1346)	(512)	(717)	(2682)
More important to								
(1) Keep out of war	10%	19%	15%	12%	28%	41%	30%	31%
(2) Help Britain	86	71	80	84	65	55	64	63
No opinion	4	10	5	4	7	4	6	6

a Includes Jews, other white non-Christians, and those who did not answer the question about church membership.

	Northeast				Midwest				West				All whites	
Prot.	Cath.	Unaf.	Tot.	Prot.	Cath.	Unaf.	Tot.	Prot.	Cath.	Unaf.	Tot.	Prot.	Cath.	Unaf.
(191)	(157)	(149)	(530)	(351)	(89)	(51)	(601)	(118)	(12)	(89)	(224)	(794)	(275)	(443)
79%	79%	82%	80%	85%	79%	71%	84%	89%	83%	94%	91%	84%	79%	83%
15	14	12	14	7	15	10	7	9	8	1	5	9	13	7
6	7	6	6	8	6	19	9	2	9	5	4	7	8	10
28	29	22	27	26	26	29	27	41	8	30	34	29	28	27
32	28	32	31	36	37	18	35	24	58	26	27	31	31	28
15	18	20	17	12	11	8	12	13	17	20	17	14	15	16
25	25	26	25	26	26	45	26	22	17	24	22	26	26	29
(233)	(170)	(103)	(534)	(311)	(76)	(163)	(576)	(119)	(36)	(89)	(257)	(777)	(292)	(397)
63%	48%	52%	57%	53%	47%	47%	51%	61%	47%	50%	55%	62%	48%	52%
30	41	38	34	38	42	43	40	32	41	39	35	31	40	38
7	11	10	9	9	11	10	9	7	12	11	10	7	12	10
(216)	(139)	(111)	(515)	(289)	(62)	(175)	(554)	(111)	(30)	(96)	(247)	(736)	(238)	(420)
51%	42%	47%	46%	43%	41%	42%	42%	49%	42%	44%	45%	51%	42%	46%
38	49	41	42	43	51	48	47	38	48	45	43	36	48	43
11	9	12	12	14	8	10	11	13	10	11	12	13	10	11
(474)	(310)	(188)	(1015)	(632)	(139)	(329)	(1134)	(240)	(65)	(133)	(452)	(1631)	(539)	(736)
12%	19%	15%	15%	26%	21%	28%	26%	18%	21%	20%	19%	16%	19%	18%
50	51	52	50	50	51	49	51	52	50	49	51	51	51	50
31	24	28	29	16	21	14	16	21	20	25	24	26	23	25
7	6	5	6	8	7	7	7	9	9	6	6	7	7	7
34	35	39	35	26	34	33	29	31	33	38	33	34	36	37
56	55	50	54	63	56	56	62	59	58	56	59	56	54	52
11	10	11	11	11	10	11	9	11	11	11	8	10	10	11
(473)	(309)	(207)	(1049)	(631)	(137)	(329)	(1130)	(242)	(66)	(181)	(503)	(1592)	(533)	(791)
21%	41%	26%	28%	34%	42%	34%	34%	27%	39%	28%	29%	25%	40%	29%
73	54	68	67	58	54	60	58	67	59	67	66	68	55	66
6	5	6	5	8	4	6	8	6	2	5	5	7	5	5

Table 7-4.   Regional differences (whites only)

	Northeast		Midwest		West	
	Cath.	Prot.	Cath.	Prot.	Cath.	Prot.
AIPO 408, Sept.'47						
(N)	(334)	(502)	(184)	(752)	(67)	(325)
Heard or read of trade agreements signed at Geneva	25%	34%	33%	39%	40%	42%
Favor agreement for reciprocal reduction of tariffs	67	65	63	66	72	71
Oppose	9	12	16	14	15	13
No opinion	24	23	21	20	13	16
AIPO 454, 3-2-50						
(N)	(186)	(294)	(100)	(390)	(34)	(157)
Increase Marshall Plan	19%	12%	11%	13%	6%	5%
Decrease it	46	45	44	44	67	55
Maintain current level	35	36	36	33	21	33
No opinion	10	7	9	10	6	7
Summit meeting with Stalin a good idea	54	44	30	45	59	39
Fair idea	6	7	13	7	3	10
Poor idea	36	42	51	39	32	42
No opinion	4	7	6	9	6	9
Such a Summit session likely to be successful	23	17	16	19	29	11
Not	65	70	75	70	59	78
No opinion	12	13	9	11	12	11
Increase national defense	76	60	71	60	53	67
Decrease	2	9	7	8	18	6
Maintain current level	18	27	17	26	26	24
No opinion	4	4	5	6	3	3
AIPO 514, 4-17-53						
(N)	(178)	(246)	(84)	(340)	(49)	(146)
Favor international con- trol of atomic energy providing for U.N. in- spection of atomic plants in all countries, in- cluding U.S. and USSR	55%	60%	62%	64%	61%	62%
Oppose	34	29	31	27	29	30
No opinion	11	11	7	9	10	8
Approve of giving less economic and military aid to Europe, more to allies in Asia	47	50	50	42	51	45
Disapprove	33	27	32	26	27	28
Qualified	2	4	5	6	0	5
No opinion	18	19	13	26	22	22

Total	Non-South	South	
Cath.	Prot.	Cath.	Prot.
(585)	(1579)	(26)	(304)
30%	39%	39%	36%
66	67	42	67
12	13	15	5
22	20	43	28
(320)	(841)	(21)	(150)
9%	11%	24%	12%
48	46	33	54
34	34	24	21
9	9	19	13
47	43	43	37
8	8	5	7
40	40	38	45
5	9	14	11
22	16	5	17
67	72	86	63
11	11	9	20
72	61	76	60
5	8	0	3
19	26	10	29
4	5	14	8
(311)	(732)	(27)	(367)
58%	63%	30%	46%
32	28	44	34
10	9	26	20
48	45	41	42
31	27	15	21
3	5	7	1
18	23	37	36

	Northeast		Midwest		West	
	Cath.	Prot.	Cath.	Prot.	Cath.	Prot.
If can cut defense spending, use part of saving to help needy countries	61	70	55	68	53	65
Opposed	32	25	33	25	35	26
No opinion	7	5	12	7	12	9
AIPO 526, Jan.'54						
(N)	(167)	(228)	(79)	(348)	(33)	(138)
Heard or read anything of tariffs and trade discussion	36%	43%	43%	44%	42%	59%
Favor higher tariffs	16	9	10	9	12	21
Lower tariffs	30	31	19	26	27	25
Current level	19	20	33	24	12	21
No opinion	35	40	38	41	49	33
U.S. and USSR should work out agreement to buy and sell goods to each other	39	43	39	41	30	37
Shouldn't	48	46	47	46	39	51
No opinion	13	11	14	13	31	12
AIPO 540, Nov.'54						
(N)	(164)	(180)	(93)	(282)	(33)	(156)
Heard or read anything of tariffs and trade discussion	46%	49%	37%	52%	58%	62%
Favor higher tariffs	23	21	14	20	18	16
Lower tariffs	35	28	31	33	40	32
Current level	13	23	24	21	24	26
No opinion	29	28	31	26	18	26
AIPO 546, 4-12-55						
(N)	(193)	(226)	(115)	(342)	(49)	(137)
Good idea to send economic aid to non-communist Asian countries	58%	58%	51%	56%	55%	63%
Poor idea	27	26	35	26	27	23
No opinion	15	16	14	18	18	14
Heard or read of trouble in Formosa area	83	83	81	90	92	91
Knew Quemoy and Matsu in noncommunist control	39	45	43	54	39	46
USSR, Com. China, and all other interested nations should meet to try to work out peaceful solution on Formosa	76	73	74	76	74	74
Should not	14	20	10	16	18	21
No opinion	10	7	16	8	8	5

Non-South		South	
Cath.	Prot.	Cath.	Prot.
58	68	41	62
33	25	55	19
9	7	4	19
(279)	(714)	(28)	(311)
39%	47%	39%	42%
14	12	11	6
27	27	50	31
22	22	11	21
37	39	28	42
39	41	39	41
47	46	39	44
14	13	22	15
(290)	(618)	(21)	(267)
45%	54%	48%	46%
20	19	14	20
34	31	48	26
18	23	24	24
28	27	14	30
(357)	(705)	(23)	(353)
55%	58%	78%	50%
30	25	13	27
15	17	9	23
84	88	74	68
40	50	17	35
75	75	78	69
14	18	13	17
11	7	9	14

	Northeast Cath.	Prot.	Midwest Cath.	Prot.	West Cath.	Prot.
Roper 939, April 1957						
(N)						
Eisenhower policy to resist communist agression in Mideast with force:						
A good policy						
Could be improved						
Not adequate						
Stay out						
No opinion						
NORC 404, 4-26-57						
(N)						
Could name no countries or colonies (dependencies) in Africa						
One correct mention						
Two correct						
Three correct						
Four correct						
Five or more correct						
AIPO 614, 5-27-59						
(N)	(177)	(208)	(115)	(307)	(33)	(160)
Heard or read anything of tariffs and trade discussion	38%	45%	36%	40%	45%	41%
Favor higher tariffs	22	18	12	11	15	11
Lower tariffs	7	18	9	16	12	14
Current level	6	4	11	7	9	13
No opinion	3	5	4	6	9	3
Never heard of it	62	55	64	60	55	59
AIPO 653, 12-5-61						
(N)	(184)	(208)	(103)	(329)	(51)	(167)
Heard or read anything of tariffs and trade discussion	51%	58%	60%	51%	69%	59%
Favor higher tariffs	18	19	21	16	16	22
Lower tariffs	21	23	24	21	34	23
Current level	7	7	8	9	12	8
No opinion	5	9	7	5	7	6
Never heard of it	49	42	40	49	31	41
AIPO 655, Feb.'62						
(N)	(188)	(197)	(116)	(295)	(52)	(180)
In general, rather more imports than now	8%	10%	11%	8%	12%	13%
Prefer more restrictions on imports	63	58	47	42	66	52
Do about as do now	14	16	25	27	16	14
Depends	9	6	6	6	5	2
No opinion	6	10	11	17	1	19

Total Cath. (301)	Non-South Prot. (611)	South Cath. (38)	Prot. (431)
24%	25%	13%	24%
36	37	24	23
6	9	10	9
22	17	24	22
12	12	29	22
(285)	(496)	(22)	(369)
57%	52%	68%	70%
17	22	14	16
13	11	9	6
4	6	4	5
4	5	5	1
5	4	0	2
(325)	(819)	(26)	(269)
38%	35%	54%	29%
18	11	19	4
8	14	19	16
8	6	8	5
4	4	8	4
62	65	46	71
(338)	(704)	(24)	(269)
56%	52%	53%	50%
19	17	21	15
24	21	0	19
8	7	4	4
5	7	28	12
44	48	47	50
(356)	(672)	(30)	(306)
10%	12%	15%	8%
58	46	39	58
18	21	29	14
7	5	11	4
7	16	6	16

	Northeast		Midwest		West	
	Cath.	Prot.	Cath.	Prot.	Cath.	Prot.
Prefer more restrictions						
on textile imports	41	34	31	34	44	26
About as are now	33	39	46	39	30	38
Encourage more imports	9	13	7	8	20	14
No opinion	17	14	16	19	6	22
Prefer more restrictions						
on oil imports	28	21	28	26	35	25
About as are now	35	32	31	31	47	25
Encourage more imports	19	27	23	20	11	21
No opinion	18	20	18	23	7	29
Prefer more restrictions						
on automobile imports	55	49	56	54	68	51
About as are now	29	29	35	30	27	21
Encourage more imports	6	12	3	8	2	12
No opinion	10	10	6	8	3	16
Prefer more restrictions						
on steel imports	47	44	45	42	62	38
About as are	30	30	32	24	19	24
Encourage more imports	10	11	11	13	13	12
No opinion	13	15	12	21	6	26
AIPO 656, 3-6-62						
(N)	(142)	(203)	(112)	(354)	(47)	(165)
Important for U.S. to in-						
crease goods it buys						
and sells abroad	64%	70%	68%	72%	71%	76%
Not important	20	17	19	14	17	14
No opinion	16	13	13	14	12	10
Favor higher tariffs	23	14	17	15	10	13
Lower	35	39	38	27	38	30
About as are now	12	19	11	20	26	20
No opinion	30	28	34	38	26	37
AIPO 657, 4-4-62						
(N)						
Continue military and						
economic aid to						
Yugoslavia						
Opposed						
No opinion						
SRC 473, Sept.-Oct.'64						
(N)	(132)	(124)	(91)	(302)	(53)	(124)
Give economic aid if						
need help	57%	43%	57%	51%	55%	58%
Depends	17	26	22	19	25	18
Each country should make						
own way as best can	14	21	14	19	15	21
No opinion	12	10	7	11	5	3

Total	Non-South	South	
Cath.	Prot.	Cath.	Prot.
38	29	50	42
37	39	30	37
10	12	10	6
15	20	10	15
29	22	37	35
36	31	35	32
19	22	10	11
16	25	18	22
57	48	36	49
31	29	45	29
5	11	11	7
7	12	8	15
49	39	47	37
29	26	18	29
11	14	21	11
11	21	14	23
(301)	(722)	(44)	(302)
68%	69%	59%	62%
19	17	21	16
14	14	20	22
18	13	11	17
37	30	23	23
14	19	15	15
31	38	51	45
(358)	(681)	(39)	(308)
28%	28%	19%	17%
39	43	35	34
33	29	46	49
(276)	(550)	(37)	(307)
57%	50%	70%	49%
19	20	14	18
14	20	13	22
10	10	13	11

	Northest		Midwest		West	
	Cath.	Prot.	Cath.	Prot.	Cath.	Prot.
Favor negotiations with communist leaders to						
try to settle differences	70	67	78	76	72	68
Depends	3	5	3	4	8	7
Refuse to have anything to						
do with them	12	11	9	9	11	15
No opinion	15	17	10	11	9	10
Trade nonmilitary goods with						
communist countries	25	21	43	26	25	27
Depends	7	6	6	5	8	6
Forbid trade	46	52	34	42	47	44
No opinion	22	21	17	27	20	23
Knew Mainland China						
communist and not in U.N.	72%	77%	74%	69%	79%	80%
Admit her to U.N.	17	18	25	14	17	11
Do not but stay in if						
admitted	35	38	28	34	28	44
Pull out if admitted	6	9	9	5	2	6
Don't know if should be admitted or what U.S.						
should do if admitted	14	12	12	16	32	19
Did not know China communist						
and not in U.N.	28	23	26	31	21	20
POS 655, 2-17-65						
(N)	(166)	(176)	(103)	(293)	(61)	(295)
1/200 of U.S. GNP for						
foreign aid too much	30%	39%	33%	35%	46%	40%
Too little	11	9	14	11	15	6
About right or depends	37	37	45	40	31	32
No opinion	22	18	8	14	8	22
U.S. obligated to help poor						
nations	58	44	56	48	44	37
No obligation	23	29	20	24	30	27
Depends	18	23	23	27	24	33
No opinion	6	4	1	1	1	3
Extremely well satisfied						
with aid to poor nations	30	26	19	17	15	12
Considerably well						
satisfied	24	19	28	29	30	19
Somewhat satisfied	31	32	27	31	26	34
Not at all satisfied	15	23	26	23	29	35
AIPO 706, 2-17-65						
(weighted N) [a]	(350)	(453)	(180)	(677)	(91)	(382)
For foreign aid	55%	63%	67%	57%	65%	54%
Against it	32	30	23	34	34	42
No opinion	13	7	10	9	1	4

Total Non-South		South	
Cath.	Prot.	Cath.	Prot.
73	72	81	72
4	5	3	4
11	11	8	8
12	12	8	16
31	25	30	22
7	6	0	4
42	45	49	50
21	25	21	24
74%	73%	92%	72%
20	14	11	6
32	37	43	35
4	6	8	5
18	16	30	26
26	27	8	28
(330)	(754)	(22)	(233)
34%	37%	36%	39%
12	9	9	6
38	36	46	37
16	18	9	18
55	43	64	49
23	27	18	24
21	28	18	25
1	2	–	2
24	17	14	17
26	23	27	24
29	33	23	29
21	27	36	28
(756)	(1966)	(76)	(725)
60%	58%	70%	50%
30	35	24	38
10	7	6	12

	Northeast		Midwest		West	
	Cath.	Prot.	Cath.	Prot.	Cath.	Prot.
Increase foreign aid above President's request of $3.4 billion	3	4	6	3	5	8
Keep the same	35	30	52	33	48	29
Decrease aid	50	52	34	55	46	57
No opinion	12	14	8	9	1	6
Heard or read of recent developments in Vietnam	92	89	88	87	88	85
Asked of only those who had heard or read:						
Favor U.S. calling conference with heads of Southeast Asia and Communist China	66	65	74	72	71	57
Oppose	17	17	9	10	11	22
No opinion	9	7	5	5	6	6
Had not heard	8	11	12	13	12	15
Admit Communist China to U.N.	23	19	29	23	33	18
Should not	62	68	57	65	58	75
No opinion	15	13	13	12	9	7
Go along with U.N. majority vote on China	52	52	63	51	71	50
Do not	33	34	24	32	26	42
No opinion	15	14	13	17	2	8

a Weighted samples of AIPO 706 were approximately twice the number of interviewees.

Total Cath.	Non-South Prot.	South Cath.	Prot.
4	5	12	6
42	31	37	32
45	54	45	49
9	10	6	13
91	87	96	82
69	66	84	61
14	15	9	11
7	6	3	11
9	13	4	18
26	20	21	14
60	68	63	73
14	12	16	13
58	51	45	35
30	35	33	48
12	14	22	17

Table 7-5.   Education and social class (whites only)

Which of these two things do you think is more important for the United States to try to do -- to keep out of war ourselves, or to help Britain, even at the risk of getting into the war?

| | Composite of AIPO 217, 10-22-40, and 220, 11-5-40 | | | | AIPO 248, 9-17-41[a] | | | |
	(N)	Keep out	Help Britain	No opinion	(N)	Keep out	Help Britain	No opinion
All Catholics	(1071)	56%	39%	5%	(518)	40%	55%	5%
All Protestants	(3411)	45	50	5	(1579)	25	68	7
All Jews	(206)	25	71	4				
All unaffiliated	(1791)	43	50	7	(777)	29	66	5
Education								
College								
Catholics	(202)	54	43	3	(98)	46	53	1
Protestants	(1115)	35	63	2	(516)	21	75	4
Jews	(82)	16	83	1				
Unaffiliated	(399)	35	63	2	(173)	28	68	4
High school								
Catholics	(455)	54	42	4	(220)	36	59	5
Protestants	(1317)	44	51	5	(609)	25	69	6
Jews	(93)	27	68	5				
Unaffiliated	(645)	40	53	7	(276)	25	71	4
Grade school								
Catholics	(414)	58	36	6	(200)	42	54	4
Protestants	(979)	49	44	7	(454)	31	60	9
Jews	(11)	36	55	9				
Unaffiliated	(747)	50	41	9	(324)	32	60	8
Socioeconomic situation								
Upper								
Catholics	(98)	53	43	4	(47)	34	64	2
Protestants	(527)	36	61	3	(267)	23	71	6
Jews	(37)	19	76	5				
Unaffiliated	(194)	34	63	3	(91)	23	75	2
Middle								
Catholics	(541)	54	40	6	(142)	35	61	4
Protestants	(1833)	43	51	5	(601)	23	72	5
Jews	(130)	24	72	4				
Unaffiliated	(792)	40	54	6	(244)	25	69	6
Lower								
Catholics	(432)	58	36	6	(332)	43	52	5
Protestants	(1051)	48	44	8	(687)	29	64	7
Jews	(39)	33	64	3				
Unaffiliated	(805)	51	40	9	(428)	32	62	6

a Jews were too few in AIPO 248 for comparison of education and socioeconomic subgroups.

Table 7-6.   Average annual incomes of families (1964)

	(N)	Below $1000	1000– 1999	2000– 2999	3000 3999	4000– 4999	5000– 5999	6000– 7499	7500– 9999	10000– 14999	15000– up	No answer
White Catholic	(334)	1%	4%	5%	7%	6%	10%	19%	19%	18%	9%	2%
Southern white Protestant	(240)	4	9	4	13	12	15	11	12	11	6	3
Northern white Catholic in towns > 2500	(287)	1	3	4	6	6	10	20	20	19	10	1
Northern white Protestant in towns > 2500	(543)	1	4	6	7	10	9	14	18	17	9	3
Negro Catholic	(16)	19	6	19	19	6	0	6	13	6	6	0
Negro Protestant	(148)	16	11	11	12	9	14	7	7	6	2	5
Northern white Protestant	(690)	2	7	9	8	9	11	13	17	13	8	3

Table 7-7.   Education and income (whites only)

	At least some college		Some H.S., No college		Grade school or less	
	Cath.	Prot.	Cath.	Prot.	Cath.	Prot.
SRC 473, Sept.-Nov.'64						
(N)	(69)	(209)	(180)	(435)	(64)	(209)
Give economic aid if need						
help	58%	55%	62%	54%	47%	37%
Depends	35	25	16	20	13	14
Each country should						
make own way as best it can	6	16	15	17	20	33
No opinion	1	4	7	9	20	16
Trade nonmilitary goods with						
Communist countries	46	31	27	21	23	22
Depends	4	9	7	6	5	-
Forbid trade	38	44	47	50	38	42
No opinion	12	16	19	23	34	36
Knew Mainland China communist						
and not in U.N.	93	89	76	75	58	52
Admit China to U.N.	23	21	16	13	19	6
Do not admit, but stay in if						
admitted	39	43	38	40	14	22
Do not admit, pull out if						
admitted	9	11	5	6	5	8
Do not admit, don't know if						
U.S. should stay in if						
admitted	7	5	4	6	1	6
Do not know if China should						
be admitted	14	10	13	10	19	8
Did not know China communist						
and not in U.N.	7	11	24	25	42	48
POS 655, 2-15-65						
(N)	(66)	(254)	(215)	(515)	(69)	(216)
1/200 of U.S. GNP for foreign						
aid is too much	42%	34%	34%	40%	28%	38%
Too little	9	8	14	8	10	7
About right or depends	38	41	36	33	46	37
No opinion	11	17	16	19	16	18
U.S. obligated to help						
poor nations	56	48	54	45	60	38
No obligation	20	19	24	28	23	29
Depends	24	32	21	25	17	28
No opinion	-	1	1	2	-	5
Extremely well satisfied with						
aid to poor nations	9	12	27	21	15	16
Considerably well satisfied	30	23	21	22	39	24
Somewhat satisfied	32	36	30	31	19	30
Not at all satisfied	29	29	22	26	17	30

	$10,000 or more		Less than $10,000	
	Cath.	Prot.	Cath.	Prot.
POS 655, 2-15-65				
(N)	(51)	(161)	(295)	(809)
1/200 of U.S. GNP for foreign aid too much	41%	38%	33%	38%
Too little	16	11	12	7
About right or depends	41	39	38	36
No opinion	2	12	17	19
U.S. obligated to help poor nations	67	48	54	44
No obligation	21	24	23	26
Depends	12	27	22	27
No opinion	–	1	1	3
Extremely well satisfied with aid to poor nations	18	17	24	18
Considerably well satisfied	27	16	26	24
Somewhat satisfied	24	37	29	31
Not at all satisfied	31	30	21	27

	At least some college		Some H.S., No college		Grade school or less	
	Cath.	Prot.	Cath.	Prot.	Cath.	Prot.
AIPO 706, 2-17-65 (weighted N) [a]	(145)	(420)	(346)	(1081)	(204)	(732)
For foreign aid	78%	68%	62%	54%	49%	51%
Against it	20	28	29	38	37	37
No opinion	2	4	9	8	14	12
Pres. Johnson's request for $3.4 billion for aid should be:						
Increased	4	5	4	3	8	8
Kept same	57	37	41	34	31	24
Decreased	31	47	46	56	53	51
No opinion	8	11	9	7	8	17
Heard or read of recent Vietnam developments	99	98	93	91	83	71
Haven't heard of developments	1	2	7	9	17	29
Asked only of those who had heard or read: U.S. should negotiate with Chinese and Southeast Asian communist leaders	77	72	73	68	63	56
Should not	20	39	13	16	11	6
No opinion	3	7	7	6	9	9
Favor Peking's membership in U.N.	43	29	23	19	17	13
Oppose	54	64	67	74	54	67
No opinion	3	8	10	7	29	20
Go along with U.N. majority vote	65	64	57	49	50	32
Do not	30	29	31	41	29	43
No opinion	5	7	12	10	21	25

[a] Actual N's were approximately one-half these weighted N's.

Table 7-8.   Age (whites only)

	21-39 years		40-59 years		60 years up	
	Cath.	Prot.	Cath.	Prot.	Cath.	Prot.
SRC 473, Sept.-Nov.'64						
(N)	(138)	(301)	(118)	(351)	(57)	(205)
Give economic aid if need						
help	60%	56%	57%	52%	56%	37%
Depends	20	20	23	18	10	21
Each country should make own						
way as best it can	14	17	13	20	18	30
No opinion	6	7	7	10	16	12
Favor discussions with						
communist leaders to						
settle differences	80	76	77	70	69	58
Depends	2	5	2	4	7	7
Refuse to have anything to						
do with them	8	8	9	13	12	13
No opinion	10	11	12	13	12	22
Trade nonmilitary goods with						
communist countries	30	23	28	26	37	22
Depends	7	6	5	5	5	4
Forbid trade	45	45	48	50	28	44
No opinion	18	26	19	19	30	30
Knew Mainland China communist						
and not in U.N.	76	72	75	78	77	64
Admit China to U.N.	20	18	16	13	18	7
Do not admit, but stay in if						
admitted	33	36	36	40	28	31
Do not admit, pull out if						
admitted	5	6	6	9	7	8
Do not admit, don't know if						
U.S. should stay if admitted	3	3	6	5	5	11
Don't know if China should be						
admitted	15	9	11	11	19	7
Did not know China communist						
and not in U.N.	24	28	25	22	23	36
AIPO 706, 2-17-65						
(weighted N)[a]	(113)	(334)	(343)	(813)	(224)	(999)
For foreign aid	71%	64%	62%	60%	57%	50%
Against it	25	29	27	33	34	39
No opinion	4	7	11	7	9	11
Pres. Johnson's request for						
$3.4 billion for foreign						
aid should be						
Increased	5	5	4	4	7	6
Kept same	42	40	41	33	39	27
Decreased	45	46	45	54	47	54
No opinion	8	9	10	9	7	13

	21-39 years		40-59 years		60 years up	
	Cath.	Prot.	Cath.	Prot.	Cath.	Prot.
Heard or read of recent						
Vietnam developments	97	87	91	89	89	83
Haven't	3	13	9	11	11	17
Asked only of those who had						
heard or read:						
U.S. should negotiate with						
Chinese and Southeast						
Asian communist leaders	84	62	71	65	73	61
Should not	11	17	14	16	11	13
No opinion	3	8	5	9	5	9
Favor Peking's membership in U.N.	31	29	23	18	26	15
Oppose	51	59	67	74	54	70
No opinion	18	12	10	8	20	15
Go along with U.N. majority vote	71	58	52	46	57	43
Do not	20	27	36	43	28	39
No opinion	9	15	12	11	15	18
POS 655, 2-17-65						
(N)	(86)	(187)	(150)	(386)	(115)	(409)
1/200 of U.S. GNP for foreign						
aid is too much	37%	36%	36%	37%	30%	39%
Too little	14	9	12	8	11	7
About right or depends	40	38	37	38	40	34
No opinion	9	17	15	17	19	20
U.S. obligated to help poor						
nations	52	50	57	46	55	40
No obligation	21	23	23	24	25	29
Depends	26	26	19	28	19	27
No opinion	11	1	1	2	1	4
Extremely well satisfied with						
aid to poor nations	19	16	23	18	24	18
Considerably well satisfied	30	27	25	25	26	19
Somewhat satisfied	29	29	30	33	27	32
Not at all satisfied	22	28	22	4	23	31

a Weighted N's were approximately twice actual N's.

Table 7-9.   Partisan preferences (whites only)

	Democrats		Republicans	
	Cath.	Prot.	Cath.	Prot.
SRC 473, Sept.-Nov.'64				
(N)	(220)	(467)	(65)	(327)
Give economic aid if need help	61%	51%	49%	48%
Depends	17	17	30	23
Each country should make own way as best				
it can	13	22	15	21
No opinion	9	10	6	8
Trade nonmilitary goods with communist				
countries	28	27	36	20
Depends	4	4	9	6
Forbid trade	44	43	45	54
No opinion	24	26	10	20
Knew Mainland China communist and not in U.N.	72	70	83	78
Admit China to U.N.	18	13	25	12
Do not admit, but stay in if admitted	35	36	25	38
Do not admit, pull out if admitted	4	7	11	9
Do not admit, don't know if U.S. should				
stay in if admitted	3	4	9	9
Do not know if China should be admitted	12	10	13	10
Did not know China communist and not in U.N.	28	30	17	22
AIPO 706, 2-15-65				
(weighted N)[a]	(407)	(980)	(122)	(706)
For foreign aid	64%	62%	62%	48%
Against it	25	28	29	47
No opinion	11	10	9	5
President Johnson's request for $3.4				
billion for aid should be				
Increased	7	9	2	3
Kept same	43	38	47	27
Decreased	40	42	45	61
No opinion	10	11	6	9
Heard or read of recent Vietnam developments	89	83	94	90
Haven't	11	17	6	10
Asked only of those who had heard or read:				
U.S. should negotiate with Chinese and				
Southeast Asian communist leaders	71	66	75	65
Should not	12	9	12	21
No opinion	6	8	7	4
Favor Peking's membership in U.N.	23	18	35	15
Oppose	63	71	46	74
No opinion	14	11	19	11
Go along with U.N. majority vote	55	11	66	49
Do not	29	41	28	3
No opinion	16	15	7	13

| | Democrats | | Republicans | |
	Cath.	Prot.	Cath.	Prot.
POS 655, 2-17-65				
(N)	(191)	(412)	(51)	(318)
1/200 of U.S. GNP for foreign aid too				
much	27%	34%	43%	43%
Too little	13	9	12	8
About right or depends	41	39	33	33
No opinion	19	18	12	16
U.S. obligated to help poor nations	61	43	33	41
No obligation	20	28	31	26
Depends	18	26	16	30
No opinion	1	3	-	3
Extremely well satisfied with aid to				
poor nations	30	22	20	15
Considerably well satisfied	30	24	20	20
Somewhat satisfied	26	31	33	35
Not at all satisfied	14	23	27	30

a Weighted N's were approximately twice actual N's.

Table 8-1.   Liberalism-conservatism

| | | ALL | | WHITES ONLY | | | | |
| | | | | | | North | South | |
	Jews	Cath.	Prot.	Cath.	Prot.	Prot.	Prot.	Negroes
AIPO 133, 9-23-38								
(N)	(56)	(528)	(1690)	(527)	(1643)	(1359)	(284)	(75)
During next two years, like to see Roosevelt administration continue along present lines or become more liberal	75%	46%	43%	46%	43%	44%	43%	41%
Like it to become more conservative	19	31	36	31	37	38	30	12
No opinion	6	23	21	23	20	18	27	47
NORC 230, Nov.'44								
(N)	(85)	(388)	(1493)	(382)	(1445)	(1147)	(298)	(61)
In politics, regard self as a liberal	62%	46%	40%	46%	40%	41%	36%	54%
Conservative	21	27	36	27	36	37	34	18
Neither	1	1	1	1	1	1	1	0
Don't know	16	26	23	26	23	21	29	28
NORC S-089, May '48[a]								
(N)	(207)	(886)	(1796)	(870)	(1663)			(166)
In politics, call self a liberal	53%	21%	18%	20%	18%			30%
Conservative	17	19	20	20	21			12
Middle of the roader	21	36	43	36	44			28
Don't know	9	24	19	24	17			30
AIPO 454, 3-24-50								
(N)	(78)	(341)	(989)	(336)	(946)	(805)	(141)	(54)
Consider self a liberal	74%	29%	26%	29%	26%	26%	25%	32%
Conservative	5	17	31	17	32	33	25	17
Neither	5	19	13	19	13	12	15	11
No opinion, don't know	16	35	30	35	29	29	35	40
AIPO 527, 2-23-54								
(N)	(39)	(349)	(1062)	(342)	(977)	(626)	(351)	(98)
In general think of self as liberal	67%	34%	30%	34%	31%	32%	31%	26%
Conservative	18	32	36	32	38	38	37	17
Neither or don't know	15	34	34	34	31	30	32	57
AIPO 547, 5-10-55								
(N)	(48)	(372)	(1022)	(361)	(965)	(642)	(323)	(70)
Consider self more of a liberal in politics	79%	33%	33%	34%	33%	34%	31%	24%
Conservative	15	30	34	29	35	37	31	20
Neither or don't know	6	37	33	37	32	29	38	56

	ALL			WHITES ONLY		North	South	
AIPO 577, 1-15-57	Jews	Cath.	Prot.	Cath	Prot.	Prot.	Prot.	Negroes
(N)	(53)	(385)	(1025)	(368)	(893)	(599)	(294)	(156)
Consider self more of a liberal in politics	62%	26%	26%	27%	26%	30%	19%	26%
A conservative	15	25	28	26	29	29	28	19
In between	13	16	18	16	19	18	23	8
Don't know	10	33	28	31	26	23	29	47
AIPO 694, 6-23-64								
(weighted N) [b]	(83)	(850)	(2435)			(789)	(1498)	(327)
Would prefer liberal party (if only two in U.S., one for liberals, one for conservatives)	65%	43%	32%			42%	35%	56%
Prefer conservative party	25	27	38			29	38	9
Don't know	10	30	30			29	27	35
AIPO 702, 11-18-64								
(weighted N) [b]	(97)	(903)	(2423)			(1521)	(786)	(323)
Prefer liberal party	77%	45%	28%			45%	32%	46%
Prefer conservative party	13	27	41			28	39	17
Don't know	10	28	31			27	29	37
SRC 473, Sept.-Nov.'64								
(N)	(38)			(313)	(857)			(147)
Favorable feelings toward liberals	50%			28%	26%			27%
Neutral	42			51	51			43
Unfavorable feelings	5			19	22			10
No opinion	3			2	1			20
Favorable feelings toward conservatives	11			36	42			25
Neutral	48			46	45			37
Unfavorable feelings	38			16	12			16
No opinion	3			2	1			22
AIPO survey of March '70 [c]								
Classify self as liberal		34%	24%					
Conservative		39	48					
No opinion		27	28					

	Cath.	Prot.
AIPO survey of Oct.'70[d]		
Describe self as very		
conservative	8%	9%
Fairly conservative	28	34
Middle-of-the-road	38	36
Fairly liberal	18	14
Very liberal	5	3
No opinion	3	4

a Sample included only California, Illinois, and New York states.

b Weighted N's were approximately twice actual N's.

c *Gallup Opinion Index*, April 1970.

d *Gallup Opinion Index*, Nov. 1970.

Table 8-2.   Liberalism-conservatism vs. international attitudes (whites only)

	Like to see Roosevelt Administration continue along present lines or become more liberal		Prefer that it become more conservative	
	Cath.	Prot.	Cath.	Prot.
AIPO 133, 9-23-38				
(N)	(242)	(706)	(163)	(608)
U.S. failure to join League partly				
responsible for European troubles	16%	20%	14%	17%
Not at all responsible	62	60	66	64
No opinion	22	20	20	19
England and France mistaken to accept				
Germany's demands on Czechoslovakia	52	53	49	51
Not a mistake	26	27	31	31
No opinion	22	20	20	18
Would like F.D.R. to openly criticize				
Hitler and Mussolini	29	31	26	29
Would not	64	62	68	67
No opinion	7	8	6	7
Would join movement to stop buying				
German goods	54	51	50	47
Would not	35	40	41	44
No opinion	11	9	9	9

	Consider self a liberal		Neither and in between		A conservative	
	Cath.	Prot.	Cath.	Prot.	Cath.	Prot.
AIPO 454, 3-24-50						
(N)	(98)	(244)	(63)	(121)	(57)	(299)
U.S. gov't spending on						
ERP should be increased	11%	18%	10%	9%	7%	8%
Decreased	47	47	46	46	61	55
Kept same	33	31	35	38	28	32
No opinion	9	4	9	7	4	5
Good idea for Pres. Truman to						
lead in arranging meeting						
with Stalin and other chiefs						
of state to try to settle						
cold war	44	38	45	42	46	43
Fair idea	10	10	8	8	9	6
Poor idea	43	46	44	44	44	47
No opinion	3	6	3	6	1	4

AIPO 577, 1-15-57	Consider self a liberal		Neither and in between		A conservative	
	Cath.	Prot.	Cath.	Prot.	Cath.	Prot.
(N)	(98)	(235)	(60)	(173)	(94)	(258)
Approve sending economic help to friendly Middle Eastern countries	79%	75%	72%	73%	81%	70%
Disapprove	17	18	22	18	15	21
Neither	3	3	3	3	0	2
No opinion	1	4	3	6	4	7
Approve sending war materials to help build up their armies	60	55	55	54	55	52
Disapprove	37	36	33	31	44	37
Neither	2	3	7	5	0	3
No opinion	1	6	4	10	1	8
Chances of U.N. keeping peace in world are good	41	38	38	36	36	38
Fair	30	42	42	41	41	36
Poor	26	15	15	18	18	23
No opinion	3	5	5	5	5	3

	Prefer that Pres. Kennedy should					
	Go more to left, following views of labor and other liberal groups		Follow policies halfway between two		Go more to right, following views of business nad conservative groups	
	Cath.	Prot.	Cath.	Prot.	Cath.	Prot.
AIPO 647, 6-21-61 (weighted N)[a]	(137)	(385)	(347)	(268)	(115)	(947)
Communism would be in greater position of world power if Congress had not appropriated $3.4 billion a year for aid abroad	69%	57%	72%	69%	65%	54%
Would not or no difference	19	25	19	20	24	32
No opinion	12	18	9	11	11	15

	Reactions to conservatives					
	Favorable		Neutral		Unfavorable	
	Cath.	Prot.	Cath.	Prot.	Cath.	Prot.
SRC 473, Sept.-Nov.'64						
(N)	(112)	(360)	(143)	(307)	(49)[b]	(100)
Give economic aid if need help	60%	48%	59%	50%	56%	58%
Depends	25	23	14	17	20	20
Each country should make own way as best it can	8	23	19	19	16	14
No opinion	7	6	8	14	8	8
Favor discussions with communist leaders to settle differences	68	72	81	71	67	79
Depends	5	7	1	2	8	3
Refuse to have anything to do with them	14	13	6	8	19	7
No opinion	13	8	12	19	6	11
Trade nonmilitary goods with communist countries	33	25	27	22	39	30
Depends	5	7	6	3	8	6
Forbid trade	42	49	46	43	39	51
No opinion	20	19	21	32	14	13
Knew Mainland China communist and not in U.N.	80	84	72	64	78	71
Admit China to U.N.	15	13	18	13	25	17
Do not admit, but stay in if admitted	35	44	31	31	39	32
Do not admit, pull out if admitted	10	11	4	5	2	10
Do not admit; don't know if U.S. should pull out if admitted	7	7	4	5	-	2
Do not know if China should be admitted	13	9	15	10	12	10
Did not know China communist and not in U.N.	20	16	28	36	22	29

	Reactions to liberals					
SRC 473, Sept.-Nov.'64						
(N)	(86)	(225)	(161)	(433)	(59)[b]	(189)
Give economic aid if need help	64%	60%	58%	47%	53%	45%
Depends	20	17	18	18	24	28
Each country should make own way as best it can	7	17	16	21	22	22
No opinion	9	6	8	14	2	5

	Reactions to liberals					
	Favorable		Neutral		Unfavorable	
Favor discussions with communist	Cath.	Prot.	Cath.	Prot.	Cath.	Prot.
leaders to settle differences	70	78	81	71	61	68
Depends	7	4	1	2	5	9
Refuse to have anything to						
do with them	12	8	6	9	24	14
No opinion	11	10	12	18	10	9
Trade nonmilitary goods with						
communist countries	35	30	30	24	27	17
Depends	8	7	6	4	2	6
Forbid trade	42	41	39	43	58	62
No opinion	15	22	25	29	13	15
Knew Mainland China communist						
and not in U.N.	79	79	73	65	80	86
Admit China to U.N.	26	17	15	12	15	11
Do not admit, but stay in if						
admitted	33	43	35	31	32	42
Do not admit, pull out if						
admitted	3	8	4	5	14	15
Do not admit, don't know if						
U.S. should pull out if						
admitted	1	2	5	6	9	9
Do not know if China should be						
admitted	16	9	14	11	10	9
Did not know China communist						
and not in U.N.	21	21	27	35	20	14

a Actual N's were approximately one-half these weighted N's.

b Owing to the small numbers in these two Catholic groups, comparisons of
  their replies with those of other groups appear rather erratic and
  should be interpreted with caution.

Table 8-3.   Domestic economics, welfare, and related issues

	All			Whites only				
	Jews	Cath.	Prot.	Cath.	Prot.	North Prot.	South Prot.	Negroes
AIPO 123, 5-20-38								
(N)	(52)	(521)	(1634)	(526)	(1584)	(1318)	(266)	(63)
Gov't should provide medical care for those unable to pay for it	88%	82%	76%	81%	75%	74%	78%	89%
Should not	8	14	20	15	21	22	17	6
No opinion	4	4	4	4	4	4	5	5
Willing to pay higher taxes for this purpose	64	49	50	48	49	47	55	56
AIPO 145, 1-20-39								
(N)	(72)			(590)	(1601)	(1319)	(282)	(32)
Extend old age pensions and unemployment insurance to household help, bank workers, sailors, farmhands, others now not covered	85%			78%	71%	71%	72%	69%
Do not	11			13	20	20	19	16
No opinion	4			9	9	9	9	15
Federal gov't should increase spending on relief	25			23	12	12	12	19
Should decrease it	23			30	46	46	44	34
Should keep same	46			42	36	35	39	38
No opinion	6			5	6	7	15	9
Federal gov't should increase spending on old age pensions	38			51	41	42	33	47
Should decrease it	8			5	8	9	6	5
Keep same	46			34	41	39	47	43
No opinion	8			10	10	10	14	5
Federal gov't is spending too much in general	28			40	60	62	51	52
Too little	8			10	5	5	4	7
Right amount	42			40	26	23	39	31
No opinion	22			10	9	10	6	10

		All		Whites only				Negroes
AIPO 445, 7-21-49	Jews	Cath.	Prot.	Cath.	Prot.			
(N)	(91)	(532)	(1875)	(516)	(1745)			(167)
Agree with Pres. Truman that federal gov't should borrow more money to increase spending on public works and like to avoid depression	52%	48%	34%	48%	31%			56%
Disagree--should balance budget	33	33	49	34	53			20
No opinion	15	19	17	18	16			24
AIPO 454, 3-24-50								
(N)	(78)	(341)	(991)	(335)	(909)	(870)	(139)	(89)
Federal spending on public works should be increased	65%	60%	49%	60%	48%	50%	41%	47%
Decreased	5	10	16	11	17	15	21	16
Keep same	22	23	29	23	29	29	26	29
No opinion	8	7	6	6	6	6	12	8
Spending on federal housing should be increased	83	60	38	60	36	38	35	61
Decreased	6	16	28	16	29	29	25	18
Kept same	7	19	23	19	24	24	21	14
No opinion	4	5	11	5	11	9	19	7
Federal spending on social welfare, health, social security should be increased	68	52	36	52	35	36	35	44
Decreased	8	11	19	12	19	18	24	18
Kept same	20	33	39	32	40	41	33	35
No opinion	4	4	6	4	6	5	8	3
Federal farm subsidies should be increased	13	20	15	21	15	12	29	23
Decreased	51	48	54	47	55	58	36	42
Kept same	23	21	22	21	21	21	25	25
No opinion	13	11	9	11	9	9	10	11
Federal gov't should provide greater security for masses-- increase old age pensions and unemployment insurance, provide health insurance, etc.	42	38	23	38	22	21	25	45

		All			Whites only			
							North	South	
	Jews	Cath.	Prot.	Cath.	Prot.	Prot.	Prot.	Negroes

Rather should provide greater individual opportunities by encouraging business opportunities, reducing federal spending, letting people stand on own feet

	Jews	Cath.	Prot.	Cath.	Prot.	North Prot.	South Prot.	Negroes
on own feet	50	57	71	57	72	73	69	47
Neither and no opinion	8	5	6	5	6	6	6	8

AIPO 639, 12-6-60[a]

	Jews	Cath.	Prot.	Cath.	Prot.	North Prot.	South Prot.	Negroes
(weighted N)[a]	(74)	(718)	(1953)	(692)	(1621)	(1118)	(503)	(371)

New (Kennedy) administration and new Congress should

	Jews	Cath.	Prot.	Cath.	Prot.	North Prot.	South Prot.	Negroes
Institute stricter control of corporations	26%	42%	39%	43%	42%	43%	37%	25%
Raise the minimum wage	55	48	45	48	40	42	38	65
Institute Medicare	64	60	46	61	44	45	44	50
Channel more federal aid to education	57	44	35	43	32	34	30	54
Help farmers more	35	29	39	30	35	31	48	54
Expand federal housing and slum clearance	59	38	36	38	32	32	33	56
Keep big companies from getting bigger	42	24	24	24	24	26	22	23
Spend more to reduce unemployment	36	34	26	35	24	23	26	43
Hold down prices and inflation	62	66	60	67	62	61	64	53
Institute stricter controls of labor unions	26	43	40	43	42	43	35	29
Cut federal spending	14	39	36	38	37	37	36	33
Reduce taxes on people like myself	42	48	47	48	46	42	51	62

SRC 473, Sept.-Nov.'64

	Jews	Cath.	Prot.	Cath.	Prot.	North Prot.	South Prot.	Negroes
(N)				(313)	(857)			
Favor passage of Medicare				54%	40%			
Depends				6	7			
Opposed				23	36			
No opinion				17	17			
Federal gov't should see that all have jobs and good living standards				29	24			
Depends				11	12			
Gov't should let each person get ahead on own				45	49			
No opinion				15	15			

	All			Whites only		North	South	Negroes
	Jews	Cath.	Prot.	Cath.	Prot.	Prot.	Prot.	
Favor expanded federal aid to education				34	24			
Depends				7	4			
Opposed				42	54			
No opinion				17	18			
Federal gov't too powerful				24	37			
Depends				3	3			
Not too powerful				41	30			
No opinion				32	30			
Favorable feelings toward labor unions				53	43			
Neutral				23	28			
Unfavorable				21	27			
No opinion				3	2			

AIPO 702, 11-18-64

	All			Whites only		North	South	Negroes
(weighted N)[a]	(97)	(903)	(2423)	(882)	(2121)			(323)
Lack of individual effort more often to blame for person's poverty	19%	30%	31%	31%	36%			8%
Circumstances beyond his control more often to blame	37	34	29	34	27			39
Both	43	31	34	31	32			42
No opinion	1	5	6	4	5			11

AIPO 704, Jan. '65

	Jews	Cath.	Prot.	Cath.	Prot.			
Favor compulsory medical care for elderly		72%	59%					
Opposed		22	31					
No opinion		6	10					

POS 655, 2-15-65

	All			Whites only		North	South	Negroes
	Jews	Cath.	Prot.	Cath.	Prot.	Prot.	Prot.	
(N)	(46)	(359)	(1152)	(352)	(987)	(626)	(361)	(182)
Federal gov't does too much for people in U.S.	18%	21%	27%	22%	32%	32%	33%	2%
Not enough	42	34	32	32	28	30	25	56
About right	35	37	32	38	32	30	34	33
No opinion	5	8	9	8	8	8	8	9
Extremely well satisfied with opportunity for individual to get ahead in U.S.	36	37	27	38	30	27	35	11
Considerably satisfied	33	34	39	35	40	42	36	31
Somewhat satisfied	30	21	22	20	20	21	18	32
Not at all satisfied	1	7	11	6	9	9	10	22
No opinion	0	1	1	1	1	1	1	4

		All			Whites only			Negroes
						North	South	
	Jews	Cath.	Prot.	Cath.	Prot.	Prot.	Prot.	
Big business is biggest								
threat to this country	26	21	15	20	14	16	10	24
Big labor is	43	30	27	33	29	32	23	19
Big gov't is	9	31	39	30	41	35	53	22
No opinion	22	18	19	17	16	17	14	35
AIPO 716, 8-25-65								
(weighted N)[a]	(133)	(773)	(2496)	(701)	(2101)	(1332)	(769)	(513)
Increase minimum wage								
above present								
$1.25 per hour	74%	65%	50%	63%	47%	47%	47%	75%
Decrease the minimum	3	(0.1)	2	(0.2)	2	1	2	0
Keep as is	19	31	43	33	47	48	46	18
No opinion	4	4	5	4	4	4	5	7
AIPO 717, 9-14-65								
(weighted N)[a]	(114)	(914)	(2360)	(890)	(2091)	(1372)	(719)	(319)
A person should be								
required to join a								
union if he works								
in a unionized								
factory or business	51%	50%	40%	50%	38%	42%	29%	57%
Should not	42	40	51	41	53	50	59	33
No opinion	7	10	9	9	9	8	12	10
Gov't should guarantee								
every family a mini-								
mum annual income	37	26	25	25	20			50
Opposed	44	51	59	52	65			28
No opinion	19	23	16	23	15			22
AIPO 723, 12-29-65								
(weighted N)[a]	(148)	(959)	(2284)	(937)	(2033)	(1332)	(701)	(303)
Laws regulating labor								
are not strict								
enough	47%	38%	40%	38%	44%	44%	44%	27%
Too strict	6	11	10	13	11	11	10	4
About right	39	29	23	29	23	26	17	29
No opinion	8	22	27	20	22	19	29	40
Laws regulating busi-								
ness are not strict								
enough	13	23	19	25	20	21	17	13
Too strict	17	17	22	17	25	24	25	5
About right	47	35	30	34	28	28	30	41
No opinion	23	25	29	24	27	27	28	41
Favor a law making all								
strikes illegal	15	22	30	23	32	30	36	23
Opposed	81	67	56	65	57	60	49	47
No opinion	4	11	14	12	11	10	15	30

	All			Whites only				Negroes
	Jews	Cath.	Prot.	Cath.	Prot.	North Prot.	South Prot.	
Labor unions which cover whole industries are monopolies and should come under antitrust laws	55	40	43	41	47	47	45	22
Should not come under antitrust laws	38	30	24	31	26	28	22	16
No opinion	7	30	33	28	27	25	33	62
A person should be required to join a union if he works in a unionized factory or business	55	45	40	45	37	43	24	60
Should not	33	45	51	45	54	50	64	17
No opinion	12	10	9	10	9	7	12	23
Despite Vietnam war, gov't should continue aid to education, medical care, cleaning up water pollution, war against poverty, Great Society programs generally in U.S.	82	62	55	62	52	53	51	64
Cut them back	7	24	27	25	29	29	30	18
No opinion	11	14	18	13	19	18	19	18
Lack of individual effort more often to blame if a person is poor	31	40	42					
Circumstances beyond his control	41	26	24					
Combination of both	28	29	24					
No opinion	0	5	10					
AIPO 726, 3-22-66 (weighted N)[a]	(85)	(878)	(2451)	(856)	(2162)	(1430)	(732)	(383)
Favorable opinion of antipoverty program nationwide	57%	49%	38%	50%	37%	38%	34%	41%
Unfavorable opinion	28	20	28	20	31	30	34	11
No opinion	15	31	34	30	32	32	32	48
AIPO survey of March '67[b] Every person employed in a unionized factory or business should be required to join a union	50%	46%	39%					65%
Should not	47	49	55					23
No opinion	3	5	6					12

	All Cath.	Prot.
AIPO survey of Oct.'67[c]		
In general approve of		
labor unions	74%	63%
Disapprove	19	25
No opinion	7	12
AIPO survey of Nov.'67[d]		
Favor guaranteed		
annual wage, even		
when laid off, for		
auto workers	56%	47%
Disapprove	40	41
No opinion	4	12
Favor same for other		
industries too	56	45
Oppose	38	42
No opinion	6	13

	All Catholics	All Protestants
AIPO survey of Jan.'68[e]		
Congress should pass 10% income tax		
surcharge requested by President	14%	14%
Should reject it	79	79
No opinion	7	7
Approve idea of compulsory arbitra-		
tion after strikes have lasted		
more than 21 days	71	69
Oppose	20	22
No opinion	9	9
AIPO survey of June '68[f]		
If family of four earns less than		
$3200/year, favor gov't making		
up difference	39%	33%
Oppose	53	61
No opinion	8	6
AIPO survey of Jan.'69[g]		
If family earns less than $3200/year,		
favor gov't making up difference	39%	29%
Oppose	54	66
No opinion	7	5
As alternative, favor guarantee of		
enough work to provide $3200 annual		
wage per family	81	78
Oppose	13	17
No opinion	6	5

AIPO survey of May '69[h]	All Catholics	All Protestants
Favor giving food stamps to families earning less than $20 a week	73%	66%
Oppose	22	26
No opinion	5	8
Favor giving food stamps at much reduced rate to families earning $20-60 a week	68	56
Oppose	25	34
No opinion	7	10
AIPO survey of Oct.'70[i]		
New Congress should improve lot of poor and get at causes of social problems	41	36
Give more support to policy and get tougher with lawbreakers	56	62
No opinion	3	2

a Weighted N's were approximately twice the actual number of respondents.

b *Gallup Opinion Index,* April 1967.

c *Gallup Opinion Index,* Nov. 1967.

d *Gallup Opinion Index,* Dec. 1967.

e *Gallup Opinion Index,* Feb. 1968.

f *Gallup Opinion Index,* July 1968.

g *Gallup Opinion Index,* Jan. 1969.

h *Gallup Opinion Index,* May 1969.

i *Gallup Opinion Index,* Nov. 1970.

Table 8-4. Domestic economics and welfare vs. foreign policy

Roper survey of Mar.'40

New administration should:	Go further in New Deal	Keep as is	Modify it	Repeal most of it	Work toward gov't ownership of utilities	Should not	Turn TVA to private operation	not	Regulate unions	Should not	Balance budget	Should not
(N)	(562)	(791)	(1962)	(1029)	(1422)	(2627)	(1305)	(1889)	(3040)	(1076)	(3962)	(466)
U.S. should lend Finland money for anything, including arms	37%	30%	43%	41%	35%	44%	46%	40%	40%	38%	39%	45%
Only for food, medicine, no arms	30	32	31	27	31	29	27	31	30	29	31	25
Lend her nothing under any circumstances	24	26	19	24	26	20	21	22	22	24	22	22
No opinion	9	12	7	8	8	7	6	7	8	9	8	8
Next administration should Keep U.S. out of war unless U.S. is attacked, no matter what happens abroad should					88	84	85	86	87	87	87	81
should not					9	12	12	11	10	10	9	16
No opinion					3	4	3	3	3	3	4	3
Lower tariffs should					30	19	23	26	23	22	22	21
Should not					33	46	48	42	38	47	40	41
No opinion					37	35	29	32	39	31	38	38

	Work toward gov't owner-ship of utilities	Should not	Turn TVA to private operation	Should not	Regulate unions	Should not	Balance budget	Should not
Raise tariffs	20	27	31	22	21	28	24	20
Should not	43	37	38	45	38	39	37	41
No opinion	37	36	31	33	41	33	39	39
Continue making reciprocal trade agreements	63	64	65	63	62	61	60	64
Should not	12	15	18	12	13	16	14	13
No opinion	25	21	17	20	25	23	26	23

	Proposed income tax of $25,000 on $50,000 a year is:			Henry Ford's refusal to recognize unions in his plants:		Employers should have right to refuse jobs to union members	
	Too much	Right amount	Not enough	Approve	Disapprove	Should	Should not
AIPO 232, 3-7-41							
(N)	(1102)	(1438)	(244)	(1759)	(871)	(1398)	(1339)
Approve Lend-Lease bill	58%	62%	66%	61%	68%	62%	61%
Qualified approve	6	4	3	5	3	5	4
Disapprove	26	22	20	23	22	24	23
No opinion	10	12	11	11	12	9	12
Approve leasing 40 more destroyers to Britain	49	54	55	52	52	52	52
Qualified approve	14	13	13	14	12	14	13
Disapprove	29	26	23	26	27	26	28
No opinion	8	7	9	8	9	8	7

	Amount of own income tax:			U.S. gov't should own electric companies	Private business should	Favor law forbidding strikes in public service industries	Oppose such law
	Too high	Too low	About right				
AIPO 392, 3-12-47							
(N)	(1212)	(17)	(902)	(693)	(1669)	(1659)	(868)
Approve of U.S. lending Greece $250 million	49%	41%	54%	48%	52%	49%	49%
Disapprove	29	29	24	31	27	27	31
No opinion	22	30	22	21	21	24	20

	U.S. government should own electric utilities	Should not
AIPO 399K,6-18-47		
(N)	(402)	(904)
U.S. should increase amounts of food and supplies sent to help Europe get back on feet	24%	11%
Should send less	28	35
About same amount	38	44
No opinion	10	10
AIPO 399T,6-18-47		
(N)	(317)	(915)
Continue to give financial aid to Europe	49%	50%
Qualified approval	3	3
Have given them enough already	42	41
No opinion	6	6

AIPO 404, 9-10-47

	Favor low cost subsidized housing	Oppose	Favor higher taxes if necessary for federal aid to education	Oppose
(N)	(1306)	(103)	(1086)	(1659)
Heard or read of Marshall Plan	53%	53%	62%	52%
Approve of it	28	27	36	26
Qualified approve	1	0	2	2
Disapprove	7	14	8	8
No opinion	17	12	16	16
Never heard of Marshall Plan	47	47	38	48
Approve $5 billion a year for 4 years for Marshall Plan	32	22	41	27
Qualified approve	9	4	10	9
Oppose	47	65	39	54
No opinion	12	9	10	10

AIPO 439, 3-17-49

	Taft-Hartley unfair to labor	Not unfair	Liberalize Taft-Hartley	Keep as is	Own income tax too high	Too low	About right
(N)	(349)	(475)	(738)	(980)	(768)	(18)	(935)
Send more economic aid to Japan	34%	37%	33%	35%	30%	44%	36%
Do not	56	53	58	55	58	50	53
No opinion	10	10	9	10	12	6	11

	Taft-Hartley unfair	Not unfair	Liberalize Taft-Hartley	Keep as is	Own income tax too high	Too low	About right
Heard or read of Marshall Plan	85	89	86	88	85	89	86
Could describe it correctly	2	5	3	5	4	6	3
Congress should continue							
Marshall Plan	53	61	54	59	51	61	58
Stop it	20	17	19	17	20	11	14
No opinion	12	11	13	12	14	17	14
Never heard of it	15	11	14	12	15	11	14
Heard of North Atlantic Security Pact	62	68	61	70	65	67	63
Could describe it correctly	27	33	25	34	28	28	29
Favor NATO Pact	80	77	81	80	77	83	80
Against it	14	15	13	14	13	17	13
No opinion	6	8	6	6	10	0	7
Favor military aid to W. Europe	70	71	74	77	72	78	76
Against	22	18	19	15	16	11	16
No opinion	8	11	7	8	12	11	8

	Too high profits more important cause of high prices	Too high wages more important	Both equally	Approve increasing minimum wage to 75¢ an hour	Keep it at 40¢ an hour	Expand spending in public works to alleviate unemployment	Do not
AIPO 446, 8-12-49							
(N)	(918)	(794)	(1047)	(1860)	(1018)	(1571)	(1305)
Heard or read of England's money problems	56%	67%	68%	60%	71%	56%	73%
Think Eng. will have to have more U.S. money than Congress has provided under ERP	29	36	35	32	35	30	37
Will not need more	18	22	21	19	24	16	26
No opinion	9	9	12	9	12	10	9
Favor new loan of $1-2 billion to Britain	14	14	14	14	13	13	15
Opposed	38	48	47	41	52	38	53
No opinion	4	5	7	5	6	5	5
Never heard of England's financial difficulties	44	33	32	40	29	44	27
Makes much difference whether Britain continues a strong power	58	72	67	63	70	62	69
Little difference	22	17	19	20	19	20	18
None	10	5	8	8	5	8	7
No opinion	10	6	6	9	6	10	6

	(N)	U.S. spending on Marshall Plan should be:			
		Increased	Same	Decreased	No opinion
AIPO 454, 3-24-50					
Should repeal Taft-Hartley Law	(403)	14%	35%	43%	8%
Keep as is	(654)	11	34	49	6
Expand security of masses with larger old-age benefits, expanded unemployment compensation, health insurance, etc.	(401)	13	34	42	11
Do not, but encourage business enterprises, cut federal spending and taxes, let people stand on own feet instead	(965)	11	33	49	7
Increase farm subsidies	(235)	16	27	47	10
Keep as are	(312)	12	44	36	8
Decrease them	(764)	11	32	53	4
Increase social welfare, health, social security	(606)	15	31	44	10
Keep as are	(535)	10	39	43	8
Decrease them	(238)	10	24	63	3
Increase spending on federal housing	(670)	15	34	42	9
Keep as is	(305)	9	45	40	6
Decrease it	(349)	9	24	63	4
Increase federal spending on public works	(764)	15	33	45	7
Keep at current level	(389)	7	43	43	7
Decrease it	(207)	11	23	62	4

In current steel strike, sympathize in general with:

AIPO 490, 4-11-52	United Steelworkers	Steel companies	Neither
(N)	(859)	(546)	(33)
U.S. should continue giving money and arms to W. Europe	58%	60%	61%
$8 billion from U.S. for W. Europe next year is			
Too much	24	34	25
Too little	1	2	0
About right	20	14	12
No opinion	13	10	24
Should stop all such aid	35	37	33
No opinion	7	3	6

AIPO 541, 12-29-54	U.S. should start big public works program to relieve unemployment	Not necessary	Federal taxes should not take more than 35% of individual's income	Oppose such a limit
(N)	(623)	(663)	(761)	(528)
U.S. should withdraw aid to nations which refuse to cooperate with us	75%	75%	79%	71%
Should continue aid	17	19	15	22
No opinion	8	6	6	7

SRC 417, Sept.-Nov.'56

	(N)	U.S. should send aid to poor countries				U.S. should give help to foreign countries even if not as much against communism as we			
		Agree	Not sure	Disagree	No opinion	Agree	Not sure	Disagree	No opinion
U.S. gov't ought to cut taxes even if it means putting off important things that need to be done									
Agree	(451)	26%	10%	52%	12%	23%	9%	59%	9%
Disagree	(787)	31	11	43	15	33	11	46	10
U.S. gov't ought to see that everybody who wants to work can find a job									
Agree	(995)	61	7	27	5	53	8	34	5
Disagree	(471)	55	6	31	8	60	7	27	6
U.S. gov't should provide money cities and towns need to help build schools									
Agree	(484)	74	7	15	4	73	9	15	3
Disagree	(259)	67	8	18	7	67	7	20	6
U.S. gov't should help people get doctors and hospital care at low cost									
Agree	(949)	58	8	27	7	52	9	33	6
Disagree	(458)	52	8	29	11	56	7	28	9
U.S. gov't should see to it big business doesn't have much to say about how gov't is run									
Agree	(890)	56	7	18	19	60	6	18	16
Disagree	(284)	59	4	15	22	62	5	16	17

		U.S. should send aid to poor countries				U.S. should give help to countries even if not as much against Communists			
	(N)	Agree	Not sure	Disagree	No opinion	Agree	Not sure	Disagree	No opinion
U.S. gov't should see to it unions don't have much to say about how gov't is run									
Agree	(874)	52	6	23	19	58	7	23	12
Disagree	(343)	56	5	20	19	60	6	20	14
Gov't should leave things like electric power and housing for private businessmen to handle									
Agree	(731)	45	7	26	22	47	9	28	16
Disagree	(398)	45	5	27	23	47	7	28	18

AIPO 577, 1-15-57	Approve of labor unions		Approve federal aid to build schools		Approve raising minimum wage to $1.25	
	Approve	Disapprove	Approve	Disapprove	Approve	Disapprove
(N)	(1118)	(211)	(1138)	(282)	(980)	(417)
Approve sending economic aid to friendly Middle Eastern gov'ts	72%	67%	73%	64%	69%	74%
Qualified approve	2	2	2	2	3	2
Disapprove	17	23	16	26	18	18
No opinion	9	8	9	8	10	6
Approve sending them military aid	53	52	54	50	53	50
Qualified approve	3	2	3	4	3	3
Disapprove	34	36	33	40	33	37
No opinion	10	10	10	6	11	10

Roper 939, April '57

	Eisenhower request for 1958 budget should be:			Favor federal aid to education, both buildings and salaries	For buildings only	Leave both to local government
	Passed as is	Cut a little	Cut a good deal			
(N)	(410)	(321)	(580)	(654)	(444)	(245)
Foreign economic aid should						
be increased	7%	5%	2%	6%	2%	2%
Kept at current level	38	25	15	23	27	25
Cut a little	29	42	29	30	36	29
Cut drastically	16	18	44	28	25	36
Stopped	2	3	5	3	2	3
No opinion	8	7	5	10	8	5
Foreign military aid should						
be increased	9	5	4	6	6	5
Kept at current level	58	47	42	49	50	43
Cut a little	16	26	23	18	24	21
Cut drastically	5	12	22	12	11	21
Stopped	2	2	3	4	1	2
No opinion	10	8	6	11	8	0

AIPO 593, 12-31-57

	Higher prices caused primarily by:			Willing to have income taxes raised to:			
	Labor's demands for higher wages	Employers' demands for higher profits	Both equally	Build schools and increase teachers' salaries	Not willing	Give more aid to farmers	Not willing
(N)	(405)	(394)	(592)	(991)	(450)	(415)	(942)
Willing to have income taxes raised to meet Soviet economic competition and Soviet promises for economic aid to Asia & Africa	34%	33%	31%	42%	16%	47%	28%
Not willing	56	55	55	46	78	38	65
No opinion	10	12	14	12	6	15	7

Roper 963 Jan. '58

	Cut back costs of domestic programs	Do not
(N)	(377)	(891)
Expand aid and loans to less-developed countries in Asia and Africa	17%	19%
Keep at current level	41	45
Cut back	25	20
No opinion	17	16

AIPO 617, 8-18-59	In general, approve of unions	Disapprove	Side with unions in steel strike	Neutral	Side with steel companies
(N)	(1070)	(208)	(406)	(364)	(466)
Good idea for U.S. to fit out hospital ships, food ships, training-school ships, etc., and send them abroad where needed	74%	75%	74%	71%	73%
Also favor Congress appropriating funds therefor	58	57	57	57	58
Oppose use of federal funds	9	12	9	8	9
No opinion	7	6	7	6	6
Poor idea	17	19	16	17	20
No opinion	9	6	10	12	7

New President and Congress should:

AIPO 639, 12-6-60 (weighted N)[a]

	Control big corporations more strictly (656)	Raise minimum wage (1308)	Institute Medi-care for aged (1416)	Increase aid to education (1077)	Control unions more strictly (1134)	Balance budget by cutting spending (1030)	Help farmers more (1028)	Reduce taxes for people like me (1338)	Expand federal housing, slum clearance (1069)	Keep big companies from getting bigger (696)	Spend more to re-duce unemployment (811)	Hold down prices and inflation (1746)
Believe possible to reach peaceful settlement of differences with USSR	54%	54%	55%	56%	49%	51%	52%	48%	56%	50%	57%	52%
Impossible	25	25	25	25	34	29	26	28	24	27	25	28
No opinion	21	21	20	19	17	20	22	24	20	23	18	20

AIPO 640, 1-10-61 (weighted N)[a]

	In general, approve of unions (1834)	Disapprove (486)
Favor proposed Peace Corps	75%	66%
Oppose	15	27
No opinion	10	7

AIPO 641, 2-8-61 (weighted N)[a]	Feel own income tax:			Favor raising minimum wage from $1.00 an hour	
	Too high	About right	Too low		Opposed
	(1307)	(1306)	(31)	(2183)	(512)
Favor sending food to Communist China if requests it	50%	56%	52%	54%	53%
Opposed	41	35	35	37	38
No opinion	9	9	13	9	9

AIPO 647, 6-21-61 (weighted N)[a]	Big businessmen have more power in U.S. than should	Right amount	Less	Unions have more power in U.S. than should	Right amount	Less
	(1233)	(794)	(328)	(1580)	(487)	(352)
Communism would be in greater position of world power if Congress had not appropriated $3-4 billion a year for aid abroad	64%	64%	57%	62%	65%	64%
Would not or no difference	23	25	29	25	22	23
No opinion	13	11	14	13	13	13

AIPO 652, 11-15-61

	Federal money going into welfare programs is:		
(weighted N)[a]	Too much	About right	Not enough
	(616)	(973)	(753)
U.S. and the West are doing enough to help less-developed countries with financial and technical assistance	76%	71%	65%
Not doing enough	11	14	21
No opinion	13	15	14
U.S. interests have been helped by U.S. foreign-aid program during last five years	47	57	54
Have not	33	24	29
No opinion	20	19	17

AIPO 659, 11-15-61

	Higher prices caused mostly by demands for higher:		Favor Medicare under social security	Leave to private insurance	Prefer Kennedy administration to follow policies:		
(weighted N)[a]	Wages by labor	Profits by employers			to Right, advocated by Business	Middle	to Left, advocated by Unions
	(1353)	(1048)	(1543)	(1332)	(652)	(1650)	(590)
Send food to Communist China if requests it	50%	46%	50%	47%	46%	53%	46%
Do not	43	46	41	47	47	39	46
No opinion	7	8	9	6	7	8	8

AIPO 667, 1-9-63 (weighted N)ᵃ

	Approve of unions	Dis-approve	Strikes in communications, press, telephone, radio, TV should be:	
			Forbidden by law	Permitted, as they are
(weighted N)	(2942)	(971)	(1465)	(1672)
In general for foreign aid	62%	57%	58%	64%
Against it	28	36	34	28
No opinion	10	7	8	8

AIPO 682, 12-10-63ᵇ (weighted N)ᵃ

	Don't cut income taxes until budget balanced	Cut taxes only if expenditures kept as are and not increased	Cut taxes, without regard to expenditures	Favor present system of progressive income tax	Tax both rich and poor at same rate	Favor broad federal aid to education, including salaries	Against	Increase federal aid to depressed areas with long high unemployment	Kept at current level	Decrease	Favor Medicare for aged under Social Security	Disapprove	Approve of right to work laws	Disapprove
(weighted N)	(652)	(684)	(245)	(1254)	(305)	(931)	(661)	(441)	(888)	(177)	(853)	(729)	(1148)	(389)
Foreign aid should be kept at current level or increased	28%	35%	41%	34%	30%	43%	19%	35%	34%	21%	41%	25%	33%	33%
Reduce it	55	52	39	49	57	41	61	47	51	51	41	60	50	52
Terminate it	8	5	11	6	7	5	12	6	5	19	7	8	9	4
No opinion	9	8	9	11	6	11	8	12	10	9	11	7	8	11

SRC 473, Sept.-Nov. '64	Favorable impression of unions	Neutral	Unfavorable	Favor federal aid to education	Opposed	U.S. gov't getting too powerful	Not too powerful	Favor Medicare	Opposed	U.S. gov't should see that all have jobs and fair living standards	Let individual get ahead on own
(N)	(759)	(422)	(390)	(490)	(725)	(473)	(562)	(778)	(438)	(487)	(677)
Give aid to countries if need help	55%	48%	50%	57%	52%	48%	62%	56%	51%	58%	53%
Depends, not sure	17	15	23	14	21	27	15	14	25	9	21
Each country should make own way	16	22	19	17	20	21	16	18	19	21	19
No opinion	11	15	8	22	7	4	7	12	5	12	7
Favor discussions with communist leaders to settle differences	76	72	68	80	71	68	81	76	74	78	74
Depends	3	2	8	3	6	9	3	2	6	2	5
Refuse to have anything to do with them	9	7	14	7	13	14	9	9	12	7	11
No opinion	12	19	10	10	10	9	7	13	8	13	10
Trade nonmilitary goods with communist countries	30	21	25	32	26	24	34	29	27	29	28
Depends	5	3	6	5	5	6	5	5	6	3	7
Forbid trade	42	47	52	43	50	56	41	44	52	42	48
No opinion	23	29	17	20	19	14	20	22	15	26	17

Knew Mainland China communist and not in U.N.	74	66	82	72	79	86	72	71	84	68	79
Admit to U.N.	15	11	16	19	13	14	19	15	16	17	14
Do not admit, but stay in if admitted	36	35	38	35	39	43	32	34	42	29	39
Do not admit, pull out if admitted	7	6	9	6	10	13	7	7	10	8	9
Do not admit, don't know if U.S. should stay in if admitted	4	5	8	3	7	8	3	3	6	3	7
Don't know if it should be admitted	12	9	11	9	10	8	11	12	10	11	10
Did not know China communist and not in U.N.	26	34	18	28	21	14	28	29	16	32	21

	Federal government does:			Biggest future threat to U.S. is:		
	Too much for people	Too little	About right	Big business	Big labor	Big gov't
POS 655, 2-15-65 (N)	(420)	(536)	(533)	(266)	(473)	(577)
1/200 of GNP for foreign aid is						
Too much	46%	37%	23%	34%	35%	41%
Too little	7	13	11	13	12	8
About right	35	30	42	33	35	37
No opinion	12	20	24	20	18	14

<u>a</u> Weighted N's were approximately twice actual N's.

<u>b</u> Included no self-identified Democrats.

Table 8-5. Domestic economics and welfare vs. foreign policy by religion (whites only)

| | Reactions to Labor Unions | | | | | | Medicare | | | |
| | Favor | | Neutral | | Unfavorable | | Favor | | Oppose | |
SRC 473, Sept.-Nov.'64	Cath.	Prot.	Cath.	Prot.	Cath.	Prot.	Cath.	Prot.	Cath.	Prot.
(N)	(166)	(374)	(73)	(238)	(67)	(234)	(168)	(354)	(72)	(302)
Give economic aid if need help	62%	53%	60%	46%	51%	51%	65%	51%	55%	52%
Depends	17	19	12	16	31	24	16	6	28	24
Each country should make own way as best it can	12	18	21	25	14	19	12	22	13	20
No opinion	9	10	7	13	4	6	7	11	4	4
Favor discussion with communist leaders to settle differences	77	76	75	71	66	68	76	76	77	72
Depends	2	3	1	2	9	8	4	2	3	7
Refuse to have anything to do with them	12	8	3	9	16	14	10	8	12	12
No opinion	9	13	21	18	9	10	10	14	8	9
Trade nonmilitary goods with communist countries	33	29	21	21	37	20	33	28	36	23
Depends	6	5	4	3	6	6	5	5	6	6
Forbid trade	42	42	44	48	46	54	43	44	49	53
No opinion	19	24	31	28	11	20	19	23	9	18
Knew Mainland China communist and not in U.N.	75	74	73	63	82	82	77	69	85	84
Admit China to U.N.	19	14	14	10	19	15	19	14	19	15
Do not admit, but stay in if admitted	32	37	37	34	36	39	32	34	38	44

	Reactions to labor unions						Medicare			
	Favor		Neutral		Unfavorable		Favor		Oppose	
	Cath.	Prot.	Cath.	Prot.	Cath.	Prot.	Cath.	Prot.	Cath.	Prot.
Do not admit, pull out if admitted	5	8	4	6	9	9	4	8	11	10
Do not admit, don't know if U.S. should stay in if admitted	5	4	5	5	3	10	4	3	4	7
Do not know if China should be admitted	14	11	12	8	15	9	18	10	13	8
Did not know China communist and not in U.N.	25	26	27	37	18	18	23	31	15	16

	Power of Federal Government				Federal Aid to Education				Gov't should see all have jobs and good living standards		Gov't should let each get ahead on own	
	Too powerful		Not too powerful		Favor		Oppose					
	Cath.	Prot.	Cath.	Prot.	Cath.	Prot.	Cath.	Prot.	Cath.	Prot.	Cath.	Prot.
(N)	(75)	(319)	(129)	(260)	(105)	(207)	(130)	(459)	(90)	(210)	(142)	(416)
Give economic aid if need help	49%	50%	68%	58%	54%	59%	69%	49%	66%	58%	57%	52%
Depends	29	26	18	17	21	13	17	22	11	9	25	21
Each country should make own way as best it can	19	21	9	19	17	17	9	23	1	24	13	21
No opinion	3	3	5	6	8	11	5	6	22	9	5	6
Favor discussions with communist leaders to settle differences	65	70	84	80	73	83	77	69	81	77	74	74
Depends	8	9	3	3	3	3	4	6	1	2	4	5

SRC 473, Sept.-Nov. '64

	Too powerful		Not too powerful		Favor		Oppose					
	Cath.	Prot.	Cath.	Prot.	Cath.	Prot.	Cath.	Prot.	Cath.	Prot.	Cath.	Prot.
Refuse to have anything to do with them	21	11	7	9	12	5	11	14	9	7	12	11
No opinion	6	10	6	8	12	9	8	11	9	14	10	10
Trade nonmilitary goods with communist countries	28	22	40	31	39	29	29	25	31	28	36	25
Depends	5	7	8	4	8	4	5	5	3	3	7	6
Forbid trade	56	56	39	42	34	47	48	50	40	43	44	50
No opinion	11	15	13	24	19	20	18	20	26	26	15	14
Knew Mainland China communist and not in U.N.	88	86	76	71	77	70	83	78	78	74	77	80
Admit China to U.N.	16	14	24	17	20	19	17	12	26	24	15	14
Do not admit, but stay in if admitted	37	46	30	33	34	35	39	39	30	28	33	41
Do not admit, pull out if admitted	15	12	4	8	6	6	8	10	4	10	6	9
Do not admit, don't know if U.S. should stay in if admitted	9	7	2	4	2	3	7	7	2	3	8	6
Do not know if China should be admitted	11	7	16	9	15	7	12	10	16	9	15	10
Did not know China communist and not in U.N.	12	14	24	29	23	30	17	22	22	26	23	20

POS 655, 2-17-65	U.S. gov't does too much for people		About right amount		Not enough		Biggest threat to country is Big business		Big labor		Big gov't	
	Cath.	Prot.	Cath.	Prot.	Cath.	Prot.	Cath.	Prot.	Cath.	Prot.	Cath.	Prot.
(N)	(77)	(317)	(135)	(311)	(112)	(280)	(72)	(134)	(115)	(285)	(106)	(409)
1/200 of U.S. GNP for foreign aid too much	46%	47%	24%	25%	38%	45%	33%	42%	37%	37%	39%	43%
Too little	10	5	12	9	17	11	14	10	24	10	12	7
About right or depends	38	35	46	44	28	30	38	33	57	36	37	37
No opinion	6	13	18	22	17	14	15	15	12	17	12	13
U.S. obligated to help poor nations	56	43	56	50	55	40	56	43	62	50	57	42
No obligation	23	23	23	18	23	38	23	29	21	22	22	29
Depends	21	33	19	29	22	19	21	26	17	27	20	28
No opinion	-	1	2	3	-	3	-	2	-	1	1	1
Extremely well satisfied with aid to poor nations	20	15	23	24	25	14	26	14	22	22	19	15
Considerably well satisfied	23	15	33	31	20	22	24	24	28	25	21	18
Somewhat satisfied	25	33	30	28	34	31	39	29	29	29	34	32
Not at all satisfied	32	37	14	17	26	30	19	23	21	24	31	35

Opportunity for individual to get ahead

	Extremely satisfied		Considerably satisfied		Somewhat satisfied		Not at all satisfied	
	Cath.	Prot.	Cath.	Prot.	Cath.	Prot.	Cath.	Prot.
POS 655, 2-17-65 (N)	(135)	(297)	(123)	(400)	(69)	(200)	(25)	(90)
1/200 of U.S. GNP for foreign aid too much	33%	33%	29%	37%	36%	40%	60%	56%
Too little	15	10	11	7	12	6	4	8
About right or depends	36	39	44	37	42	25	20	24
No opinion	16	18	16	19	10	19	16	12
U.S. obligated to help poor nations	57	51	55	47	61	37	36	26
No obligation	26	21	19	23	19	30	40	43
Depends	17	27	25	27	19	28	24	28
No opinion	-	1	1	3	1	5	-	3
Extremely well satisfied with aid to poor nations	34	28	16	11	14	15	16	18
Considerably well satisfied	21	24	34	28	25	19	20	8
Somewhat satisfied	24	28	33	34	35	36	20	29
Not at all satisfied	21	20	17	27	26	30	44	45

Table 8-6. Civil rights

	All			Whites only				
	Jews	Cath.	Prot.	Cath.	Prot.	North Prot.	South Prot.	Negroes
AIPO survey of 9-16-37								
(N)	(64)	(529)	(1435)	(527)	(1401)	(972)	(429)	(55)
Past membership in the KKK should bar one from becoming a Supreme Court judge	75%	69%	44%	69%	44%	48%	31%	64%
Should not	22	21	45	21	46	41	60	22
No opinion	3	10	11	10	10	11	9	14
AIPO 181, 1-10-40								
(N)	(41)	(537)	(1638)					
Congress should enact antilynching bill	77%	52%	44%					
Should not	21	43	52					
No opinion	2	5	4					
AIPO 407, 11-5-47								
(N)	(72)	(653)	(1781)					
Favor a federal FEPC law	58%	47%	37%					
Opposed	28	34	42					
No opinion	14	19	21					
AIPO 557, 12-6-55								
(N)	(63)	(386)	(1059)	(376)	(949)	(638)	(301)	(132)
Approve ICC ruling ending segregated transportation	67%	58%	54%	58%	50%	53%	38%	72%
Disapprove	28	34	38	33	43	39	55	19
No opinion	5	8	8	9	7	8	7	9
SRC 417, Sept.-Nov.'56								
(N)	(56)			(359)	(1149)	(801)	(348)	(147)
U.S. gov't should stay out of question whether whites and Negroes should go to same school	25%			35%	49%	40%	64%	23%
Depends, not sure	5			5	7	8	5	7
Disagree	61			43	35	42	24	53
No opinion	9			17	9	10	7	17
Gov't should see that Negroes get fair treatment in jobs and housing	66			63	56	57	52	93
Depends	13			5	7	6	9	2
Disagree	16			17	23	23	24	1
No opinion	5			15	14	14	15	4

| | All | | | Whites only | | | | Negroes |
	Jews	Cath.	Prot.	Cath.	Prot.	North Prot.	South Prot.	
AIPO 639, 2-6-60								
(weighted N)[a]	(74)	(718)	(1953)	(683)	(1347)	(835)	(512)	(371)
New President (Kennedy) and new Congress should do more to end racial segregation	66%	46%	43%	46%	38%	44%	23%	78%
AIPO 646, 5-26-61								
(weighted N)[a]	(110)	(817)	(2466)	(788)	(2284)	(1626)	(658)	(281)
Approve 1954 Supreme Court school desegregation decision	97%	77%	56%	78%	54%	70%	17%	69%
Disapprove	3	20	38	20	40	23	79	22
No opinion	0	3	6	2	6	7	4	9
Approve Supreme Court decision desegregating transportation	97	81	60	81	54	69	20	71
Disapprove	3	15	33	15	35	17	74	19
No opinion	0	4	7	4	11	14	6	10
Approve of "Freedom Riders"	62	17	14	17	11	13	2	39
Disapprove	31	42	47	42	53	48	66	7
No opinion	7	41	39	41	36	39	32	54
Pres. Kennedy right to send U.S. marshals to Alabama	95	78	66	78	65	74	49	73
Wrong	1	8	16	8	16	8	30	11
No opinion	4	14	18	14	19	18	21	16
"Sit ins," "freedom rides," other Negro demonstrations help chances of integration in South	63	28	25	28	21	24	16	58
Hurt chances	27	52	60	52	65	58	76	21
No opinion	10	20	15	20	14	18	·8	21
AIPO 674, 6-19-63								
(weighted N)[a]	(138)	(771)	(2411)	(720)	(1982)	(1340)	(642)	(421)
Kennedy administration pushing integration too fast	13%	29%	47%	29%	52%	40%	72%	5%
Not fast enough	38	13	13	13	8	11	4	37
About right	36	45	26	45	28	35	15	42
No opinion	13	13	14	13	12	14	9	16

	All			Whites only				Negroes
						North	South	
AIPO 676, 8-13-63	Jews	Cath.	Prot.	Cath.	Prot.	Prot.	Prot.	
(weighted N)[a]	(134)	(861)	(2466)	(822)	(2091)	(1395)	(696)	(464)
Congress should pass civil rights bill providing that Negroes be served in hotels,								
restaurants, etc.	86%	63%	49%	63%	43%	51%	20%	89%
Should not	6	27	44	27	50	42	72	6
No opinion	8	10	7	10	7	7	8	5
AIPO 679, 11-8-63								
(weighted N)[a]	(110)	(925)	(3073)	(879)	(2478)	(1801)	(677)	(651)
Kennedy administration pushing inegration								
too fast	11%	40%	48%	41%	58%	48%	71%	6%
Not fast enough	19	10	11	10	6	8	3	36
About right	64	40	31	40	27	34	17	43
No opinion	6	10	10	9	9	10	9	15
AIPO 694, 6-23-64								
(weighted N)[a]	(83)			(803)	(2409)			(492)
Prefer candidate in own party who took strong stand for								
civil rights	84%			76%	48%			93%
Against civil rights	0			12	36			3
No opinion	16			12	16			4
SRC 473, Sept.-Nov.'64								
(N)				(334)		(690)	(240)	
Prefer desegregation				29%		28%	8%	
Something between desegregation and								
segregation				53		46	4	
Strict segregation				14		23	51	
No opinion				4		3	1	
POS 655, 2-15-65								
(N)	(46)	(359)	(1152)	(342)	(987)	(626)	(369)	(182)
Federal gov't has moved too fast to enforce Negro rights to vote and be served in public places under								
new civil rights law	27%	30%	46%	30%	52%	40%	72%	6%
Not fast enough	28	31	24	31	18	22	2	62
About right (volunteered)	40	34	25	34	24	33	20	26
No opinion	5	5	5	5	6	5	6	6

	All			Whites only				Negroes
						North	South	
	Jews	Cath.	Prot.	Cath.	Prot.	Prot.	Prot.	
Federal gov't doing too much for Negroes	25	27	36	29	44	32	64	2
Not enough	25	23	24	22	16	23	5	60
About right (volunteered)	45	43	34	42	33	38	25	32
No opinion	5	7	6	7	7	7	6	6
AIPO 709, 3-31-65 (weighted N)[a]	(119)	(878)	(2393)	(849)	(2071)	(1326)	(745)	(340)
Johnson administration pushing integration too fast	25%	36%	49%	37%	53%	46%	71%	7%
Not fast enough	22	17	12	16	9	11	4	43
About right	48	39	28	40	26	30	16	40
No opinion	5	8	11	7	12	13	9	10
AIPO 716, 8-22-65 (weighted N)[a]	(133)	(773)	(2496)	(701)	(2101)	(1332)	(769)	(513)
Johnson administration pushing integration too fast	24%	43%	49%	45%	54%	46%	70%	6%
Not fast enough	10	8	8	7	5	6	3	25
About right	47	34	31	32	28	32	19	53
No opinion	19	15	12	16	13	16	8	16
AIPO survey of Aug.'66 Johnson administration pushing integration too fast	18%	49%	56%	50%	61%			5%
Not fast enough	12	9	9	8	4			32
About right	64	31	28	32	29			50
No opinion	6	11	7	10	6			13
Highly favorable rating for M. L. King	20	12	11	12	4			29
Mildly favorable	24	23	18	24	20			21
Mildly unfavorable	31	24	18	25	20			1
Highly unfavorable	21	35	49	34	53			18
No opinion	4	6	4	5	3			31
AIPO survey of May '67[b] Would vote for well-qualified Negro for President if nominated by my party	80%	64%	49%	62%	44%			92%
Would not	16	29	46	31	49			6
Don't know	4	7	5	7	7			2

		All		Whites only		Negroes
	Jews	Cath.	Prot.	Cath.	Prot.	
AIPO survey of Aug.-67[c]						
Johnson administration pushing integration too						
fast	18%	39%	47%	40%	52%	8%
Not fast enough	11	20	14	18	11	27
About right	64	24	20	24	16	53
No opinion	7	17	19	18	21	12

	All	
	Cath.	Prot.
AIPO survey of April '68[d]		
Johnson administration pushing integration		
too fast	31%	43%
Not fast enough	30	24
About right	24	18
No opinion	15	15
AIPO survey of June '68[e]		
Johnson administration pushing integration		
too fast	38%	48%
Not fast enough	21	19
About right	27	21
No opinion	14	12
AIPO survey of July '68[f]		
Approve of marriage between whites and		
nonwhites	25%	16%
Disapprove	68	77
No opinion	7	7
AIPO survey of Oct.'68[g]		
Favor opening-housing laws	46%	39%
Oppose	30	41
No opinion	24	20
Johnson administration pushing integration		
too fast	54	57
Not fast enough	17	15
About right	22	21
No opinion	7	7
AIPO survey of March '69[h]		
Would vote for otherwise well-qualified		
Negro presidential candidate	78%	61%
Would not	11	29
No opinion	11	10

	All	
AIPO survey of March '70[i]	Cath.	Prot.
Integration of U.S. schools going too fast	40%	53%
Not fast enough	21	14
About right	24	20
No opinion	15	13

<u>a</u> Weighted N's were approximately twice the actual number of interviewees.

<u>b</u> *Gallup Opinion Index*, June 1967.

<u>c</u> *Gallup Opinion Index*, Sept. 1967.

<u>d</u> *Gallup Opinion Index*, May 1968.

<u>e</u> *Gallup Opinion Index*, July 1968.

<u>f</u> *Gallup Opinion Index*, Nov. 1968.

<u>g</u> *Gallup Opinion Index*, Oct. 1968.

<u>h</u> *Gallup Opinion Index*, April 1969.

<u>i</u> *Gallup Opinion Index*, April 1970.

Table 8-7.   Race relations vs. foreign policy by region (whites only)

	Favor federal antilynching law		Oppose	
	South	North	South	North
AIPO 181, 1-10-40				
(N)	(100)	(710)	(252)	(602)
Approve Finnish loan	74%	54%	65%	54%
Disapprove	25	40	31	41
No opinion	1	6	4	5
Give Hull power to make more reciprocal trade treaties	28	24	23	22
Opposed	14	24	16	20
No opinion	58	52	61	58
Change Constitution to require national vote before Congress can draft men for overseas war	52	63	59	63
Do not	45	33	34	32
No opinion	3	4	7	5

	U.S. gov't should be able to deal directly with lynching		Leave to states	
	South	North	South	North
AIPO 439, 2-17-49				
(N)	(80)	(745)	(178)	(770)
Heard or read of Marshall Plan	82%	85%	81%	84%
Congress should vote funds to continue it	56	59	46	52
Should not	13	13	24	20
No opinion	13	13	11	12
Never heard of it	18	15	19	16
Heard or read of N. Atlantic Security Pact	56	65	62	63
U.S. should join	81	80	80	80
Should not	8	13	15	13
No opinion	11	7	5	7
U.S. should supply arms to European members	78	73	75	76
Should not	11	17	15	15
No opinion	11	10	10	9
U.S. should do more to help Japan get back on feet	42	37	27	32
Should not	49	54	65	57
No opinion	9	9	8	11

AIPO 439, 2-17-49	Abolish poll taxes		Do not	
	South	North	South	North
(N)	(114)	(959)	(148)	(555)
Heard or read of Marshall Plan	85%	84%	88%	79%
Congress should vote funds	50	60	45	43
Should not	18	13	23	22
No opinion	11	11	17	15
Never heard of it	20	16	15	21
Heard or read of N. Atlantic Security Pact	62	66	57	53
U.S. should join	81	80	79	78
Should not	11	13	14	14
No opinion	8	7	7	8
U.S. should supply arms to European members	79	77	74	73
Should not	8	15	17	18
No opinion	13	8	9	9
U.S. should do more to help Japan get back on feet	35	33	28	31
Should not	60	56	59	57
No opinion	5	11	13	12

AIPO 439, 2-17-49	Desegregate interstate transportation		Keep segregated	
	South	North	South	North
(N)	(40)	(959)	(228)	(555)
Heard or read of Marshall Plan	83%	84%	81%	79%
Congress should vote funds	63	60	45	43
Should not	15	13	21	22
No opinion	5	11	16	14
Never heard of it	17	16	19	21
Heard or read of N. Atlantic Security Pact	68	69	57	58
U.S. should join	75	79	79	79
Should not	7	14	14	14
No opinion	8	7	7	7
U.S. should supply arms to European members	75	73	78	77
Should not	15	18	14	16
No opinion	10	9	8	7

U.S. should do more to help Japan get	Desegregate		Keep segregated	
	South	North	South	North
back on feet	43	37	31	28
Should not	40	52	62	63
No opinion	17	11	7	9

	Approve Supreme Court decision desegregating education		Disapprove	
	South	North	South	North
AIPO 541, 12-29-54				
(N)	(42)	(596)	(280)	(304)
Withdraw aid to nations which refuse				
to cooperate with us	69%	72%	78%	78%
Continue aid	24	21	14	17
No opinion	7	7	8	5
U.S. will probably be in World War III				
in five years	41	44	48	55
Probably not	33	35	28	29
No opinion	26	21	24	26
Blockade coast of Communist China	29	37	28	42
Do not	52	41	36	37
No opinion	19	22	36	21
U.S. should give strong support to U.N.	76	79	68	67
Little support	14	12	15	24
No opinion	10	9	17	9
Favor reducing general level of tariffs	29	25	25	24
Opposed	43	45	36	50
No opinion	28	33	39	26
Approve Bricker amendment to curb				
treaty-making power of President	25	30	31	34
Disapprove	23	36	26	34
No opinion	52	34	43	32

	Federal gov't should stay out of question whether white and colored go to same school			
	Disagree		Agree	
	South	North	South	North
SRC 417, Sept.-Nov.'56				
(N)	(107)	(493)	(270)	(453)
U.S. should help poorer countries	44%	49%	43%	43%
Depends	18	16	13	19
Disagree	27	24	33	28
No opinion	11	11	11	10

	Federal gov't should see that Negroes get fair treatment in jobs and housing			
	Agree		Disagree	
	South	North	South	North
SRC 417, Sept.-Nov.'56				
(N)	(222)	(706)	(105)	(232)
U.S. should help poorer countries	48%	49%	35%	38%
Depends	12	21	18	21
Disagree	25	23	41	33
No opinion	15	7	6	8
U.S. should give aid even to countries less anticommunist than we	32	32	28	31
Depends	13	14	13	14
Disagree	31	34	44	37
No opinion	24	20	15	18

	Approve Supreme Court decision desegregating education		Disapprove	
	South	North	South	North
AIPO 576, 12-12-56				
(N)	(49)	(829)	(220)	(228)
Congress should appropriate $4 billion for foreign aid, as in recent years	74%	63%	52%	45%
Should not	20	26	26	42
No opinion	6	11	22	13

	Federal gov't should stay out of question whether white and colored go to same school			
	Disagree		Agree	
	South	North	South	North
SRC 440, Sept.-Nov.'60				
(N)	(129)	(589)	(333)	(402)
U.S. should help poorer countries	54%	54%	47%	49%
Depends	17	15	14	11
Disagree	22	18	27	20
No opinion	7	13	12	20

	Approve Supreme Court decisions desegregating both schools and transportation		Disapprove of both	
	South	North	South	North
AIPO 646, 5-26-61				
(weighted N)[a]	(126)	(1702)	(499)	(280)
Willing to make sacrifices, including higher taxes, for				
Foreign economic aid	26%	26%	11%	16%
Foreign military aid	10	9	5	17

	Negroes have less power in U.S. than they should		Have more power than they should	
	South	North	South	North
AIPO 647, 6-21-61				
(N)	(65)	(878)	(261)	(695)
If Congress had not appropriated $3-4 billion/year for foreign aid, communism would be more powerful	62%	64%	50%	53%
Would not	21	22	28	29
No opinion	17	14	22	16

	U.S. gov't should withhold aid from segregated schools		Should not	
	South	North	South	North
AIPO 667, 1-9-63				
(weighted N)[a]	(105)	(521)	(913)	(1937)
In general for foreign aid	65%	64%	58%	59%
Against it	30	29	30	31
No opinion	5	7	12	10

	Congress should enact laws to guarantee civil rights of Negroes, including service in hotels, restaurants, etc. All whites[b]	Should not, leave to states All whites[b]
AIPO 682, 12-10-63		
(N)	(577)	(473)
Keep foreign economic aid at present level at least	43%	20%
Reduce it	47	53
End it altogether	2	15
No opinion	8	12

	Favor de-segregation		Something in between		Favor strict segregation	
	South	North	South	North	South	North
SRC 473, Sept.-Nov.'64						
(N)	(25)	(346)	(111)	(539)	(127)	(214)
Give economic aid if need help	64%	64%	53%	52%	45%	40%
Depends	16	21	16	21	14	17
Each country should make own way as best it can	12	10	18	18	29	30
No opinion	8	5	13	9	12	13

POS 655, 2-15-65	U.S. gov't moving at about right speed or not fast enough to enforce 1964 Civil Rights Act on voting and accommodations		Too fast		U.S. gov't doing about right amount or not enough		Too much	
	South	North	South	North	South	North	South	North
(N)	(97)	(595)	(291)	(382)	(129)	(647)	(253)	(312)
1/200 of U.S. GNP for foreign aid too little	8%	11%	5%	10%	9%	12%	5%	8%
About right or depends	43	39	36	33	45	38	37	32
Too much	26	31	42	42	26	32	44	45
No opinion	23	19	17	15	20	18	17	15
Channel most aid to								
Latin America	41	47	48	45	39	45	49	47
Asia	15	10	8	7	14	11	8	6
Africa	8	12	9	9	12	12	8	8
Other	9	9	5	11	6	9	6	12
No opinion	27	22	30	28	29	23	29	27

a Weighted N's were approximately twice actual samples.

b Included no self-identified Democrats.

Table 8-8.   Race relations vs. foreign policy (whites only) by religion

| | Federal gov't should stay out of question whether white and colored go to same school | | | | | |
| | Agree | | | Disagree | | |
	Cath.	North Prot.	South Prot.	Cath.	North Prot.	South Prot.
SRC 417, Sept.-Nov.'56 (N)	(125)	(320)	(197)	(154)	(336)	(97)
U.S. should help poorer countries	43%	44%	43%	48%	49%	45%
Depends	19	18	14	16	15	18
Disagree	29	27	33	24	24	26
No opinion	9	11	10	12	12	11

| | Federal gov't should see that Negroes get fair treatment in jobs and housing | | | | | |
| | Agree | | | Disagree | | |
	Cath.	North Prot.	South Prot.	Cath.	North Prot.	South Prot.
SRC 417, Sept-Nov.'56 (N)	(226)	(457)	(197)	(61)	(184)	(97)
U.S. should give aid even to countries less anticommunist than we	31%	32%	32%	30%	30%	28%
Depends	13	12	13	15	14	13
Disagree	33	34	31	38	37	44
No opinion	23	22	24	17	19	15

| | Approve Supreme Court decisions desegregating both schools and transportation | | | Disapprove of both decisions | | |
	Cath.	North Prot.	South Prot.	Cath.	North Prot.	South Prot.
AIPO 646, 5-26-61 (weighted N)[a]	(615)	(1138)	(112)	(138)	(374)	(520)
Willing to make sacrifices, even higher personal taxes, for						
Foreign economic aid	28%	26%	26%	18%	16%	11%
Foreign military aid	16	9	8	15	17	5

	Desegregationists			In between			Strict Segregationists		
	Cath.	South Prot.	North Prot.	Cath.	South Prot.	North Prot.	Cath.	South Prot.	North Prot.
SRC 473, Sept.-Nov.'64									
(N)	(97)	(20)	(192)	(176)	(96)	(318)	(49)	(122)	(160)
Give economic aid if need help	63%	64%	64%	52%	53%	52%	41%	45%	40%
Depends	20	16	21	19	16	20	16	14	17
Each country should make own way as best it can	11	12	10	17	18	18	31	29	30
No opinion	6	8	5	12	13	10	12	13	13
Favor discussions with communist leaders to settle differences	71	80	76	76	74	71	74	66	68
Depends	4	5	5	2	–	5	4	3	3
Refuse to have anything to do with them	14	5	11	10	9	10	8	10	11
No opinion	11	10	8	12	17	14	14	21	18
(N)[b]	(90)	(17)	(179)	(167)	(88)	(295)	(44)	(115)	(149)
Trade nonmilitary goods with communist countries	34%	35%	30%	32%	26%	23%	18%	16%	23%
Depends	7	6	5	7	7	7	–	2	1
Forbid trade	39	53	44	43	52	44	57	50	48
No opinion	20	6	21	18	15	26	25	32	28
Knew Mainland China communist and not in U.N.	79	88	79	79	78	73	59	69	62
Admit China to U.N.	22	18	21	18	11	14	7	10	6
Do not admit, but stay in if admitted	33	41	35	35	43	39	34	32	31
Do not admit, pull out if admitted	7	11	8	6	6	7	5	10	10
Do not admit; don't know if U.S. should stay in if admitted	3	6	5	5	5	4	4	6	7
Don't know if China should be admitted	14	12	10	15	13	9	9	11	8
Did not know China communist and not in U.N.	21	12	21	21	22	27	41	31	38

	U.S. gov't doing about right or not enough for Negro			Too much		
	Cath.	North Prot.	South Prot.	Cath.	North Prot.	South Prot.
POS 655, 2-15-65						
(N)	(223)	(383)	(109)	(103)	(199)	(231)
1/200 of U.S. GNP for foreign aid						
Too little	13%	11%	9%	13%	7%	4%
About right or depends	43	36	43	25	35	34
Too much	27	36	28	50	43	44
No opinion	17	17	20	12	15	18
U.S. obligated to help poor nations	61	49	55	43	38	39
No obligation	16	21	13	40	34	33
Depends	22	28	29	17	26	25
No opinion	1	2	3	–	2	3
Extremely well satisfied with aid to poor nations	23	17	24	25	16	17
Considerably satisfied	27	27	28	18	16	19
Somewhat satisfied	33	34	32	22	32	26
Not at all satisfied	17	22	16	35	36	38

	U.S. gov't moving at about right speed or not fast enough to enforce 1964 Civil Rights Act on voting and accommodations			Too fast		
	Cath.	North Prot.	South Prot.	Cath.	North Prot.	South Prot.
POS 655, 2-15-65						
(N)	(222)	(406)	(131)	(103)	(250)	(254)
1/200 of U.S. GNP for foreign aid too little	10%	11%	8%	9%	10%	5%
About right or depends	40	39	43	34	33	36
Too much	29	31	26	41	42	42
No opinion	21	19	23	16	15	17

a Weighted N's were approximately twice actual N's.

b Following questions appeared on SRC 473 post-election survey only, Nov.'64.

Table 9-1.   Episcopal clergy vs. laymen, 1951-1952[a]

	Bishops (100)	Priests (259)	Parishioners (1550)
(N)			
Agree the U.N. is not worth the money the U.S. has spent on it	2%	9%	25%
Disagree	90	83	60
Uncertain or no opinion	8	8	15
Is all right for U.S. troops to serve under officers of another country appointed by U.N.	93	88	64
Disagree	5	8	28
Uncertain or no opinion	2	4	8
It would be a good thing if U.N. were some day replaced by some kind of world gov't	60	60	47
Disagree	15	22	33
Uncertain or no opinion	25	18	20
Agree that U.S. has already admitted too many refugees since end of World War II	3	8	37
Disagree	85	77	44
Uncertain or no opinion	12	15	19
The immigration laws should be changed so that the quota system does not favor certain nations as opposed to others	51	60	37
Disagree	26	23	42
Uncertain or no opinion	23	17	21
Episcopalians should recognize the right of conscientious objectors to refuse to bear arms	95	93	53
Disagree	4	6	34
Uncertain or no opinion	1	1	13
Episcopalians have a moral obligation to give financial and other assistance to conscientious objectors	60	60	26
Disagree	29	24	56
Uncertain or no opinion	11	16	18

U.S. should not spend money to help underdeveloped countries raise standards	Bishops	Priests	Parishioners
of living	2	3	16
Disagree	95	92	76
No opinion	3	5	8
U.S. should help following to get on feet economically			
India	78	76	47
England	73	78	50
West Germany	76	76	52
Iran	56	60	30
Puerto Rico	71	73	41
Japan	79	77	47
Liberia and Africa	67	73	33
None of these countries	4	3	13

a From Charles Y. Glock, Benjamin B. Ringer, and Earl R. Babbie,
   To Comfort and to Challenge (Berkeley: Univ. of California Press, 1967),
   pp. 144-51, and data provided by Charles Y. Glock.

Table 9-2. United Presbyterian ministers vs. elders, 1966-1967 [a]

	Ministers	Elders
(N)	(1019)	(618)
In general for foreign aid	61%	39%
Mixed feelings	31	53
Against it	2	5
No opinion	6	3
Important purposes of U.S. aid to:		
Help developing countries achieve economic growth	83	69
Help less fortunate to live better lives	73	68
Win friends for U.S.	10	14
Influence other nations	7	7
Build markets for U.S. products	8	12
Deter communist aggression	27	46
Most nearly agree:		
U.S. foreign aid on whole successful	33	24
U.S. has made mistakes, but now doing much better	56	47
U.S. aid has done more harm than good	4	13
U.S. aid has hurt own country	7	21
Preferred policies for U.S. economic aid:		
Give only to countries that agree to stand with us against communism	11	30
Continue to some countries like India that have not joined us as allies against communism	58	44
Offer help to countries in need regardless of stand on communism	43	25
Offer help to some communist countries like Yugoslavia and Rumania that indicate political independence	37	26
U.S. should be willing to help (country) in food production, population control, health, education, etc.:		
Yugoslavia	53	28
India	79	67
Israel	62	43
Indonesia	68	44
Haiti	58	34
Cuba	37	13
Pakistan	76	54
Congo	67	41
Brazil	71	49
Paraguay	58	35
Egypt	52	27
Sudan	59	32

	Ministers	Elders
Dominican Republic	64	43
North Vietnam	25	15
People's Republic of China	37	20
Channeling of U.S. aid:		
On whole should go directly to recipient countries (bilateral)	32	43
Most should go through U.N. agencies	41	20
U.S. Gov't should provide incentives for U.S. business and industry in international development	47	33
U.S. gov't should encourage church-related and other philanthropic aid programs	58	55
More aid through private programs, less through gov't	23	31
Know aid position of own congressman or of one of two senators	32	28
Have general idea	32	36
Only vaguely	10	11
Don't know and no opinion	24	25
Knew U.S. per capita aid budget smaller than that of some other countries	18	8
Knew U.S. gives less of GNP than some other countries	32	18
Strongly agree U.S. better off if stayed home, did not concern self with problems abroad	2	4
Mildly agree	2	5
Mildly disagree	5	16
Strongly disagree	81	61
No opinion	10	14
Strongly agree good for U.S. to help other countries raise living standards	78	70
Mildly agree	12	21
Mildly disagree	1	1
Strongly disagree	2	1
No opinion	7	7
Strongly agree U.S. economic aid should be on long-term basis so recipients can borrow for projects which take more than one year to finish	29	21
Mildly agree	39	31
Mildly disagree	10	16
Strongly disagree	4	11
No opinion	18	21

	Ministers	Elders
Strongly agree economic aid should be appropriated one year at a time, with annual congressional review of U.S. aid program	17	32
Mildly agree	20	21
Mildly disagree	28	20
Strongly disagree	26	9
No opinion	9	18
Strongly agree economic aid more important than military aid	60	56
Mildly agree	23	26
Mildly disagree	3	4
Strongly disagree	2	2
No opinion	12	12
Strongly agree technical assistance good idea	82	58
Mildly agree	10	13
Mildly disagree	0	1
Strongly disagree	1	1
No opinion	7	27
Strongly agree U.S. capital aid for dams, steel mills, highways, other large-scale programs a good idea	47	30
Mildly agree	34	35
Mildly disagree	5	1
Strongly disagree	2	5
No opinion	12	19
Strongly agree Peace Corps good idea	72	52
Mildly agree	17	28
Mildly disagree	1	5
Strongly disagree	1	4
No opinion	9	11
Strongly agree gift and sale of surplus foods (P.L. 480) good idea	80	63
Mildly agree	12	25
Mildly disagree	1	2
Strongly disagree	0	1
No opinion	7	9
Strongly agree U.S. gov't should help solve overpopulation through family planning and birth control	79	60
Mildly agree	10	20
Mildly disagree	1	3
Strongly disagree	1	8
No opinion	9	9

	Ministers	Elders
Strongly agree growing gap in living standards between U.S. and Asia, Africa, and Latin America should be matter of great concern to us, both morally and pragmatically	70	44
Mildly agree	18	29
Mildly disagree	1	6
Strongly disagree	2	3
No opinion	9	18
Strongly agree present U.S. aid level (under 1% GNP) not enough	37	12
Mildly agree	23	18
Mildly disagree	9	21
Strongly disagree	4	14
No opinion	27	35
Strongly agree Americans should be willing to pay higher taxes for expanded foreign aid	29	9
Mildly agree	28	15
Mildly disagree	15	28
Strongly disagree	9	29
No opinion	19	19
Strongly agree U.S. should spend less on foreign aid to have more money for domestic programs like schools, roads, conservation, housing, reduction of poverty	6	9
Mildly agree	6	17
Mildly disagree	27	33
Strongly disagree	49	24
No opinion	12	17
Strongly agree Presbyterian Church should take positions on national issues with moral or ethical connotations, like foreign aid	55	41
Mildly agree	23	27
Mildly disagree	5	9
Strongly disagree	6	9
No opinion	11	14
Strongly agree church should seek to inform members such issues	65	50
Mildly agree	20	23
Mildly disagree	2	7
Strongly disagree	2	5
No opinion	11	15

a Derived from *A Survey of Attitudes on Foreign Aid* (Philadelphia: Office of Church and Society, Board of Christian Education of the United Presbyterian Church, U.S.A., 1968), pp. 8-14.

Table 9-3.   Protestant clergymen in local parishes, 1960[a]

(N)	Clergy of N.C.C. de- nominations[b] (4013)	Missouri Lutherans (93)	Southern Baptists (67)
Very interested in news of national and international affairs	61%	58%	57%
Strongly approve of purposes of:			
U.N.	54	24	37
W.C.C.	44	2	6
Would dislike very much for clergy to restrict its activities to religious problems of congregations	34	5	18
Would like very much to see church-sponsored examination of ethical issues	56	31	31
Give great emphasis to social implications of Christian faith	54	46	52
Frequently or occasionally include currently controversial topics in sermons	76	66	49
Agree with N.C.C. goals in:			
Relief and world service	82	60	35
International affairs and peace	69	18	22
Disagree N.C.C. too concerned with national and international problems	61	16	18
Agree N.C.C. has right to issue pronouncements for member denominations	30	15	10
N.C.C. pronouncements are far to left	13	22	33
Pronouncements in agreement with own views to great or considerable extent	41	8	11

a Derived from *The Clergy Views the National Council of Churches* (Report of the Bureau of Applied Social Research, Columbia University, 1960), Tables 2:12, 3:2, 4:1, 4:3, IV-9a, 5:1, and A-2 through A-7.

b Combination of Episcopalians, United Presbyterians, Presbyterians U.S., Methodists, Disciples of Christ, Congregationalists, United Lutherans, and American Baptists.

Table 9-4. Denominations vs. foreign policy: 1938-41 (whites only)

	Epis.	Pres.	Cong.	All Meth.	So. Meth.	E+R	Luth.	Bapt.	So. Bapt. and other Fundamentalists	Other Non-Fundamentalist denominations	Cath.
AIPO 145, 1-20-39											
(N)	(119)	(233)	(85)	(442)	(90)	(23)[a]	(150)	(259)	(153)	(238)	(571)
Prefer Fascism over Communism	41%	24%	33%	21%	17%	22%	29%	19%	14%	24%	34%
Prefer Communism over Fascism	22	28	23	26	25	22	17	24	23	28	17
No opinion, neither	37	48	44	53	58	56	54	57	63	48	49
Return colonies to Germany											
Germany	20	12	18	12	3	17	24	9	6	14	20
Do not	71	77	70	75	83	83	63	72	70	74	66
No opinion	9	11	12	13	14	0	13	19	24	12	14
AIPO 133, 9-23-38											
(N)	(143)	(193)	(78)	(431)	(77)	(26)[a]	(151)	(294)	(228)	(246)	(519)
Britain and France mistaken in accepting Germany's demands on Czechoslovakia	45%	50%	53%	51%	49%	58%	52%	50%	45%	52%	51%
Not mistaken	43	37	33	31	31	19	26	31	30	30	28
No opinion	12	13	14	18	20	23	22	19	25	18	21
U.S. failure to join League partly responsible for Europe's troubles	20	20	27	18	23	23	11	14	18	20	15
Not responsible	65	64	60	60	57	46	69	65	59	60	64
No opinion	15	16	13	22	16	31	20	21	23	20	21

	Epis.	Pres.	Cong.	All Meth.	So. Meth.	E & R	Luth.	Bapt.	Fund.	Non-fund.	Cath.
Like to see F.D.R. openly criticize Hitler and Mussolini	29	22	29	28	35	27	33	32	32	29	28
Would not	66	73	63	63	57	73	60	58	57	64	65
No opinion	5	5	8	9	8	0	7	10	11	7	7
AIPO 149 A, 2-22-39											
(N)	(42)	(88)	(29)[a]	(223)	(54)	(20)[a]	(86)	(113)	(89)	(101)	(258)
Rather USSR win if war with Japan	64%	61%	38%	48%	52%	40%	45%	57%	72%	41%	45%
Rather Japan win	3	7	14	11	7	25	9	8	7	10	14
No choice	26	24	45	30	33	30	33	18	9	38	30
No opinion	7	8	3	11	8	5	13	17	12	10	11
AIPO 213, 9-30-40											
(N)	(53)	(97)	(50)	(210)	(47)	(12)[a]	(77)	(122)	(81)	(142)	(275)
Forbid sale of strategic goods to Japan	81%	93%	84%	86%	86%	84%	81%	81%	82%	82%	80%
Do not	13	5	12	8	6	8	8	11	6	10	13
No opinion	6	2	4	6	8	8	11	8	12	8	7
Risk war to prevent Japan from getting control of China	28	39	22	29	28	17	23	32	30	27	28
Let Japan take China	38	29	44	26	13	17	35	26	24	34	31
Other isolationist replies	13	16	16	16	19	25	10	11	10	14	15
No opinion	21	16	18	29	40	41	32	31	36	25	26
Would vote to enter war against Germany and Italy	21	17	12	19	21	17	12	17	21	12	16
Would vote to stay out	73	74	86	70	64	67	83	68	65	79	75
No opinion	6	9	2	11	15	16	5	15	14	9	9

Composite of AIPO 209, 213, 216, 217, 220, 229, and 248, Sept. '40–Sept. '41

	Epis.	Pres.	Cong.	Meth.	All So. Meth.	E & R	Luth.	Bapt.	Fund.	Non-fund.	Cath.
(N)	(361)	(680)	(351)	(1403)	(315)	(96)	(521)	(860)	(573)	(903)	(2981)
More important to keep out of war	29%	31%	34%	34%	26%	35%	39%	35%	25%	35%	37%
To help Britain	65	61	59	60	65	57	51	57	63	59	53
No opinion	6	8	7	6	9	8	10	8	12	6	10

a Percentages derived from samples of less than fifty cases syould be interpreted with caution.

Table 9-5.   Denominations vs. postwar foreign policy (whites only)

	Quakers, Unit., Univ., Un.Breth.	Epis.	Meth.	Pres.	Cong.; E.and R.; other mod. Prot.	Luth.	Am. Bapt.	S. Bapt.	Fund. sects	Cath.
AIPO 307, 11-23-43										
(N)	(10)	(51)	(201)	(90)	(87)	(49)	(32)	(100)	(43)	(220)
Democrats and Republicans should both take stands for active part in world affairs in platforms	80%	71%	63%	70%	66%	69%	64%	62%	58%	66%
Should not	0	16	16	20	17	6	12	12	13	13
No opinion	20	13	21	10	17	25	24	26	29	21
NORC 280, April '50										
(N)		(46)	(172)	(102)	(170)	(93)	(46)	(160)	(25)	(301)
Expect war in 10 years		61%	65%	72%	70%	61%	71%	78%	76%	63%
Do not expect it		24	25	23	22	30	20	12	8	29
No opinion		15	10	5	8	9	9	10	16	8
Expect war in 2 years		24	25	18	22	15	27	30	30	17
Approve continuing ERP		76	55	62	55	52	52	49	46	58
Disapprove		17	32	31	35	44	32	35	31	32
No opinion		7	13	7	10	4	16	16	23	10
SRC 440, Sept.-Nov.'60										
(N)	(15)	(64)	(278)	(133)	(64)	(138)	(88)	(210)	(100)	(355)

	Quakers, etc.	Epis.	Meth.	Pres.	Cong., etc.	Luth.	Am. Bapt.	So. Bapt.	Fund.	Cath.
Agree U.S. would be better off if we just stayed home and did not concern ourselves with problems abroad	13%	5%	14%	14%	14%	18%	19%	22%	27%	17%
Depends or uncertain	7	22	7	7	5	5	6	7	4	2
Disagree	73	73	66	75	61	70	63	60	56	71
No opinion	7	0	13	4	20	7	12	11	13	10
Agree U.S. should give economic help to poorer countries	53	59	57	57	73	51	45	39	34	58
Depends or uncertain	13	16	14	21	13	20	11	12	16	12
Disagree	20	23	17	18	6	12	29	34	17	17
No opinion	14	2	12	4	8	7	15	15	33	13
SRC 473, Sept.-Nov.'64 (N)	(17)	(49)	(206)	(73)	(53)	(119)	(50)	(180)	(85)	(313)
Give economic aid if need help	71%	68%	49%	58%	42%	50%	50%	47%	40%	58%
Depends or uncertain	16	16	22	18	28	24	16	17	15	20
Each country should make its own way as best it can	7	16	19	17	17	14	24	27	27	14
No opinion	6	0	10	7	13	12	10	9	18	8
Spending too much on aid		37	53	56	57	56	50	52	54	50
Right amount		41	27	30	27	27	33	31	31	33
Not enough		11	5	4	3	1	5	4	0	5
Don't know		11	15	10	13	16	12	13	15	12
Good policy to aid backward countries		83	69	76	76	76	67	65	61	75
No concern of our gov't		15	23	24	20	18	28	29	28	21
No opinion		2	8	0	4	6	5	6	11	4

	Quakers, etc.	Epis.	Meth.	Pres.	Cong., etc.	Luth.	Am. Bapt.	So. Bapt.	Fund.	Cath.
Spend all aid through										
U.S. gov't		39	26	27	37	39	35	33	32	34
Some through U.N.		44	36	40	33	32	26	24	15	37
Don't know		0	7	9	6	5	6	8	14	4
Aid to backward countries would										
really help us		80	69	70	67	69	65	63	51	75
Would not		16	22	24	25	20	27	27	33	17
No opinion		4	9	6	8	11	8	10	16	8
Heard of Point Four program		37	26	28	26	23	17	15	12	19
Correct knowledge of it		9	6	9	3	3	3	2	3	3
Favor negotiations with										
communist leaders	89	78	73	77	70	72	72	70	61	74
Depends or uncertain	0	8	4	3	2	3	3	4	6	4
Oppose negotiations	6	10	8	12	11	9	12	13	11	10
No opinion	5	4	15	8	17	16	13	13	22	12
Favor trade with communist countries										
in nonmilitary goods	30	36	24	26	20	21	22	20	18	31
Depends or uncertain	6	4	6	6	7	5	4	3	1	6
U.S. gov't should prohibit trade	52	53	46	45	54	45	46	47	45	43
No opinion	12	7	24	23	19	29	28	30	36	20
Knew Mainland China communist and not in U.N.	82	93	75	76	78	75	68	61	58	76
Should admit to U.N.	18	20	15	15	15	13	12	10	9	18
If admitted, U.S. should stay in	46	44	42	30	30	34	37	21	21	34

	Quakers, etc.	Epis.	Meth.	Pres.	Cong., etc.	Luth.	Am. Bapt.	So. Bapt.	Fund.	Cath.
If admitted, don't know what U.S. should do	6	7	6	8	13	6	3	9	7	5
If admitted, U.S. should get out	12	9	4	15	13	6	9	10	11	5
Don't know if China should be admitted	0	13	8	8	7	16	7	11	10	12
Did not know China communist and not in U.N.	18	7	25	24	22	25	32	39	42	24
AIPO 706, 2-17-65 (weighted N)[a]	(25)	(96)	(481)	(212)	(402)	(284)	(292)	(421)	(290)	(756)
For foreign aid	72%	72%	60%	61%	56%	55%	56%	49%	46%	60%
Against it	20	27	31	32	34	35	32	41	38	29
No opinion	8	1	9	7	10	10	12	10	16	11
Increase foreign aid	8	8	6	6	5	2	7	5	1	6
Keep same	40	41	38	22	30	39	30	26	18	41
Decrease	44	45	46	59	53	46	45	49	60	43
No opinion	8	6	10	13	12	13	18	20	21	10
Most important purpose of aid										
Economic development	28	33	24	22	24	25	17	19	13	29
To aid needy	16	17	27	26	19	19	24	28	28	22
U.S. self-interest	12	9	13	16	16	12	14	14	15	16
Admit Communist China to U.N.	28	36	20	27	21	20	19	15	11	26
Do not	60	57	66	60	65	65	66	68	71	59
No opinion	12	7	14	13	14	15	15	17	18	15

	Quakers, etc.	Epis.	Meth.	Pres.	Cong., etc.	Luth.	Am. Bapt.	So. Bapt.	Fund.	Cath.
Go along with U.N. majority on China	56	63	45	50	47	46	46	42	39	56
Do not	32	27	38	36	37	37	38	40	42	29
No opinion	12	10	17	14	16	17	16	18	19	15
Negotiate with Peking and Southeast Asian leaders on Vietnam	64	72	64	65	64	63	63	60	58	68
Do not	20	10	13	12	12	15	13	16	17	13
No opinion	16	18	23	23	24	22	24	24	25	19
Approximately correct estimate of population of Communist China	16	19	12	14	13	12	12	10	9	12

a Weighted N's were approximately twice actual N's.

Table 9-6.[a]   Theological orientations vs. world affairs
attitudes in   clergy of eight N.C.C. denominations, 1960[b]

	Theological liberalism–conservatism scores[c]				
	Liberals		Conservatives		All
	(0)	(1)	(2)	(3)	
Strongly approve of purposes of U.N.	67%	57%	42%	30%	54%
Strongly approve of purposes of W.C.C.	62	45	26	18	14
Very interested in national and international news	66	58	59	52	61
Would like very much to see church-sponsored examination of major ethical issues	68	56	47	41	56
Would dislike very much for clergy to restrict its activities to religious problems of congregations	48	35	22	14	34
Agree with N.C.C.'s goal in:					
Relief and world service	90	82	77	76	82
International affairs and peace	80	72	58	50	69
Foreign missions	69	62	.46	40	58
Disagree that N.C.C. is too concerned with national and international social problems	80	62	46	34	61
N.C.C. has right to issue pronouncements for member denominations	40	31	21	15	30
N.C.C. has right to recommend legislation to Congress	88	83	67	59	78
Pronouncements of N.C.C. are far to left	9	8	20	35	13
Agree personally with views in N.C.C.'s pronouncements to great or considerable extent	84	63	33	23	63
Could recall content of N.C.C. pronouncement on Communist China	54	48	47	41	48
Agreed with it[d]	58	42	35	27	43

	N.C.C. is too liberal in its theological interpretations	
	Agree	Disagree
Agree N.C.C. too concerned with national and international social problems	42%	9%
N.C.C. pronouncements too far to left	33	9

<u>a</u> Derived from *The Clergy Views the National Council of Churches* (report of the Bureau of Applied Social Research, Columbia University, 1960), Tables 2:12, 3:2, 4:1, 4:3, 5:1, 5:3, 5:5, 6:6, 6:10, and 7:15.

<u>b</u> Episcopalians, United Presbyterians, Presbyterians U.S., Methodists, Disciples of Christ, Congregationalists, United Lutherans, and American Baptists.

<u>c</u> A composite of replies to three questions: (1) Whether Bible is (a) infallible revelation of God's will, (b) inspired by God, but subject to historical criticism, or (c) great history of religious experience, but not necessarily inspired by God; (2) whether questioned traditional interpretations of doctrine or creed: (a) frequently, (b) occasionally, or (c) whether emphasized biblically conservative Christianity (aa)frequently, (bb)occasionally, or (cc)rarely.

<u>d</u> Percentages only among ministers who could recall China pronouncement.

Table 9-7.   Theological orientations, 1939-1941 (whites only)

	National Prohibition Favor	Oppose	CATHOLICS Read Bible last month	Did not	Prefer Old Test.	New	Equally	Clergy Should discuss foreign policy	Should not
AIPO 149, 2-22-39									
(N)			(130)	(462)	(130)	(207)	(72)		
Prefer Japan win if war with USSR			9%	14%	10%	19%	3%		
Prefer USSR win			50	46	51	46	46		
Neither			26	30	27	27	43		
No opinion			15	10	12	8	8		
Permit Britain and France to buy warplanes here			43	51	50	52	58		
Do not			40	37	39	37	31		
Undecided			8	7	8	4	8		
No opinion			9	5	3	7	3		
Permit Germany and Italy to do so too			15	17	15	20	14		
Do not			68	75	76	70	76		
Undecided			8	5	8	3	6		
No opinion			9	3	1	7	4		
AIPO 180, 12-22-39									
(N)	(119)	(371)							
Lend Finland money for war supplies	49%	55%							
Do not	37	36							
No opinion	14	9							
Lend Britain and France money for war supplies	12	18							
Do not	77	73							
No opinion	11	9							
AIPO 253, 11-13-41									
(N)	(110)	(350)						(165)	(291)
More important to help defeat Germany, even if means getting into war ourselves	51%	60%						46%	63%
More important to stay out of war, even at risk of letting Germany win	40	34						46	29
No opinion	9	6						8	8

		PROTESTANTS					Clergy	
National Prohibition Favor	Oppose	Read Bible last month	Did not	Prefer Old Test.	New	Equally	Should discuss foreign policy	Should not
		(1015)	(1062)	(357)	(1101)	(328)		
		9%	9%	12%	9%	6%		
		48	52	54	51	43		
		30	27	22	30	34		
		13	12	12	10	17		
		49	53	53	53	42		
		38	34	38	36	36		
		7	7	7	5	10		
		6	6	2	6	12		
		13	14	12	14	12		
		78	76	80	78	74		
		3	4	4	3	4		
		6	6	4	5	10		
(801)	(919)							
54%	59%							
31	31							
13	10							
18	24							
72	69							
10	7							
(736)	(885)						(649)	(906)
68%	75%						72%	70%
18	16						18	18
14	9						10	12

Table 9-8.   Biblical literalism vs. foreign policy (whites only)

	Bible literally God's word; literally true		Bible inspired by God; written by men; some error		Good book or not; written by men; God not involved	
	Cath.	Prot.	Cath.	Prot.	Cath.	Prot.
SRC 473, Sept.-Nov.'64 (N)	(147)	(456)	(140)	(353)	(15)	(18)
Favor economic aid	61%	49%	57%	54%	60%	28%
Depends or uncertain	18	17	22	23	27	28
Each country make own way	11	22	16	18	13	35
No opinion	10	12	5	5	0	11
Favor negotiations with communist leaders to settle differences	75	72	75	73	86	72
Depends or uncertain	1	3	5	6	7	6
Oppose negotiations	11	9	8	10	7	11
No opinion	13	16	12	11	0	11
Favor trade with communist countries in nonmilitary goods	26	22	35	25	20	55
Depends or uncertain	7	5	5	6	47	0
U.S. gov't should prohibit trade	44	43	44	53	33	28
No opinion	23	30	16	16	0	17
Knew Mainland China communist and not in U.N.	69	62	86	87	80	89
Should admit to U.N.	13	9	23	18	27	17
If admitted, U.S. should stay in	30	29	40	47	27	39
If admitted, don't know what U.S. should do	3	6	6	5	0	5
If admitted, U.S. should get out	7	8	5	8	0	11
Don't know if China should be admitted	16	10	12	9	26	17
Did not know China communist and not in U.N.	31	38	14	13	20	11

Table 9-9.   Ecumenicism vs. foreign policy (whites only)

	Favor idea of forming single U.S. Prot. church		Oppose	
	Cath.	Prot.	Cath.	Prot.
AIPO 454, 3-24-50				
(N)	(105)	(471)	(76)	(351)
U.S. spending on Marshall Plan should be increased	11%	12%	9%	11%
Decreased	46	44	48	48
Kept same	34	37	33	32
No opinion	9	7	10	9

	Jews have more power than they should in U.S.		Right amount or less	
	Cath.	Prot.	Cath.	Prot.
AIPO 647, 6-21-61				
(weighted N)[a]	(100)	(289)	(426)	(937)
If Congress had not appropriated $3-4 billion a year in recent years for aid, communism would be in greater position of world power	59%	52%	69%	60%
No difference or less	28	31	20	22
No opinion	13	17	11	18

	Feelings about Jews					
	Unfavorable		Neutral		Favorable	
	Cath.	Prot.	Cath.	Prot.	Cath.	Prot.
SRC 473, Sept.-Nov.'64						
(N)	(20)	(89)	(99)	(369)	(186)	(389)
Favor economic aid	55%	38%	46%	47%	67%	57%
Depends	15	19	20	20	19	20
Each country make own way	25	32	26	21	7	17
No opinion	5	11	8	12	7	6

	White Protestants only: feelings about Catholics			White Catholics only: feelings about Protestants		
	Unfavorable	Neutral	Favorable	Unfavorable	Neutral	Favorable
SRC 473, Sept.-Nov.'64 (N)	(112)	(296)	(438)	(8)	(80)	(217)
Give economic aid if need help	45%	49%	53%	38%	51%	63%
Depends	15	20	21	12	19	19
Each country should make own way as best can	30	19	18	25	23	11
No opinion	10	12	8	25	7	7
Favor discussion with communist leaders to settle differences	67	71	75	25	72	77
Depends	4	5	5	-	5	3
Refuse to have anything to do with them	14	8	9	38	8	11
No opinion	15	16	11	37	15	9
Trade nonmilitary goods with communist countries	22	26	24	13	28	33
Depends	4	4	6	12	4	6
Forbid trade	44	40	52	25	46	43
No opinion	30	30	18	50	22	18
Knew Mainland China communist and not in U.N.	70	66	79	50	74	78
Admit China to U.N.	13	11	15	13	15	19
Do not admit but stay in if admitted	30	31	42	-	39	34

	Unfavorable	Neutral	Favorable	Unfavorable	Neutral	Favorable
Do not admit, pull out if admitted	12	8	7	-	5	6
Do not admit, don't know if U.S. should stay in if admitted	6	6	5	25	1	5
Do not know if China should be admitted	9	10	10	12	14	14
Did not know China communist and not in U.N.	30	34	21	50	26	22

	Feelings about Jews					
	Unfavorable		Neutral		Favorable	
	Cath.	Prot.	Cath.	Prot.	Cath.	Prot.
Favor negotiations with communist leaders to settle differences	50%	69%	72%	70%	75%	75%
Depends or uncertain	0	4	3	4	4	5
Oppose negotiations	30	10	8	8	10	12
No opinion	20	17	17	18	11	8
Favor trade with communist countries in nonmilitary goods	25	27	27	21	33	27
Depends or uncertain	5	2	5	3	7	7
U.S. gov't should prohibit trade	45	45	46	44	42	50
No opinion	25	26	22	32	18	16
Knew Mainland China communist and not in U.N.	75	70	70	65	80	82
Should admit to U.N.	25	10	13	12	20	16
If admitted, U.S. should stay in	25	37	35	29	35	44
If admitted, don't know what U.S. should do	5	2	4	6	5	6
If admitted, U.S. should get out	10	12	5	7	5	8
Don't know if China should be admitted	10	9	13	11	15	8
Did not know China communist and not in U.N.	25	30	30	35	20	18

a Weighted N's were approximately twice actual N's.

Table 9-10.   Demographic differences among religious denominations

	Epis.	Pres.	Meth.	Luth.	Bapt.	Cath.	Jews
Education:							
College	45%	34%	20%	20%	10%	17%	44%
High School	45	50	54	53	49	56	40
Grade School	10	16	26	27	41	27	16
Occupation:							
Professional							
& Business	37	31	24	24	15	23	51
White Collar	16	15	11	11	7	13	18
Farmers	1	4	8	9	9	3	0
Manual	24	29	36	38	50	47	14
Non-Labor Force	22	21	21	18	19	14	17
Income:							
$7000 up	55	50	42	49	26	47	69
$5000-6999	20	19	21	20	21	23	14
$3000-4999	14	17	17	15	23	16	9
Under $3000	9	12	18	15	28	12	6
Urban-Rural:							
Half-million							
and up	41	30	21	28	19	51	80
50,000-499,999	19	29	22	24	23	25	17
2500-49,999	16	17	19	16	16	10	2
Under 2500,							
Rural	24	24	38	32	42	14	1

Table 9-11. Church attendance and international opinions
(whites only)

	Catholics				Protestants			
	Last Sunday	Not last Sunday	At least weekly	Less often	Last Sunday	Not last Sunday	At least weekly	Less often
AIPO 149, 2-22-39								
(N)	(384)	(206)	(444)	(144)	(783)	(1274)	(888)	(1155)
Prefer Japan win if war with USSR	14%	10%	15%	6%	9%	8%	11%	8%
Prefer USSR win	44	52	42	59	47	53	47	52
Neither	32	25	31	27	32	27	29	28
No opinion	10	13	12	8	12	12	13	12
Permit Britain and France to buy warplanes here	50	51	49	51	49	53	48	53
Do not	37	38	37	39	37	36	40	34
Undecided	7	6	8	4	8	5	6	7
No opinion	6	5	6	6	6	6	6	6
Permit Germany and Italy to buy warplanes here	17	15	17	14	13	14	12	15
Do not	71	78	71	79	76	78	80	75
Undecided	6	3	6	4	5	3	3	4
No opinion	6	3	6	3	6	5	5	6

	Regularly		Attend Church Often		Seldom or Never	
	Cath.	Prot.	Cath.	Prot.	Cath.	Prot.
SRC 417, Sept.-Nov.'56						
(N)	(256)	(392)	(47)	(229)	(56)	(521)
Agree U.S. would be better off if we just stayed home and did not concern ourselves with problems abroad	23%	21%	17%	23%	25%	26%
Depends or uncertain	5	5	4	8	5	6
Disagree	57	65	47	60	59	57
No opinion	15	9	32	9	11	11
Agree best way to deal with USSR and Communist China is to act just as tough as they do	69	62	49	69	70	70
Depends or uncertain	4	6	6	5	4	5
Disagree	10	16	13	13	7	12
No opinion	17	16	32	13	19	13
Agree U.S. should give economic help to poorer countries	42	48	34	41	45	39
Depends or uncertain	14	18	11	17	18	16
Disagree	27	21	21	28	25	31
No opinion	17	13	34	14	12	14
Agree U.S. should help countries not as much against communism as we are	28	33	23	28	25	28
Depends or uncertain	12	14	13	13	12	13
Disagree	37	31	26	29	34	34
No opinion	23	22	38	30	29	25
SRC 431, Sept.-Nov.'58						
(N)	(241)	(435)	(63)	(217)	(58)	(526)
Agree U.S. would be better it we just stayed home and did not concern ourselves with problems abroad	25%	19%	22%	17%	17%	28%
Depends or uncertain	9	8	6	6	21	7
Disagree	58	63	43	65	45	53
No opinions	8	10	29	12	17	12

	Attend church					
Agree U.S. should	Regularly		Often		Seldom	
	Cath.	Prot.	Cath.	Prot.	Cath.	Prot.
give economic help						
to poorer countries	53	52	38	48	43	48
Depends or uncertain	12	15	12	14	17	13
Disagree	22	17	15	19	19	24
No opinion	13	16	35	19	21	15

SRC 440, Sept.-Nov.'60

	Cath.	Prot.	Cath.	Prot.	Cath.	Prot.
(N)	(263)	(449)	(50)	(232)	(42)	(524)
Agree U.S. would be better off if we just stayed home and did not concern ourselves with problems abroad	17%	13%	16%	13%	24%	22%
Depends or uncertain	3	4	2	4	2	11
Disagree	71	74	70	72	57	56
No opinion	9	9	12	11	17	11
Agree U.S. should give economic help to poorer countries	58	56	74	55	40	46
Depends or uncertain	13	13	2	15	24	17
Disagree	19	18	6	20	12	26
No opinion	10	13	18	10	24	11

SRC 417, 431, and 440 combined

	Cath.	Prot.	Cath.	Prot.	Cath.	Prot.
(N)	(760)	(1276)	(160)	(678)	(156)	(1571)
Agree U.S. would be better off if we just stayed home and did not concern ourselves with problems abroad	22%	18%	19%	17%	22%	25%
Depends or uncertain	6	6	4	6	10	8
Disagree	62	67	53	66	53	56
No opinion	10	9	24	11	15	11
Agree U.S. should give economic help to poorer countries	51	52	48	48	43	44
Depends or uncertain	13	15	9	16	19	15
Disagree	23	18	14	22	19	27
No opinion	13	15	29	14	19	14

	Attended Church in last 7 days		Did not	
	Cath.	Prot.	Cath.	Prot.
AIPO 653, 12-5-61				
(N)	(250)	(380)	(108)	(589)
Had heard or read anything about tariffs and trade	58%	55%	51%	53%
Favor higher tariffs	20	17	15	18
Same	7	5	10	9
Lower	23	24	21	18
No opinion	8	9	5	8
Never heard or read of them	42	45	49	47

	Attend Church					
	Regularly		Often		Seldom or Never	
	Cath.	Prot.	Cath.	Prot.	Cath.	Prot.
SRC 473, Sept.-Nov.'64						
(N)	(203)	(325)	(42)	(148)	(65)	(367)
Favor economic aid	62%	51%	57%	53%	51%	48%
Depends or uncertain	21	21	17	21	15	18
Each country should make own way	11	18	17	15	20	25
No opinion	6	10	9	11	14	9
Favor negotiations with communist leaders to settle differences	75	73	69	75	75	69
Depends or uncertain	4	5	5	4	2	4
Oppose negotiations	11	9	12	11	9	10
No opinion	10	13	14	10	14	17
Favor trade with communist countries in nonmilitary goods	33	23	21	20	28	26
Depends or uncertain	6	6	10	7	3	3
U.S. gov't should prohibit trade	41	45	52	48	43	47
No opinion	20	26	17	25	26	24

| | Attend church | | | | | |
| Knew Mainland China | Regularly | | Often | | Seldom | |
is communist and not	Cath.	Prot.	Cath.	Prot.	Cath.	Prot.
in U.N.	79	77	69	70	72	71
Should admit to U.N.	21	13	24	14	17	14
If admitted, U.S. should stay in	37	37	29	29	24	38
If admitted, don't know what U.S. should do	1	7	5	6	0	4
If admitted, U.S. should get out	7	9	5	10	8	7
Don't know if China should be admitted	13	11	7	11	23	8
Did not know China communist and not in U.N.	21	23	31	30	28	29

| | Attended Church in last 7 days | | Did not | |
	Cath.	Prot.	Cath.	Prot.
AIPO survey of June '66				
Continue war in Vietnam	43%	52%	42%	50%
Withdraw U.S. troops in next few months	39	31	41	34
No opinion	18	17	17	16

INDEX